GIRAFFES

◆ ON ◆ HORSEBACK SALAD

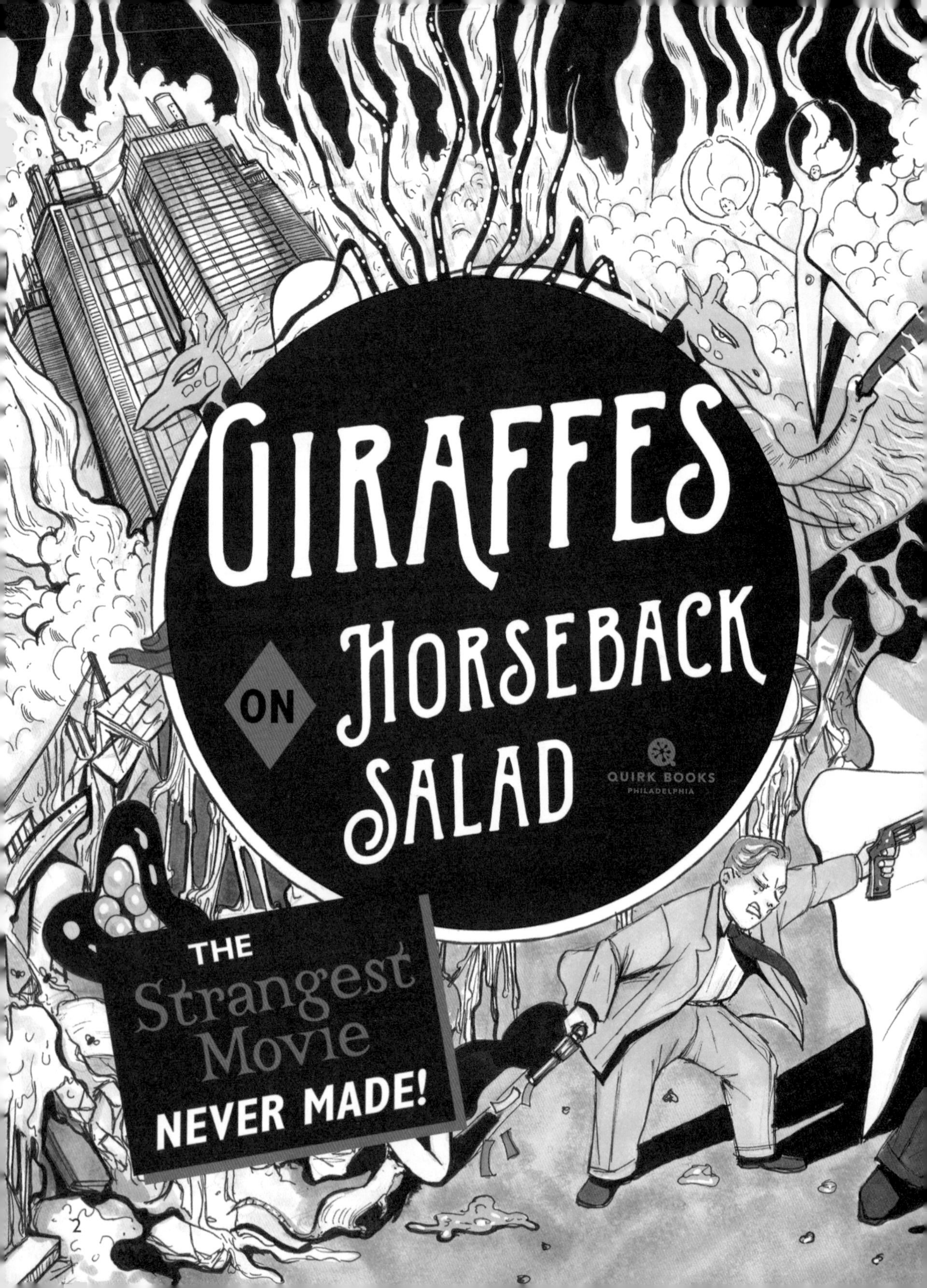
GIRAFFES ON HORSEBACK SALAD
QUIRK BOOKS
PHILADELPHIA
THE Strangest Movie NEVER MADE!

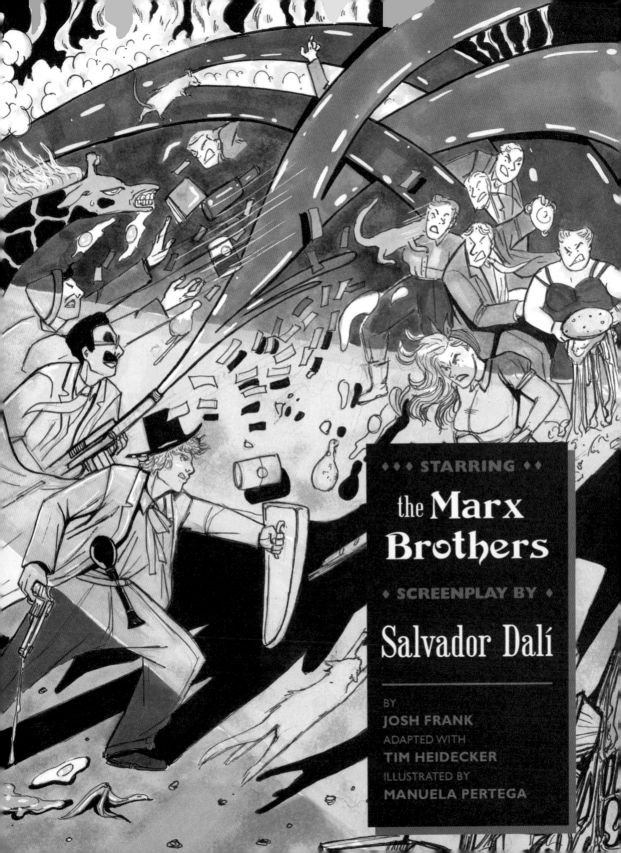

◆◆◆ STARRING ◆◆

the Marx Brothers

◆ SCREENPLAY BY ◆

Salvador Dalí

BY
JOSH FRANK
ADAPTED WITH
TIM HEIDECKER
ILLUSTRATED BY
MANUELA PERTEGA

The publisher would like to thank Bill Marx and his family,
Robert Bader, John Tefteller, The Gala and Salvador Dali
Foundation, The Centre Pompidou, and Artists Rights Society
for their invaluable help in creating this book.

Library of Congress Cataloging in Publication Number: 2017961243

ISBN: 978-1-59474-923-0

Printed in China

Typeset in Duper Pro, Chaloops, and Adobe Garamond Pro

Cover Designed by Doogie Horner
Lettering by Molly Rose Murphy
Production management by John J. McGurk

Quirk Books
215 Church Street
Philadelphia, PA 19106
quirkbooks.com

10 9 8 7 6 5 4 3 2 1

This book is dedicated to Mom and Grandma Shirley, who collectively taught me an early appreciation of music, poetry, fine art, and the satisfying sound a typewriter makes.

To Jessica Shapiro Frank, my wife, who has given me all the meaning, love, and confidence that keeps me young, inspired, and hopeful. Without you, Dalí and Harpo's movie would never have been made.

As well as to my loving father, who has taught me so much, and to my son Austin Joseph, who will continue to teach me the rest.

And to Harpo and Bill.

Photo of author Josh Frank, age 12, Halloween 1987

LADIES AND GENTLEMEN.

THE MANAGEMENT REMINDS YOU THAT LOUD TALKING AND WHISTLING ARE NOT ALLOWED DURING THE PRESENTATION.

POPCORN AND SODA POP ARE AVAILABLE FOR PURCHASE IN THE LOBBY.

KINDLY REMOVE ALL HATS AND REFRAIN FROM SMOKING.

ENJOY THE SHOW!

◆ ◆ ◆ THE PROGRAM ◆ ◆ ◆

◆ ◆ ◆ ◆ ◆ *More surprises and extras on view at HorsebackSaladBook.com* ◆ ◆ ◆ ◆ ◆

How a Group of Storytellers and Artists Brought a Lost Dalí Film, Starring the Marx Brothers, to Life

By Josh Frank

I like to think of myself as an archaeologist of forgotten pop culture. I have always been intrigued by lost histories, especially the untold stories behind music, art, and film. As the great-grandson of Jewish ancestors, some of whom escaped the Holocaust but most of whom did not, I'm haunted by the idea that the amazing acts of people—whether famous or obscure—can simply fall away from our collective memory.

This is my fourth book to explore such lost histories, but perhaps the one I was most destined to write. Ever since I was a kid growing up in Houston, Texas, in the 1980s, I've been beguiled by the zany antics of those comic geniuses known as the Marx Brothers. Back then, *Star Wars* may have ruled the cinemas, but I sat enthralled by *Duck Soup* on my family's TV. When I was ten years old, my father took me, along with my two best friends Greg and Michael, fellow Marx Brothers diehards, to see Harpo's son Bill play piano at the local Jewish Community Center. We wore our Harpo trenchcoats despite the hundred-degree temperature and swamp-like humidity, and we got to shake hands and have our picture taken with a guy who, to us, was the son of a god.

Two years later, my father took me to visit his twenty-eight-year-old friend from his law firm, a guy who, for some reason, had an entire house full of Marx Brothers memorabilia. An entire house! Obscure and valuable stuff. Upon discovering that grown-ups could also be as obsessed with the Marx Brothers, and that they could collect and fill their living space with artifacts from that zany world, I was hooked for life.

And so, while everyone else dressed up as Hulk Hogan, Freddy Krueger, and Ronald Reagan for Halloween, I went as Harpo Marx. None of my friends had any idea who I was, and most of their parents didn't either (they thought I was a clown who couldn't afford face paint). Harpo had passed away eleven years before I was even born, and his last Marx Brothers big-screen appearance was made thirty-five years before my first glimpse of the quartet on the small screen, but in the mid-1980s they were still alive in my home during our many late-night Marx Brothers movie marathons.

Flash-forward thirty years. While researching and writing *The Good Inn*, an illustrated novel that re-creates the making of the first narrative adult-only film in France, I fell in love with the process of bringing to life a forgotten story in collaboration with artists, musicians, and illustrators. We felt like we were breathing life into an overlooked piece of the past, recasting it for a modern audience. In search of a story that spoke to me, I started searching for articles that listed the greatest unmade or long-vanished scripts. Any online blog of merit had just such a list: Indiewire, Den of Geeks, Insider, Screen Rant, Film Comment, Gizmodo, and Business Insider, among many others. Every article mentioned the same mythical movies gone missing: a sci-fi epic by Stanley Kubrick, a Superman movie by Tim Burton, Werner Herzog's *The Conquest of Mexico*, Clair Noto's H. R. Giger–designed *The Tourist*, and, of course, David Lynch's *Ronny Rocket*. And near the top of almost every list was Salvador Dalí's *Giraffes on Horseback Salad, (also known simply as) "The Surrealist Woman,"* starring my beloved Marx Brothers.

Just like a real archaeologist, the first task of a pop-cultural archaeologist is to dig. So I dug into every source I could find about Dalí's proposed movie featuring the greatest surrealistic comics who ever lived, as envisioned by the greatest Surrealist painter on the planet. I started by mining film history blogs, which eventually led me to a piece that Dalí wrote for *Harper's Bazaar* in 1937, in which he described his first meeting with Harpo. It was also relatively easy to locate the sketches and other drawings that Dalí had created in preparation for pitching the movie to Harpo and, later, to MGM. (They're scattered across the Web, but you can find them if you search for "Dalí" and "Giraffes on Horseback Salad.") Yet I found it difficult to track down the full-length film treatment, if one even existed. It was rumored that something resembling a script had been in Harpo's possession after he and Dalí pitched the project to MGM Studios, but supposedly the document had disappeared sometime in the following decade. Others claimed it was merely a few paragraphs of an idea. It seemed to me, at first, that the latter was true. I was able to locate these paragraphs, which *Harper's* ran in their May 1996 issue, but it wasn't enough. I had to find out if there was more; if not, my project would be over before it had even begun.

I wrote to the Gala-Salvador Dalí Foundation in Figueres, Spain, and asked the research department if they knew of a documented version of the complete manuscript for *Giraffes on Horseback Salad*. They wrote back and provided two leads. Yes, they possessed a version of Dalí's script, but it was available only in an out-of-print compilation of Dalí's film projects that had been translated into Portuguese. They generously agreed to share the Portuguese version with me. They noted, however, that this version had been translated from an original and larger document: Dalí's *Giraffes* notebook, handwritten in French and currently housed at the Centre Pompidou in Paris. The Dalí Foundation kindly provided me with contact information for the museum, so with the Portuguese version in hand, I awaited word from the Centre Pompidou.

As a pop-culture archaeologist, I have had to overcome many obstacles. While writing my book *In Heaven Everything Is Fine*, which chronicled the unsolved murder of Peter Ivers, I needed to convince the Los Angeles Police Department to reopen the case after thirty years. Now I had a new and unique challenge: translating a Portuguese fragment of a French handwritten notebook into English. Fortunately, we live in the age of the internet. I posted a Craigslist ad for a translator and crossed my fingers. I received one response and hired that person on the spot. Two weeks later, I had fifteen pages of text.

The material was exciting: amazing visual ideas, a clear story, specific characters. In essence, *Giraffes* is a surreal love story about a man lost in the trappings of modern life, adrift without the social grounding of reality, and a woman who, thanks to the help of her friends the Marx Brothers, lives a truly surreal life by literally manifesting her dreams, fantasies, and wishes onto the world (whether the world likes it or not). There wasn't enough for a full-length movie, but it was a start—and proof that more existed than had been previously speculated. This was all the fuel I needed to look for more clues, find more answers, and spend more time on the case.

I could only hope that whatever the Centre Pompidou sent me would provide more insight than these fifteen pages of translated text. While I waited for the French connection, I decided to focus on another angle: Dalí's personal life during this time, which I thought might shed light on the inspiration for his script. The version of Dalí who painted the canvas he's most known for, *The Persistence of Memory*, has been well documented and studied by academics, art critics, and cinephiles alike. But the Dalí who created the foundational drawings for a never-made Marx Brothers movie has not. In fact, aside from a brief chapter in *Dalí, Surrealism and Cinema* by Elliot H. King, *Giraffes* tends to be relegated to the footnotes of history. It was important to understand what Dalí was going through between 1936 and 1939, when he wrote the film treatment, if only so that I could take the little available material and turn the shards of inspiration into a complete pane of glass.

On to Amazon to buy every memoir, biography, museum catalogue, and film history that mentioned Surrealist cinema or Dalí himself. I occupied my time by reading everything that the artist had to say about his stay in America, his improbable visits with and adoration of Harpo, his financial and personal struggles during the Spanish Civil War, and any moment that could shed light on what might have inspired the characters and story behind *Giraffes*. What I discovered was exciting stuff. The ideas in *Giraffes* seem to mirror Dalí's own life struggles during this period. Its story also brought these disjointed and seemingly disconnected scenes and characters into a clearer vision and new light. I was starting to understand the backbone of the movie, the recurring themes, and, most important, the seemingly unrelated episodes that formed a cohesive narrative arc. In essence, to put it into modern "superhero" terms, this was an origin story—for Dalí the artist, for the true "Super-Hero" in the screen story, the Surrealist woman, and for the character of Harpo as well. This was the story of how Harpo became Harpo!

The first thing I did was to rearrange the Portuguese translation into the structure for a Hollywood-style movie. I also established the "rules" of the adaptation. This step was important because if I was going for authenticity, I needed to create guidelines. Who was "making" this movie? Was it Dalí in the 1930s, or was it someone like the Zucker Brothers, Judd Apatow, or even Quentin Tarantino today? Although the latter option intrigued me, the choice was obvious: the movie had to be produced in 1937 by MGM, and the only way to do it right would be to bring Irving Thalberg, head of production and cofounder of MGM, back to life long enough to green-light the idea and oversee production.

In reality, Thalberg might have allowed Harpo and Dalí to make this movie. Unfortunately, after Thalberg's untimely death, MGM was not in the mindset of taking chances, and company executives could not see past the insanity that oozed and melted across all of Dalí's works, including the pitch for *Giraffes*. Not to mention that Louis B. Mayer was *not* a fan of the Marxes. At all. He had recently taken over Thalberg's responsibilities, including dealing with those damn brothers, whose contract was set to end shortly after Thalberg's death. (Ultimately, this is probably the reason *Giraffes* never stood a chance, aside from the flaming giraffes.) I absolutely needed Thalberg—and luckily, since I was directing this picture, I could bring him back from the great beyond for one more production.

I began to adapt the story as if I were Dalí working under the watchful eye of Thalberg, the genius at MGM who elevated the Marx Brothers into big-budget cinema stars with hits like *A Night at the Opera.* The adaptation would have to take into account the person Dalí was during the months he wrote these scenarios and spent time with Harpo, what he was experiencing in his personal life, and his journey as an artist. In my mind, this is what *Giraffes on Horseback Salad* is really about.

I now had the framing device, but I still needed the notebook from the Centre Pompidou to fill in the story. While I waited, I imagined the warehouse in *Indiana Jones and the Raiders of the Lost Ark,* with an old docent slowly rolling a rickety cart down impossibly long aisles of lost histories, each locked away in giant wooden boxes stacked to the rafters. In my imagination, he would stop at one and crack open the lid with a crowbar, sending decades of dust exploding into the air; then he'd reach in and pull out a glowing manuscript with a giraffe on the cover.

When the package from Paris finally arrived, it wasn't glowing and it did not bear a TOP SECRET stamp. It certainly had not been stored in a secret warehouse at an undisclosed location. It wasn't even a package, but an ordinary email attachment. Nevertheless, to me this message held the same weighty and mysterious significance as the Holy Grail. The moment of truth had arrived: Either the text was just the original French document that I already had in Portuguese (now translated into English), or there was more here and I would be able to write the missing pieces of the story. I opened the file and immediately scrolled to the last of the eighty-four pages. All were handwritten by Dalí in a frenzied script, like graffiti scrawled across the worn and age-stained notebook pages. Some of the margins contained tiny worlds and objects doodled by Dalí.

The document was substantial, but I couldn't read a word of it! Luckily, I knew a guy who could. I wrote to a friend in France, Louis Collin, and asked if he could translate eighty-four pages of French text into English. He agreed.

As I waited for this next translation, I wondered how many fewer pages the English text would be. Were there really eighty-four pages, or was it a trompe l'oeil, a trick of the eye? Would it all boil down to the same fifteen pages I already had?

When the translation arrived a few weeks later, I was not disappointed. The translation amounted to forty-two pages, some detailing specific storylines, others containing surreal gag ideas for the Marx Brothers, and several describing specific characters. Lacking a final script, which, it seemed, simply did not exist, here was everything I could hope for—and more. Most thrilling were the liner notes to the script scenario, in which Dalí wrote personal mini-manifestos that I knew were related to his tumultuous artistic journey at the time.

I now needed to find a collaborator who could help me ensure that the surrealist comedy of Marx and Dalí melded into something truly authentic—an accurate and faithful treatment of the people and the period that would speak to today's audiences. Where could I find a comic writer who would rise to the challenge? Who was the Harpo Marx of today?

If it weren't for my first book, *Fool the World: The Oral History of a Band Called Pixies*, this book would never have existed. I would not have been able to reach out to my friend and co-author of *The Good Inn*, Black Francis of the Pixies, who knows some very funny people. Francis is the man famous for screaming the lyrics "slicing up eyeballs" in his song "Debaser," a tribute to *Un chien andalou*, Dalí's surreal film collaboration with the Spanish director Luis Buñuel. He immediately suggested Tim Heidecker, the comedian best known for *Tim and Eric Awesome Show, Great Job!* Tim is the modern incarnation of a surrealist, absurdist performance artist. The proof? On August 11, 2017, a year after we finished working together, the *Washington Post* published a profile about "millennial humor," calling Tim's comedic style "a digital update to the surreal and absurd genres of art and literature that characterized the tumultuous early-twentieth century." The Harpo Marx of today, indeed.

When I completed the first draft of the screenplay, Tim and I met in Los Angeles and worked on filling in the missing gags and one-liners. Dalí had left notes about where "Marx Brothers antics" would ensue, but gave no specific direction. The dialogue would need to be invented from the ground up. Tim put together a roundtable writers' room of sorts, inviting many mainstays from *Tim and Eric Awesome Show, Great Job!* to chime in with ideas. It was very cool, especially for this researcher-writer, who had been alone on the journey for a long time.

The final task? Hire a "cinematographer" who could breathe life into this incomplete work. I posted an ad online to find an illustrator in Spain, Dalí's home country, and found Manuela Pertega, an artist from Barcelona whose work was breathtaking: lush, passionate, magical, and, of course, surreal. I knew immediately that she was the person for the job. Together, with the help of Google Translate (neither of us speak the other's language particularly well; Harpo and Dalí had exactly the same problem when they worked together some eighty years ago), we created sample pages that led us magically into the hands of Quirk Books. And to our delight, Quirk got it!

But what is a Marx Brothers movie without songs? I knew from the start that I wanted to address the musical element of a film that would have been championed by Irving Thalberg. I wrote a handful of ideas for lyrics and titles and sprinkled them throughout the script, but I returned to the question of authenticity and wondered how I might ensure that they remained grounded in the world of Marx Brothers lore. I reached out to the one man who could help me: Noah Diamond. A year earlier, Noah had singlehandedly revived a lost Marx Brothers Off-Broadway musical called *I'll Say She Is*. Similar to my project, he had filled in the blanks from a lost work. If anyone could help sculpt my ideas into genuine Marx Brothers show-stoppers, it was Noah.

Several filmmakers I admire and respect have been trying to make a new Marx Brothers movie for decades. The Zucker brothers came closest with *Brain Donors*, an 1980s interpretation of a Marx Brothers movie that, as a child, I cherished. Robert B. Weide went so far as to make a Marx Brothers movie with his definitive documentary *Marx Brothers in a Nutshell*, aka the holy grail for a ten-year-old collector and fan (aka me in 1985). The folks behind the Andy Kaufman biopic, *Man on the Moon*, were also rumored to be creating a movie, with Danny DeVito on board to produce, though that one never came to fruition.

So I am thrilled and humbled to be able to say that my team of incredible creatives have made the first *new* Marx Brothers movie in seventy years. We hope you enjoy it.

ACKNOWLEDGMENTS

This book would not have been possible without the absurdist, surreal friendship and skills of my agent, Michael Harriot at Folio Literary Management; the trust and interest of the Gala-Salvador Dalí Foundation; the Centre Pompidou; and the Marx Estate's director, Robert Bader, whose own Marx Brothers book is a gift to fans both new and old. And, of course, special thanks to Harpo's son Bill Marx and to Rick Chillot, our enthusiastic editor at Quirk, without whom *Giraffes on Horseback Salad* never would have made it into your hands.

Thanks to the writers' round table at Tim Heidecker's office for additional gags: Mark Proksch, Doug Lussenhop, Mikey Kampmann, Matthew Carlin, and Vic Berger.

And now, as Groucho would say:

"Let there be dancing in the streets, drinking in the saloons, and necking in the parlor. Play, Don!"

A Note from Tim Heidecker

I'm so excited to be a part of this project because my own work is so connected to the humor and spirit of the Marx Brothers. I grew up watching them along with other classic comedies. Some may find them dusty, old-fashioned, and not cool anymore, but I see the marvelous sense of anarchy and absurdism that exists in all their movies. And there's an anti-authoritarian quality that also exists in my own work, a point of view that sees the world as ridiculous and deserving of ridicule. Slapstick, quick wit, absurdism—all are core elements of what I do as a comedian and a writer. It's very exciting and rewarding to have imagined new ideas and situations for *Giraffes on Horseback Salad*. Enjoy the show.

SHORT #3

Dalí and Harpo

By Bill Marx

Some may wonder how it is that my father, Arthur "Harpo" Marx, a vaudevillian, stage performer, and movie comedian, got on so well with the Spanish painter Salvador Dalí, a modern art luminary. The truth is, the Marx Brothers were a perfect fit for Dali's perception of reality. From the very first time Dalí saw their act, the Brothers must have appealed deeply to his ragingly rebellious and absurdly cantankerous visual and emotional view of the world.

Dalí was one-of-a-kind, and my father and his brothers (Groucho, Chico, and Zeppo, as they're known to millions) were four of one-of-a-kind. They all shared an appreciation of their own ever-present human uniqueness. That individuality exists within all of us, and perhaps we should all have the courage to call upon it now and then, to soothe our own personal reality.

I'm convinced that Dalí considered Harpo Marx to be the ultimate depiction of Dali's way of dealing with life and its vicissitudes. In his art, Dalí used breathtaking draftsmanship to show us the world that he saw, the surreal world that was his reality. In the Marx Brothers films, Harpo imposed his absurd reality onto the blank canvas of the mundane world. From beneath the long coat he wore, Harpo retrieved whatever was necessary according to the dream-logic of the moment: a cup of piping hot coffee from his pocket; 300 knives and a teapot tumbling out of his sleeve; scissors, a carrot, a rubber chicken, a blow torch.

One day not long before their fateful meeting at our home (which you'll read more about elsewhere this book), Dad received a real—or perhaps I should say surreal—harp, sent with compliments of Dalí. Its frame was covered with silverware and wrapped in cellophane. To assure its musical functionality, the harp had strings made of barbed wire. Dad could not have been more pleased. In a famous staged photo, he

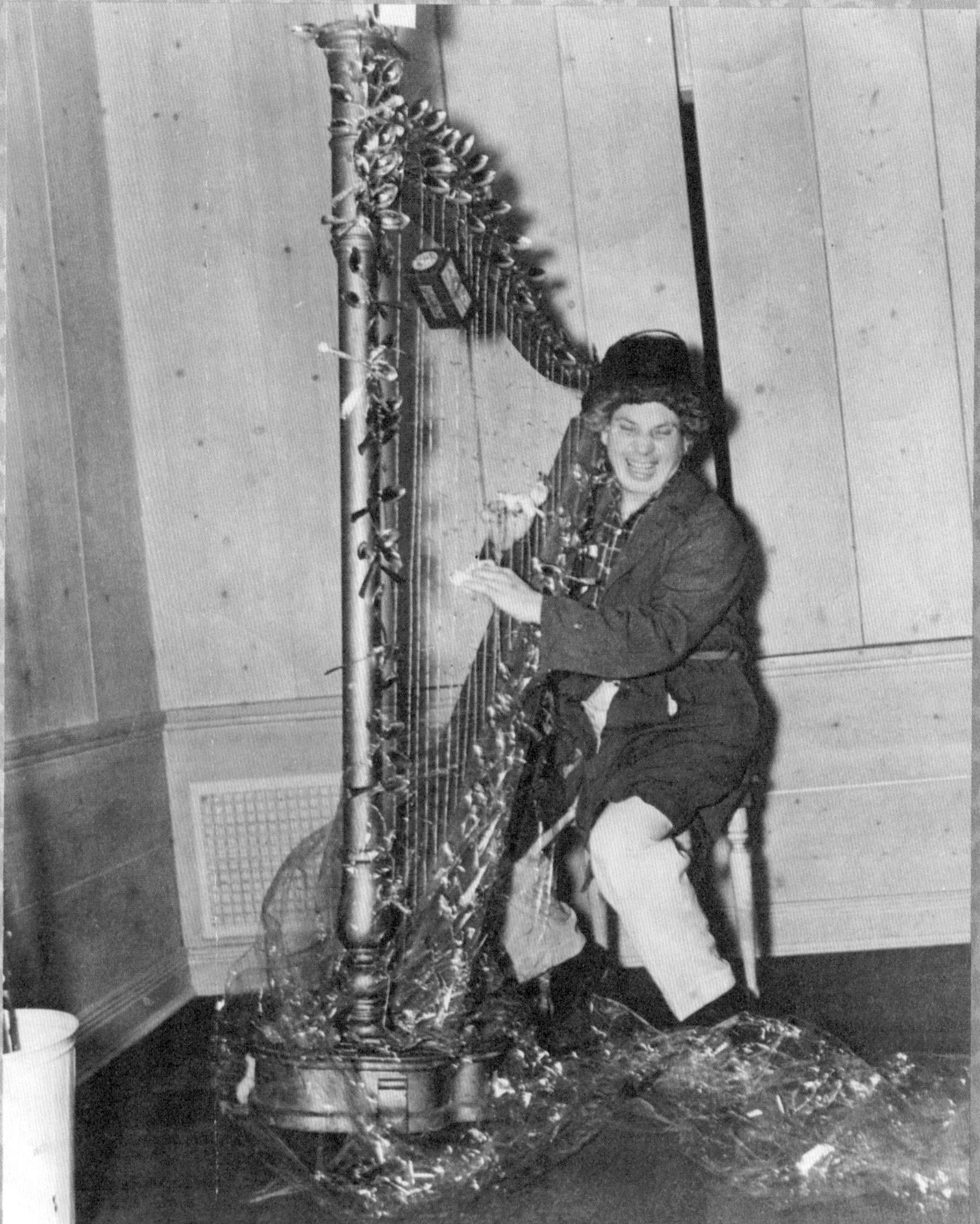

Photographs this page and opposite courtesy of the Marx family

posed at the harp with all of his fingers wrapped in bandages. Of course my mother, Susan, a card-carrying pragmatist, saw to it that Dad never actually played even a single note on it, ever.

So given their shared worldview, it's perhaps the smallest of all possible wonders that Dad became, to my knowledge, the first and only entertainer ever to sit for Salvador Dalí. The result was a pencil-and-ink portrait, showing dad sitting at his beloved harp, a lobster on top of his wig, and his heavenly instrument's frame topped with a piece of raw liver. In the true spirit of reciprocity, Harpo—who took up painting as a hobby—convinced Dalí to become *his* portrait subject. Their tit-for-tat was another first, Salvador Dalí being painted by an entertainer.

The pair's mutual admiration would surely have led to greater things, had they been able to create the film that Dalí envisioned. But now, for the first time—another first!—we all have a chance to enjoy what might have been.

HALLUCINATORY CELLULOID

The Real and Surreal History of
Giraffes on Horseback Salad

Nothing seems to be more suited to be devoured by the surrealist fire than those mysterious strips of "hallucinatory celluloid" turned out so unconsciously in Hollywood, and in which we have already seen appear, stupefied, so many images of authentic delirium, chance and dream.

—SALVADOR DALÍ,
"SURREALISM IN HOLLYWOOD,"
HARPER'S BAZAAR, JUNE 1937

HONK!

—HARPO MARX,
EVERY MARX BROTHERS FILM EVER

A STRANGE MEETING

MGM STUDIOS, LOS ANGELES, CA, 1937—Though never documented on film or in writing, the scene is easy to imagine in the theater of the mind: Two men are seated next to each other: a dark-haired, wide-eyed Spaniard wears an anachronistic velvet suit, while his curly haired cohort has swathed himself in a ratty trench coat. Their outlandish appearance and hand-me-down fashion, not to mention the contrast between the men themselves, paints a picture of strange characters up to no good. Anywhere else in the world, they might have been mistaken for vagrants.

But in the waiting area outside the office of film producer Louis B. Mayer, one would expect to find the most unusual people. In fact, if you weren't such a character, you probably wouldn't be waiting for a meeting with the head of MGM Pictures. Here, eccentrics were a common sight. Vikings, pirates, monsters, witches, and every other costumed type imaginable could be seen wandering the movie lot every day.

Yet, somehow, these two particular gentlemen seemed out of place. Separately, either would stand out in a crowd. Together, they created a scene simply by sharing the same space, their uniqueness magnified.

Regarding the duo cautiously from behind her desk, Mayer's secretary was convinced they had to be in the wrong office. But she was new, fresh off the bus from Ohio, and this was her first job in the exciting city of Los Angeles. If only her friends could see her now . . .

She had no idea the man with the crazy red hair had already spoken to her boss, informing him that he'd be popping over with his friend from Spain

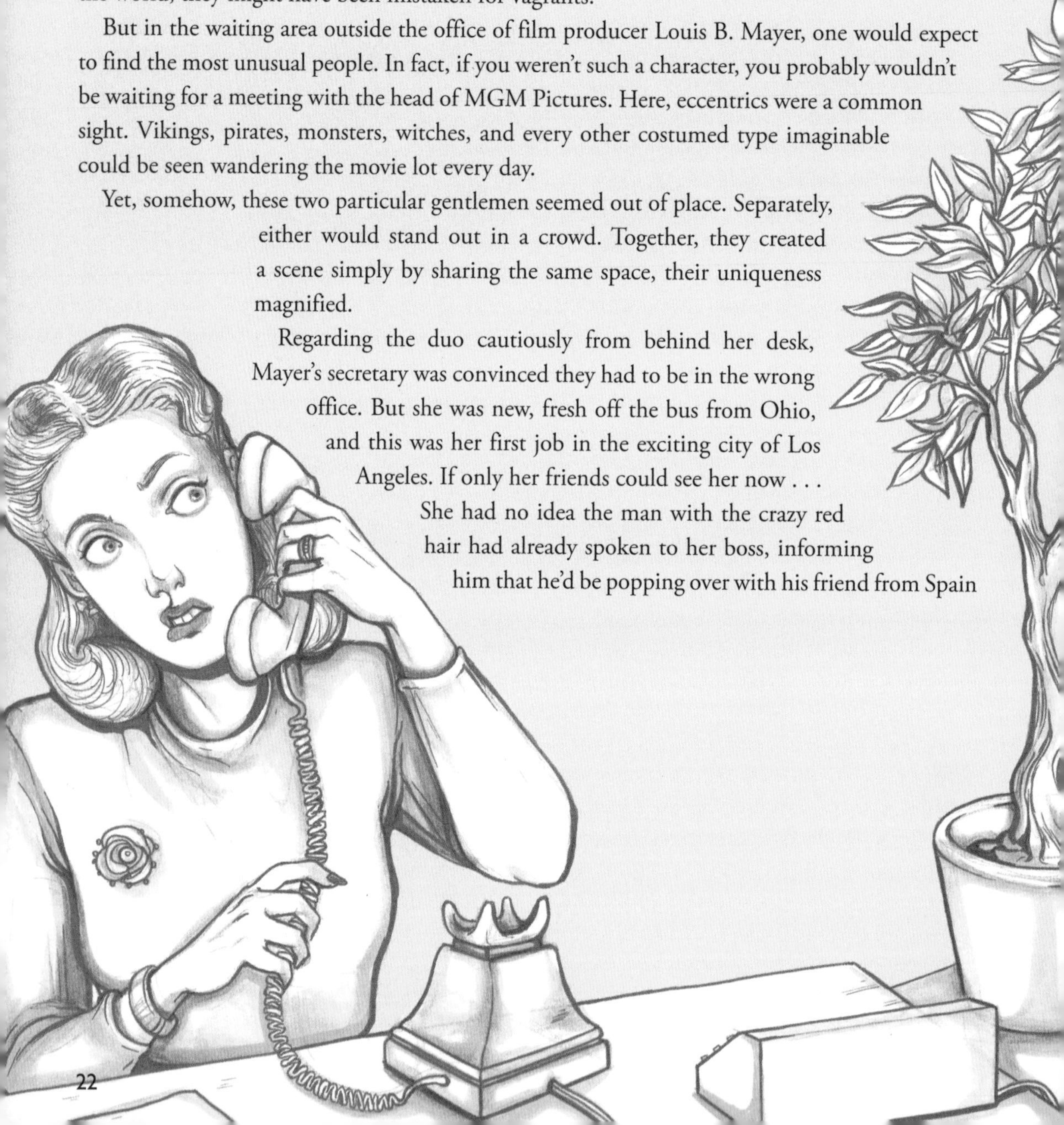

to pitch a movie idea. She would learn that this particular redheaded man could see Louis B. Mayer whenever he wanted. He—Arthur, along with his brothers Julius and Leonard—had been making Mayer and the other studio heads a lot of money. And that's why Mayer (like his predecessor, Irving Thalberg) put up with the mischief they brought to his doorstep.

Despite their names being on the list of visitors, the secretary didn't want to flub her first day of work. So she watched the pair curiously to make sure they didn't do anything . . . funny.

The buzzer rang; the secretary jumped nervously. She picked up the telephone and heard Mayer's voice. "Yes, sir. Right away, sir," she replied.

She put down the phone and stood.

"Mr. Dalí, Mr. Marx, Mr. Mayer will see you now."

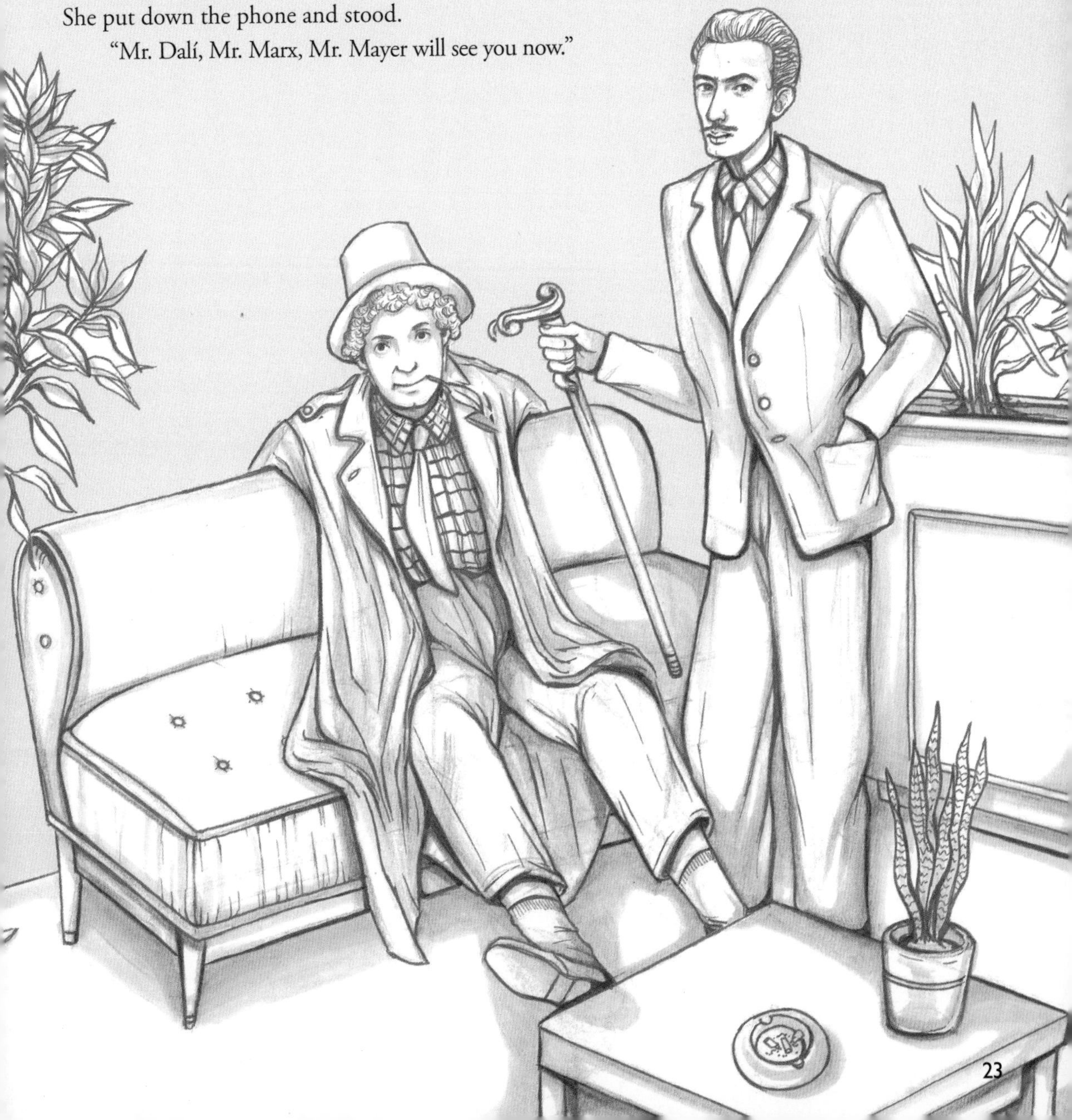

A SURREALIST IN NEW YORK

NEW YORK CITY, 1934—Salvador Dalí had made his first trip to America three years before this meeting. Numerous newspaper reports, as well as Dalí's own 1942 autobiography, *The Secret Life of Salvador Dalí*, show that he would not be mistaken for an ordinary tourist. He wore a life jacket for the entire crossing. From his home across the sea he carried a baguette, nestled under his arm and closely guarded at all times. On the day of his arrival in New York City, Dalí tripped and his loaf of stale bread landed on the pavement, crumbling into a million pieces. Dalí took this as an omen that nothing is permanent.

However, he chose not to mourn the loss. The bread had already served its purpose: every journalist, crew member, and dinner guest on his journey had been fixated on the rotting loaf from the second he stepped onto the ship till the second he walked down the gangplank onto shore. Arriving in the United States, Dalí was surprised to find the reporters "far superior" to European reporters; on U.S. soil, not one of them asked about his loaf of bread. He noted that they had an acute sense of "non-sense."

As Dalí recounts in his autobiography, it was a strange incident that had led to that journey. In an anecdote that seems calculated to cast him in a bad light, Dalí describes crossing a street in Paris, where he saw a blind, legless

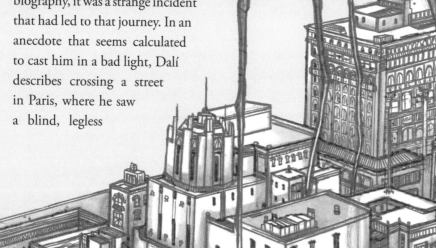

beggar in a cart who was asking passers-by for help. The beggar was ignored at every turn. Dalí kicked the man's cart so forcefully that it shot across the street; Dalí followed. He studied the cart and its bewildered passenger on the far side of the road. *Why had he done such a thing?* Dalí wondered. He could have just pushed the cart gently. But then, no one else bothered to do even that.

Dalí had another thought: it was time to go to America. No one was going to help him realize his dreams, just as no one would help this poor man cross the street. Dalí decided he would not end up like the cart . . . or like the blind beggar, for whom a kick was the only "helping hand" he received.

It was during that first visit to New York City, where he showed his famous melted-clock painting, *The Persistence of Memory*, that Salvador Dalí noticed Arthur "Harpo" Marx. In notes written at that time and later published in his autobiography, he describes his thoughts:

New York, you are an Egypt! But an Egypt turned inside out. For she erected pyramids of slavery to death, and you erect pyramids of democracy with the vertical organ-pipes of your skyscrapers all meeting at the point of infinity of liberty!

New York, granite sentinel facing Asia, resurrection of the Atlantic dream, Atlantis of the subconscious! What Piranesi invented the ornamental rites of your Roxy Theater? And what Gustave Moreau apoplectic with Prometheus lighted the venomous colors that flutter at the summit of the Chrysler Building?

New York, your cathedrals sit knitting stockings in the shadow of gigantic banks, mittens for the swallows, drunk and drenched in coca cola! New York, your beheaded manikins are already asleep, spilling all their "perpetual blood" which flows like the "surgical fountains of publicity" within the display windows dazzling with electricity, contaminated with "lethargic surrealism."

And on Fifth Avenue, HARPO MARX *has just lighted the fuse that projects from the flock of explosive giraffes stuffed with dynamite! The giraffes move in all directions, sowing panic and obliging everyone to seek refuge pell-mell within the shops. All the fire alarms of the city have gone off, but it is already too late.*

Boom! Boom!

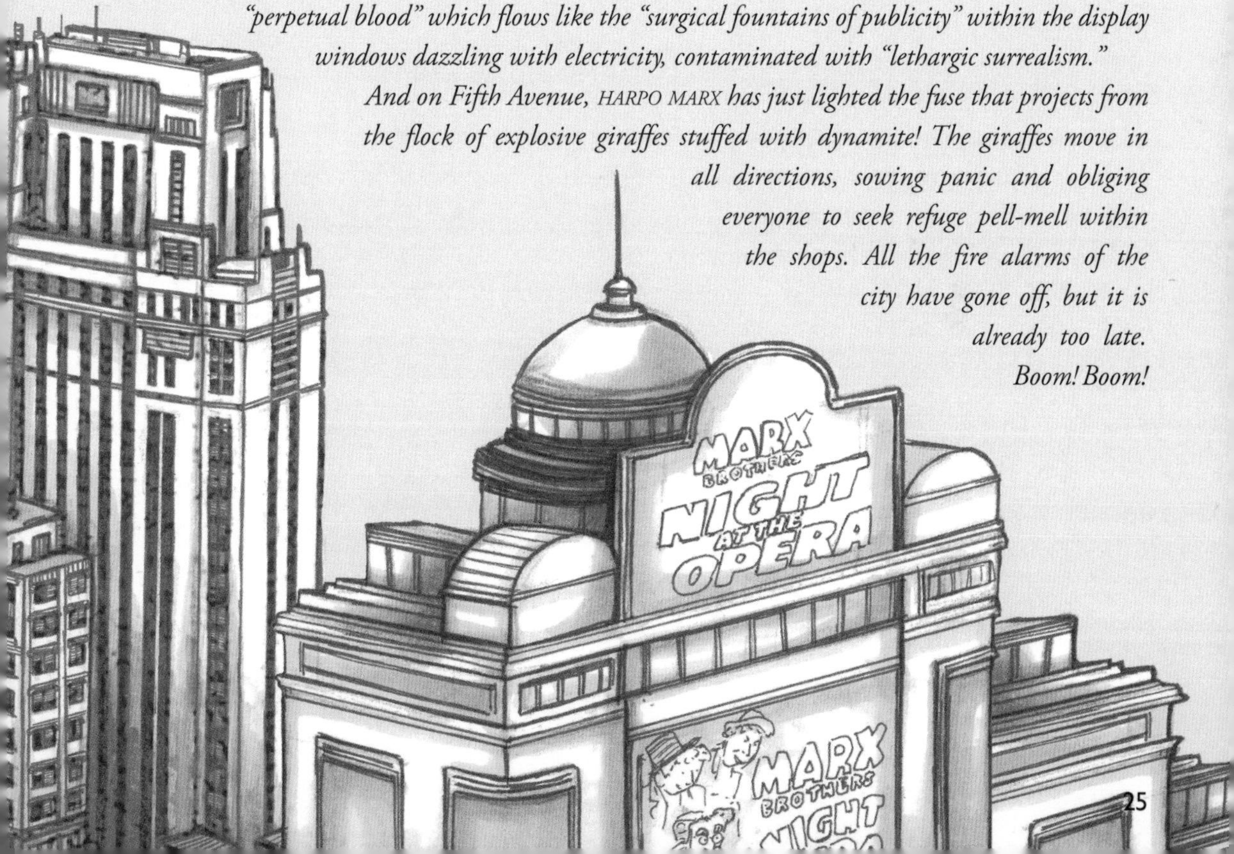
MARX
BROTHERS
NIGHT
AT THE
OPERA
MARX
BROTHERS
NIGHT

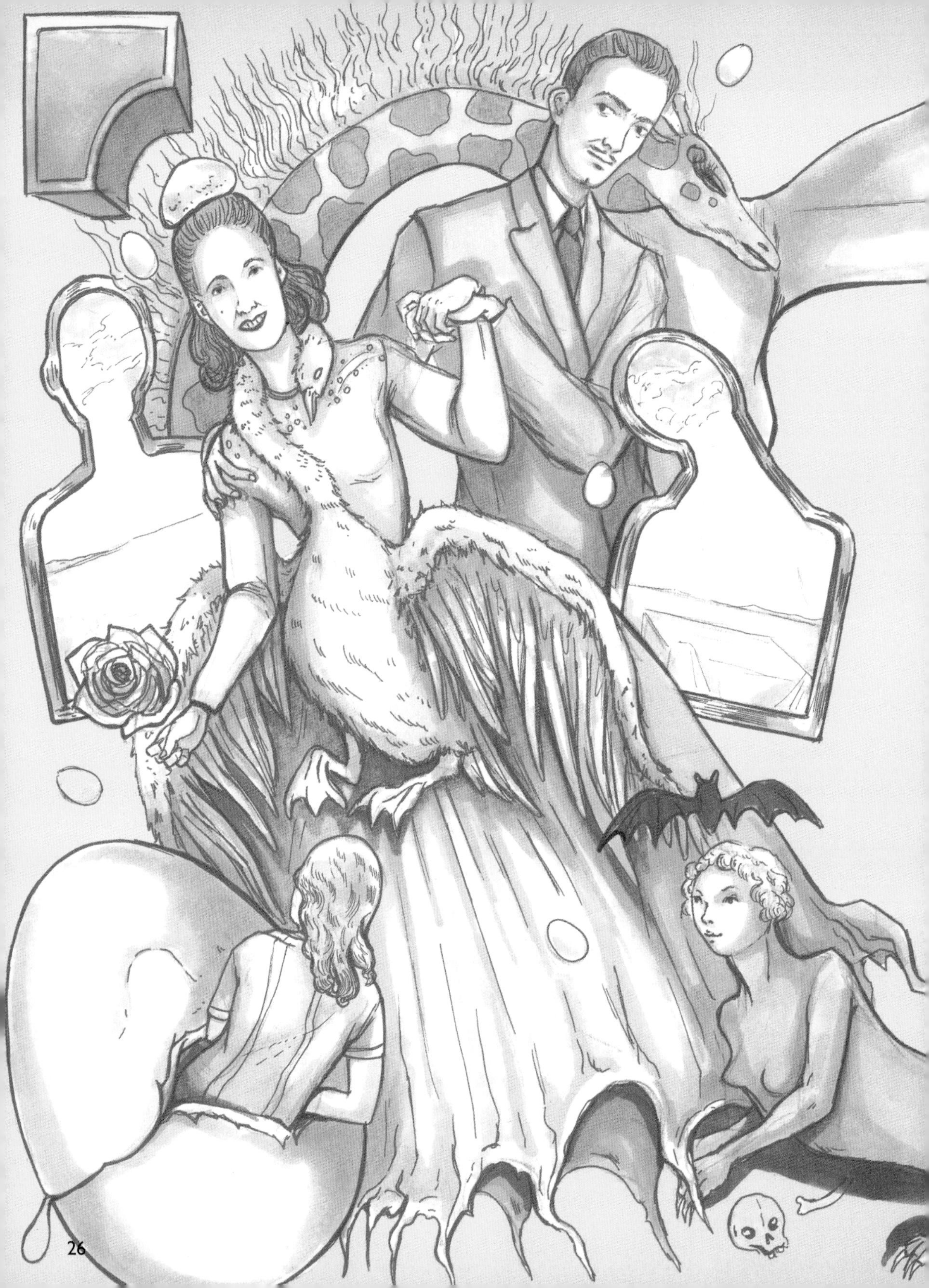

Boom! Boom! I salute you, explosive Giraffes of New York and all you forerunners of the irrational - Mack Sennett, Harry Langdon, and you too, unforgettable Buster Keaton, tragic and delirious like my rotten and mystic donkeys, desert rose of SPAIN!

It was on this trip that Dalí likely saw Harpo Marx and his brothers in *A Night at the Opera* at a movie house in Times Square.

TRIAL AND FLIGHT

SPAIN AND FRANCE, 1934—Back in Europe after his triumphant tour of the U.S. East Coast, Dalí was soon pushed into the next chapter of his life by two important events. First, he was subjected to a surreal(ist) "trial," which formally expelled him from the group of artists he'd help found. When asked if he had anything to say about the "sentence," Dalí reportedly replied, "I myself am surrealism."

Second, Dalí and his new wife, Gala (born Elena Ivanovna Diakonova), nearly found themselves trapped in the middle of the Spanish Civil War.

Theirs was a forbidden love. Dalí and Gala married in 1934 after living together since 1929. Dalí's family did not approve. Gala had been married before and was ten years older than her new husband, neither of which sat well with Dalí's stern father. Dalí's career as an artist who conjured all things absurd into existence, his flamboyant lifestyle, and his overall lack of interest in anything remotely conventional were already enough to make his middle-class family uncomfortable.

Just two years into their marriage, Spain experienced an armed uprising by Catalan separatists, whose march was closing in on Dalí and Gala's home in Port Lligat. The couple escaped to Paris, fleeing in the night just as the fighting made its way to their backyard. Dalí now found himself an expatriate from both the Surrealist movement and his own country.

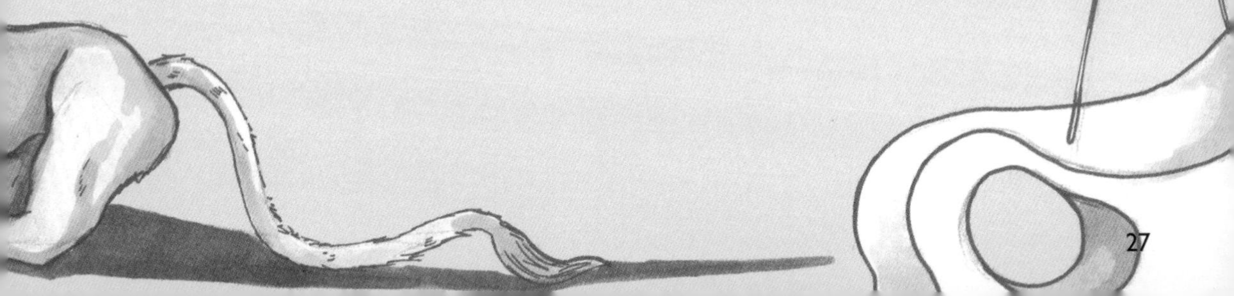

THE HALF-DEAD FISHERMEN AND THE REFUGEE

1935, THE COAST OF FRANCE—In France, wandering with no fixed address, Dalí spent many hours alone, staring at the sea. He'd attempted to give a seminar in London while wearing a deep-sea diving suit and helmet. It did not go as he had imagined. With the giant metal suit sealed tight, Dalí nearly suffocated, an embarrassing and nearly fatal incident, all for the sake of demonstrating surrealism.

Things were also getting worse for his country. As the war there spread, many of his peers made plans to leave, fearful of becoming casualties of an unstable nation. News of further unrest and revolution in Spain spread. Civil war has overtaken his faraway home.

One day Dalí sat beside two local fishermen, whose bodies were literally rotting from their damp and difficult livelihood. Dalí stared at their naked feet, bloated and cracked, as if in a trance, until one of the fishermen looked up to him and said, "We are already more than half-dead, you might say. You however, do not have to be."

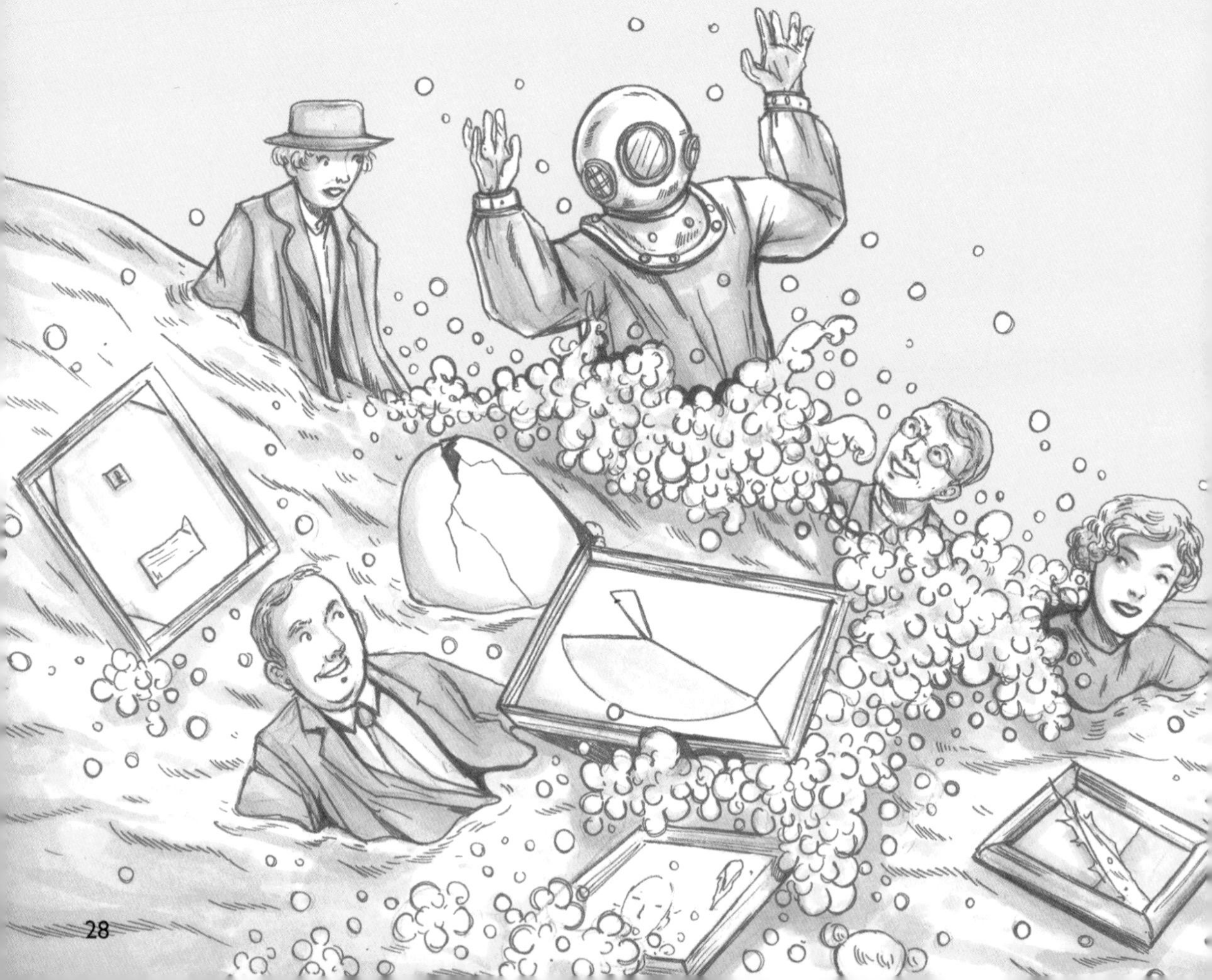

A NIGHT IN PARIS

PARIS, FRANCE, 1936—On a press tour for the new Marx Brothers film *A Night at the Opera*, Harpo Marx was spending many lonely nights wandering the streets of Paris. As he describes in his 1961 autobiography, *Harpo Speaks!*, he was looking for any distraction to take his mind off of actress Susan Fleming, whom, he was surprised to find, he missed terribly. The two had been dating for four years, and Harpo's promotional tour of Europe meant their first big good-bye.

Susan had suggested that when he returned, Harpo should leave behind his bachelor ways and find a home where they could begin a life together. Away from her for the first time, Harpo realized that her dream needed to be realized. When he returned to the United States, Arthur Marx would buy Susan that house, and they would be married.

Until then, however, Harpo needed to forget his heartache. And so one night he found himself at a wild party, and it was there that he first met the recently displaced artist Salvador Dalí.

The pair of itinerant madmen hit it off instantly, enjoying a night of drinking, dancing, and generally surreal socializing, which mostly consisted of the two smiling at each other, unable to communicate. (Of course Harpo, being Harpo, had no problem communicating without words.) After they parted, the Surrealist and the comedian became unlikely pen pals. As a token of respect and admiration, Dalí sent Harpo a surrealist harp, with strings made of barbed wire and spoons at the top in place of tuning screws. Harpo displayed his gratitude by sending Dalí a photograph of himself, holding up bandaged hands in front of the harp.

On December 31, Harpo followed with a telegram that read:

DEAR SALVADORE DALÍ

RECEIVED WIRE FROM JO FORRESTAL SAYING YOU INTERESTED IN ME AS VICTIM

THRILLED WITH IDEA

SHOOTING NOW FINISHED ABOUT SIX WEEKS

IF YOU ARE COMING WEST WOULD BE HAPPY TO BE SMEARED BY YOU

HAVE COUNTER PROPOSITION WILL YOU SIT FOR ME WHILE I SIT FOR YOU

HAPPY NEW YEAR

FROM THE GREAT ADMIRER OF PERSISTENCE OF MEMORY.

HARPO MARX

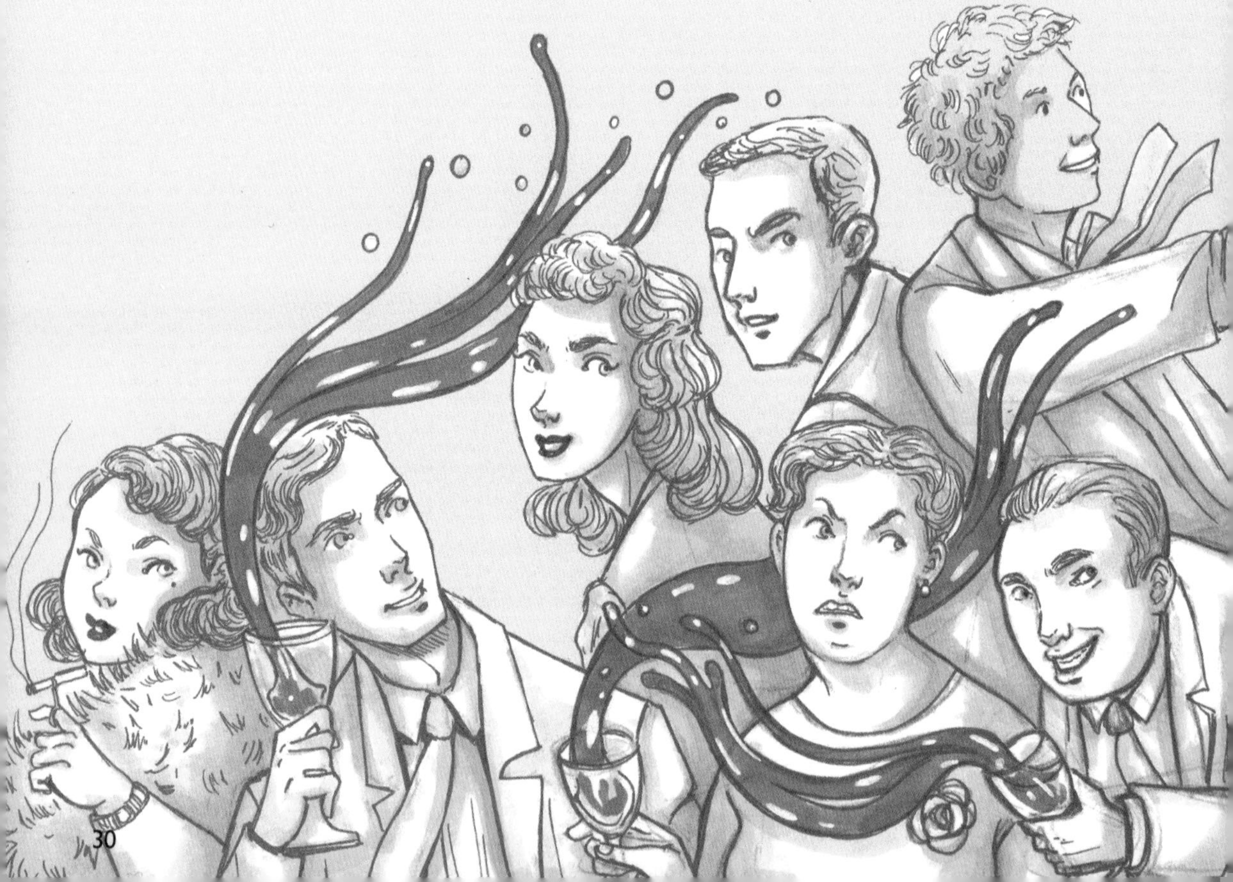

SPECTER IN THE HOUSE OF HARPS

HOLLYWOOD, CALIFORNIA, 1937—Dalí finally made a trip to California, both to conquer Hollywood and to paint his muse Harpo. With Gala by his side, he arrived on the West Coast while the situation in his own troubled country continued to worsen. In a letter to the French writer and surrealist André Breton, Dalí describes meeting kindred souls: "I'm in Hollywood, where I've made contact with the three American surrealists, Harpo Marx, Disney and Cecil B. DeMille."

Arriving at Harpo's home one sunny day, Dalí found his subject waiting for him in the garden, stripped naked and posing. Dalí documented this first visit by sketching Harpo; he also recounted the event for the June 1937 issue of *Harper's Bazaar* magazine. The account is clearly seen through his own surreal lens, but one could not imagine a better person to describe the experience of being in the presence of "the American Surrealist."

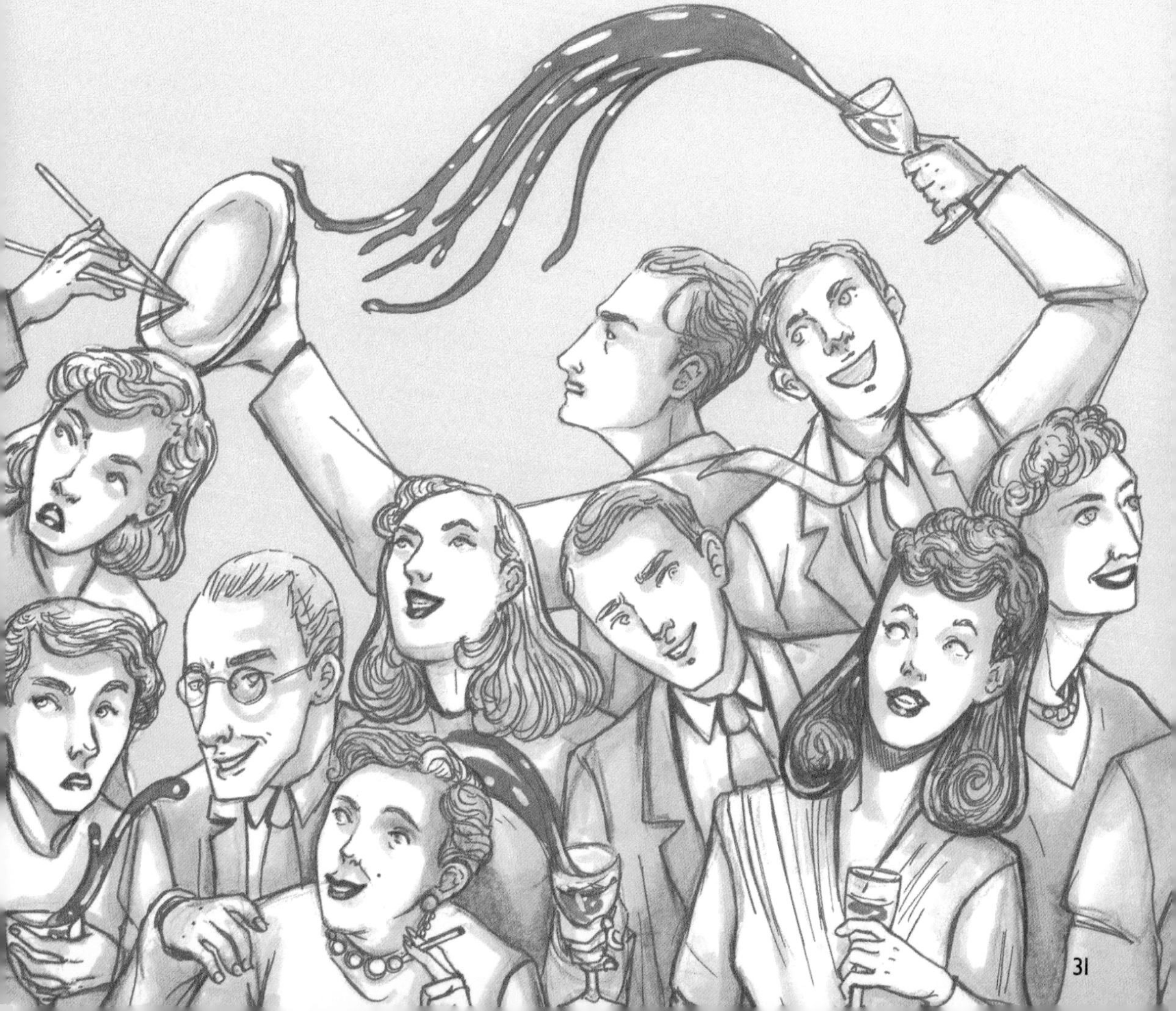

I met Harpo for the first time in his garden. He was naked, crowned with roses, and in the center of a veritable forest of harps (he was surrounded by at least five hundred harps). He was caressing, like a new Leda, a dazzling white swan, and feeding it a statue of the Venus de Milo made of cheese, which he grated against the strings of the nearest harp. An almost spring-like breeze drew a curious murmur from the harp forest. In Harpo's pupils glow the same spectral light to be observed in Picasso's.

If not for the wives of these two men, their time together would have been far less fruitful—they never would have been able to converse. The two strong women who stood next to these larger-than-life men both spoke German, which came in handy during the visits of these two unusual couples. Yet surely Harpo and Dalí communicated much of the time while saying nothing at all. Decades later, in audio recordings made for the Marx family archivist Robert Bader, Susan Marx remembered Dalí's visits to their home, as well as the first drafts of the film that the Surrealist was dreaming up:

Harpo would sit in the bay windows in the mornings and play his harp with the sun shining through. Anyone that was going to come and visit, they would have to come and sit where Harpo was playing his harp in the morning. And Dalí would visit and would sit there sketching parts of him. All in parts. A hand, his mouth, his eye, his other eye, and in the end, he put it all together. This is how he represented Harpo, how he felt he should be represented. It was a bad time for European artists. Everyone was coming over, resettling, escaping. Harpo hung all the sketches from Dalí's screenplay in the house. Beautiful sketches, but the script, terribly silly stuff, made no sense at all.

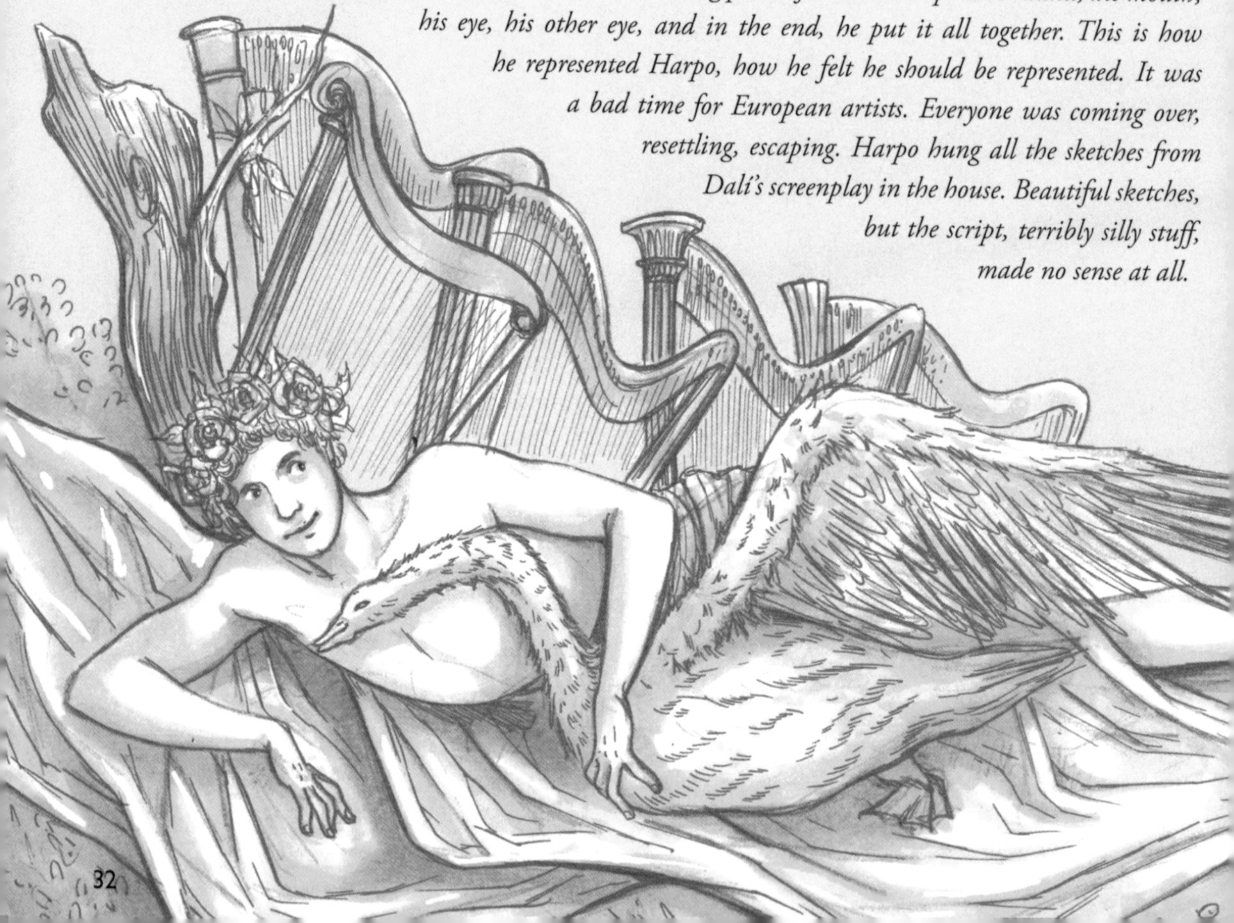

The scene continues in Dalí's words, as recorded in the 1937 Harper's Bazaar issue . . .

Because Harpo is the least modern of contemporary figures, he brings with him always that relaxed light, the duet of all those imponderable moths of the past; and this to such a point that he succeeds miraculously in transforming any place where he may be into an astounding atmosphere of legend. Harpo makes an appearance, marvelously out of his element, in the most modern gleaming apartments, nickel tubing everywhere, carrying hitched behind him all the straw, the erotic hay, all that odor composed of lambs, butterflies and heliotrope which constitutes the secret of the troubling perfume of Watteau and his century.

It was during this visit with Harpo that Dalí conceived of his desire to write a screenplay for an American audience. He envisioned a film that would bring Surrealism to the world through Hollywood. It would *have to* be scored by Cole Porter. And of course the project would star his muse, Harpo Marx. Again from the *Harper's* Bazaar article:

Harpo arrives and there, clings to his hallucinatory curly wig all the snuff, the songs of the nightingale and the swallows' droppings of the shadowed parks of the Embarkment for Cythera—that painting astounding among all others because it is painted like a true opera, with music from all the invisible harps of light and from the plain chant of the landscape, all culminating in the deep chest tones that the sinking sun exhales over the disarranged tresses of the great trees; and these in their turn are lived in by a thousand passages of Harpo, which serve as a nest for the languorous, strident, passionate duets of the thousand couples of blackbirds, canaries, lambs and minute steaks (because for Harpo there exists no essential difference between a butterfly and a minute steak, anything which bleeds with truly poetic truculence is his prey—Harpo devours all with the aid of that corrosive saliva par excellence that is "imaginative phosphorescence"). Because one must say for once and for all: "HARPO IS A SPECTER."

If one were to turn out the light, Harpo, the specter, would continue to shine, one could in the blackest night continue to read a newspaper by the phosphorescent glow of his wig alone.

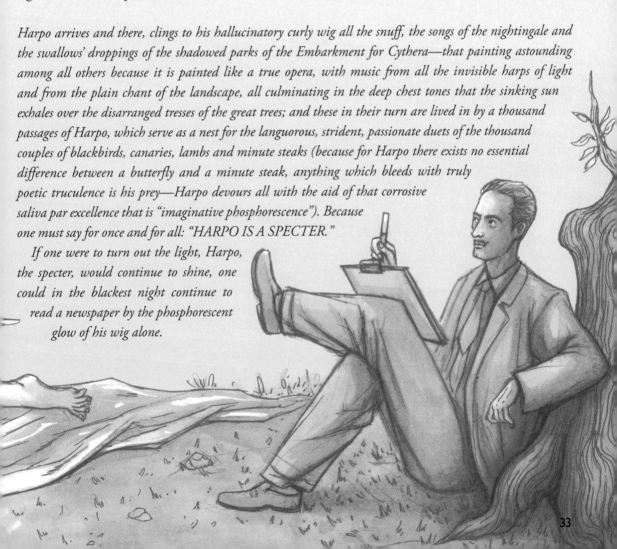

A SURREALIST IN HOLLYWOOD

LOS ANGELES, CALIFORNIA, 1937—For a short period, Salvador Dalí and Harpo Marx pranced around Hollywood together and managed to make the town of tinsel even wilder and stranger than it already was.

Spending time with Harpo seems to have sparked an unbridled, explosive burst of inspiration in Dalí, so much so that within days of their first meeting, the artist began focusing all of his solitary hours on developing his first American movie script. A letter to Harpo from that time shows that even when he was out of the country, the film project was not far from his mind:

Dear Harpo, I'm going to be spending a week in the snow and I'm going to take this advantage to write the scenario in which you are the main protagonist, after I've got to know you. I'm absolutely decided that we will do something together because we really do both think the same sort of things and we like exactly the same "type of imagination." I'm sure that a short film, with the sensational scenario made expressly for your genius, with extraordinary decorations and a very lyrical music, like Cole Porter would be something hallucinatory which in addition to amusing us could make a successful revolution in the Cinema.

When Dalí wasn't working on his movie script, he met the great filmmaker Cecil B. DeMille, and upon doing so bows at his feet. He also meets Walt Disney, and they ride miniature trains along a track that weaves through the latter's estate. The man who invented Mickey Mouse gives Dalí a peek into his own surrealist dreams, which will someday become reality at a place called Disneyland.

From Dalí's roiling imagination came the beginning of a story that mirrored his own life and struggle. This was art imitating life imitating Dalí!

As translated from Dalí's "Giraffes" notebook:

Harpo will be Jimmy, a young Spanish aristocrat who lives in the US as a consequence of the political circumstances in his country. . . . A war. He flees. But a war inside of him threatens to start an even greater world war between nothing less than the continuous struggle between the imaginative life as depicted in the old myths his "true Love" and the practical and rational life of contemporary society, of which he is most familiar.

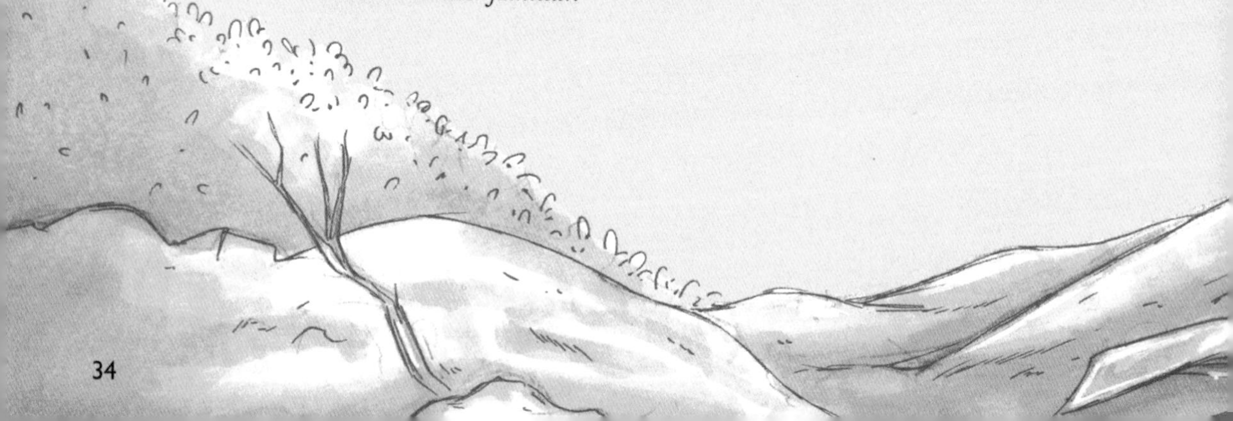

In a February 1937 letter to his friend Edward James, Dalí reveals even more details:

Many deserts, frozen Indian, horseback riding among
the cacti art world, "beautiful symmetries" blond super-platinum, etc. . .
HARPO is a delightful person and one of the finest. I'm making a drawing
with his HARP I think is lovely.

Over the following months, while Harpo was shooting the Marx Brothers film *A Day at the Races*, Dalí would work on his first Hollywood script, with his new friend as the lead character.

The general idea of the scenario consists of all the imaginative pomp splendor
and epic characters of Cecil B. DeMille's antiquity films.
For this purpose, we will have as a protagonist an immensely wealthy woman
living on the principle of fantasy and the most sensational madness and a
man, that is you, HARPO, but not yet, troubled by the pull of two worlds.

In addition to the story and characters, Dalí filled his notebook with pages of absurd moments, visual gags that he seemingly intended the Marx Brothers to infuse with their comic genius.

GAGS

1. *Waterproof jacket with stars . . .*

2. *Groucho is dancing a tango passionately, his cheek annoys him on the cheek of his partner, he removes a piece of her cheek with a spoon, as if his cheek was made of pear and pushes his chin back in that hole, and continues dancing more passionately than ever.*

3. *Various objects and walls of a room built of fresh clay, so you can rest on any object or area very comfortably and during construction one could also cut objects with a wire after a distraction he cuts off his own pants.*

4. *The butler serves cocktails on a large soft cello.*

5. *The butler throws a magnificently large piano from the top of the stairs, and then the pianos themselves take this action upon themselves, the guests pay no attention as they enter.*

6. *In a hotel's corridor, we hear behind the door some cries of terror and crazy laughs, a cave at the end and dense smoke.*

7. *Either a cut melon on a plate which slowly walks on the carpet (the plate is attached on the back of a turtle, people crossing the corridor pay no attention to this.)*

8. *Groucho offers a cigarette and instead of cigarettes there is mustache in his style.*

9. Groucho, Harpo and Chico trying by all means to save the day.

Groucho makes a sign to approach with caution to a locomotive, which gently enters the room and lies down in front of all present. He holds back the nose with clamps in front while, at the same time, Chico provides a guillotine.

Harpo fashions a blade to his face and puts his nose to cut the nose of the train in half, but just at that moment, he sees a train coming the other way.

Groucho leans through the guillotine, while resting his elbows on the ground and his hands to his cheeks on the other side.

The lights go out and Chico sees the train by using a lamp on his head.

10. Harpo appears naked with a lobster on his head while stroking a monkey. He is surrounded by a huge forest of harps, which are lost to infinity on the grass. He grates a statue with his harp as if it was cheese and gives some food to his monkey. The cold wind resonates all the harps.

11. Harpo comes out with his harp and a candle to find it filled with a little living octopus clinging to the strings. He starts playing, He opens a box and finds his usual garments completely eaten by moths.

12. Kaleidoscope, alive, with fishes inside, in which Harpo drops.

13. Waterproof watch with blinds that can open and close. Etc. etc. etc.

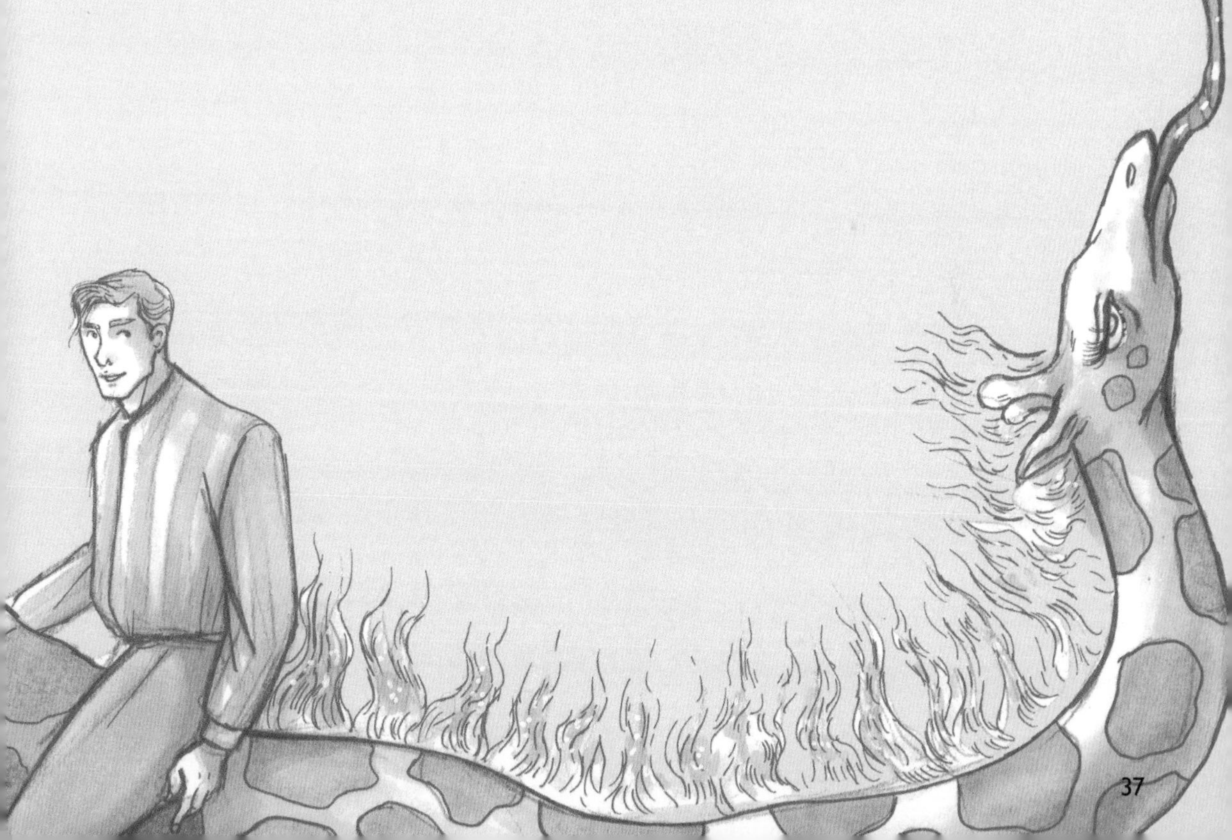

GIRAFFES ON HORSEBACK SALAD

HOLLYWOOD, CALIFORNIA, 1937—As the weeks passed, Dalí would sit in the California desert and work on his film script. The manic notes in his "Giraffes" notebook, as well as the musings in his autobiography, suggest that two worlds came together: the external world of his self-created refugee camp (i.e., the desert backlands of Hollywood, California) and his internal world of pain, fears, and visions of a land far away that was no longer safe for him to call home.

The result of that collision would become his script for a film he titled Giraffes on Horseback Salad. Again, his notebook reveals the workings of his mind:

A woman called the surrealist woman personifies the world of fantasy, dreams and imagination.

Her friends are the Marx Brothers, which are the true protagonists of everything that happens.

Linda is a snobbish woman. Intelligent but unimaginative, she personifies the struggle between the two women, i.e. between the two worlds this struggle culminates in a war in which neither world can win or escape because absurdity cannot be judged.

It is nothing less than the struggle between the world of imagination and fantasy and the conventional world.

Jimmy falls in love with the surrealist woman at the beginning of the film, but the pull of the "normal" life, "the proper path," always perseveres. However, he is intoxicated by the life that he has just discovered, with her. Who will he transform into? Something? Nothing? What will remain?

As Dalí plots the scenario, his troubles back home haunt him. In the early days of his exile he had learned that his dear friend Federico García Lorca has been executed during the war. Later, Dalí found out that his sister

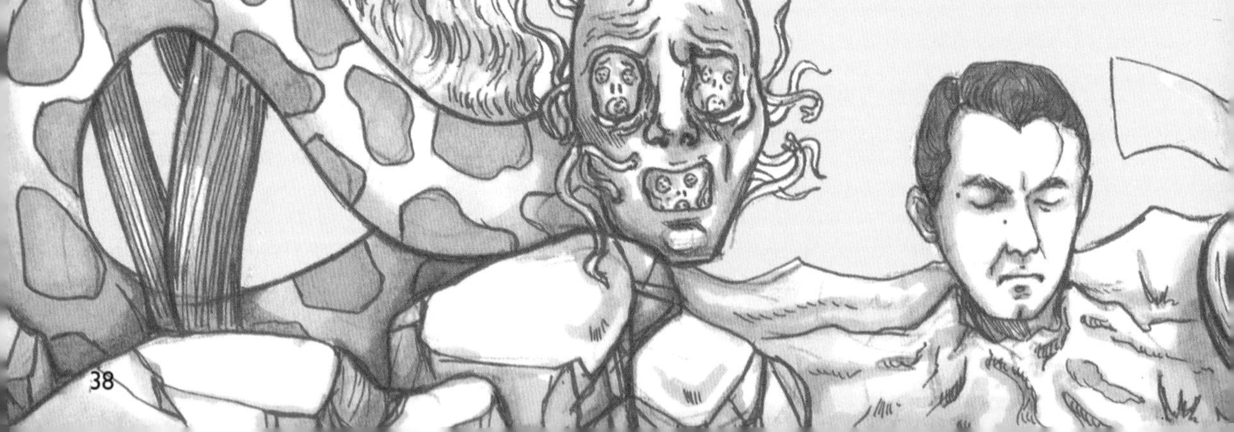

Ana Maria was imprisoned and tortured. His notes within the binding of his notebook show a man grappling with guilt, anger, fear, and frustration. Within the whirlwind of words are seeds of the imagery for the film.

Here is my space, and also here is my space, and here is the wonderful world on earth. Of course, this was incompatible with the feeling of guilt, which was the main representative.

He rescues his own face. He rescues simultaneously the architecture.

Soft structure of Apollonia. The lady plays the same role and is the equivalent to the mayonnaise sauce for the crayfish. A bicycle game with mammoth outdoor structure symbolizes the materialist notion and practice of the resurrection of the flesh. She wears her bones and her true self on her hands.

The soft structures grips around the soft marble. The soft marble smiles philosophically, stupidly.

Paranoia delirium of interpretation including the systematic structure. Paranoid critical method, spontaneous method of irrational knowledge based on the abolition interpretative critical of delirious phenomena.

With the head on the right and the tail on the left. The dead, the female and also the crescent moon crushing diagonally and the death struggle of the workers and the fishermen.

One day, alone in the desert, Dalí looks down at his own shadow. And it is there that he finds the inspiration for what the movie is really about.

(The film is preceded by a historical preface on Caligula.)

Immediately this woman appears as if she is surrounded by an atmosphere of extravagance!

All of the sentimental and dramatic development of the plot is based on the continuous struggle between the imaginative life as depicted in the old myths and the practical and national life of contemporary society. These struggles are so violent that they possess the very souls of the two main characters. Whereas HE always hopes for a normal life while being consumed by the continuous hallucination in which they live surrounded by her mysterious power!

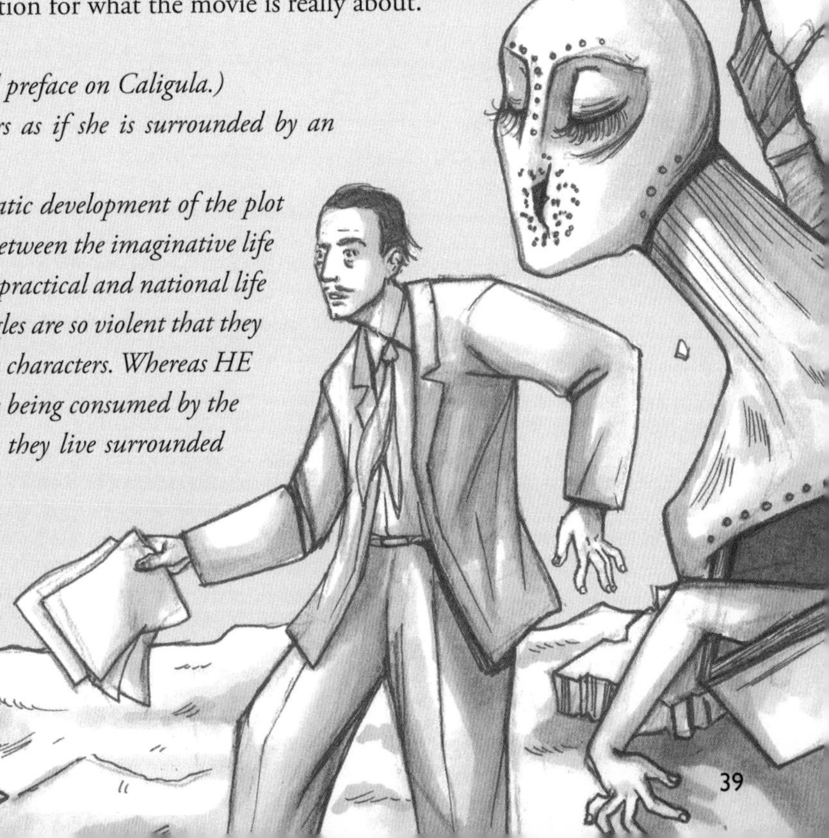

THE BIG MEETING

HOLLYWOOD, CA, 1937, IN THE SPRINGTIME—After months of work, Dalí has completed a fourteen-page treatment of *Giraffes on Horseback Salad*. Harpo arranges a meeting with Louis B. Mayer. Soon the two are in the studio head's office and, as recounted in his notebook, Dalí immediately jumps into his pitch.

I see Harpo battling a lively crayfish that jumps in a pan of boiling water to protect himself. Harpo opens an umbrella and a chicken explodes on all the onlookers. He looks at all of the chicken pieces dispersed everywhere and puts each piece carefully on a saddle that he uses as a plate . . . a saddle not for a horse . . . but for a giraffe!

The meeting did not go well.

Despite Dalí's influence in the art world, in Hollywood he was a relative unknown, and his surreal vision for what its powerful movie assembly line could do with his script was something the studios were not ready to gamble on. Harpo was unable to convince even his own brother that the project was worth donning his greasepaint mustache for. Groucho's exact words were: "It won't play."

The movie would never be made, and Dalí's script was lost to time.

It was clear from his own journal entry, on the final pages of notes for the *Giraffes* manuscript, that Dalí left Hollywood feeling defeated, unsettled, and lost—not only by the outcome of his dream project but also by his outcast status among his own movement and his ongoing life as a refugee.

He wrote:

> *Much like a snake losing its skin, we discover that the large pianos lose their skin too, because Salvador Dalí recently began peeling off the nostalgic beaches of his imagination.*

The same skins surrealists were peeling at for so long. They had hoped that by doing so, they would lose the epidermis of their own definition.

Critics rushed, enraged, now tearing up into analytical shreds the skins of the surrealists. I do not pretend to understand their private lives but it seems obvious to me that the phenomenon of aesthetic becomes impossible to be understood. —not to the surrealist— It is impossible to reduce it to a logical language. It exists outside the increasingly specialized framework offered to us nowadays by the sensational progress of the practical science.

Indeed, how could we dare use the Euclidean concepts of time and space to measure distances, or the great ones who went to the true cosmic vertigo and psychological patients, the gods of philosophical drama?

Ultimately, it's what the great surrealist artists materialize, more or less effortlessly in their works.

When Plato jokingly wrote his famous: "Let no one ignorant of geometry enter," he had more foresight than he could have known or believed. Nowadays, physics has become the new geometry of the mind. We surrealists, we rode to the gate of the glittering palace of surrealism, and found a sign that read, "no admittance to those ignorant of physics."

We will look at 5 in the morning in the true face of time, and we'll be back to sleep by a special door of the dream built in a thick white horse mane.

LADIES AND GENTLEMEN, PLEASE REMOVE YOUR HATS

For the past eighty years, descriptions of *Giraffes on Horseback Salad* have been limited to a handful of paragraphs. Fragments of Dalí's script have popped up in magazine articles and, later, in a few blogs across the internet, but the totality of his vision has remained obscured. Until now.

In 2017, the Marx family generously provided this author with access to an amazing document: a typed draft of the *Giraffes on Horseback Salad* film treatment, likely the same manuscript that Dalí handed to MGM back in 1937. And then this skeleton gained flesh, blood, and spirit from an even

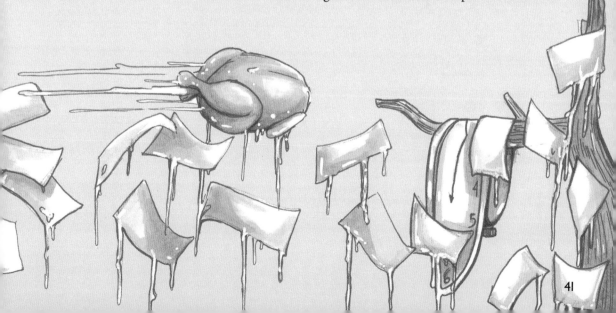

more astounding discovery: the original handwritten texts and sketches from Dalí's notebook, untouched for decades in their final resting place: the archives of the Centre Pompidou in Paris.

For all these years, the movie was hiding in those amazing pages of lost history, within the story ideas, notes, and doodles that constitute the true manuscript of *Giraffes on Horseback Salad*. The essence of the film is written between those lines and sketches, allowing an adaptation that comes as close as possible to bringing Dalí's Marx Brothers film to an eager and curious audience.

So let's imagine that things had gone differently . . .

Imagine that Irving Thalberg, producer of *A Night at the Opera* and *A Day at the Races*, had lived to see Harpo and Dalí cross the threshold of his office. Thalberg, a visionary studio head and friend of the Marxes, might just have greenlit this exceptional project. Imagine that under his watchful and creative eye, a more audience-friendly take on Dalí's vision had been released.

The year is 1939. An usher in a brass-buttoned uniform and bellhop cap has guided you to your seat. The well-heeled audience, dressed to the nines, is buzzing with excitement about the premiere of an unprecedented collaboration between creative geniuses.

The lights go down. A hush falls over the crowd.

The thick red curtain slowly rises, revealing a movie screen flickering with images. A lantern slide reminds you to remove your hats.

You settle in to your seat as *Giraffes on Horseback Salad* begins.

THE OPENING CREDITS ROLL . . .

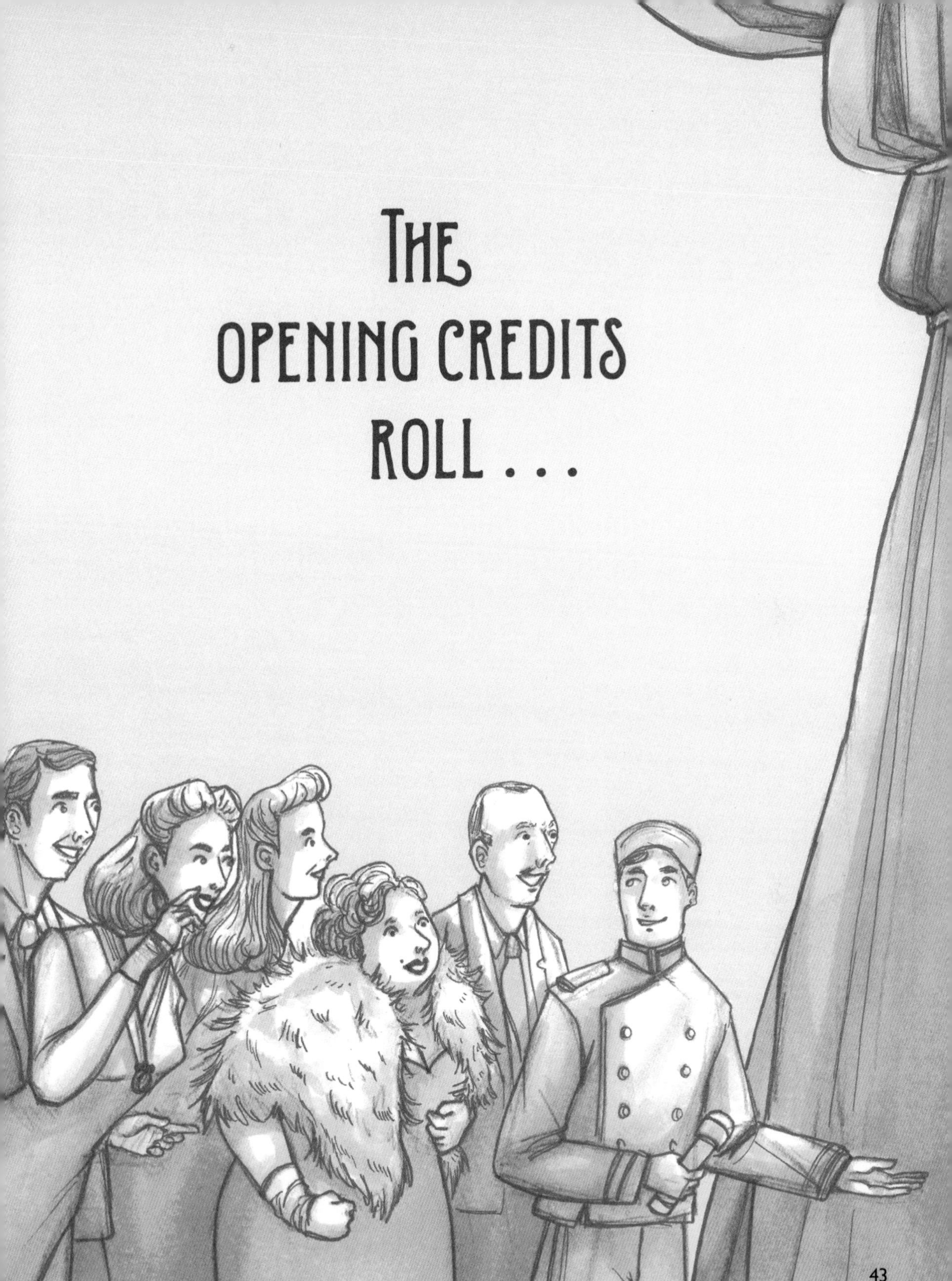

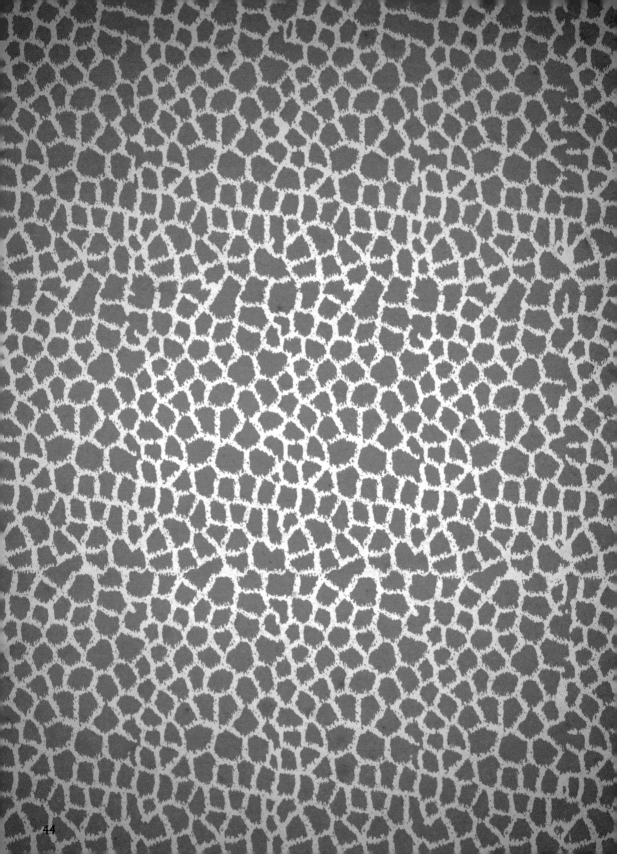

GIRAFFES
ON
HORSEBACK
SALAD

FILM BY the Marx Brothers

SCENARIO AND SETTINGS BY Salvador Dali

ADAPTED BY Josh Frank with Tim Heidecker

ILLUSTRATED BY Manuela Pertega

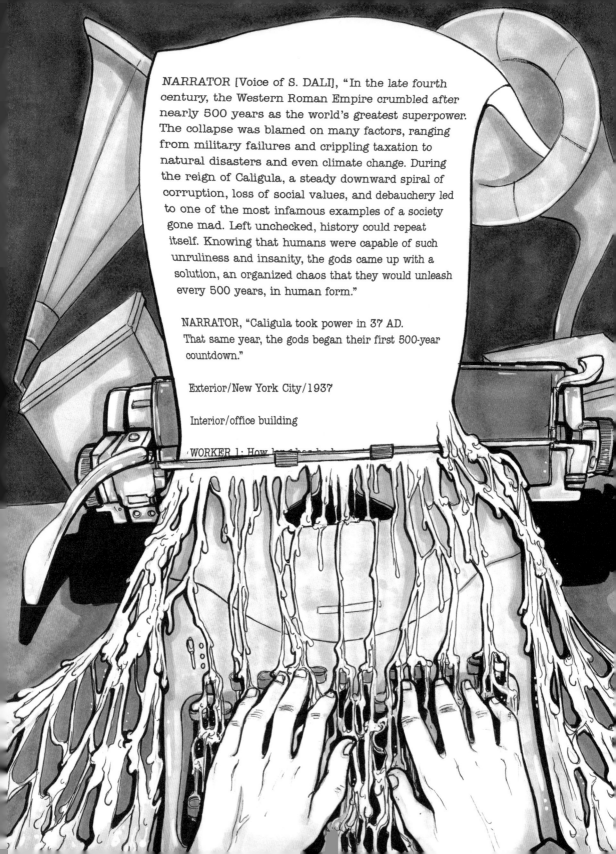

NARRATOR [Voice of S. DALI], "In the late fourth century, the Western Roman Empire crumbled after nearly 500 years as the world's greatest superpower. The collapse was blamed on many factors, ranging from military failures and crippling taxation to natural disasters and even climate change. During the reign of Caligula, a steady downward spiral of corruption, loss of social values, and debauchery led to one of the most infamous examples of a society gone mad. Left unchecked, history could repeat itself. Knowing that humans were capable of such unruliness and insanity, the gods came up with a solution, an organized chaos that they would unleash every 500 years, in human form."

NARRATOR, "Caligula took power in 37 AD. That same year, the gods began their first 500-year countdown."

Exterior/New York City/1937

Interior/office building

WORKER 1: How [illegible]

ACT 1: THE MAN FROM SPAIN

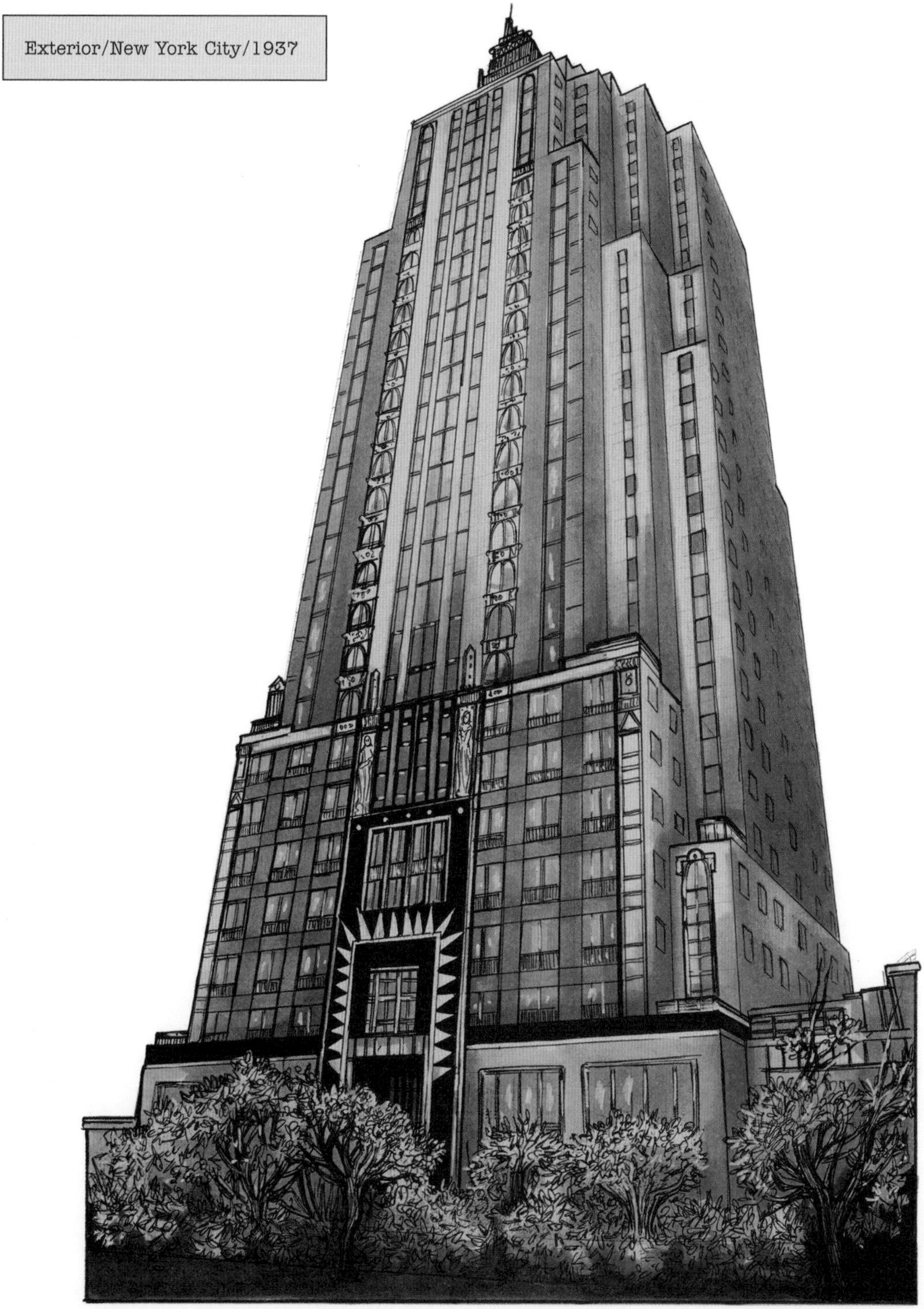
Exterior/New York City/1937

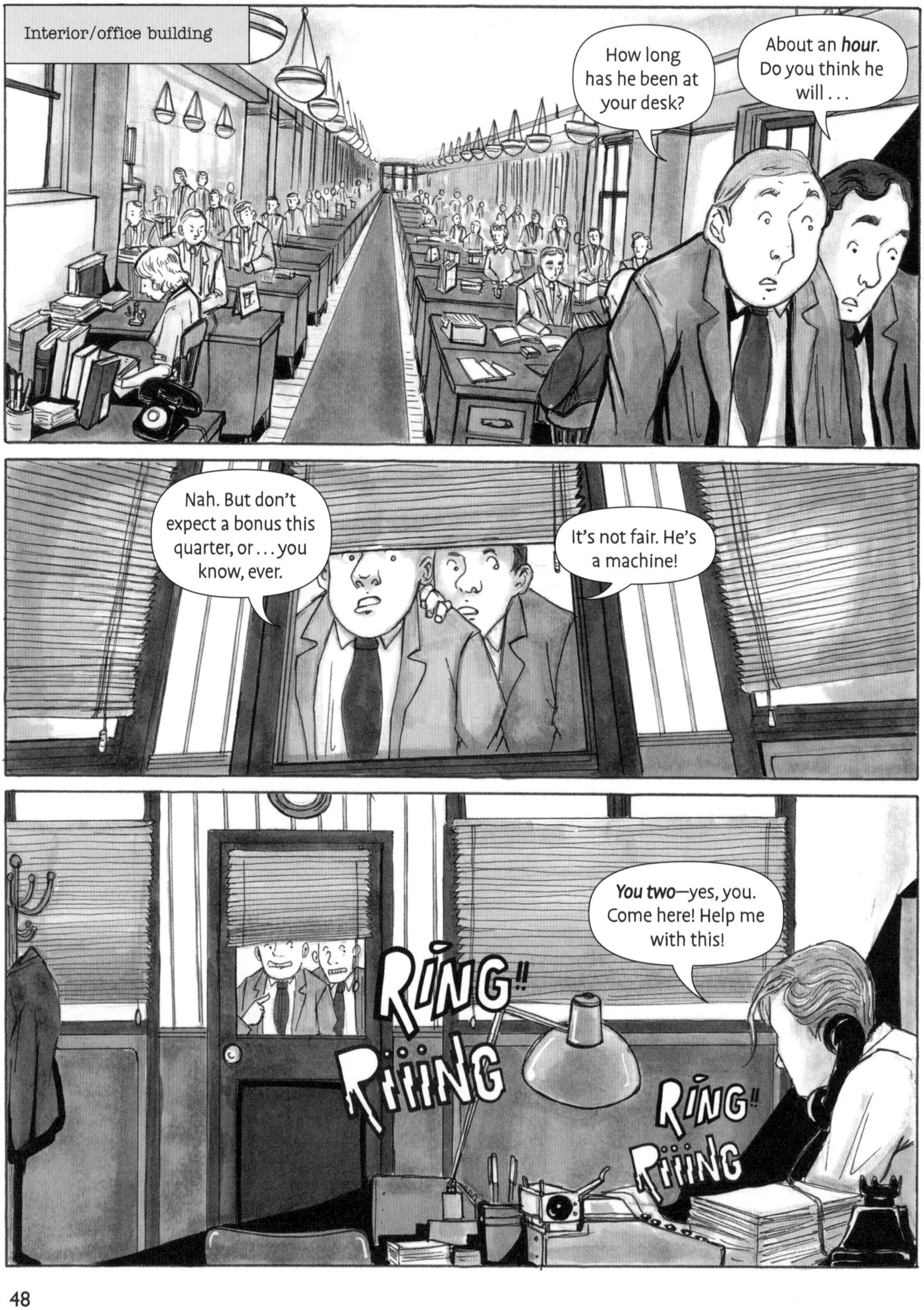
Interior/office building
How long has he been at your desk?
About an **hour**. Do you think he will . . .
Nah. But don't expect a bonus this quarter, or . . . you know, ever.
It's not fair. He's a machine!
You two—yes, you. Come here! Help me with this!
RING!! RIIING
RING!! RIIING

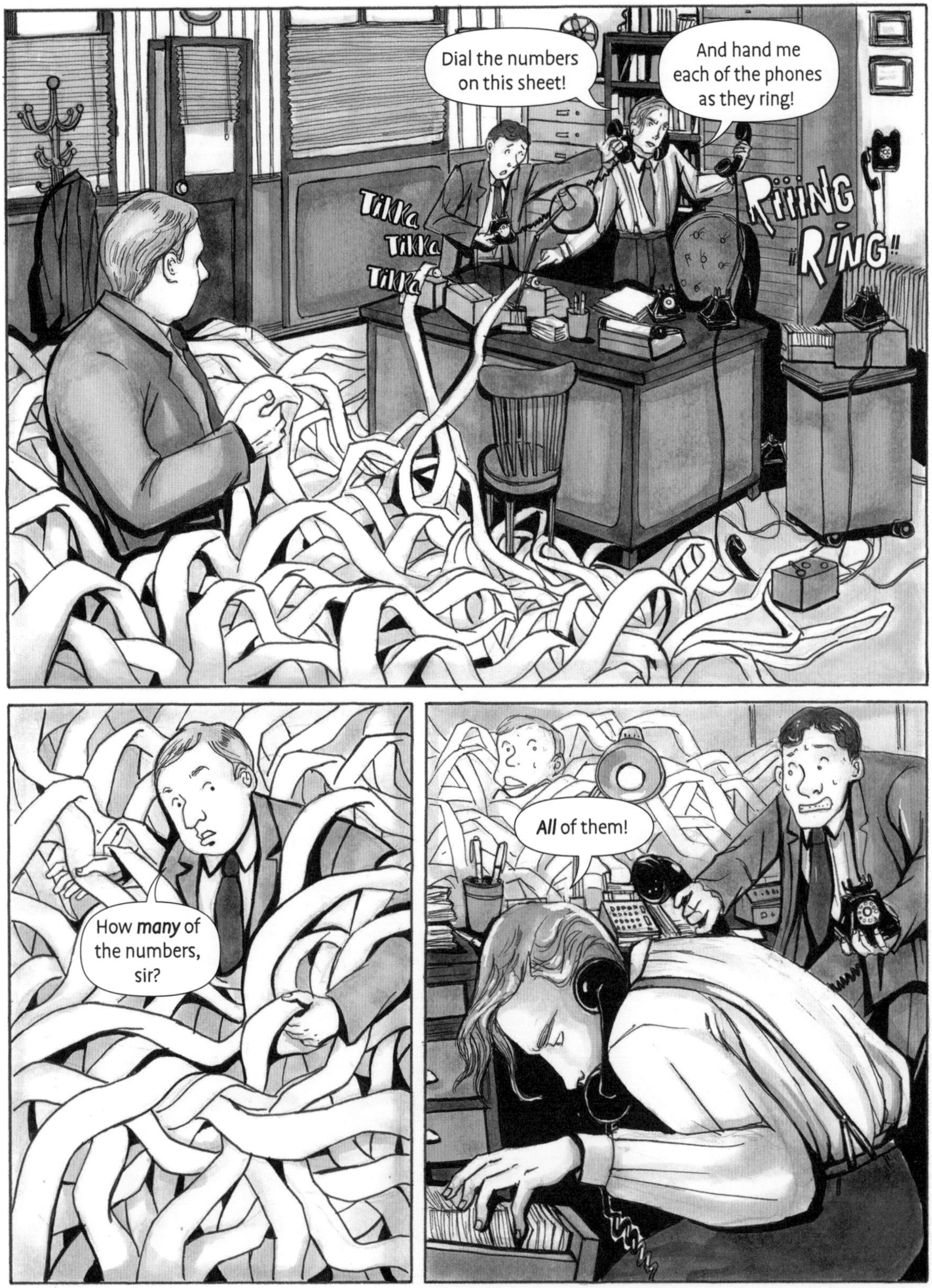
Dial the numbers on this sheet!
And hand me each of the phones as they ring!
TIKKA TIKKA TIKKA
RIIIING RING!!
How *many* of the numbers, sir?
All of them!

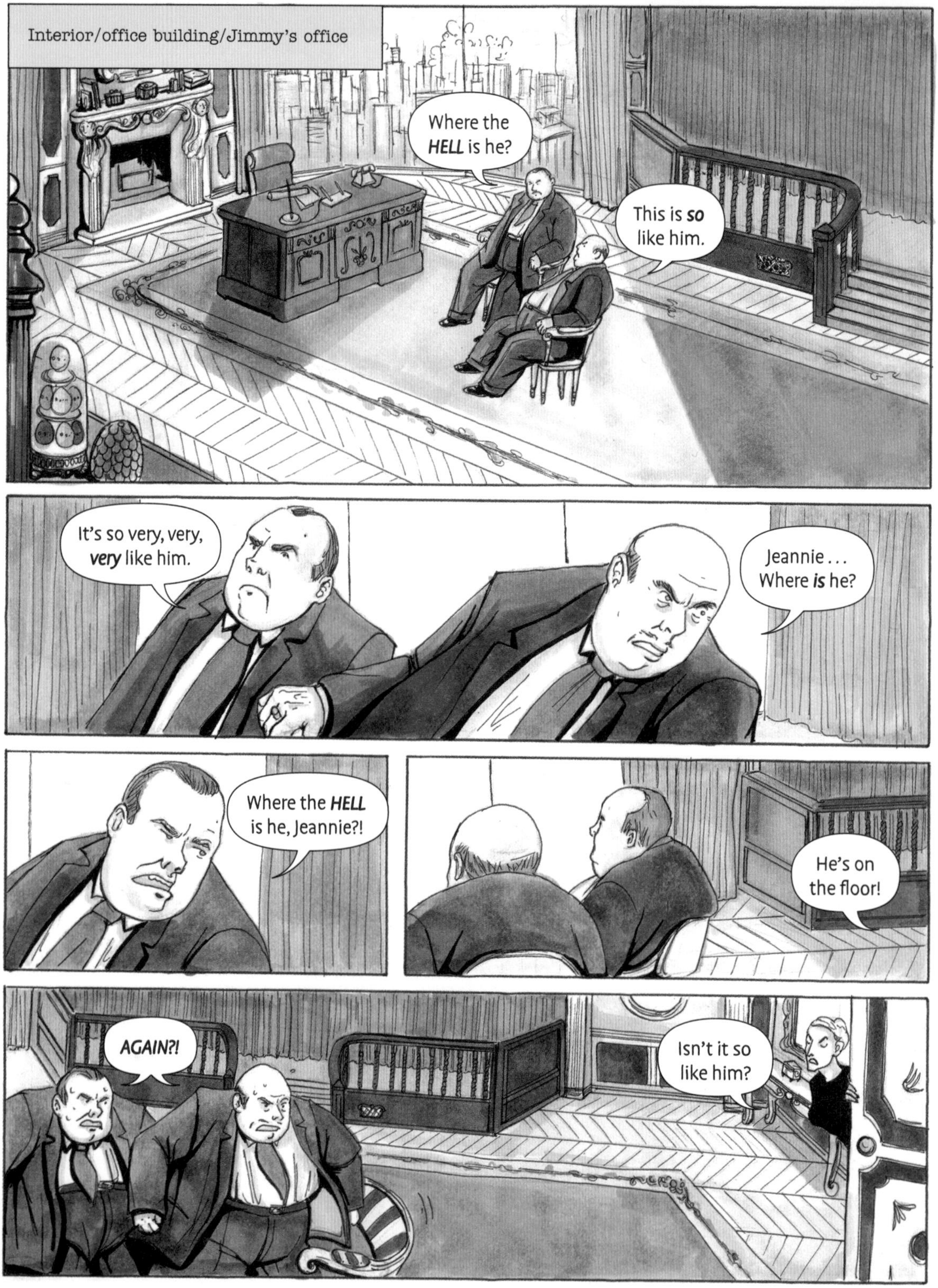
Interior/office building/Jimmy's office
Where the HELL is he?
This is so like him.
It's so very, very, very like him.
Jeannie . . . Where is he?
Where the HELL is he, Jeannie?!
He's on the floor!
AGAIN?!
Isn't it so like him?

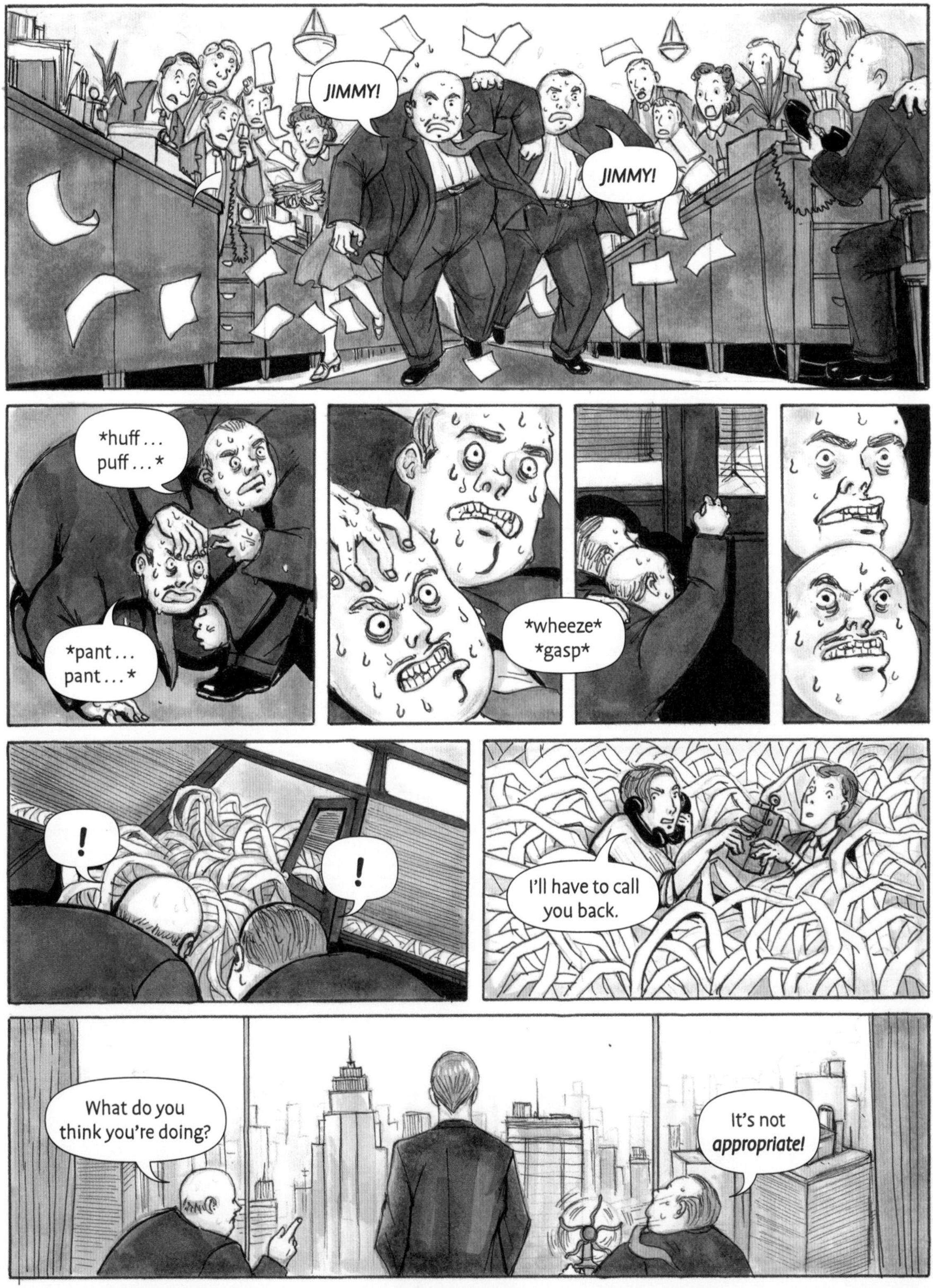
JIMMY!
JIMMY!
huff . . . puff . . .
pant . . . pant . . .
wheeze *gasp*
!
!
I'll have to call you back.
What do you think you're doing?
It's not *appropriate!*

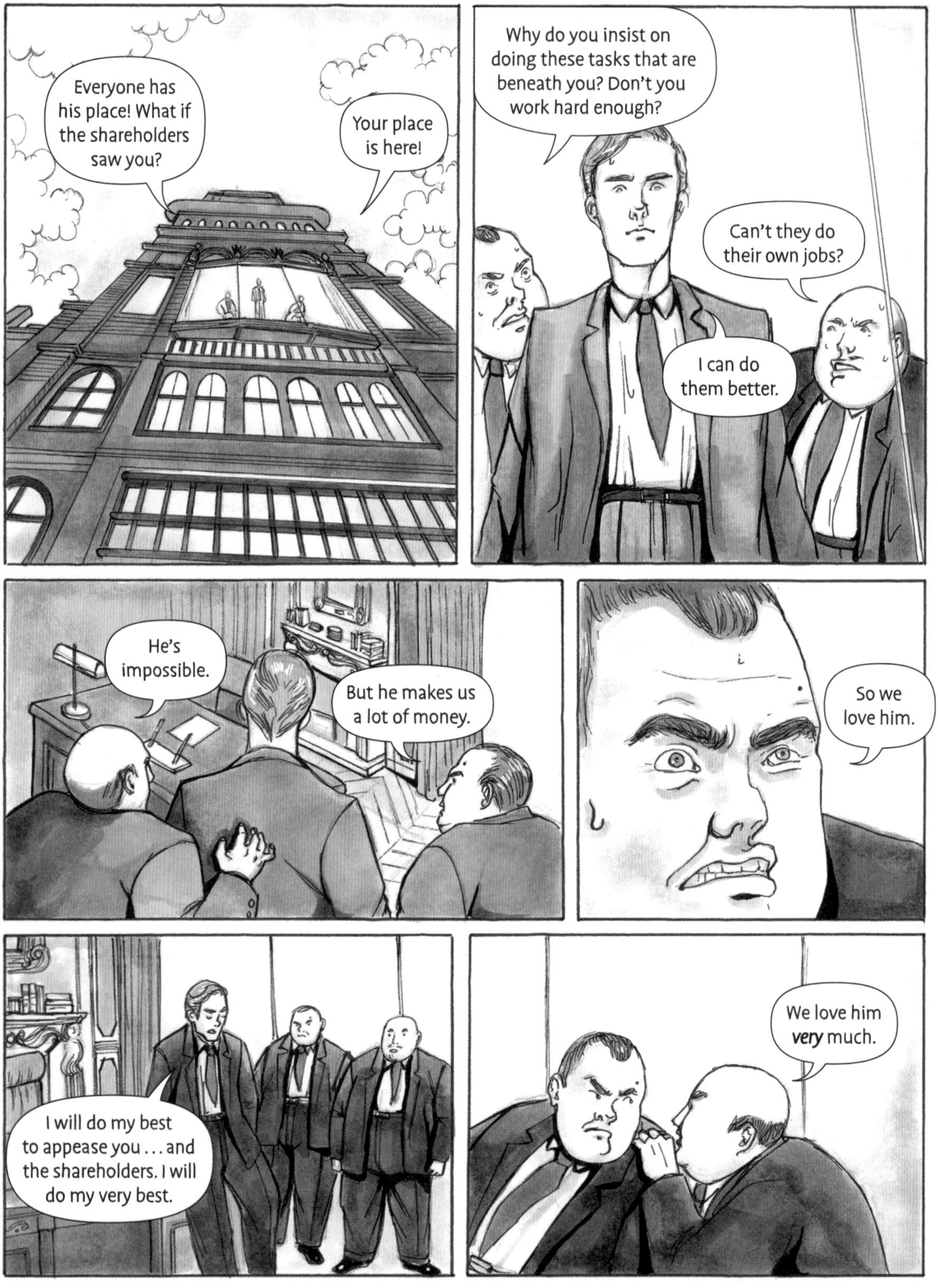
Everyone has his place! What if the shareholders saw you?
Your place is here!
Why do you insist on doing these tasks that are beneath you? Don't you work hard enough?
Can't they do their own jobs?
I can do them better.
He's impossible.
But he makes us a lot of money.
So we love him.
I will do my best to appease you . . . and the shareholders. I will do my very best.
We love him *very* much.

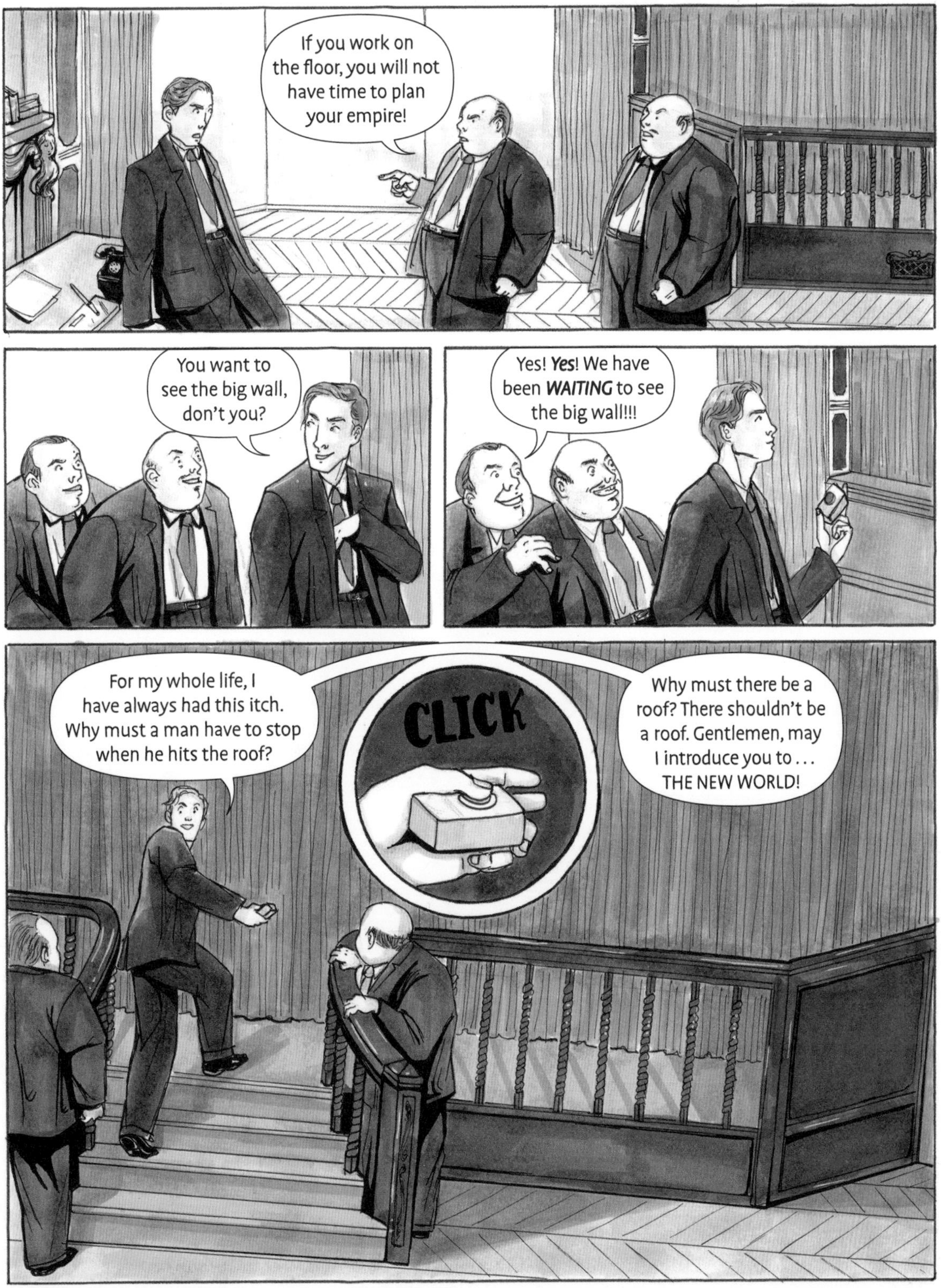
If you work on the floor, you will not have time to plan your empire!
You want to see the big wall, don't you?
Yes! **Yes**! We have been ***WAITING*** to see the big wall!!!
For my whole life, I have always had this itch. Why must a man have to stop when he hits the roof?
CLICK
Why must there be a roof? There shouldn't be a roof. Gentlemen, may I introduce you to . . . THE NEW WORLD!

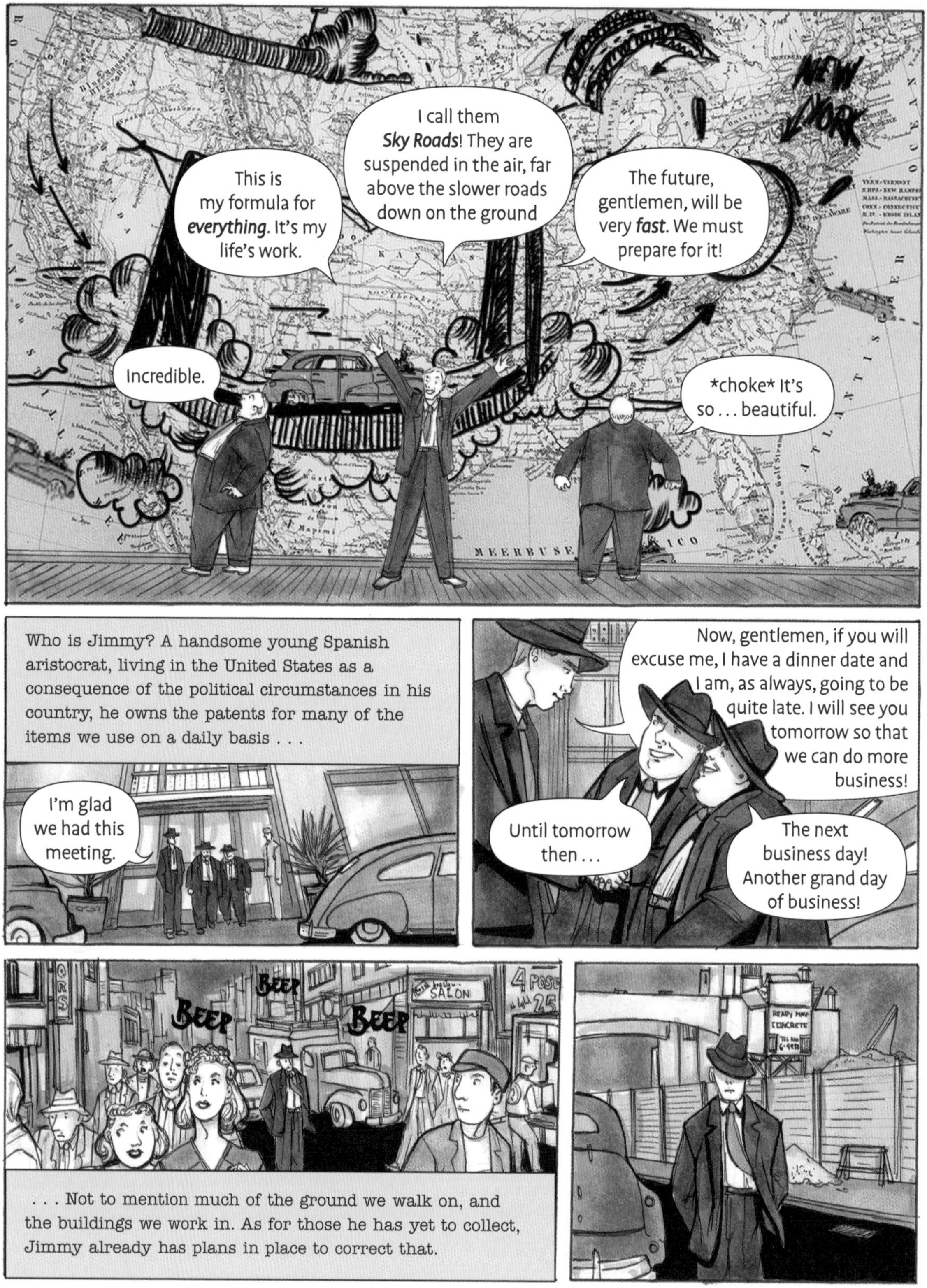
NEW YORK
This is my formula for *everything*. It's my life's work.
I call them ***Sky Roads***! They are suspended in the air, far above the slower roads down on the ground
The future, gentlemen, will be very ***fast***. We must prepare for it!
Incredible.
choke It's so . . . beautiful.
Who is Jimmy? A handsome young Spanish aristocrat, living in the United States as a consequence of the political circumstances in his country, he owns the patents for many of the items we use on a daily basis . . .
I'm glad we had this meeting.
Now, gentlemen, if you will excuse me, I have a dinner date and I am, as always, going to be quite late. I will see you tomorrow so that we can do more business!
Until tomorrow then . . .
The next business day! Another grand day of business!
BEEP
BEEP
BEEP
SALON
. . . Not to mention much of the ground we walk on, and the buildings we work in. As for those he has yet to collect, Jimmy already has plans in place to correct that.

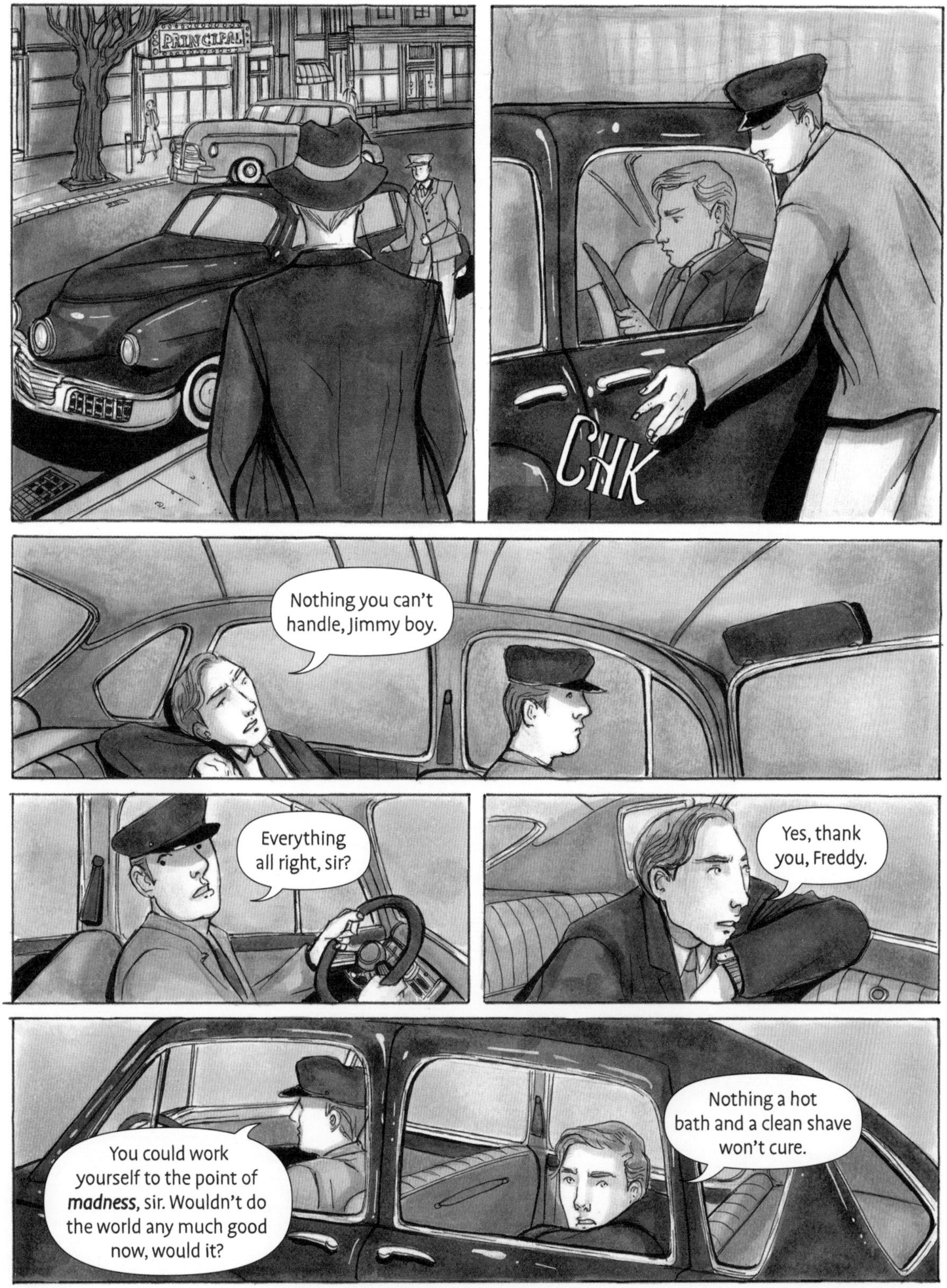
PRINCIPAL
CHK
Nothing you can't handle, Jimmy boy.
Everything all right, sir?
Yes, thank you, Freddy.
Nothing a hot bath and a clean shave won't cure.
You could work yourself to the point of *madness*, sir. Wouldn't do the world any much good now, would it?

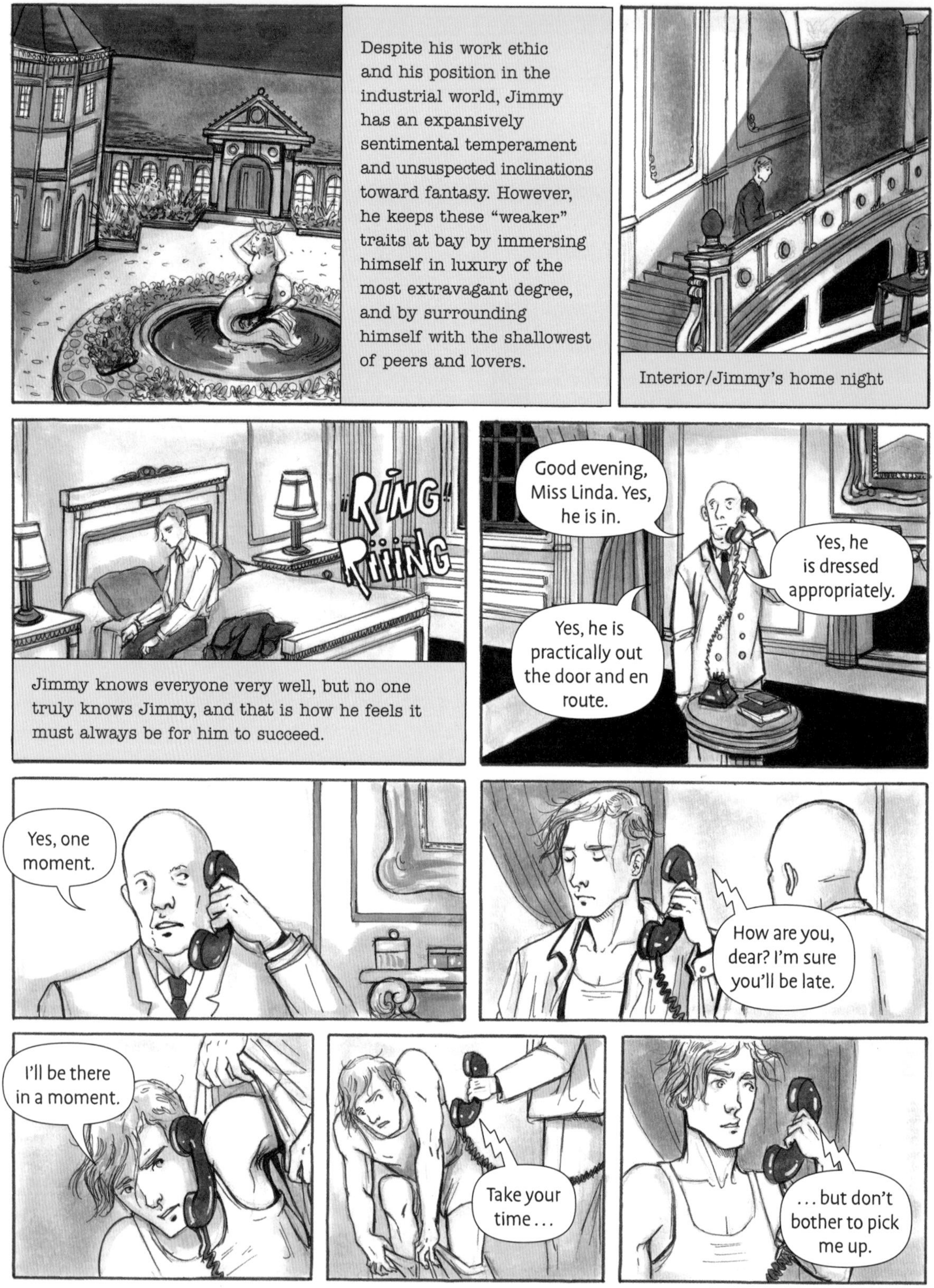
Despite his work ethic and his position in the industrial world, Jimmy has an expansively sentimental temperament and unsuspected inclinations toward fantasy. However, he keeps these "weaker" traits at bay by immersing himself in luxury of the most extravagant degree, and by surrounding himself with the shallowest of peers and lovers.
Interior/Jimmy's home night
RING!
RIIING
Jimmy knows everyone very well, but no one truly knows Jimmy, and that is how he feels it must always be for him to succeed.
Good evening, Miss Linda. Yes, he is in.
Yes, he is dressed appropriately.
Yes, he is practically out the door and en route.
Yes, one moment.
How are you, dear? I'm sure you'll be late.
I'll be there in a moment.
Take your time . . .
. . . but don't bother to pick me up.

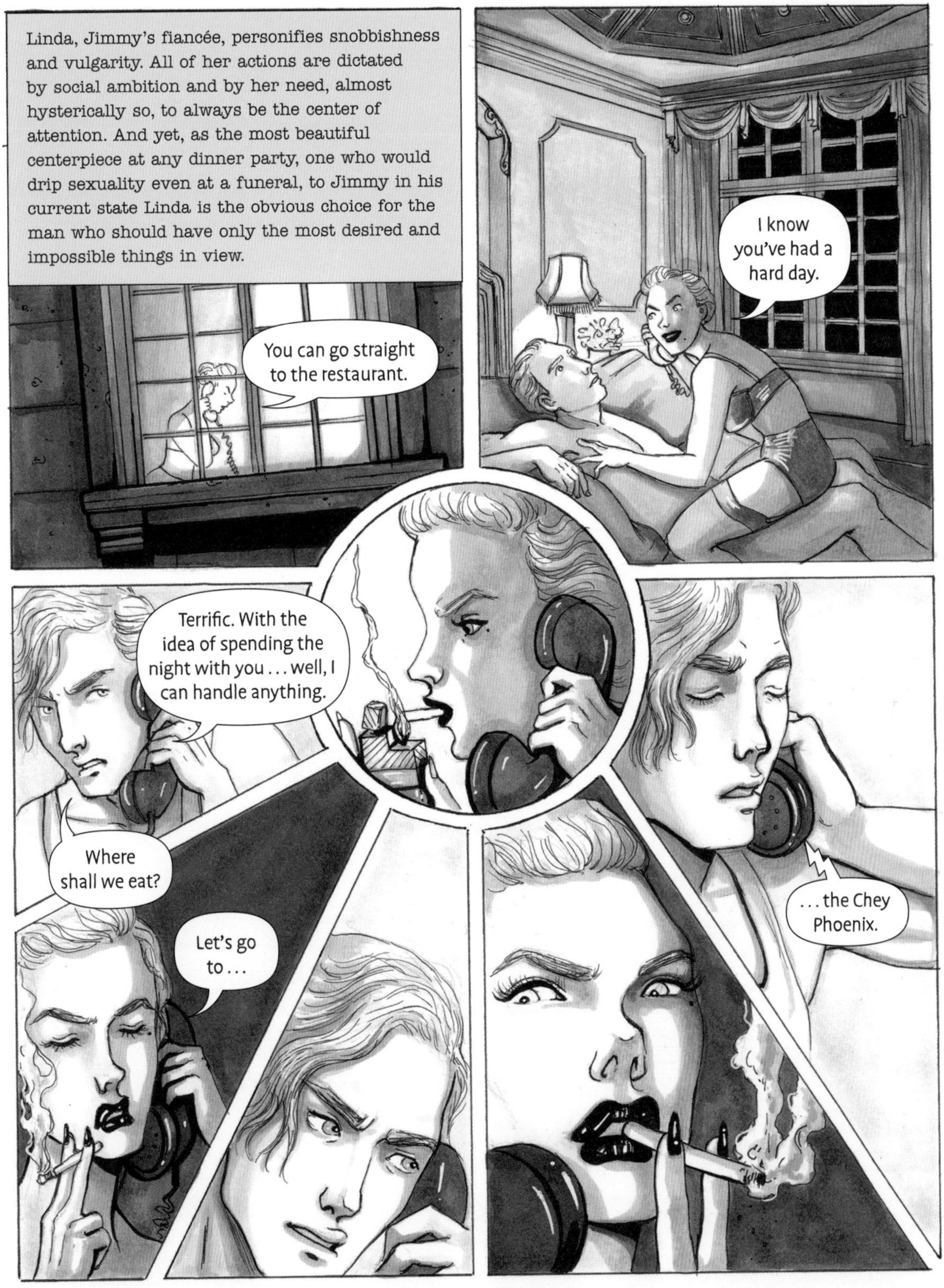
Linda, Jimmy's fiancée, personifies snobbishness and vulgarity. All of her actions are dictated by social ambition and by her need, almost hysterically so, to always be the center of attention. And yet, as the most beautiful centerpiece at any dinner party, one who would drip sexuality even at a funeral, to Jimmy in his current state Linda is the obvious choice for the man who should have only the most desired and impossible things in view.
You can go straight to the restaurant.
I know you've had a hard day.
Terrific. With the idea of spending the night with you . . . well, I can handle anything.
Where shall we eat?
Let's go to . . .
. . . the Chey Phoenix.

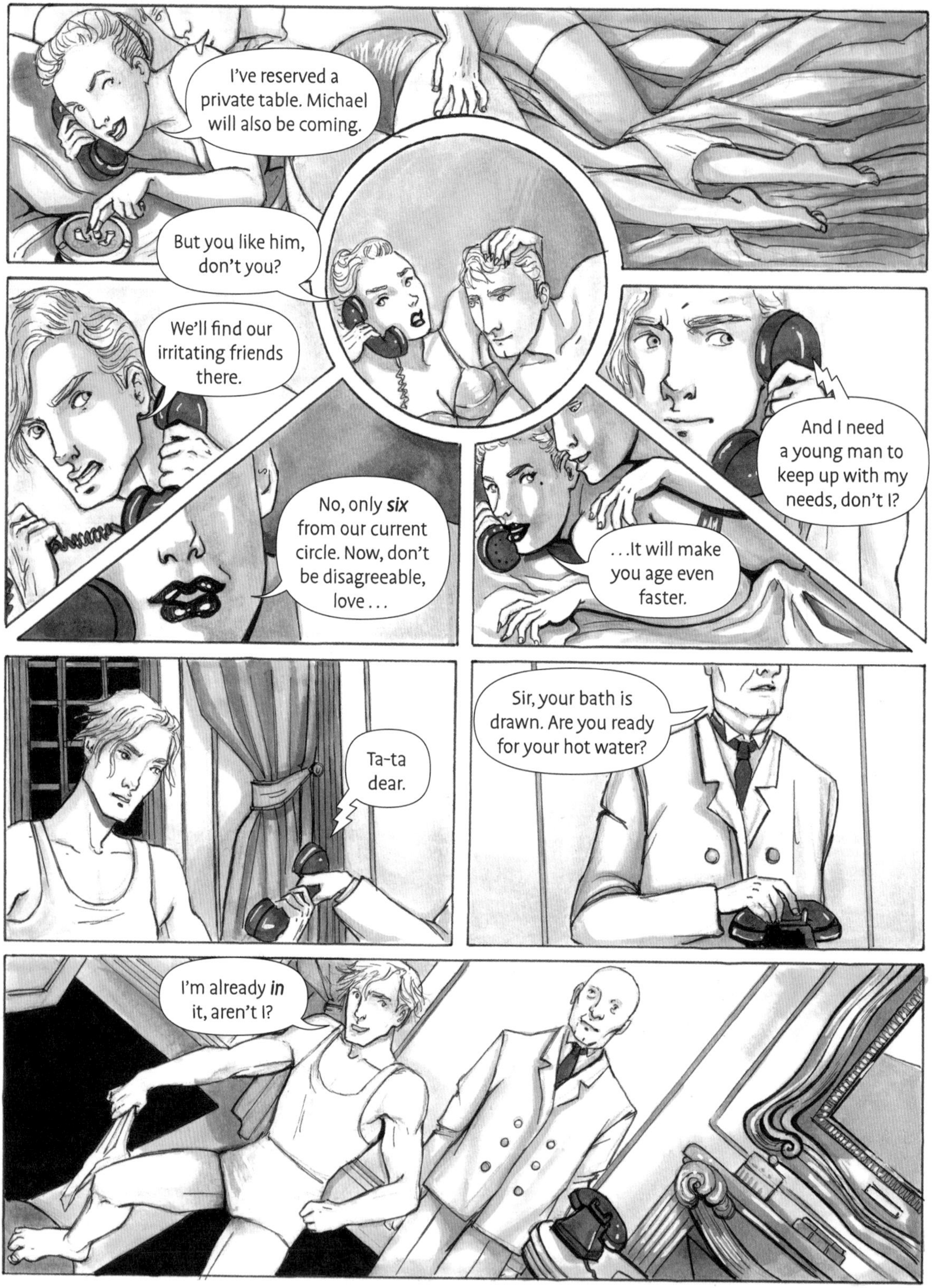
I've reserved a private table. Michael will also be coming.
But you like him, don't you?
We'll find our irritating friends there.
No, only ***six*** from our current circle. Now, don't be disagreeable, love . . .
. . .It will make you age even faster.
And I need a young man to keep up with my needs, don't I?
Ta-ta dear.
Sir, your bath is drawn. Are you ready for your hot water?
I'm already ***in*** it, aren't I?

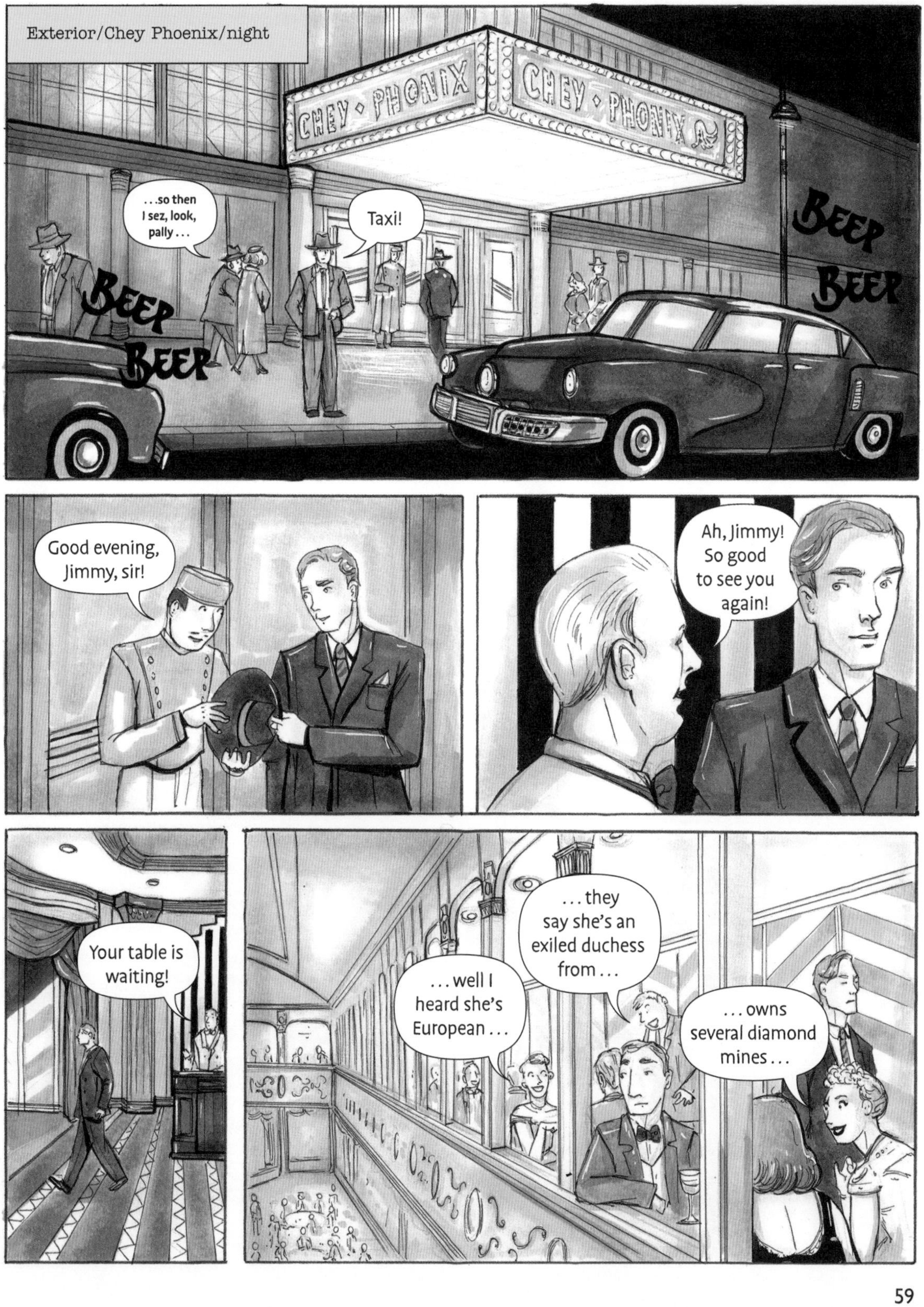
Exterior/Chey Phoenix/night
CHEY · PHONIX
CHEY · PHONIX
...so then I sez, look, pally...
Taxi!
BEEP BEEP
BEEP BEEP
Good evening, Jimmy, sir!
Ah, Jimmy! So good to see you again!
Your table is waiting!
...they say she's an exiled duchess from...
...well I heard she's European...
...owns several diamond mines...

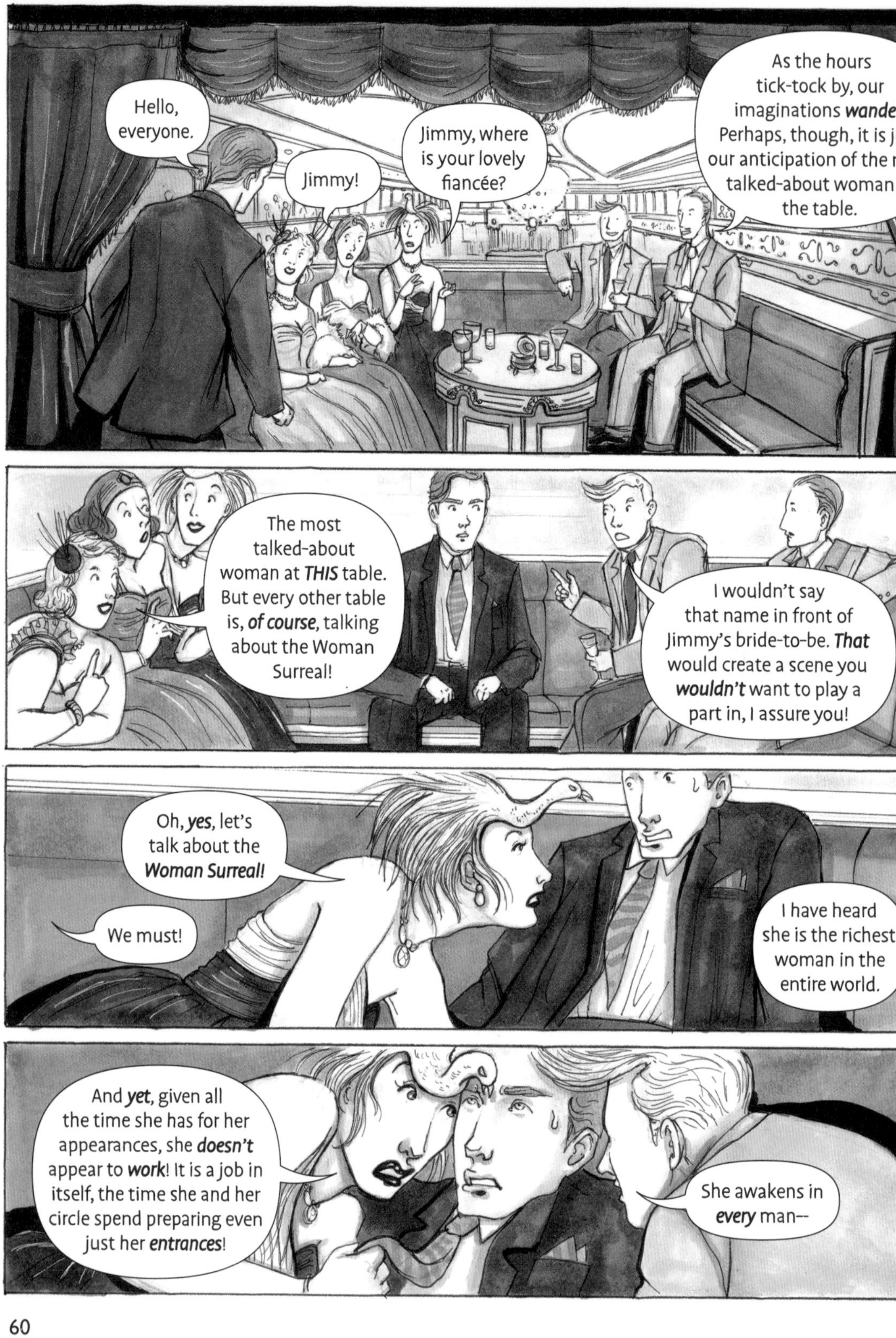
Hello, everyone.
Jimmy!
Jimmy, where is your lovely fiancée?
As the hours tick-tock by, our imaginations *wander*. Perhaps, though, it is just our anticipation of the most talked-about woman at the table.
The most talked-about woman at *THIS* table. But every other table is, *of course*, talking about the Woman Surreal!
I wouldn't say that name in front of Jimmy's bride-to-be. *That* would create a scene you *wouldn't* want to play a part in, I assure you!
Oh, *yes*, let's talk about the *Woman Surreal!*
We must!
I have heard she is the richest woman in the entire world.
And *yet*, given all the time she has for her appearances, she *doesn't* appear to *work*! It is a job in itself, the time she and her circle spend preparing even just her *entrances*!
She awakens in *every* man--

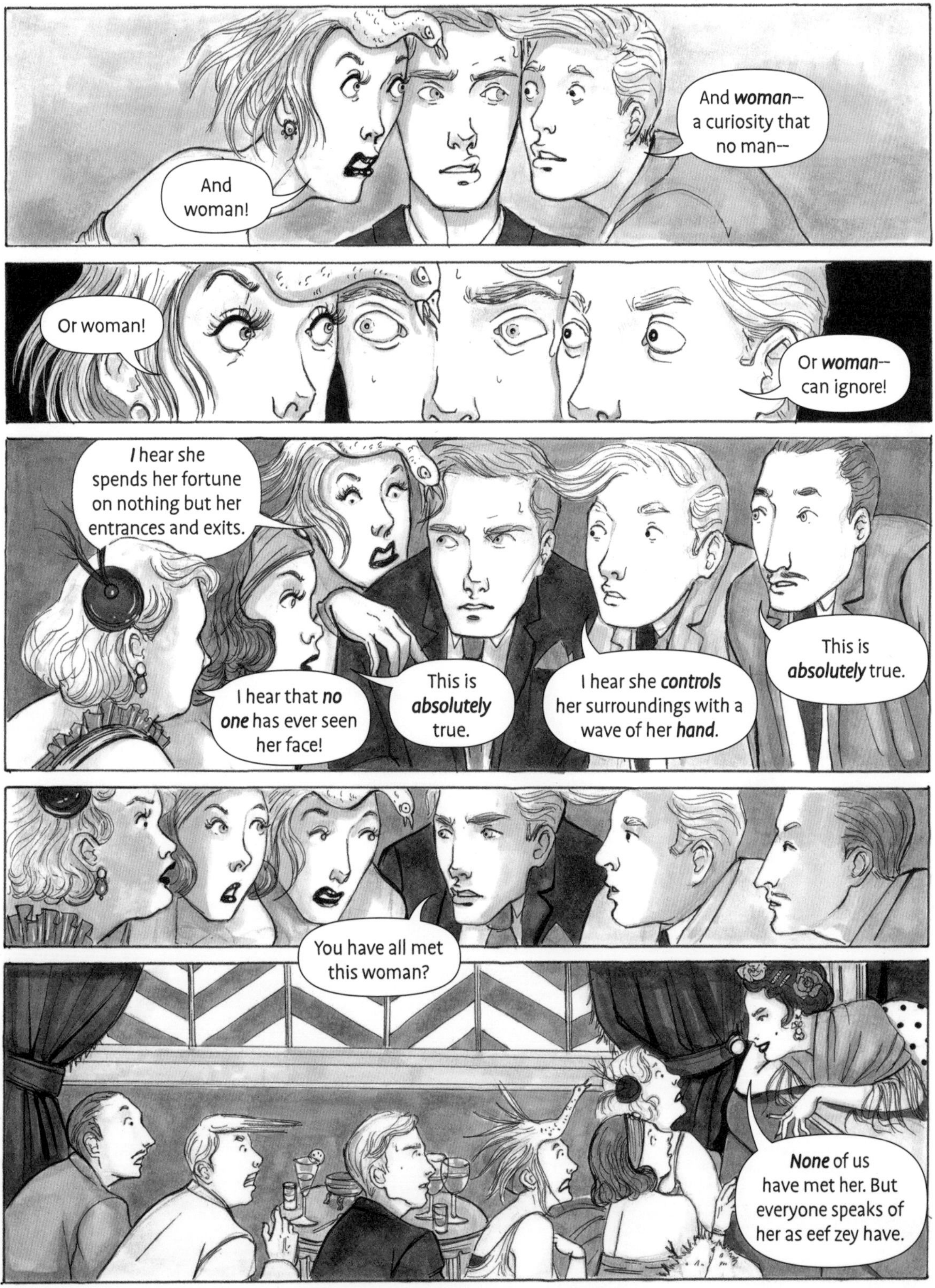
And woman!
And *woman*-- a curiosity that no man--
Or woman!
Or *woman*-- can ignore!
I hear she spends her fortune on nothing but her entrances and exits.
I hear that *no one* has ever seen her face!
This is *absolutely* true.
I hear she *controls* her surroundings with a wave of her *hand*.
This is *absolutely* true.
You have all met this woman?
None of us have met her. But everyone speaks of her as eef zey have.

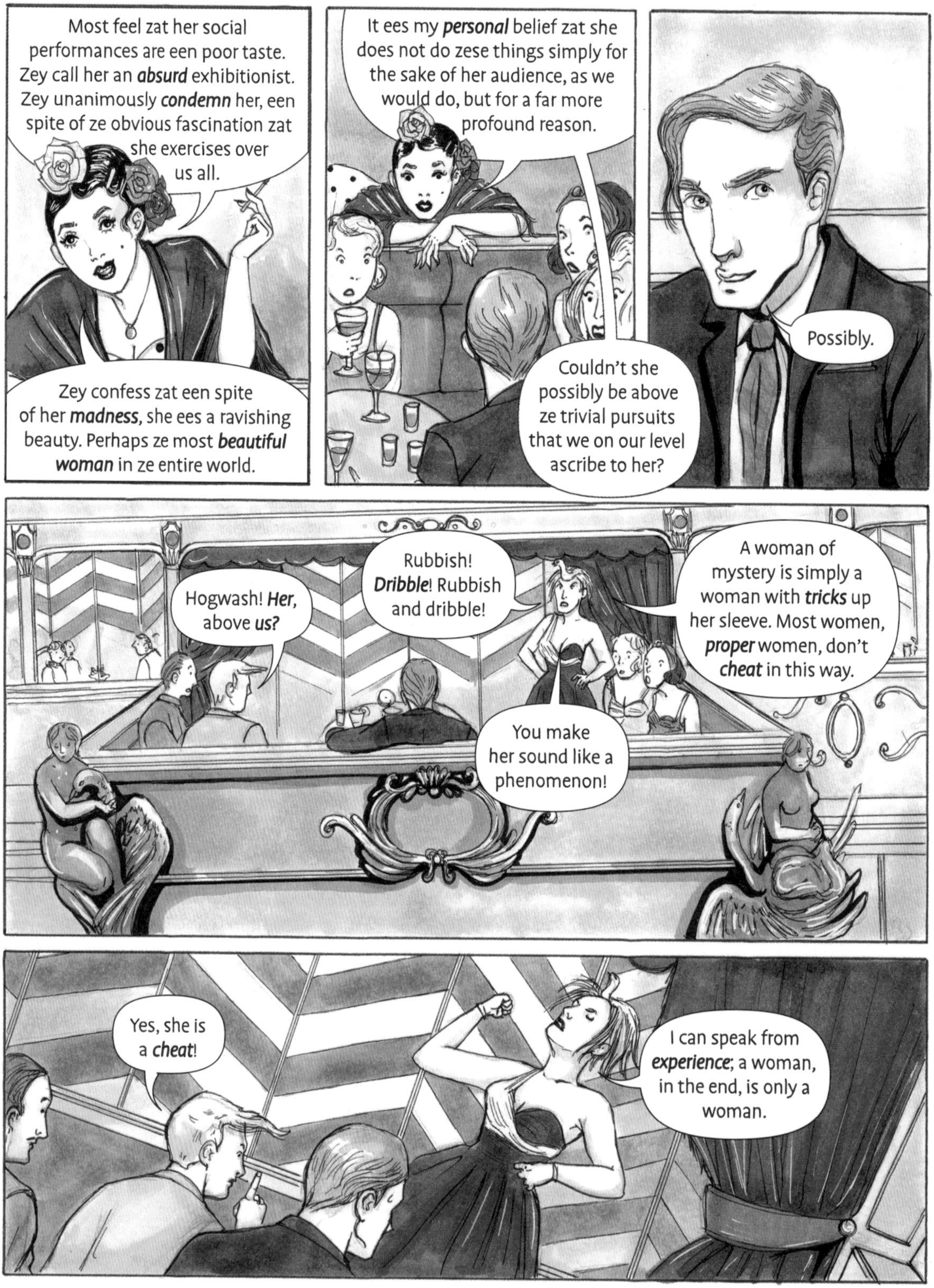
Most feel zat her social performances are een poor taste. Zey call her an absurd exhibitionist. Zey unanimously condemn her, een spite of ze obvious fascination zat she exercises over us all.
Zey confess zat een spite of her madness, she ees a ravishing beauty. Perhaps ze most beautiful woman in ze entire world.
It ees my personal belief zat she does not do zese things simply for the sake of her audience, as we would do, but for a far more profound reason.
Couldn't she possibly be above ze trivial pursuits that we on our level ascribe to her?
Possibly.
Hogwash! Her, above us?
Rubbish! Dribble! Rubbish and dribble!
A woman of mystery is simply a woman with tricks up her sleeve. Most women, proper women, don't cheat in this way.
You make her sound like a phenomenon!
Yes, she is a cheat!
I can speak from experience; a woman, in the end, is only a woman.

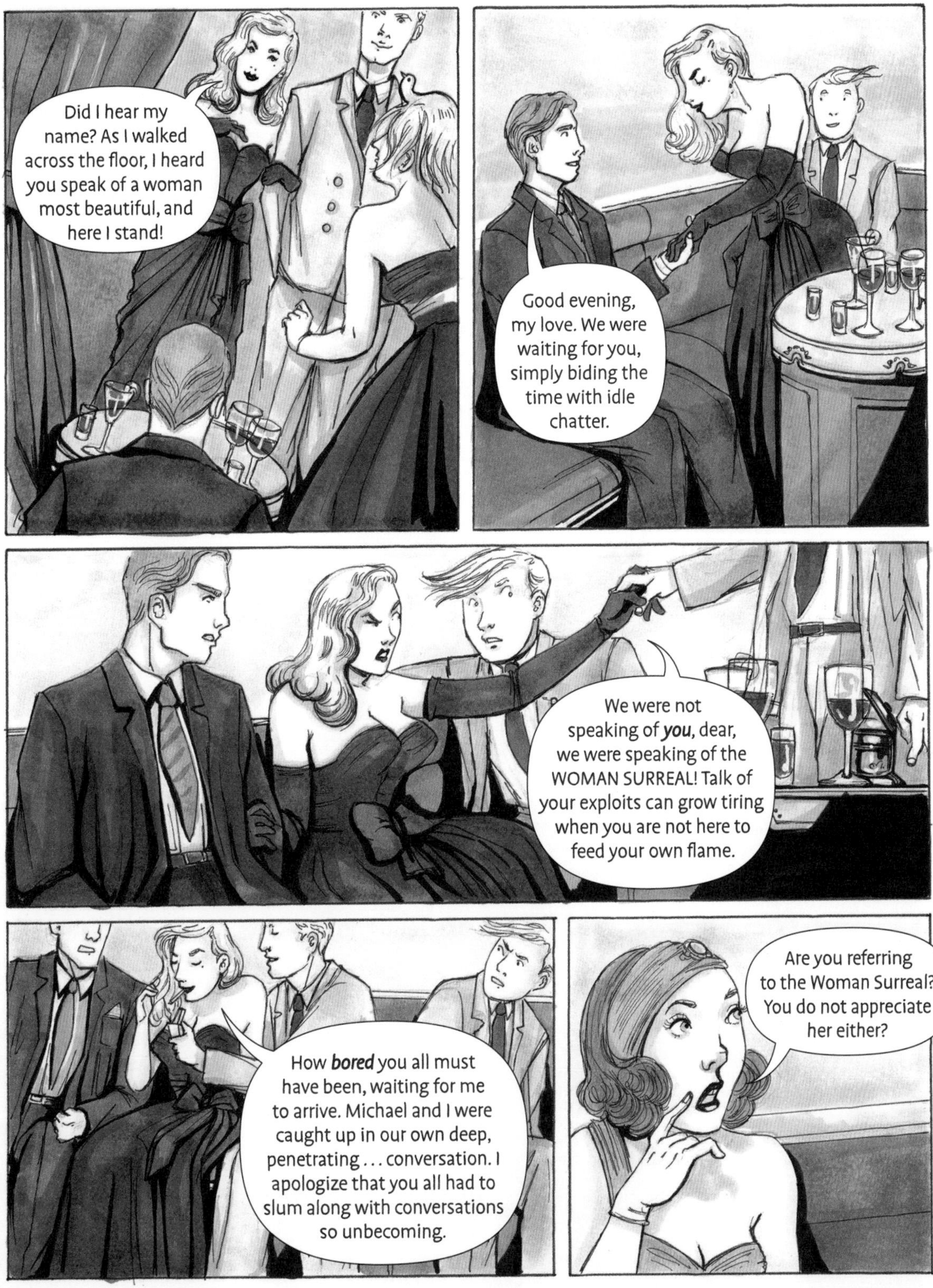
Did I hear my name? As I walked across the floor, I heard you speak of a woman most beautiful, and here I stand!
Good evening, my love. We were waiting for you, simply biding the time with idle chatter.
We were not speaking of ***you***, dear, we were speaking of the WOMAN SURREAL! Talk of your exploits can grow tiring when you are not here to feed your own flame.
How ***bored*** you all must have been, waiting for me to arrive. Michael and I were caught up in our own deep, penetrating . . . conversation. I apologize that you all had to slum along with conversations so unbecoming.
Are you referring to the Woman Surreal? You do not appreciate her either?

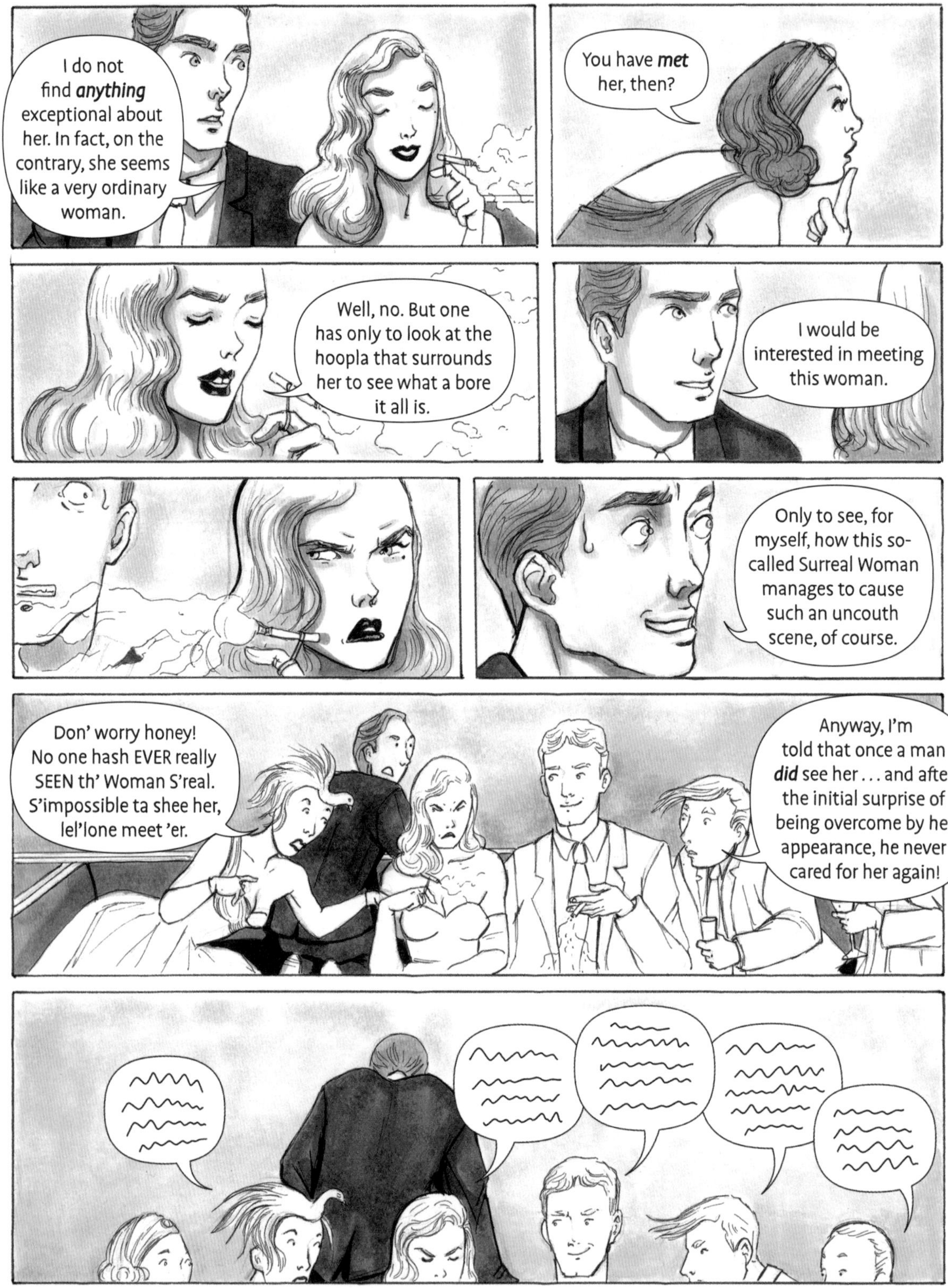
I do not find *anything* exceptional about her. In fact, on the contrary, she seems like a very ordinary woman.
You have *met* her, then?
Well, no. But one has only to look at the hoopla that surrounds her to see what a bore it all is.
I would be interested in meeting this woman.
Only to see, for myself, how this so-called Surreal Woman manages to cause such an uncouth scene, of course.
Don' worry honey! No one hash EVER really SEEN th' Woman S'real. S'impossible ta shee her, lel'lone meet 'er.
Anyway, I'm told that once a man *did* see her . . . and after the initial surprise of being overcome by her appearance, he never cared for her again!

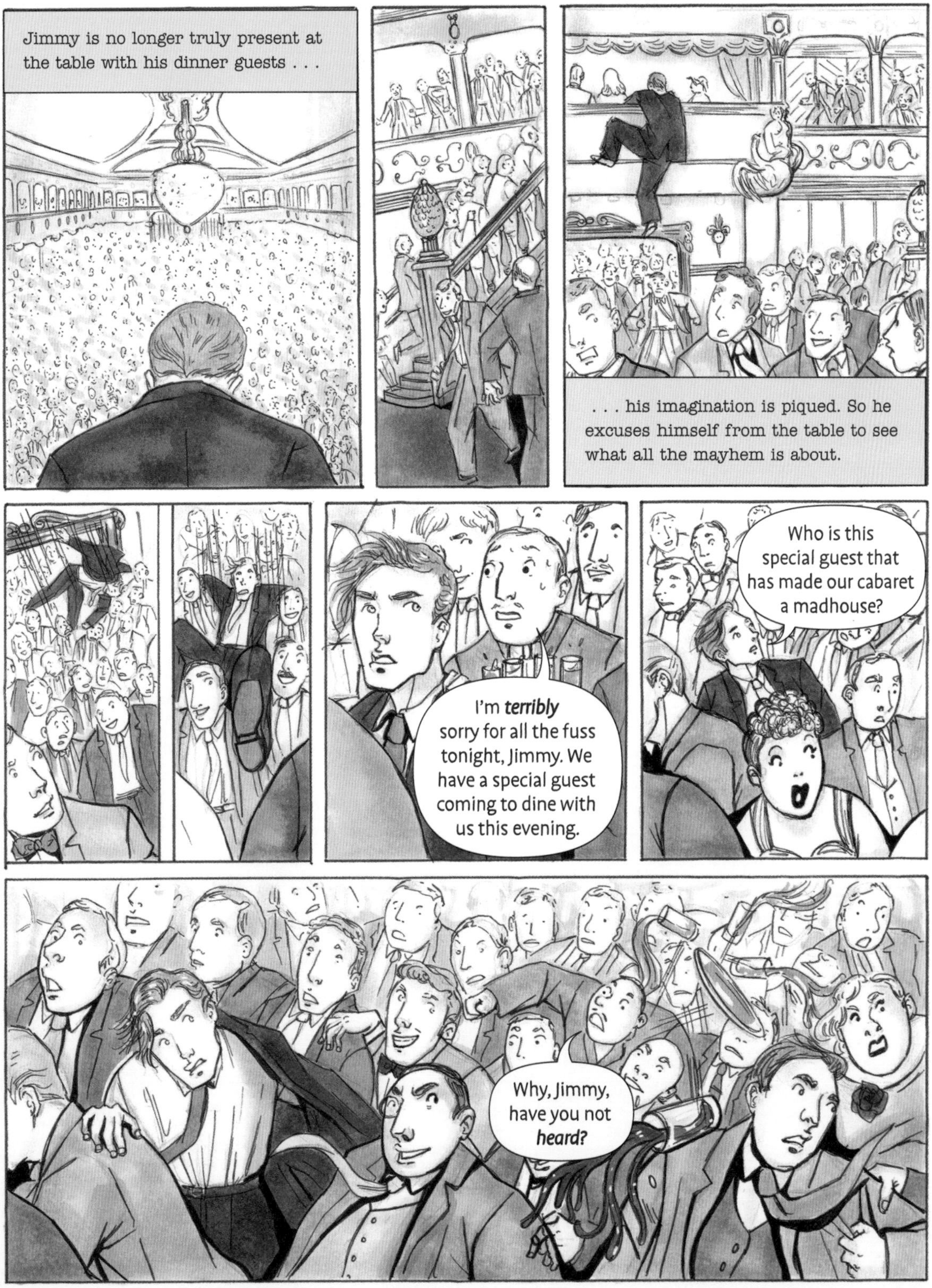
Jimmy is no longer truly present at the table with his dinner guests . . .
. . . his imagination is piqued. So he excuses himself from the table to see what all the mayhem is about.
I'm *terribly* sorry for all the fuss tonight, Jimmy. We have a special guest coming to dine with us this evening.
Who is this special guest that has made our cabaret a madhouse?
Why, Jimmy, have you not *heard?*

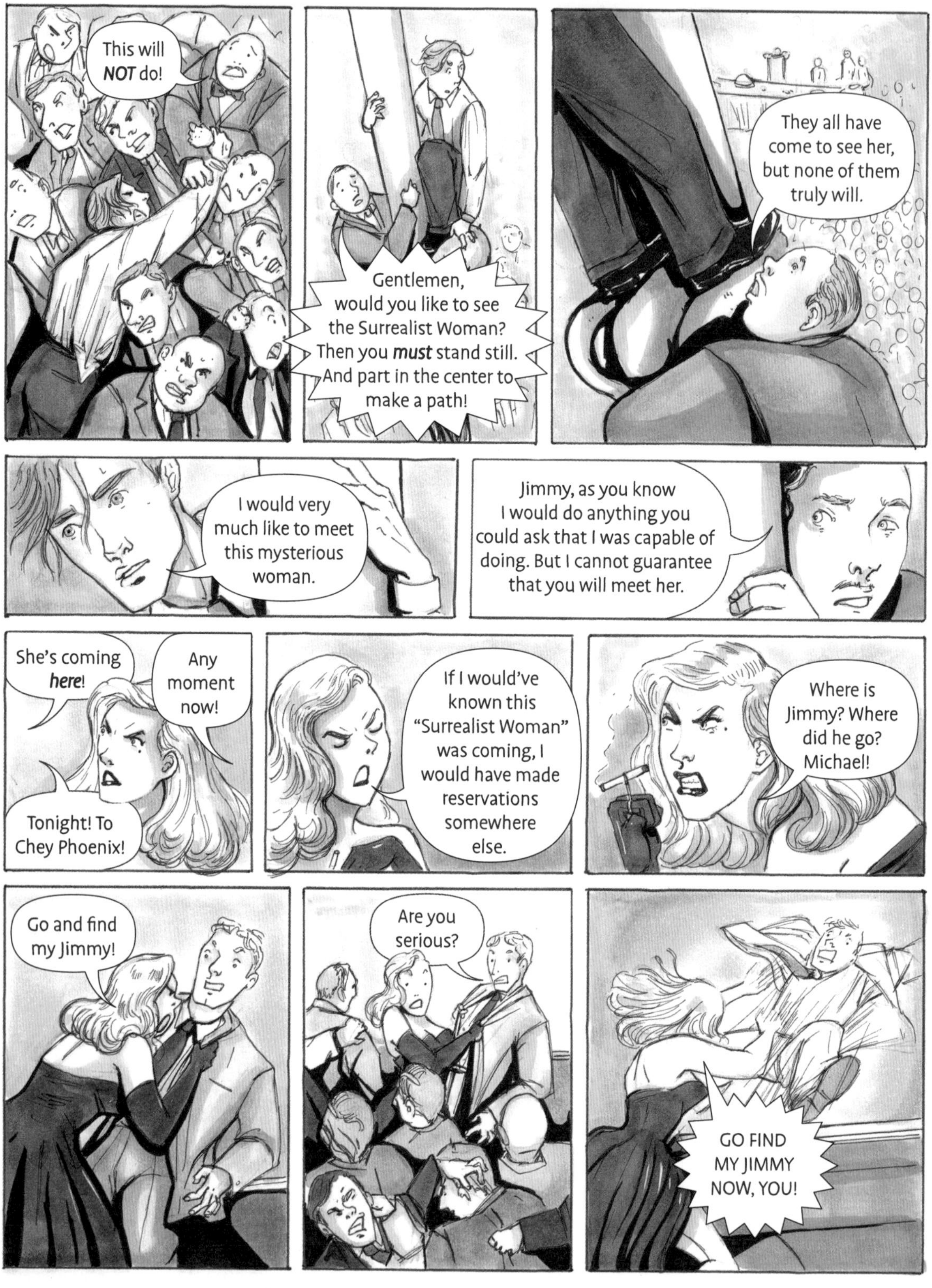
This will *NOT* do!
Gentlemen, would you like to see the Surrealist Woman? Then you *must* stand still. And part in the center to make a path!
They all have come to see her, but none of them truly will.
I would very much like to meet this mysterious woman.
Jimmy, as you know I would do anything you could ask that I was capable of doing. But I cannot guarantee that you will meet her.
She's coming *here*!
Any moment now!
Tonight! To Chey Phoenix!
If I would've known this "Surrealist Woman" was coming, I would have made reservations somewhere else.
Where is Jimmy? Where did he go? Michael!
Go and find my Jimmy!
Are you serious?
GO FIND MY JIMMY NOW, YOU!

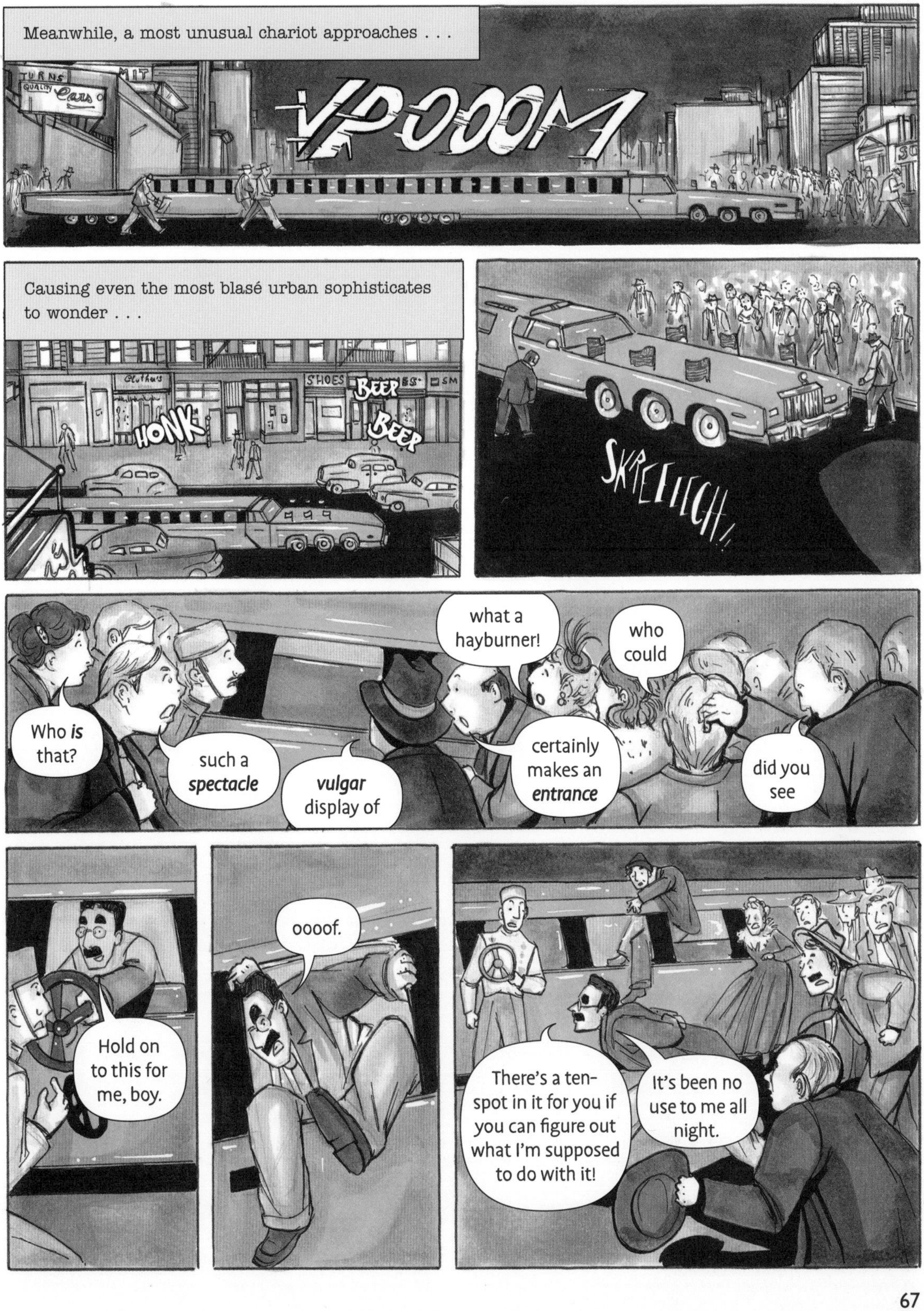

Meanwhile, a most unusual chariot approaches . . .
VROOOM
Causing even the most blasé urban sophisticates to wonder . . .
HONK
BEEP
BEEP
SKREEEECH!!
Who *is* that?
such a *spectacle*
vulgar display of
what a hayburner!
certainly makes an *entrance*
who could
did you see
Hold on to this for me, boy.
oooof.
There's a ten-spot in it for you if you can figure out what I'm supposed to do with it!
It's been no use to me all night.

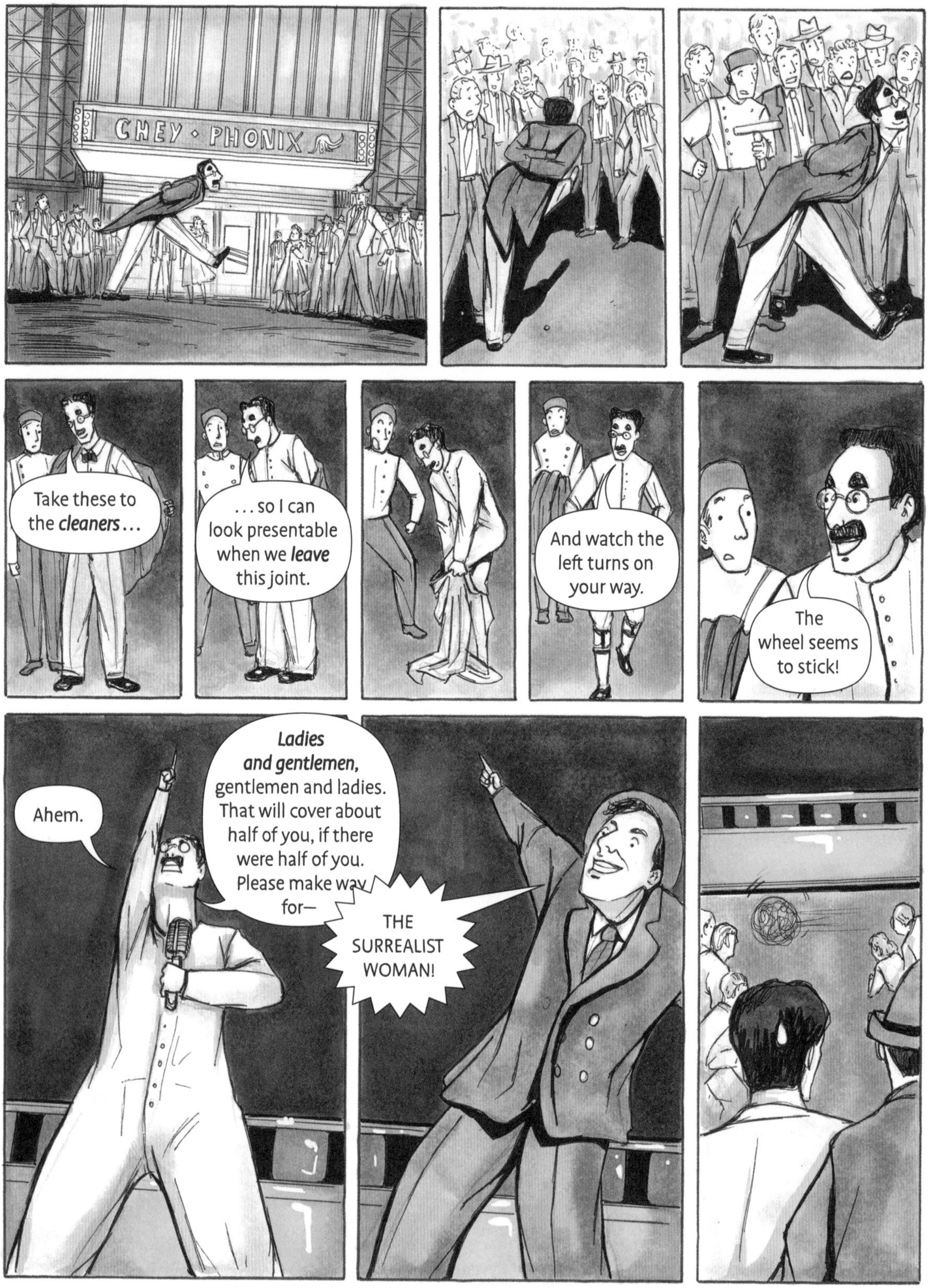
CHEY · PHONIX
Take these to the *cleaners*...
...so I can look presentable when we *leave* this joint.
And watch the left turns on your way.
The wheel seems to stick!
Ahem.
Ladies and gentlemen, gentlemen and ladies. That will cover about half of you, if there were half of you. Please make way for—
THE SURREALIST WOMAN!

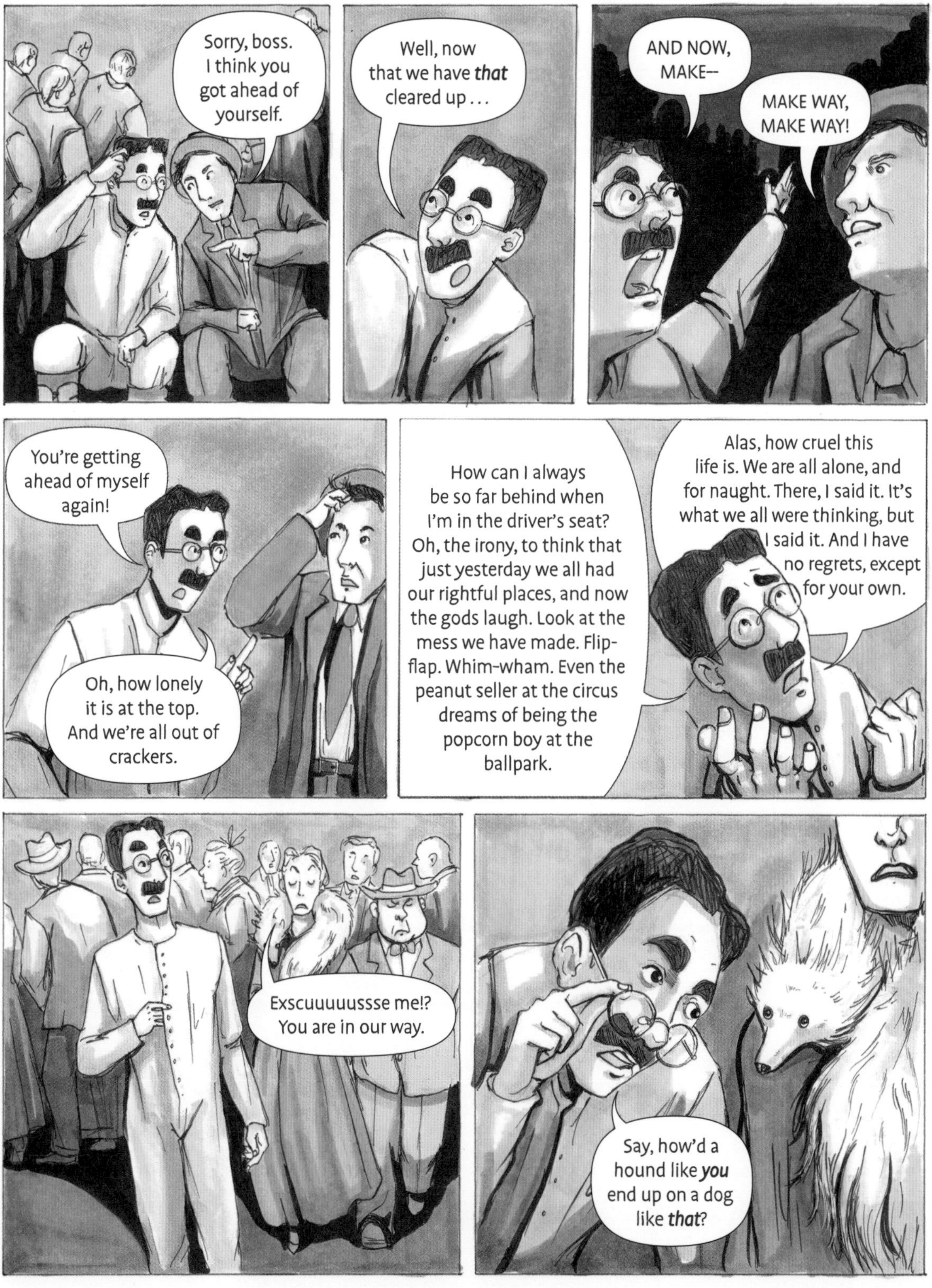
Sorry, boss. I think you got ahead of yourself.
Well, now that we have *that* cleared up . . .
AND NOW, MAKE--
MAKE WAY, MAKE WAY!
You're getting ahead of myself again!
Oh, how lonely it is at the top. And we're all out of crackers.
How can I always be so far behind when I'm in the driver's seat? Oh, the irony, to think that just yesterday we all had our rightful places, and now the gods laugh. Look at the mess we have made. Flip-flap. Whim-wham. Even the peanut seller at the circus dreams of being the popcorn boy at the ballpark.
Alas, how cruel this life is. We are all alone, and for naught. There, I said it. It's what we all were thinking, but I said it. And I have no regrets, except for your own.
Exscuuuuussse me!? You are in our way.
Say, how'd a hound like *you* end up on a dog like *that*?

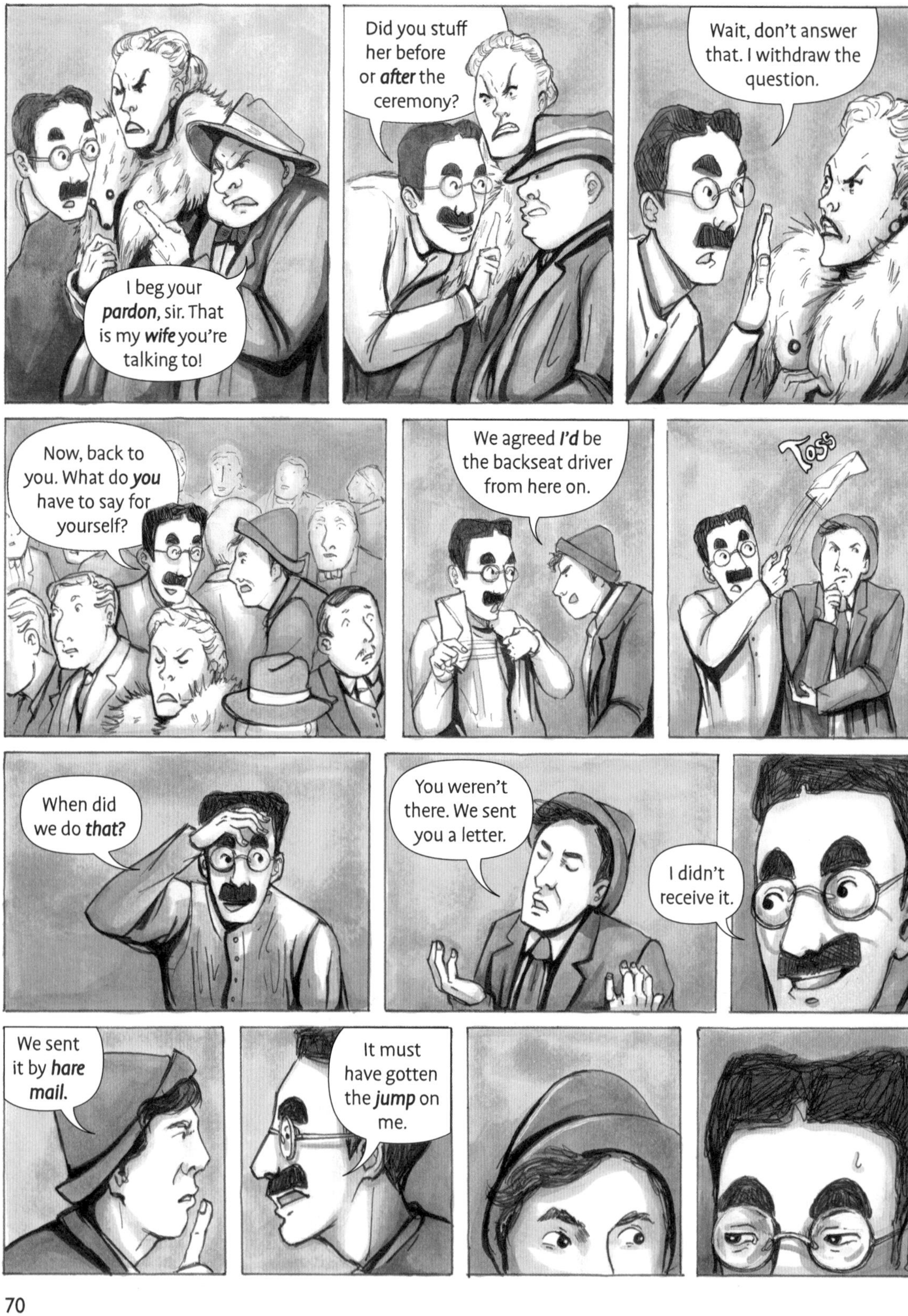
I beg your **pardon**, sir. That is my **wife** you're talking to!
Did you stuff her before or ***after*** the ceremony?
Wait, don't answer that. I withdraw the question.
Now, back to you. What do ***you*** have to say for yourself?
We agreed ***I'd*** be the backseat driver from here on.
Toss
When did we do ***that?***
You weren't there. We sent you a letter.
I didn't receive it.
We sent it by ***hare mail.***
It must have gotten the ***jump*** on me.

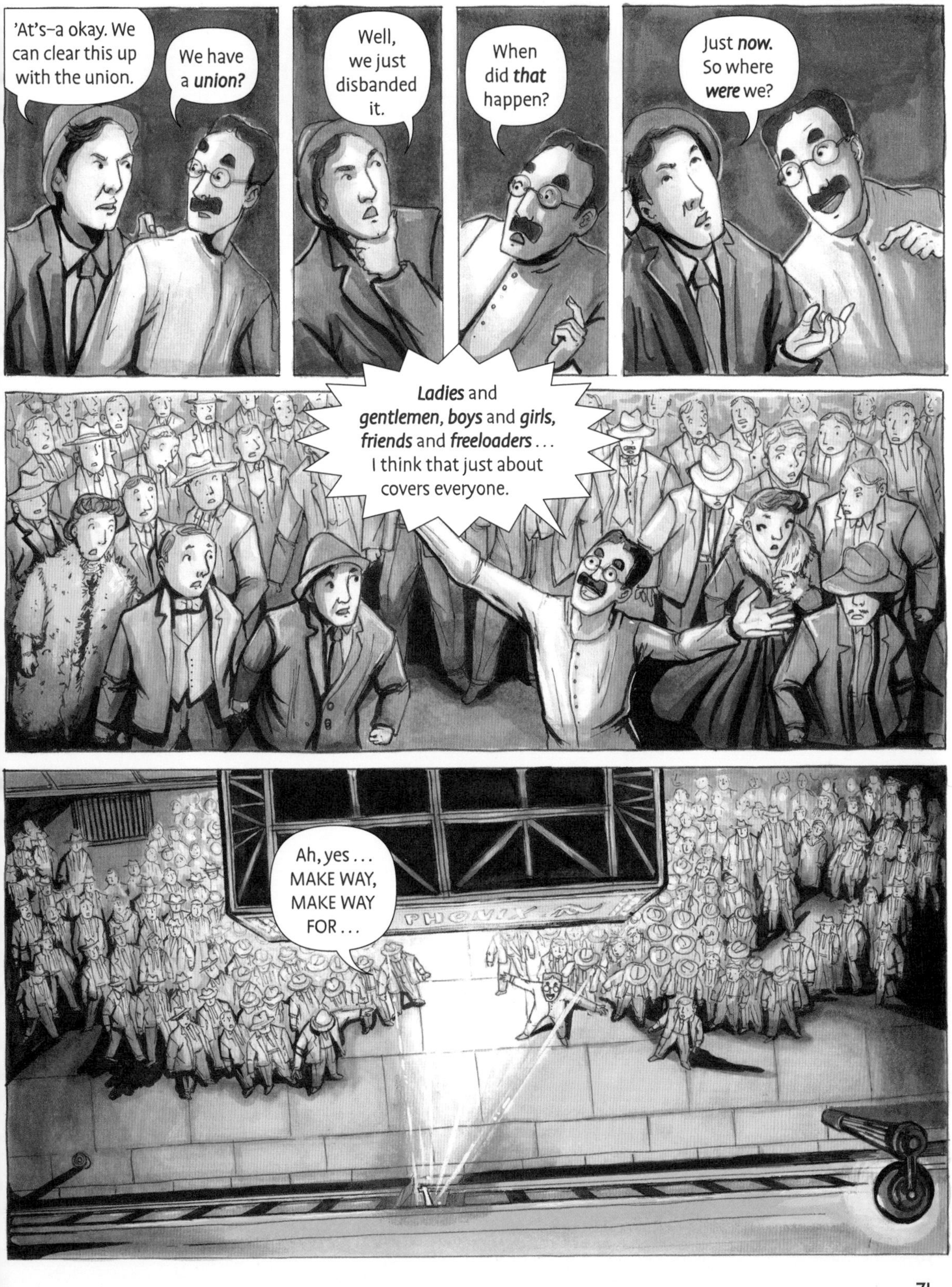
'At's–a okay. We can clear this up with the union.
We have a *union?*
Well, we just disbanded it.
When did *that* happen?
Just *now.* So where *were* we?
Ladies and *gentlemen, boys* and *girls, friends* and *freeloaders* . . . I think that just about covers everyone.
Ah, yes . . . MAKE WAY, MAKE WAY FOR . . .
PHONIX

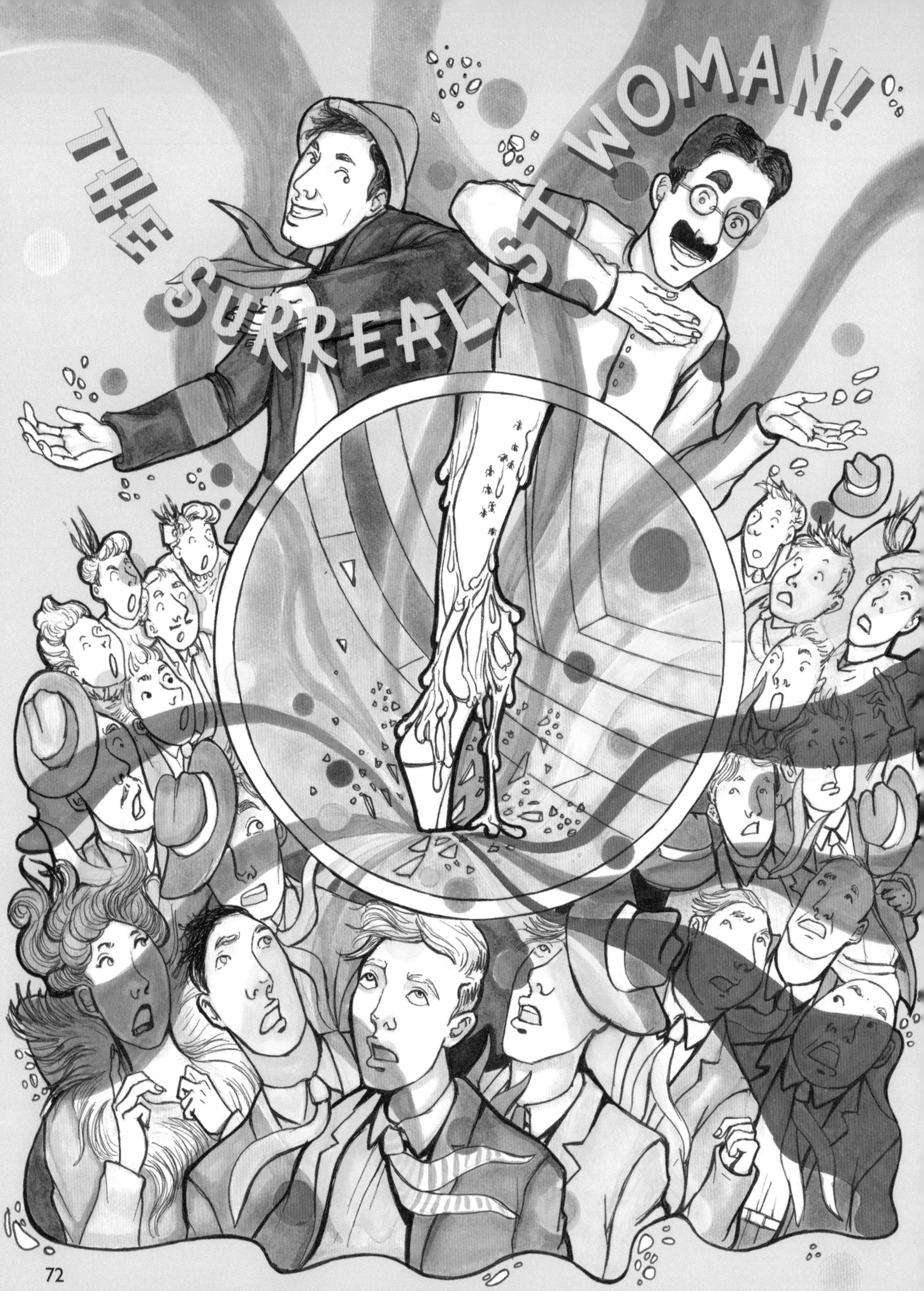
THE SURREALIST WOMAN!

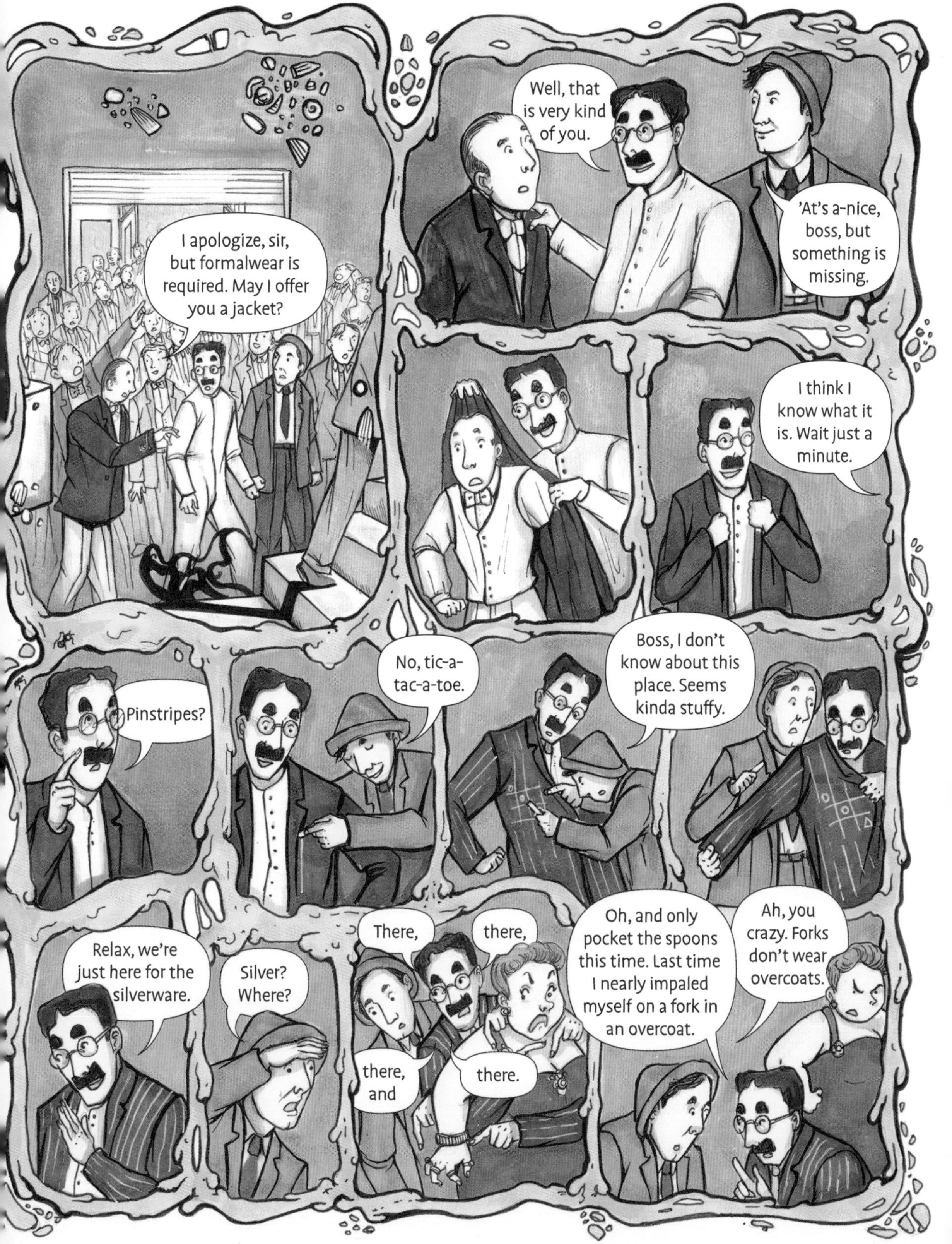
I apologize, sir, but formalwear is required. May I offer you a jacket?
Well, that is very kind of you.
'At's a-nice, boss, but something is missing.
I think I know what it is. Wait just a minute.
Pinstripes?
No, tic-a-tac-a-toe.
Boss, I don't know about this place. Seems kinda stuffy.
Relax, we're just here for the silverware.
Silver? Where?
There,
there,
there, and
there.
Oh, and only pocket the spoons this time. Last time I nearly impaled myself on a fork in an overcoat.
Ah, you crazy. Forks don't wear overcoats.

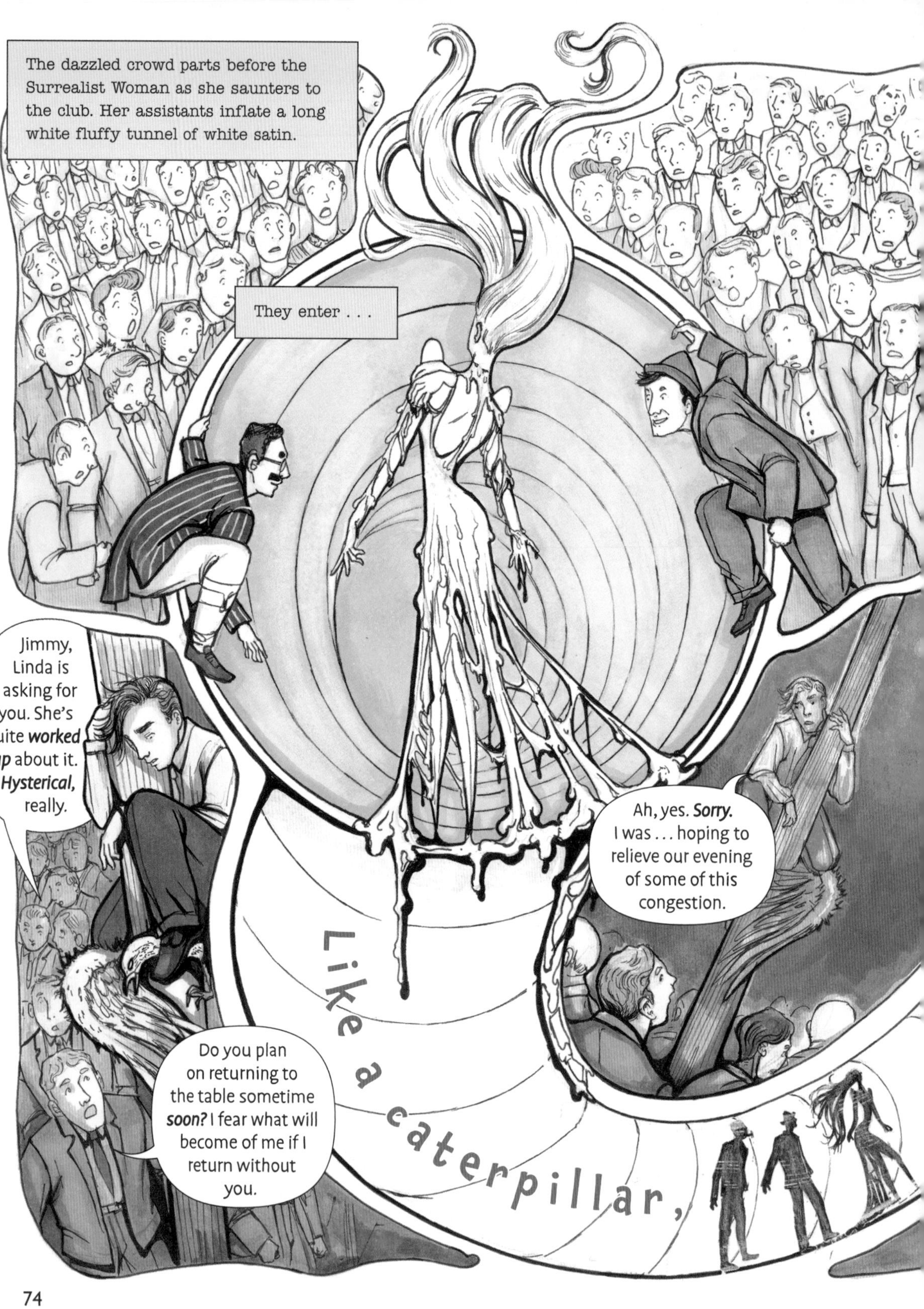
The dazzled crowd parts before the Surrealist Woman as she saunters to the club. Her assistants inflate a long white fluffy tunnel of white satin.
They enter . . .
Jimmy, Linda is asking for you. She's quite ***worked up*** about it. ***Hysterical,*** really.
Ah, yes. **Sorry.** I was . . . hoping to relieve our evening of some of this congestion.
Do you plan on returning to the table sometime ***soon?*** I fear what will become of me if I return without you.
Like a caterpillar,

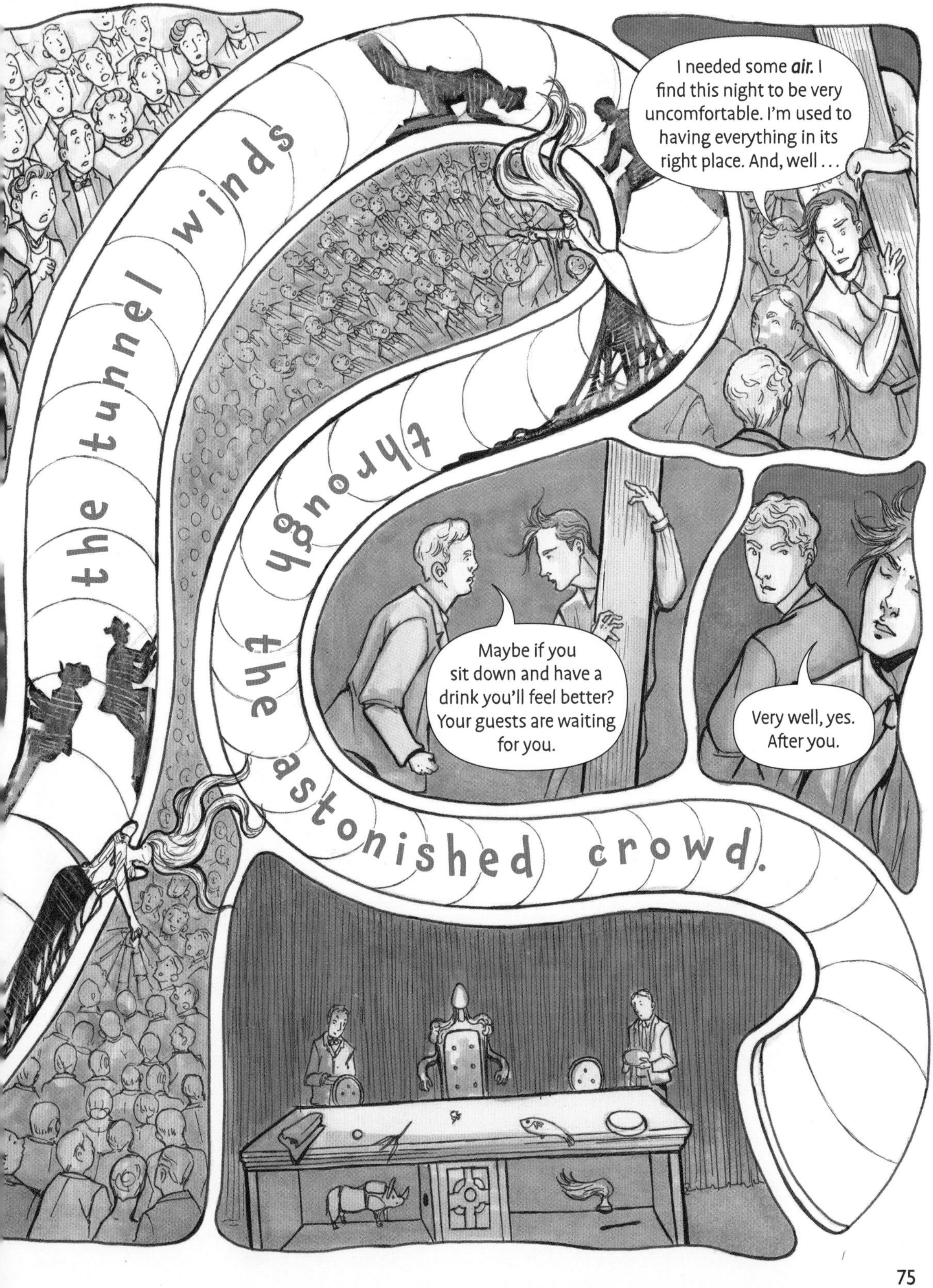

the tunnel winds through the astonished crowd.
I needed some ***air.*** I find this night to be very uncomfortable. I'm used to having everything in its right place. And, well . . .
Maybe if you sit down and have a drink you'll feel better? Your guests are waiting for you.
Very well, yes. After you.

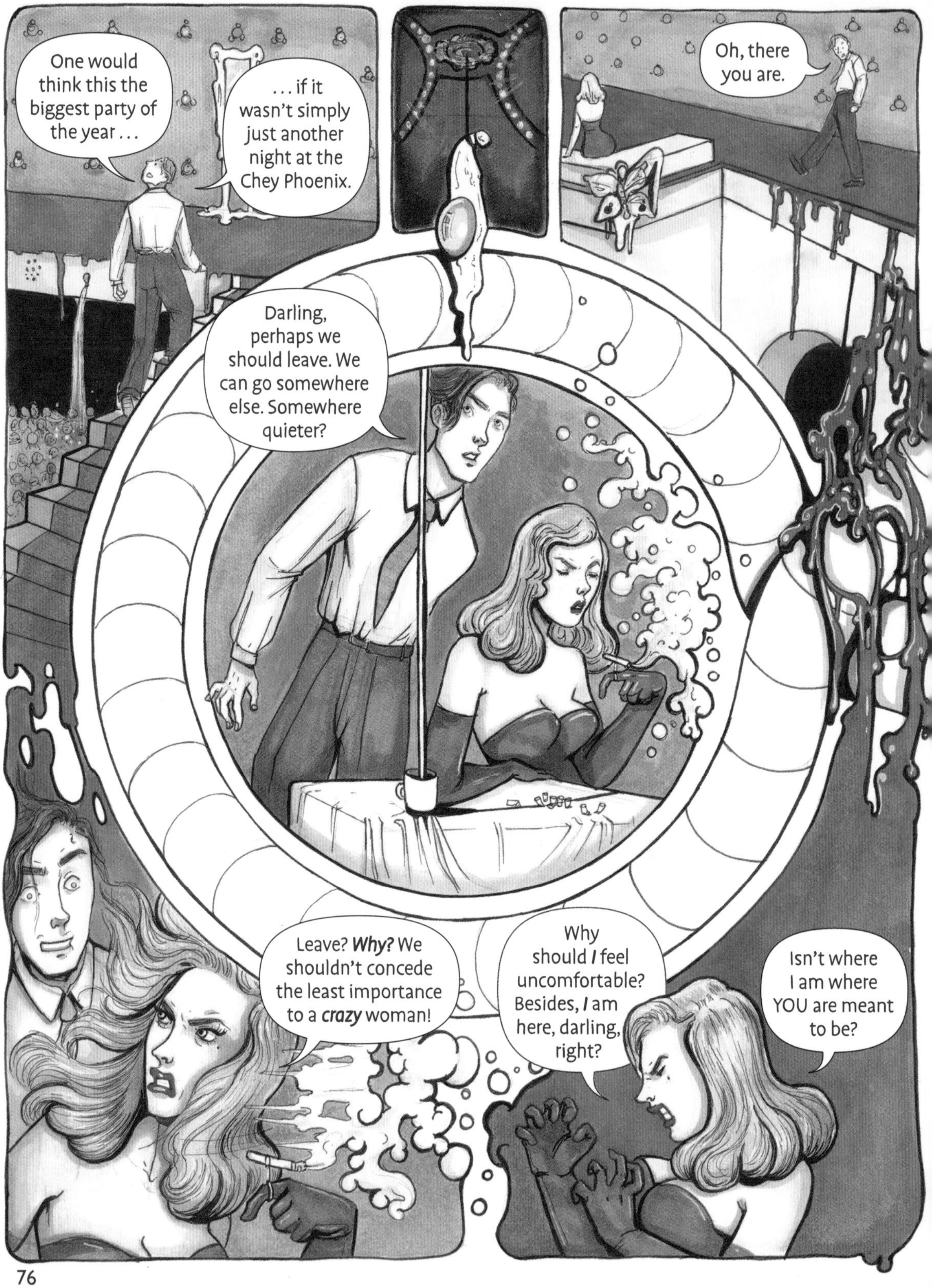
One would think this the biggest party of the year . . .
. . . if it wasn't simply just another night at the Chey Phoenix.
Oh, there you are.
Darling, perhaps we should leave. We can go somewhere else. Somewhere quieter?
Leave? ***Why?*** We shouldn't concede the least importance to a *crazy* woman!
Why should *I* feel uncomfortable? Besides, *I* am here, darling, right?
Isn't where I am where YOU are meant to be?

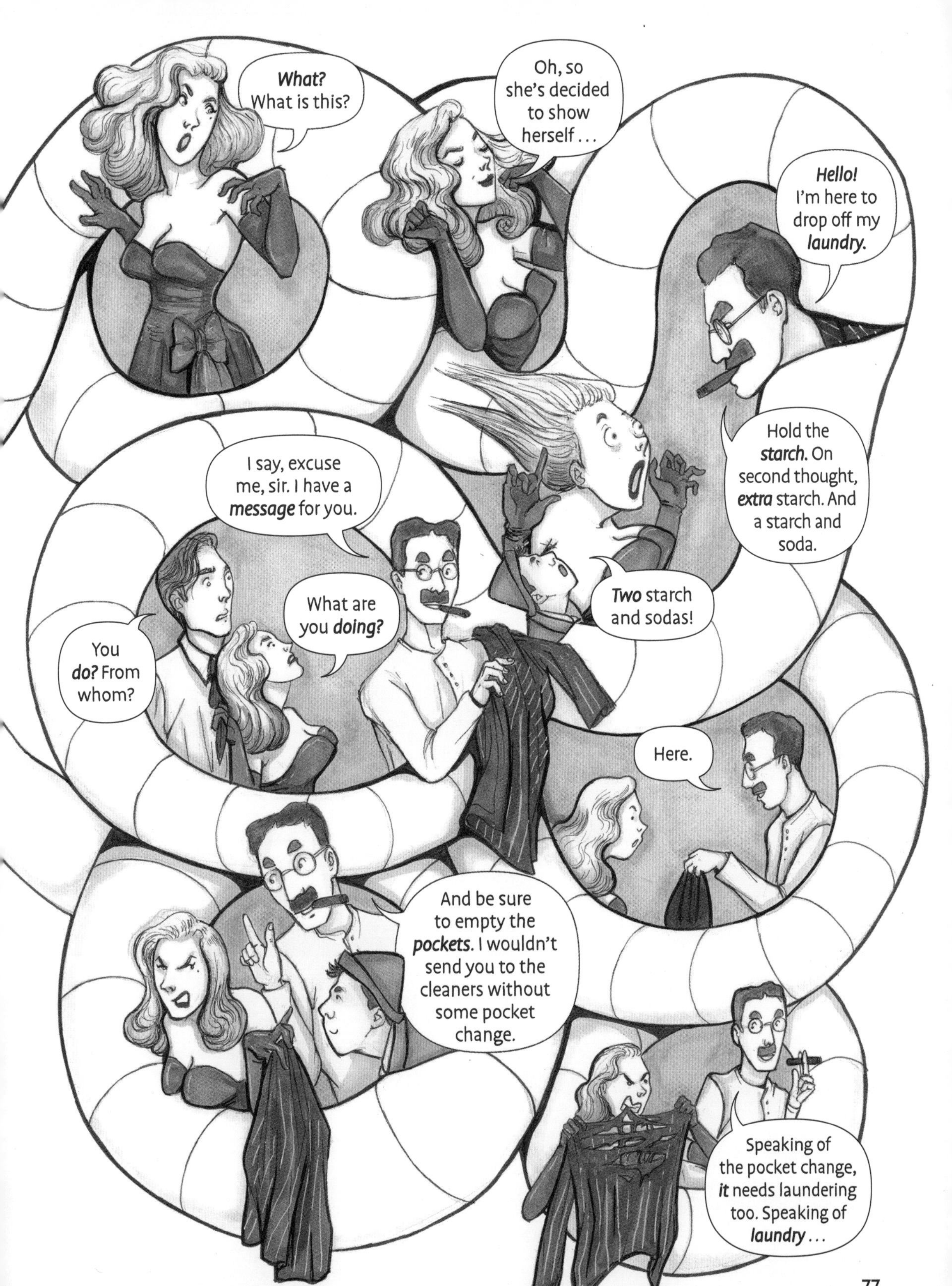
What? What is this?
Oh, so she's decided to show herself . . .
Hello! I'm here to drop off my *laundry.*
Hold the *starch.* On second thought, *extra* starch. And a starch and soda.
Two starch and sodas!
I say, excuse me, sir. I have a *message* for you.
You *do?* From whom?
What are you *doing?*
Here.
And be sure to empty the *pockets*. I wouldn't send you to the cleaners without some pocket change.
Speaking of the pocket change, *it* needs laundering too. Speaking of *laundry* . . .

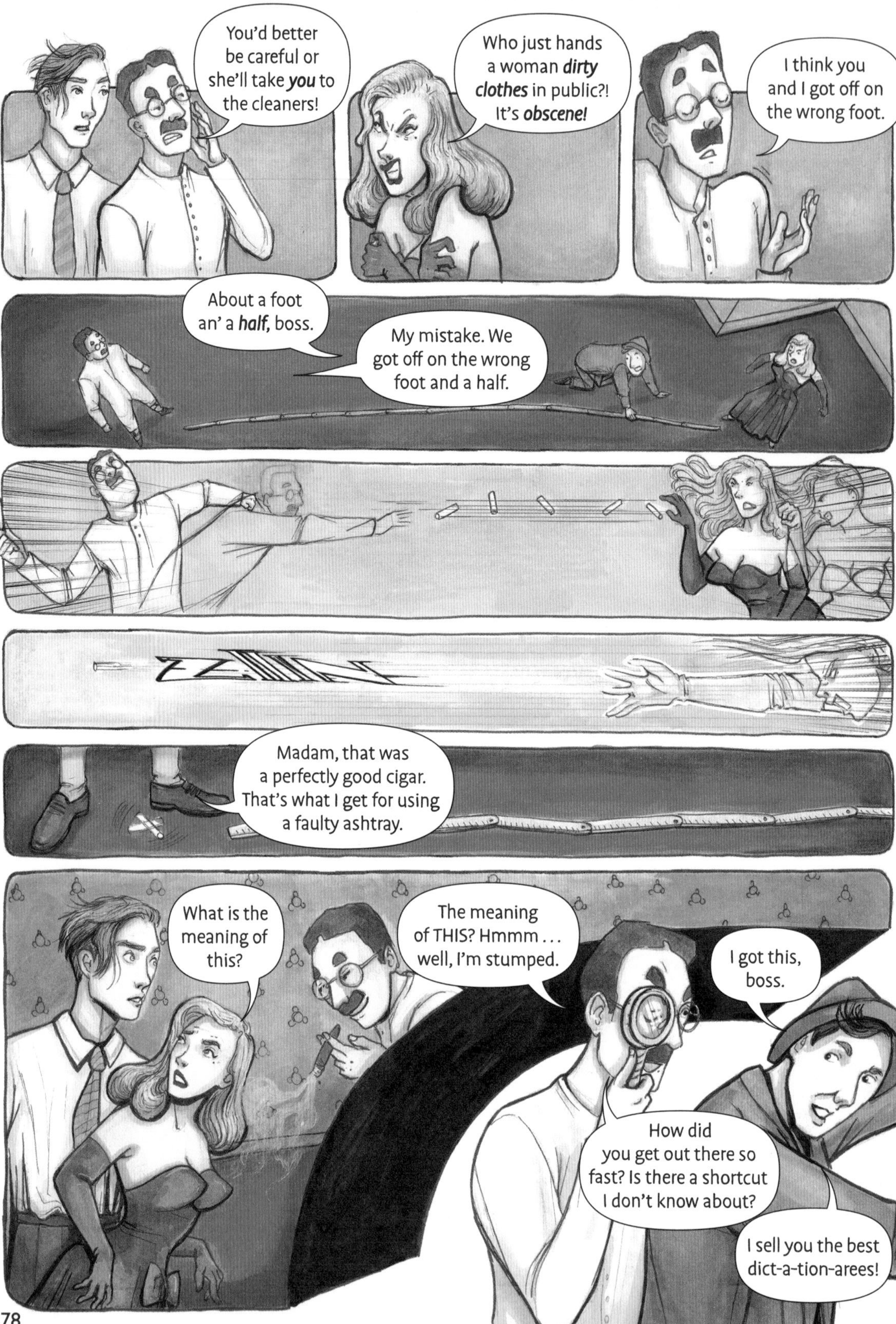
You'd better be careful or she'll take *you* to the cleaners!
Who just hands a woman *dirty clothes* in public?! It's *obscene!*
I think you and I got off on the wrong foot.
About a foot an' a *half,* boss.
My mistake. We got off on the wrong foot and a half.
ZZING
Madam, that was a perfectly good cigar. That's what I get for using a faulty ashtray.
What is the meaning of this?
The meaning of THIS? Hmmm . . . well, I'm stumped.
I got this, boss.
How did you get out there so fast? Is there a shortcut I don't know about?
I sell you the best dict-a-tion-arees!

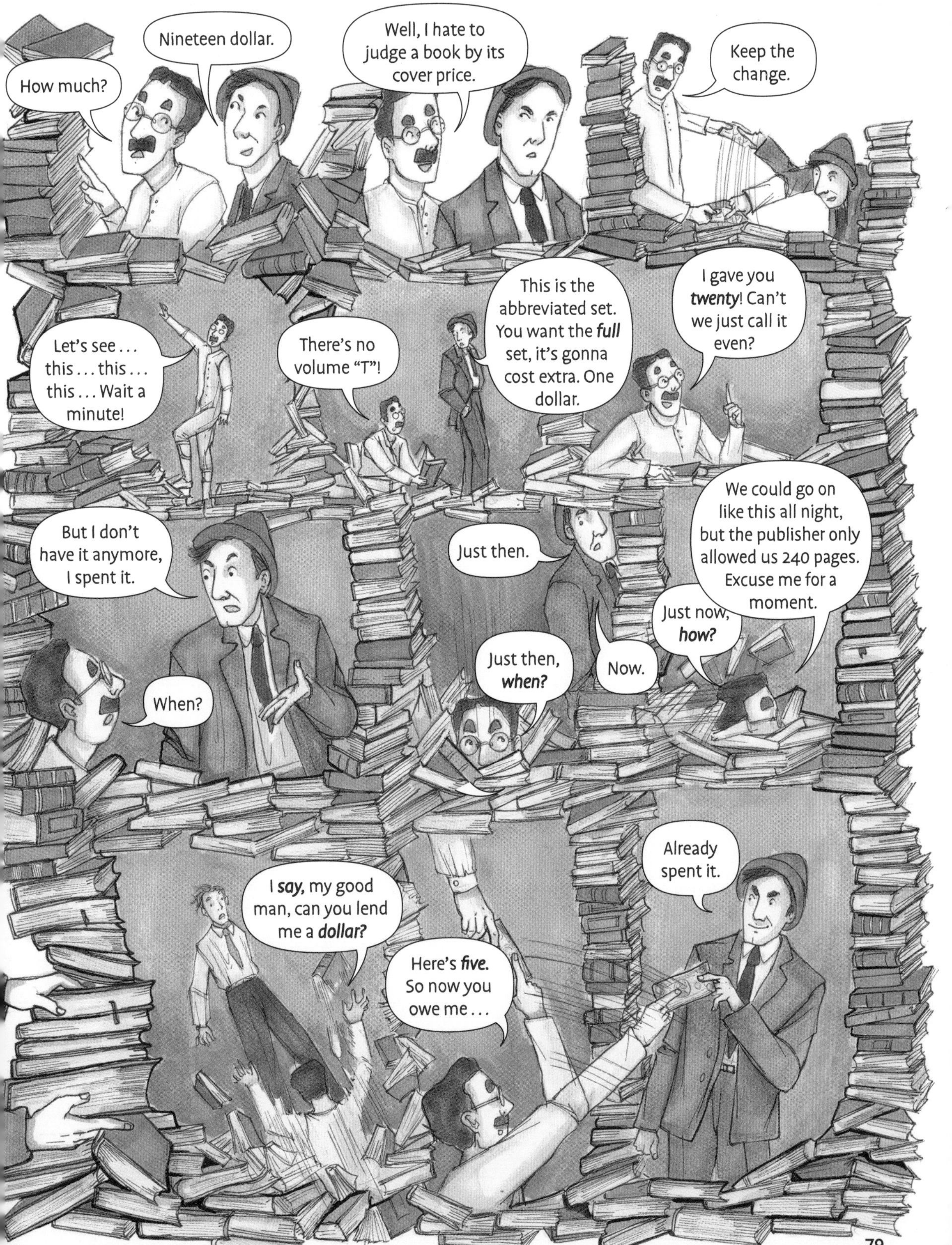
How much?
Nineteen dollar.
Well, I hate to judge a book by its cover price.
Keep the change.
Let's see . . . this . . . this . . . this . . . Wait a minute!
There's no volume "T"!
This is the abbreviated set. You want the *full* set, it's gonna cost extra. One dollar.
I gave you *twenty*! Can't we just call it even?
But I don't have it anymore, I spent it.
When?
Just then.
Just then, *when?*
Now.
Just now, *how?*
We could go on like this all night, but the publisher only allowed us 240 pages. Excuse me for a moment.
I *say,* my good man, can you lend me a *dollar?*
Here's *five.* So now you owe me . . .
Already spent it.

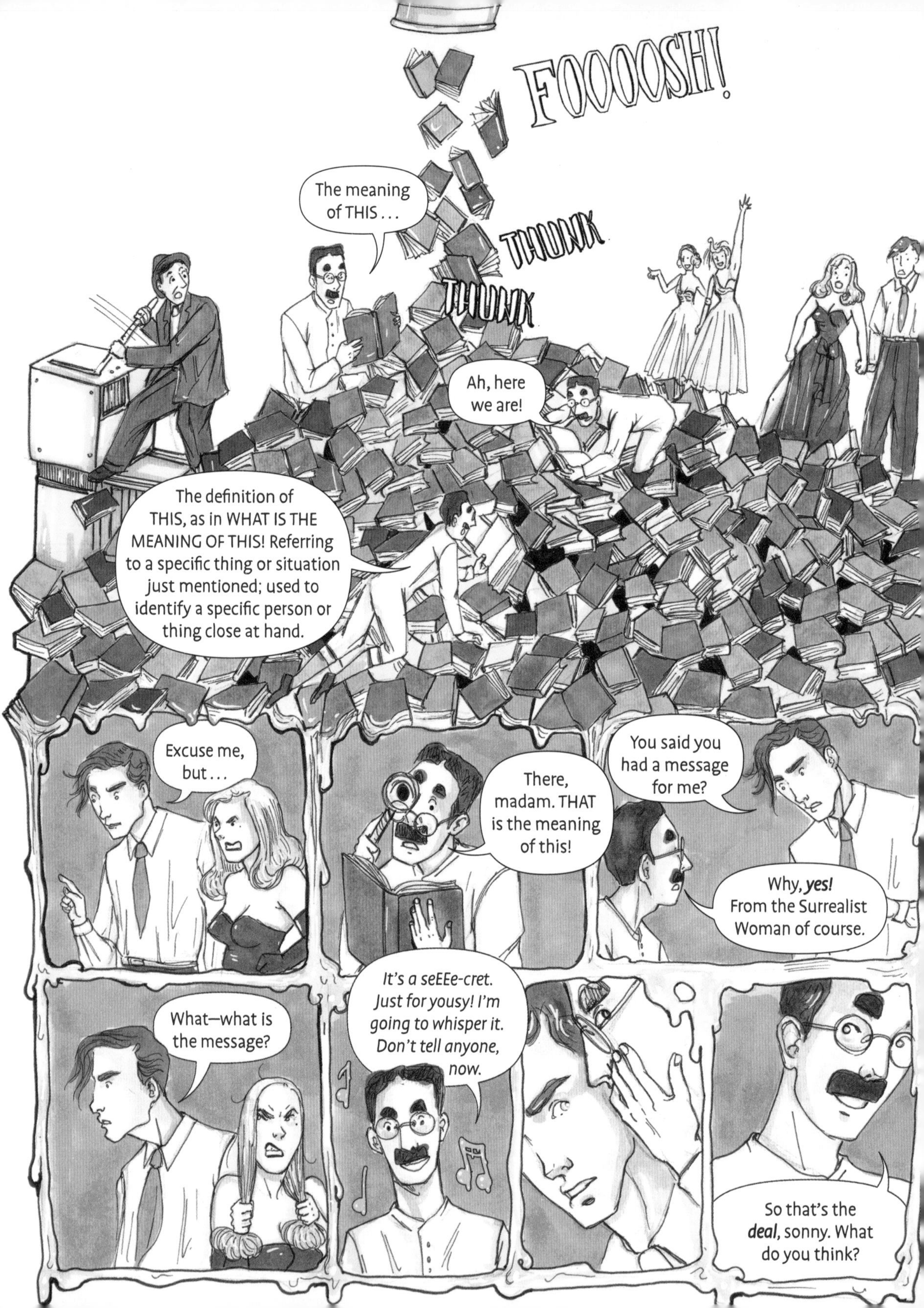
FOOOOSH!
The meaning of THIS . . .
THUNK
THUNK
Ah, here we are!
The definition of THIS, as in WHAT IS THE MEANING OF THIS! Referring to a specific thing or situation just mentioned; used to identify a specific person or thing close at hand.
Excuse me, but . . .
There, madam. THAT is the meaning of this!
You said you had a message for me?
Why, *yes!* From the Surrealist Woman of course.
What—what is the message?
It's a seEEe-cret. Just for yousy! I'm going to whisper it. Don't tell anyone, now.
So that's the ***deal***, sonny. What do you think?

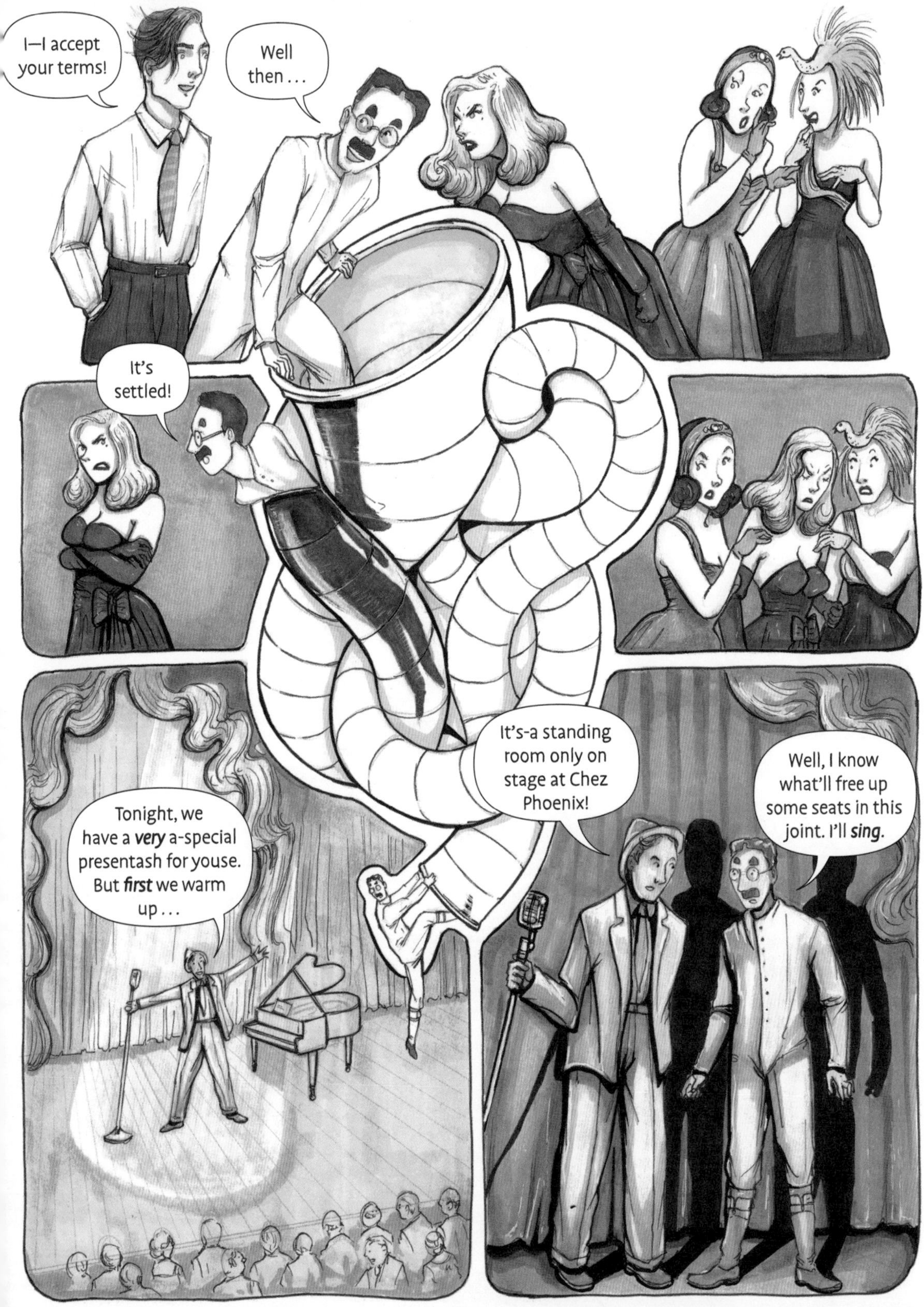

I—I accept your terms!
Well then . . .
It's settled!
Tonight, we have a *very* a-special presentash for youse. But *first* we warm up . . .
It's-a standing room only on stage at Chez Phoenix!
Well, I know what'll free up some seats in this joint. I'll *sing*.

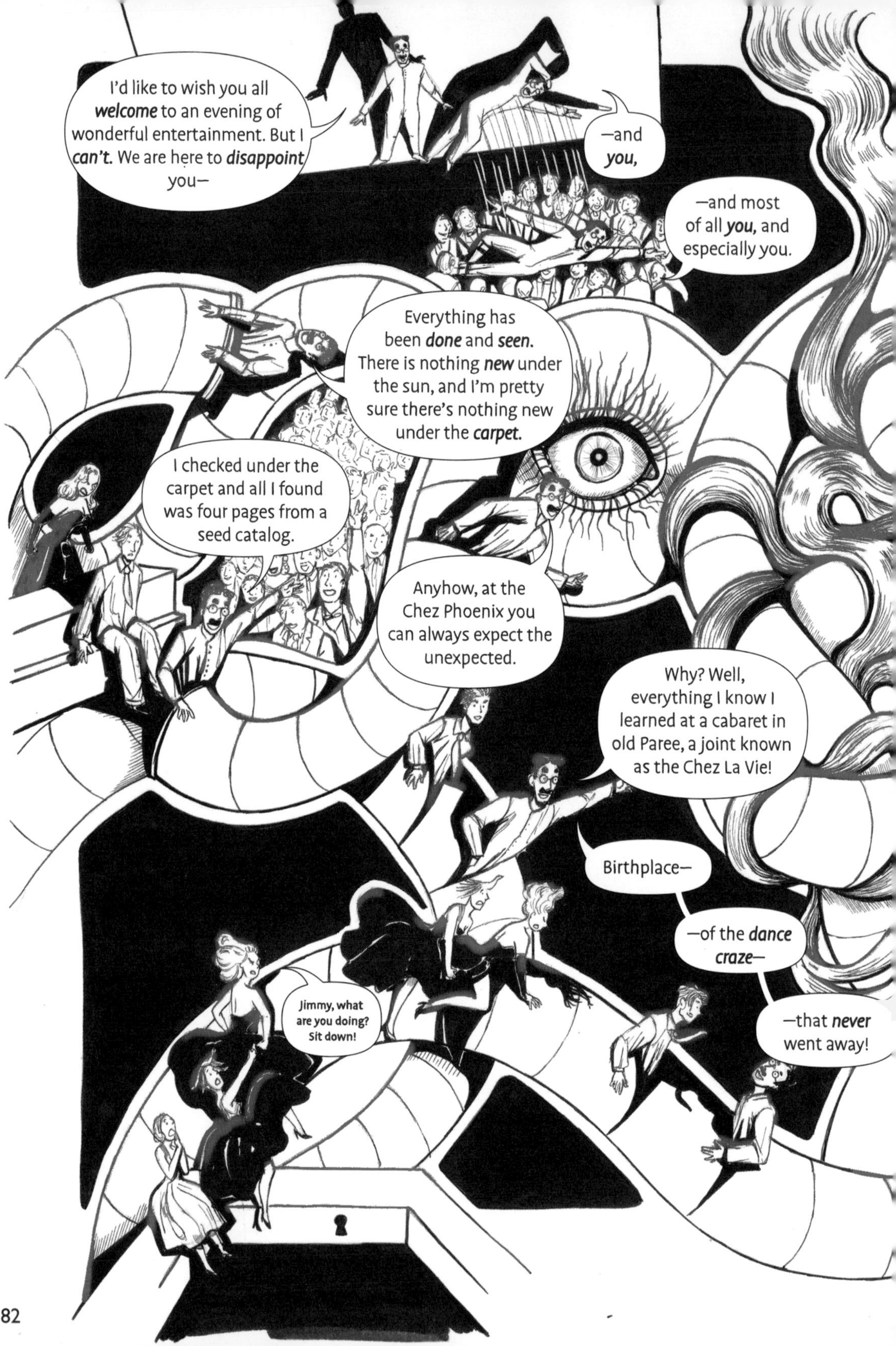
I'd like to wish you all welcome to an evening of wonderful entertainment. But I can't. We are here to disappoint you—
—and you,
—and most of all you, and especially you.
Everything has been done and seen. There is nothing new under the sun, and I'm pretty sure there's nothing new under the carpet.
I checked under the carpet and all I found was four pages from a seed catalog.
Anyhow, at the Chez Phoenix you can always expect the unexpected.
Why? Well, everything I know I learned at a cabaret in old Paree, a joint known as the Chez La Vie!
Birthplace—
—of the dance craze—
—that never went away!
Jimmy, what are you doing? Sit down!

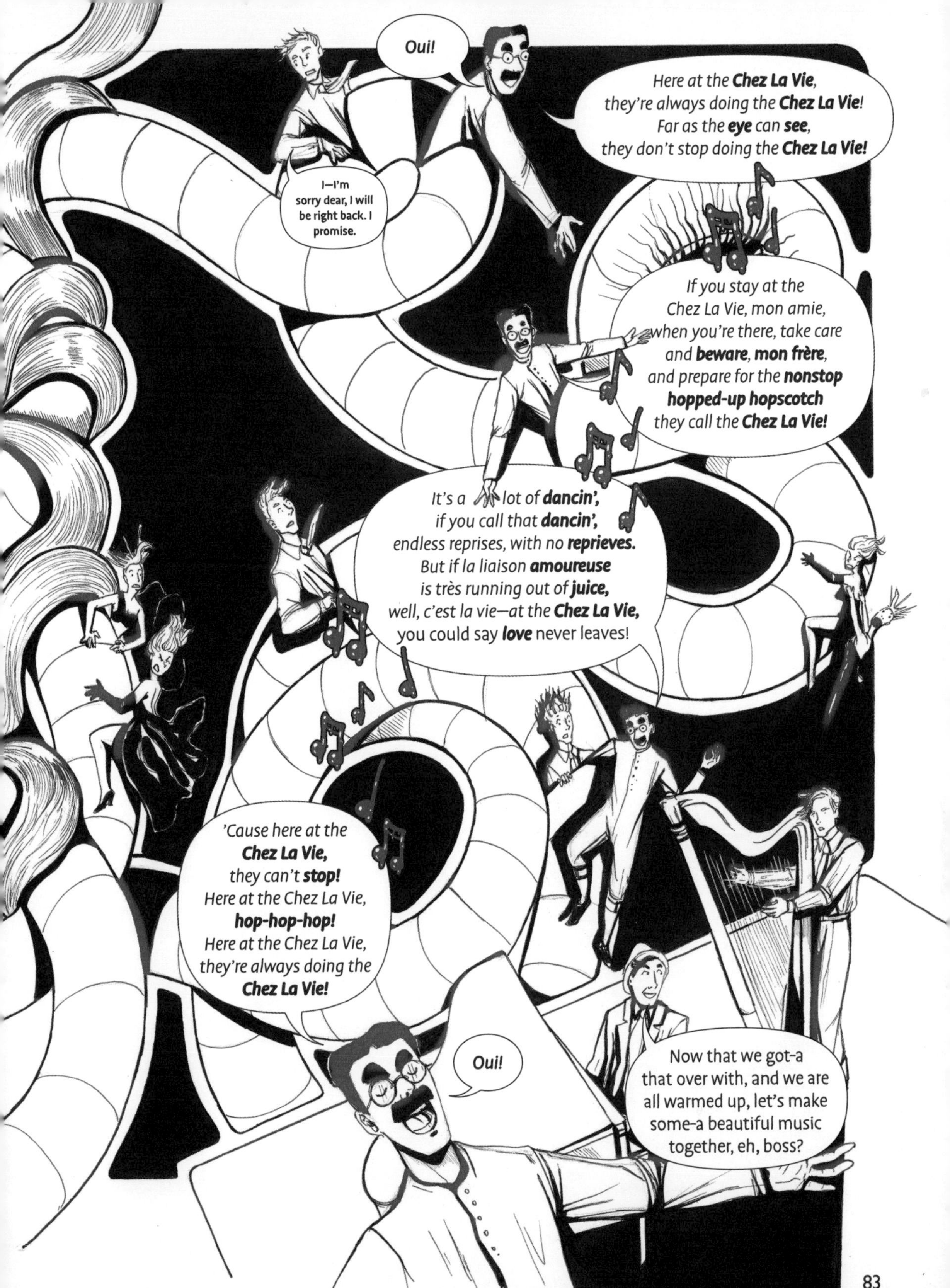
Oui!
Here at the Chez La Vie, they're always doing the Chez La Vie! Far as the eye can see, they don't stop doing the Chez La Vie!
I—I'm sorry dear, I will be right back. I promise.
If you stay at the Chez La Vie, mon amie, when you're there, take care and beware, mon frère, and prepare for the nonstop hopped-up hopscotch they call the Chez La Vie!
It's a lot of dancin', if you call that dancin', endless reprises, with no reprieves. But if la liaison amoureuse is très running out of juice, well, c'est la vie—at the Chez La Vie, you could say love never leaves!
'Cause here at the Chez La Vie, they can't stop! Here at the Chez La Vie, hop-hop-hop! Here at the Chez La Vie, they're always doing the Chez La Vie!
Oui!
Now that we got-a that over with, and we are all warmed up, let's make some-a beautiful music together, eh, boss?

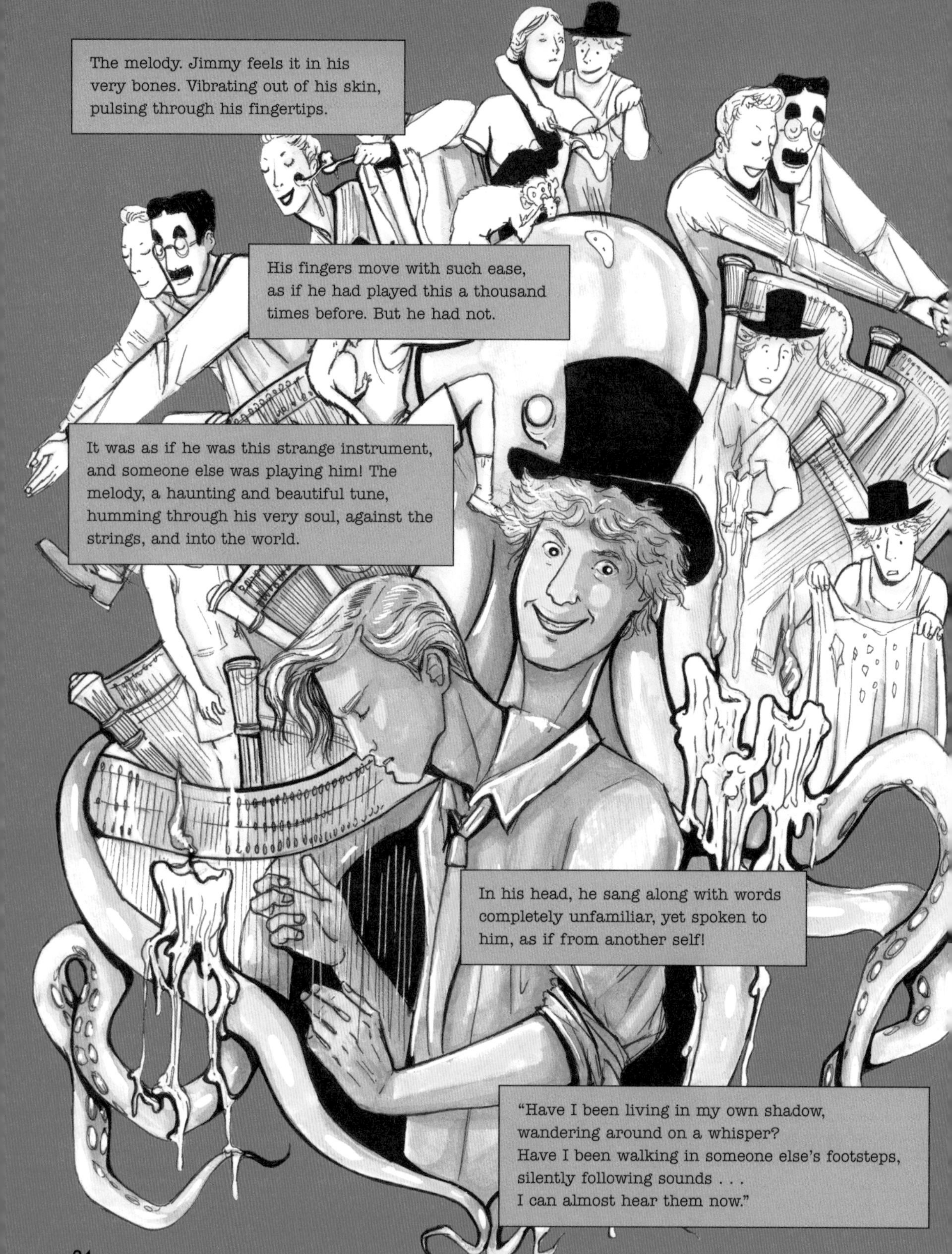
The melody. Jimmy feels it in his very bones. Vibrating out of his skin, pulsing through his fingertips.
His fingers move with such ease, as if he had played this a thousand times before. But he had not.
It was as if he was this strange instrument, and someone else was playing him! The melody, a haunting and beautiful tune, humming through his very soul, against the strings, and into the world.
In his head, he sang along with words completely unfamiliar, yet spoken to him, as if from another self!
"Have I been living in my own shadow, wandering around on a whisper? Have I been walking in someone else's footsteps, silently following sounds . . . I can almost hear them now."

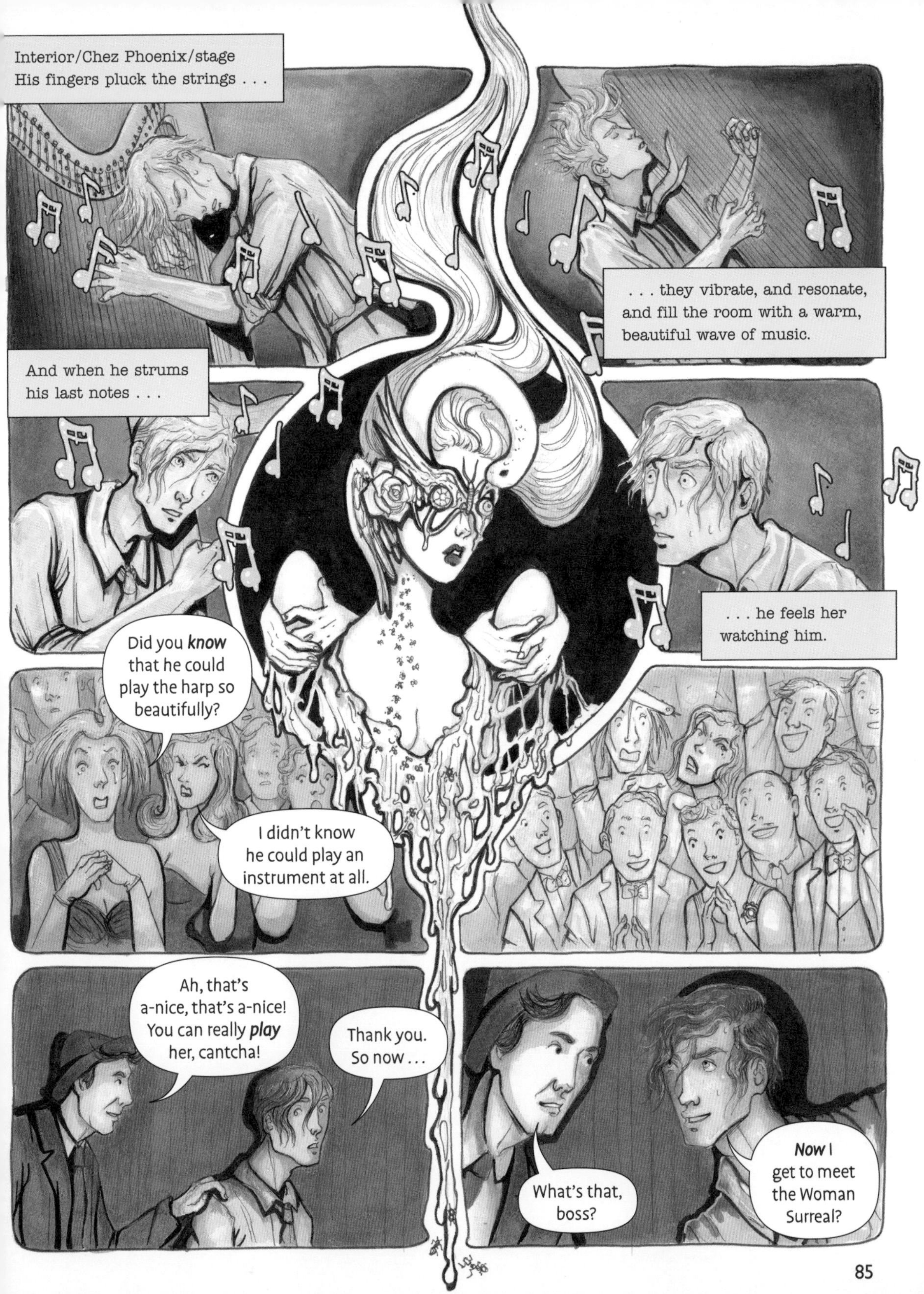
Interior/Chez Phoenix/stage
His fingers pluck the strings . . .
. . . they vibrate, and resonate, and fill the room with a warm, beautiful wave of music.
And when he strums his last notes . . .
. . . he feels her watching him.
Did you *know* that he could play the harp so beautifully?
I didn't know he could play an instrument at all.
Ah, that's a-nice, that's a-nice! You can really *play* her, cantcha!
Thank you. So now . . .
What's that, boss?
Now I get to meet the Woman Surreal?

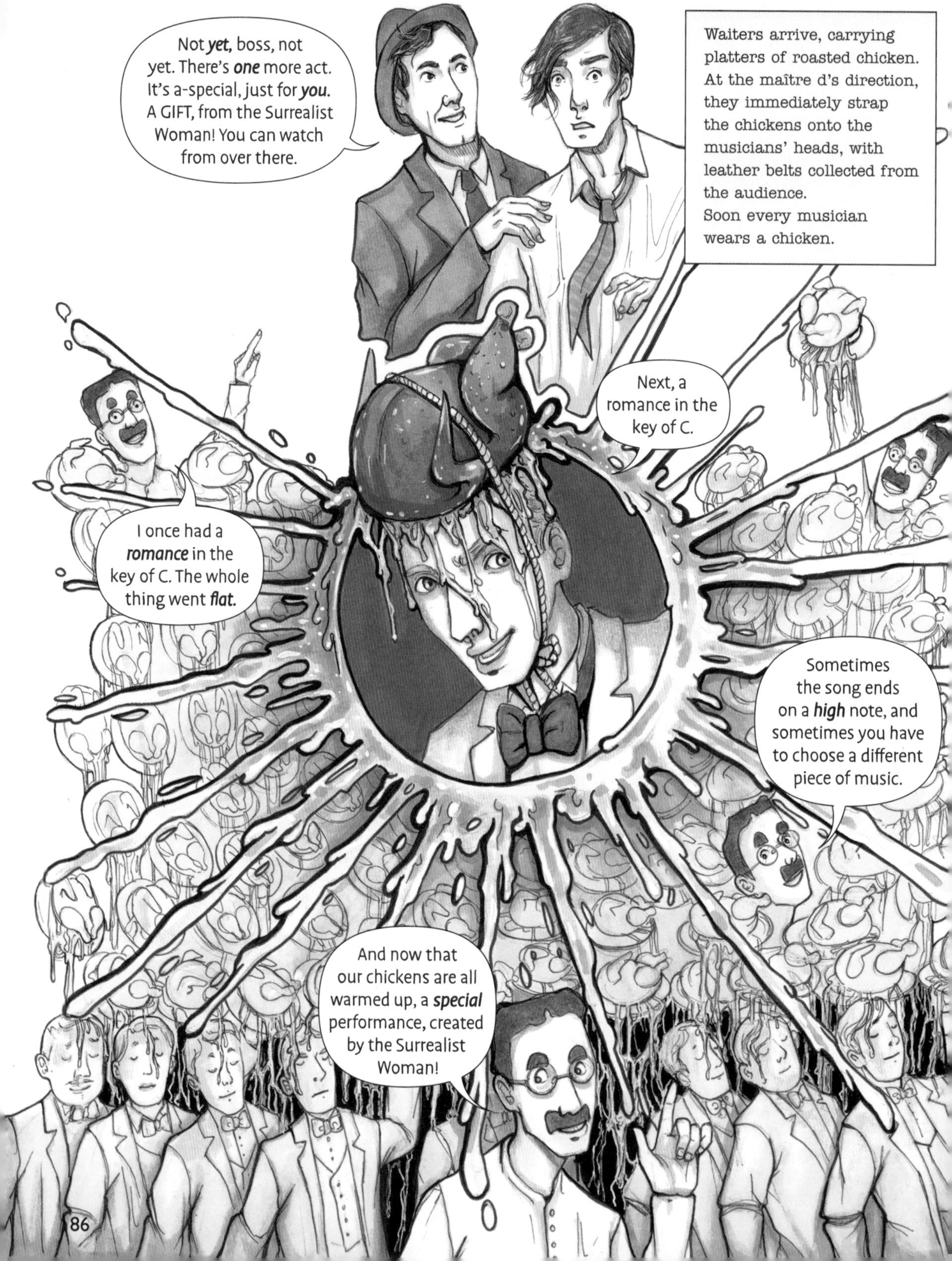
Not *yet*, boss, not yet. There's *one* more act. It's a-special, just for *you*. A GIFT, from the Surrealist Woman! You can watch from over there.
Waiters arrive, carrying platters of roasted chicken. At the maître d's direction, they immediately strap the chickens onto the musicians' heads, with leather belts collected from the audience. Soon every musician wears a chicken.
Next, a romance in the key of C.
I once had a *romance* in the key of C. The whole thing went *flat*.
Sometimes the song ends on a *high* note, and sometimes you have to choose a different piece of music.
And now that our chickens are all warmed up, a *special* performance, created by the Surrealist Woman!

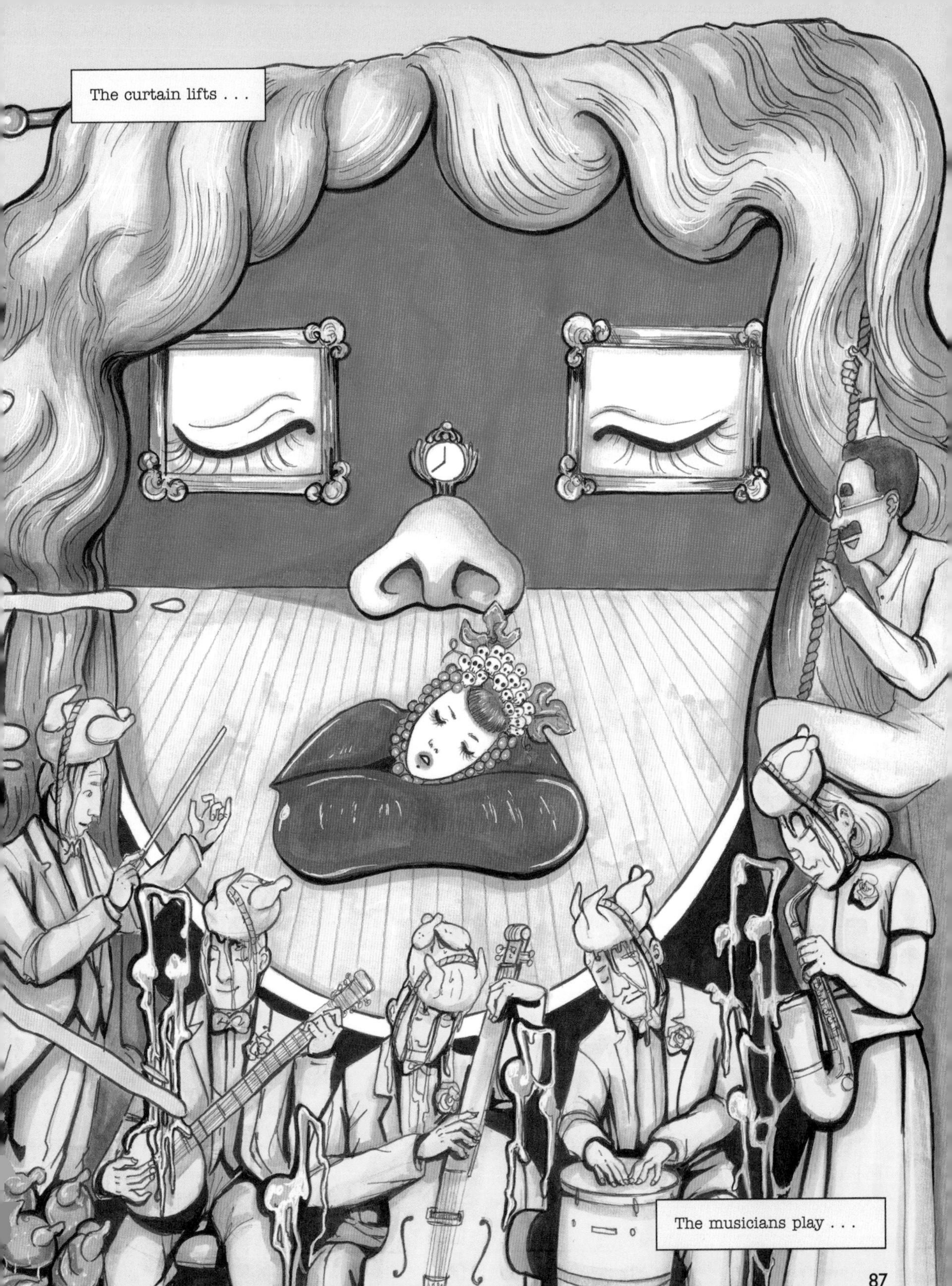
The curtain lifts . . .
The musicians play . . .

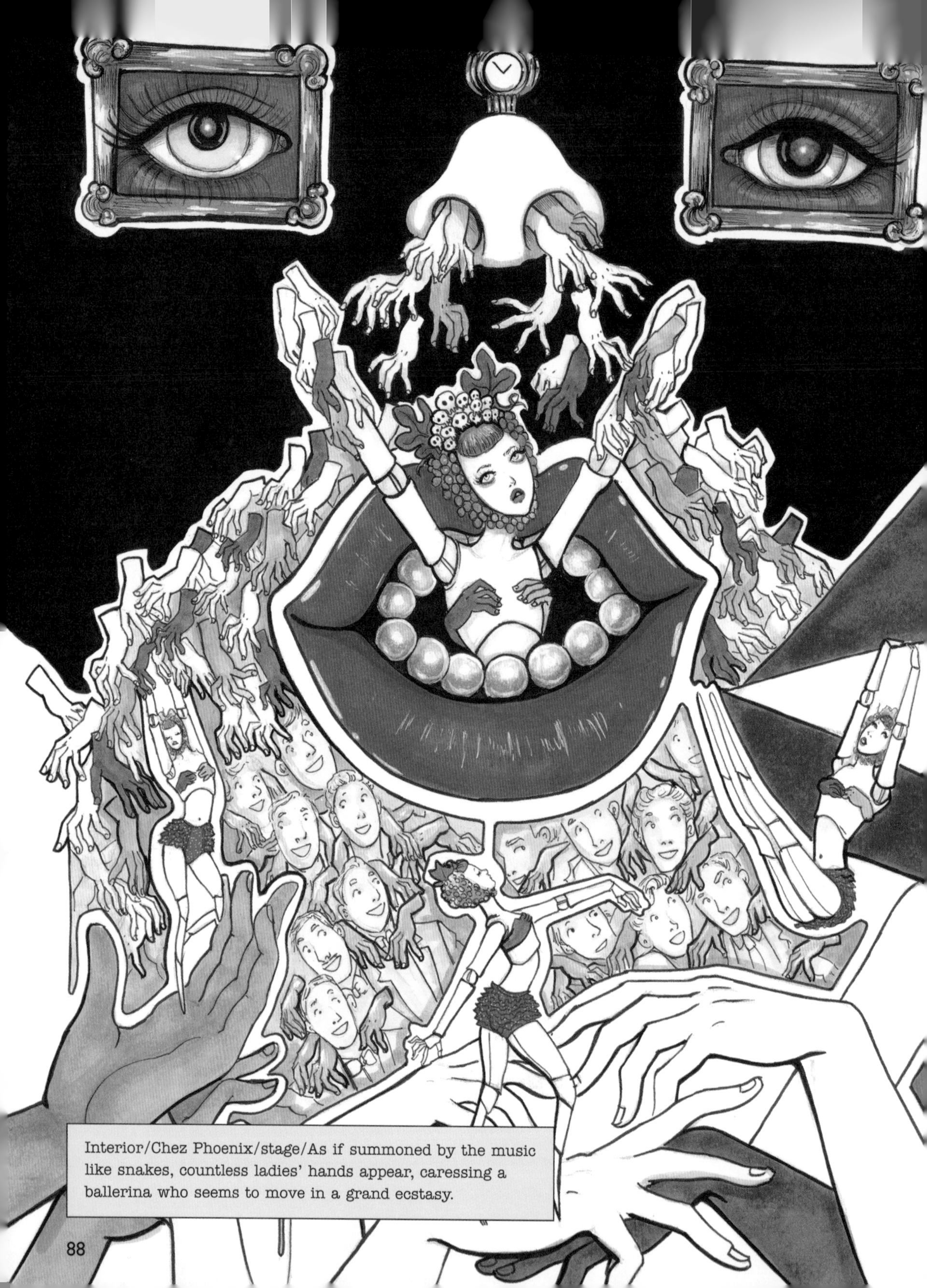
Interior/Chez Phoenix/stage/As if summoned by the music like snakes, countless ladies' hands appear, caressing a ballerina who seems to move in a grand ecstasy.

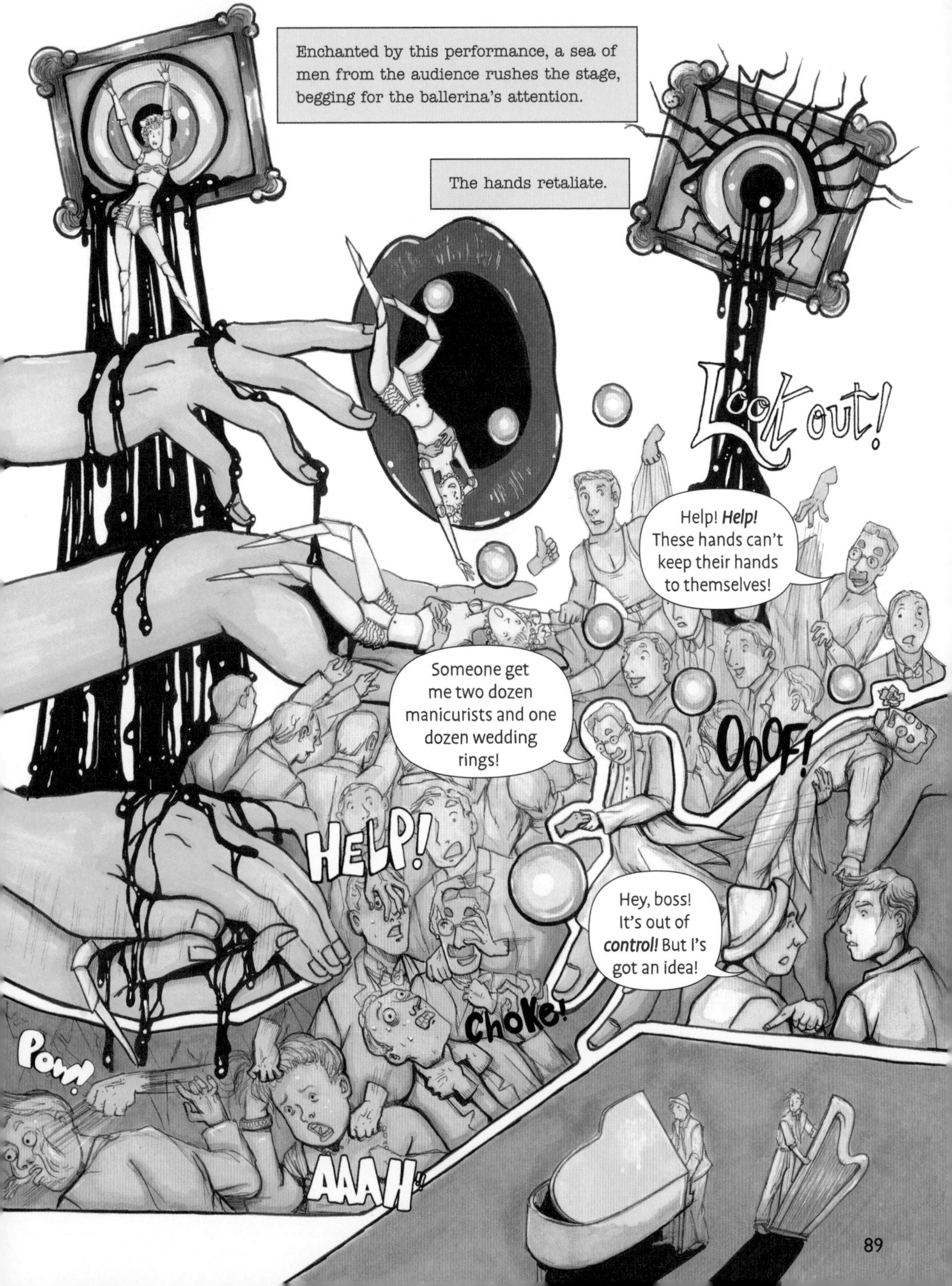
Enchanted by this performance, a sea of men from the audience rushes the stage, begging for the ballerina's attention.
The hands retaliate.
Look out!
Help! *Help!* These hands can't keep their hands to themselves!
Someone get me two dozen manicurists and one dozen wedding rings!
OOOF!
HELP!
Hey, boss! It's out of *control!* But I's got an idea!
Choke!
Pow!
AAAH!

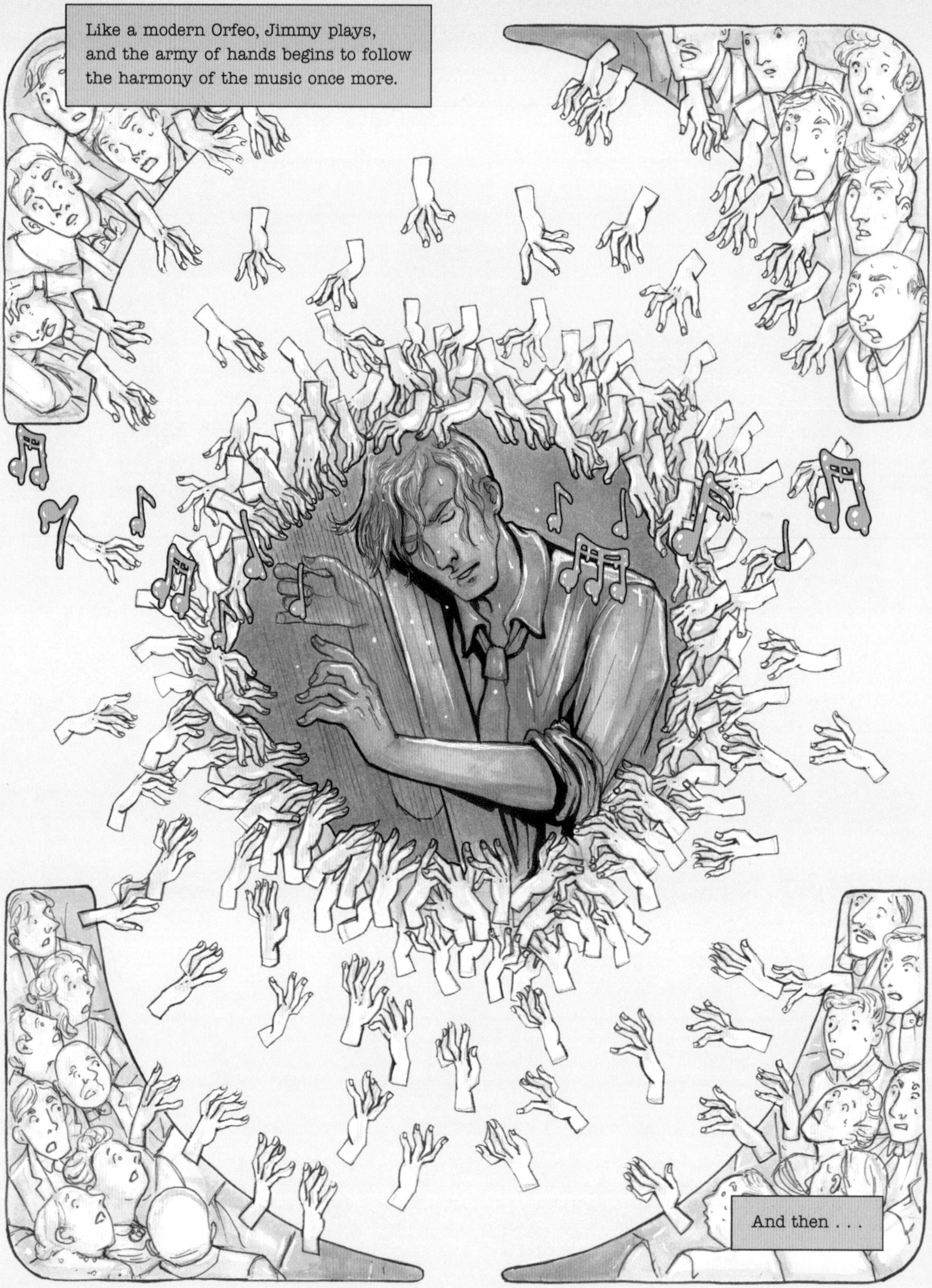
Like a modern Orfeo, Jimmy plays, and the army of hands begins to follow the harmony of the music once more.
And then . . .

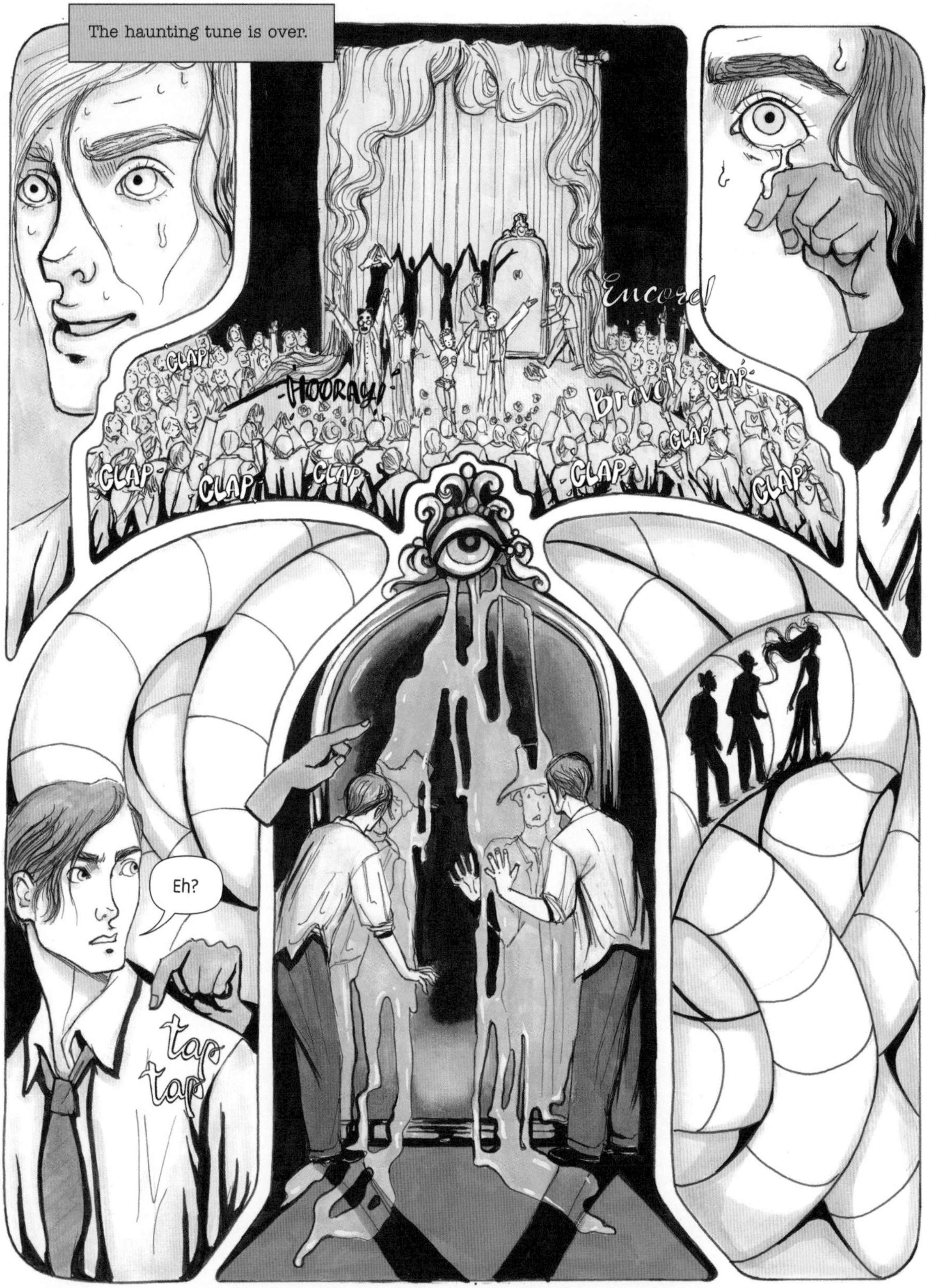
The haunting tune is over.
CLAP
HOORAY!
Encore!
Bravo!
CLAP
CLAP
CLAP
CLAP
CLAP
CLAP
CLAP
Eh?
tap tap

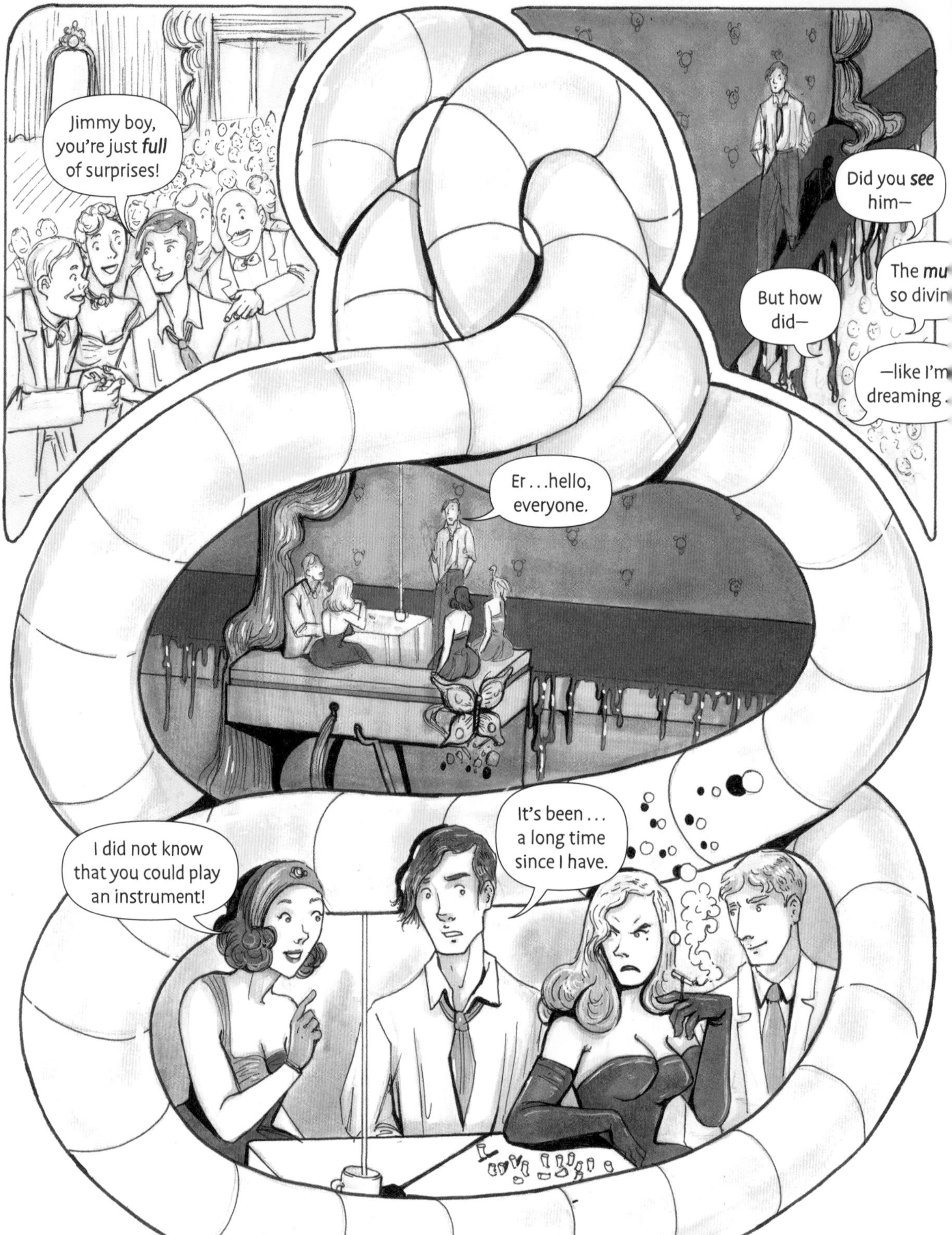

Jimmy boy, you're just *full* of surprises!
Did you *see* him—
The *mu*
so divin
But how did—
—like I'm dreaming .
Er . . . hello, everyone.
I did not know that you could play an instrument!
It's been . . . a long time since I have.

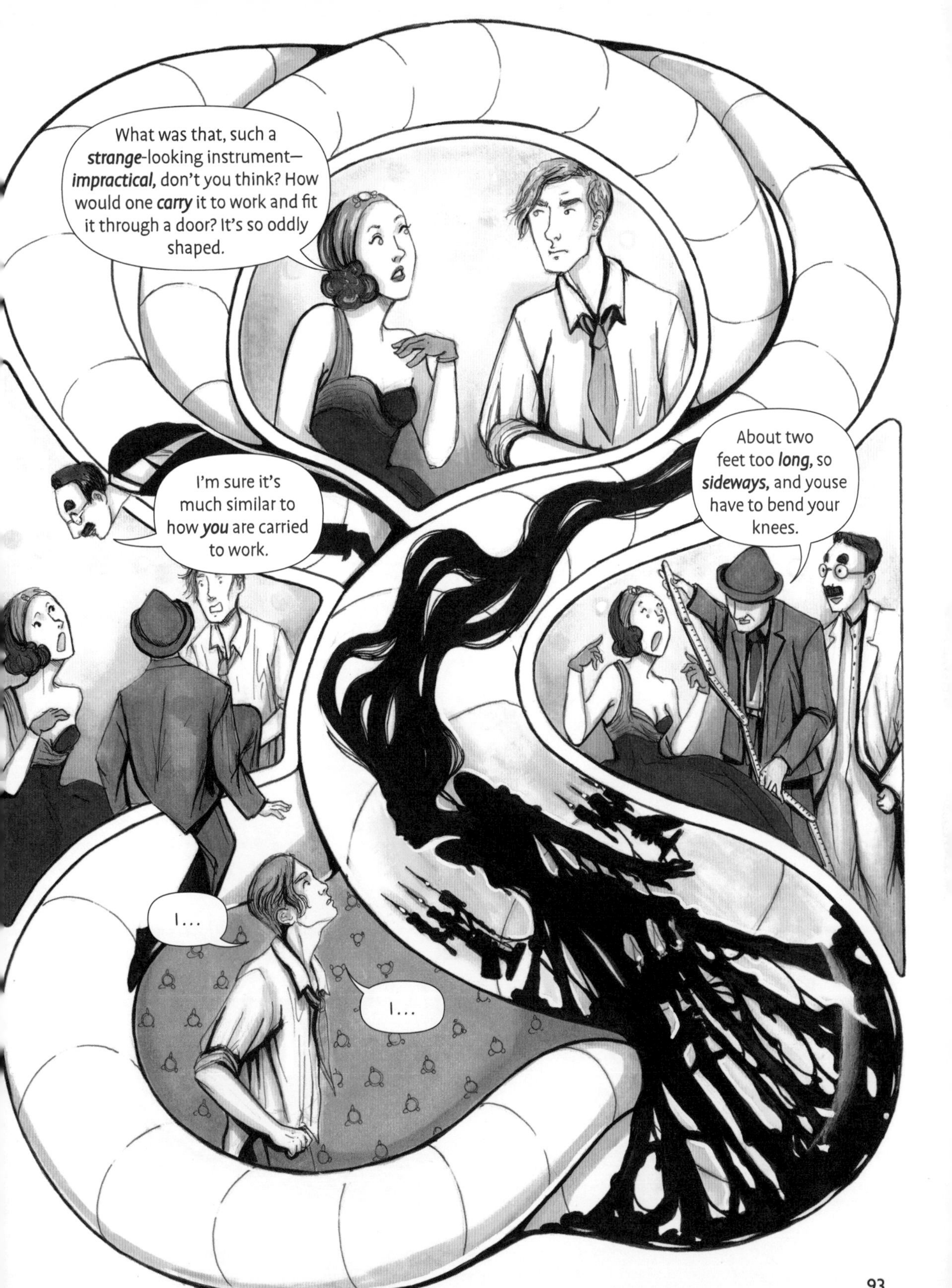
What was that, such a strange-looking instrument—impractical, don't you think? How would one carry it to work and fit it through a door? It's so oddly shaped.
I'm sure it's much similar to how you are carried to work.
About two feet too long, so sideways, and youse have to bend your knees.
I...
I...

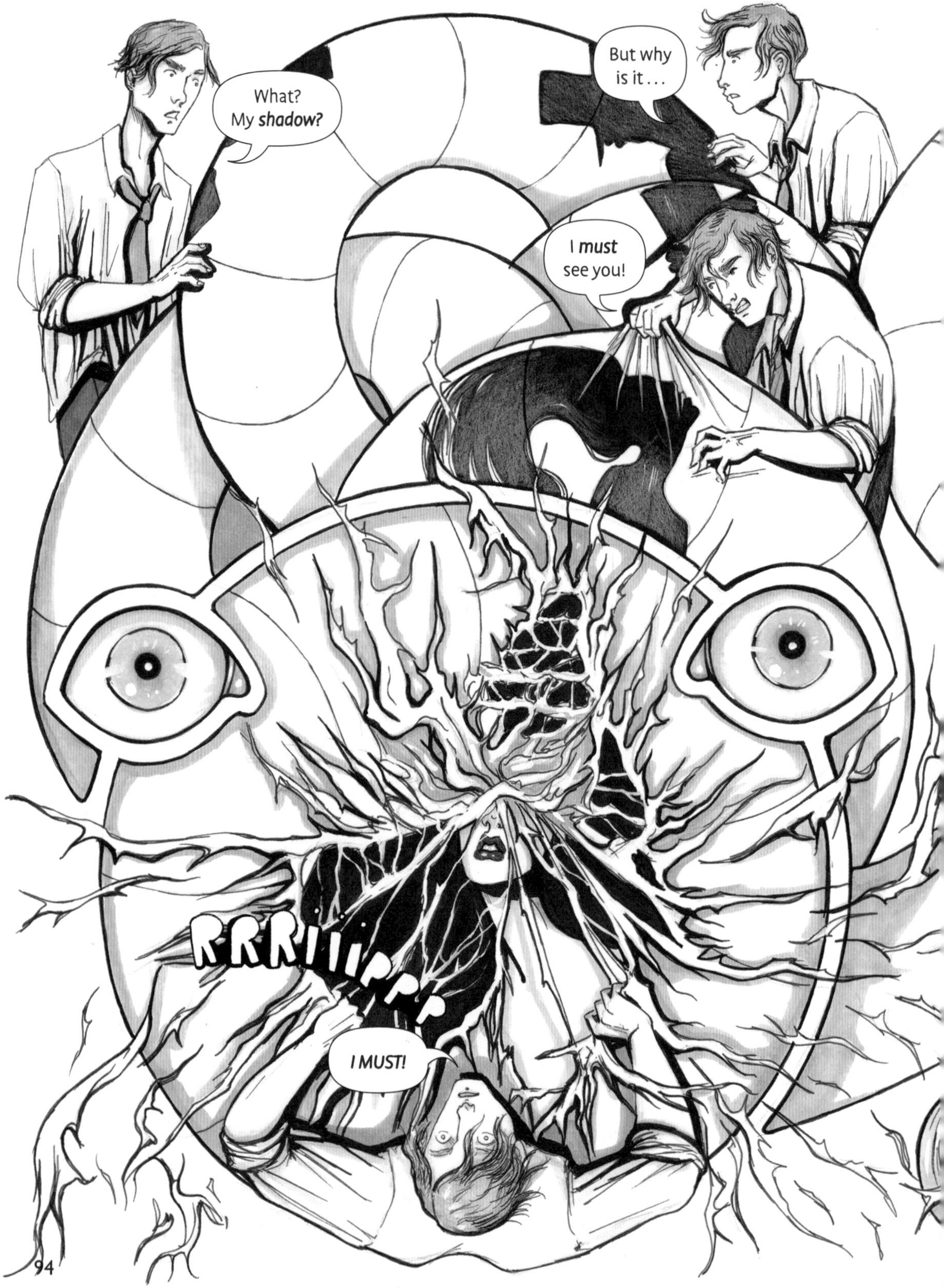
What? My *shadow?*
But why is it . . .
I *must* see you!
RRRIIIIPPP
I MUST!

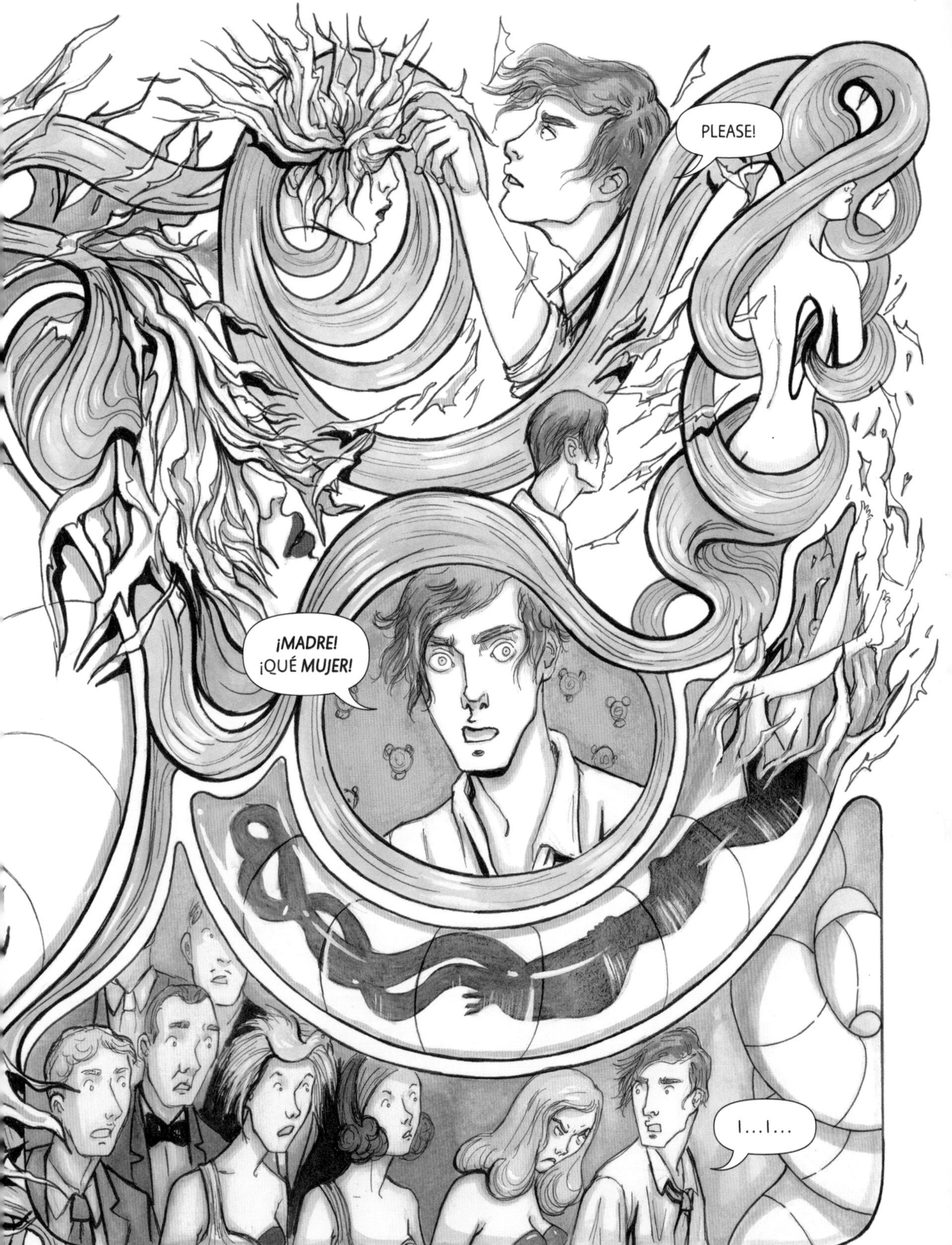
PLEASE!
¡MADRE! ¡QUÉ MUJER!
I…I…

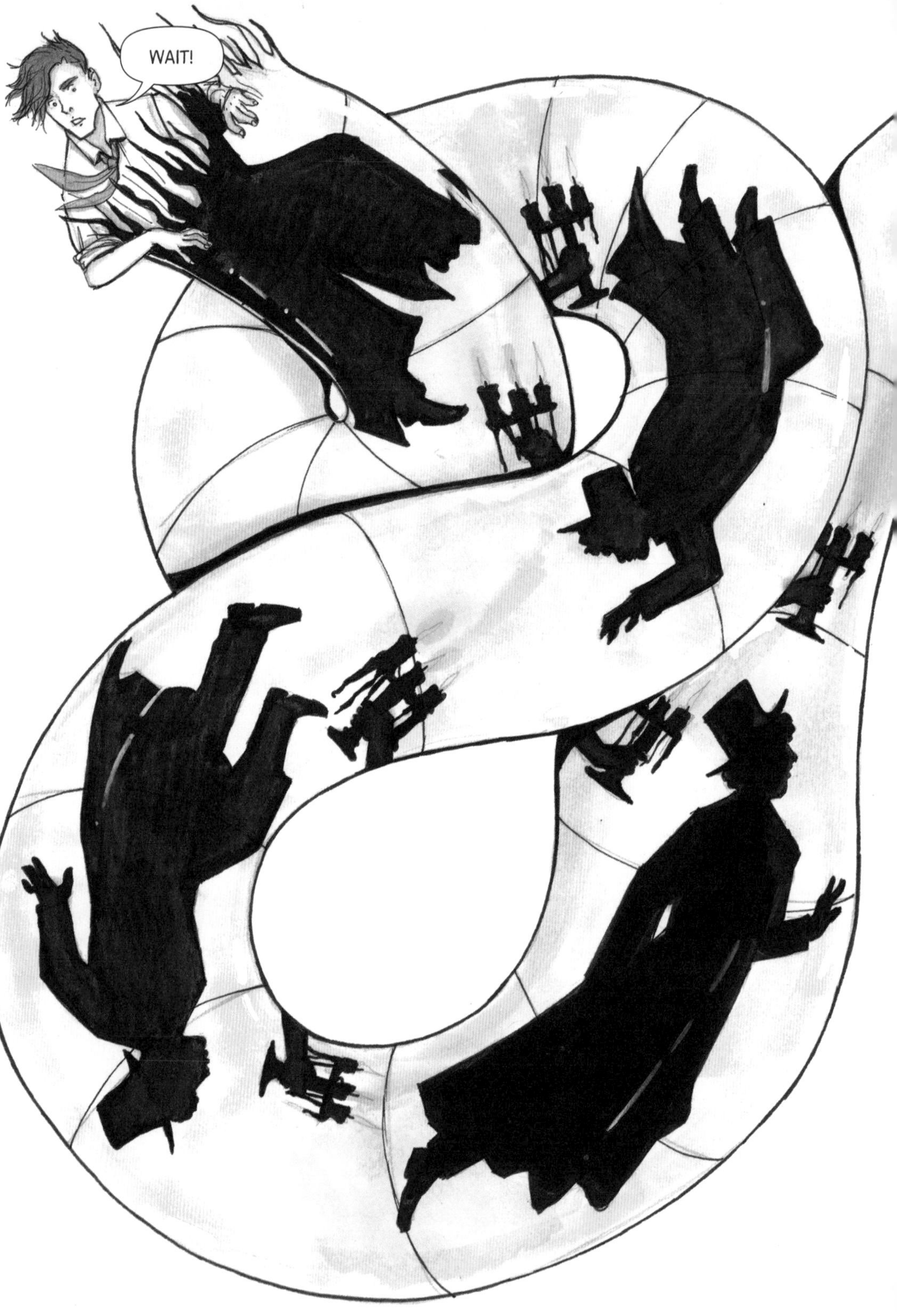
WAIT!

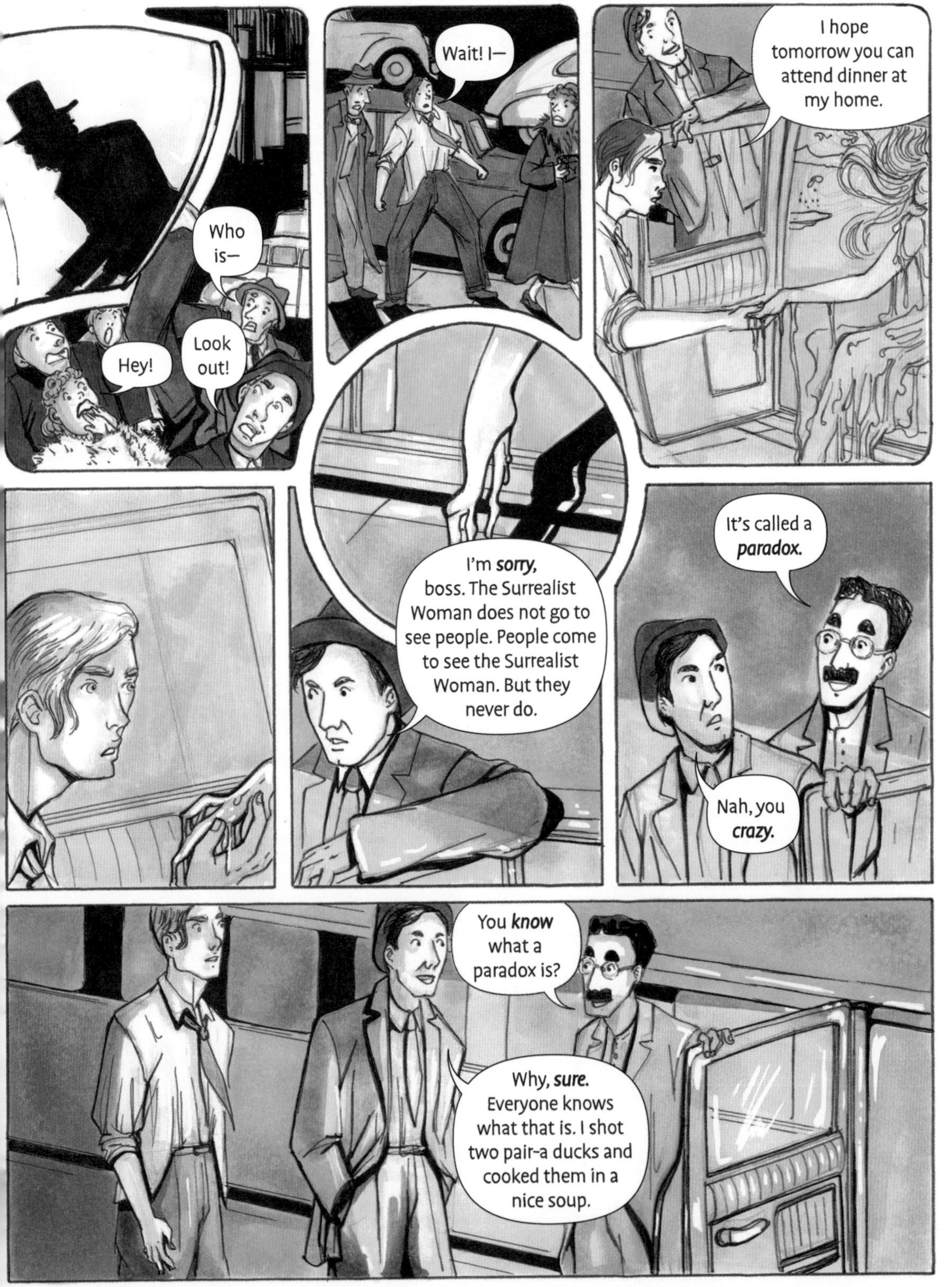
Who is—
Hey!
Look out!
Wait! I—
I hope tomorrow you can attend dinner at my home.
I'm *sorry,* boss. The Surrealist Woman does not go to see people. People come to see the Surrealist Woman. But they never do.
It's called a *paradox.*
Nah, you *crazy.*
You *know* what a paradox is?
Why, *sure.* Everyone knows what that is. I shot two pair-a ducks and cooked them in a nice soup.

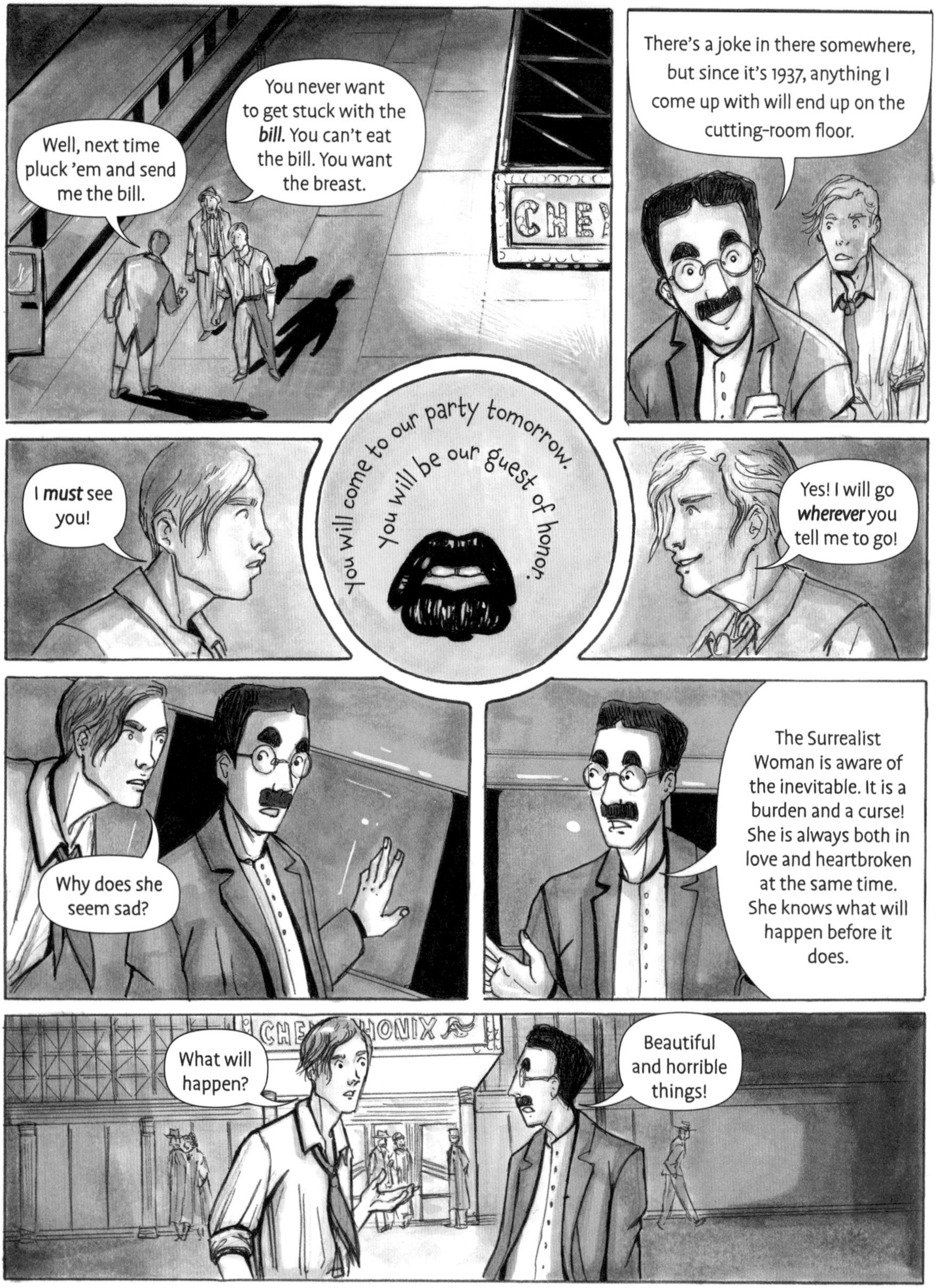
Well, next time pluck 'em and send me the bill.
You never want to get stuck with the *bill.* You can't eat the bill. You want the breast.
CHE
There's a joke in there somewhere, but since it's 1937, anything I come up with will end up on the cutting-room floor.
I *must* see you!
You will come to our party tomorrow. You will be our guest of honor.
Yes! I will go *wherever* you tell me to go!
Why does she seem sad?
The Surrealist Woman is aware of the inevitable. It is a burden and a curse! She is always both in love and heartbroken at the same time. She knows what will happen before it does.
What will happen?
Beautiful and horrible things!

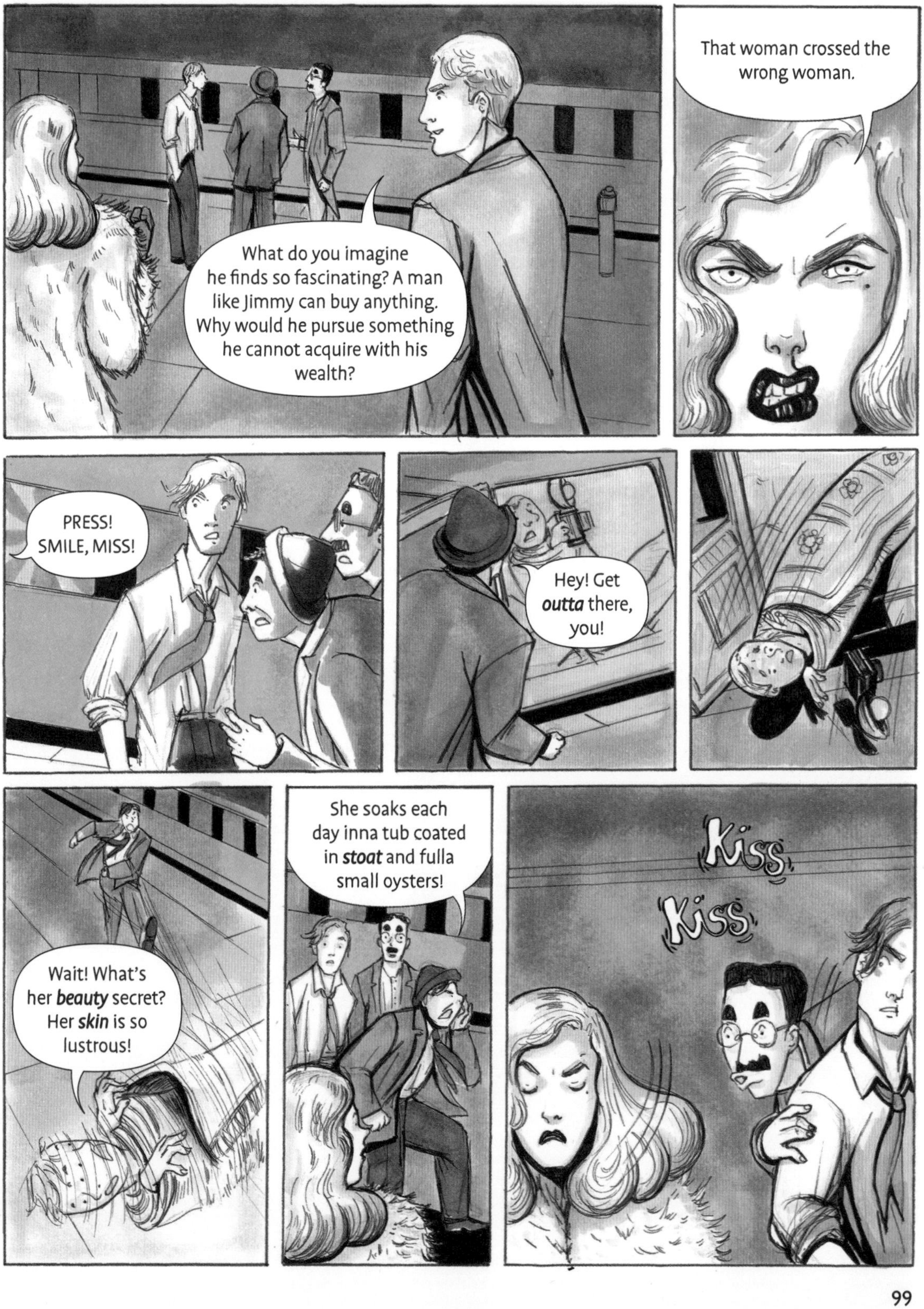
What do you imagine he finds so fascinating? A man like Jimmy can buy anything. Why would he pursue something he cannot acquire with his wealth?
That woman crossed the wrong woman.
PRESS! SMILE, MISS!
Hey! Get *outta* there, you!
Wait! What's her *beauty* secret? Her *skin* is so lustrous!
She soaks each day inna tub coated in *stoat* and fulla small oysters!
Kiss
Kiss

Ah, *love*, and its many outcomes.

Linda will be *fine*. She has simple needs that are easy to provide.

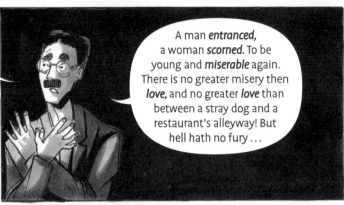

A man *entranced*, a woman *scorned*. To be young and *miserable* again. There is no greater misery then *love*, and no greater *love* than between a stray dog and a restaurant's alleyway! But hell hath no fury . . .

Love is a beautiful *butterfly* trapped in a cocoon, waiting to change into something *else*. But you must *protect* it, even when it's *ugly*, or it can never spread its wings and transform.

Thank you, my good man. I never forget a *face*, but in *your* case I'll be glad to make an exception.

Good night.

Remember, Jimmy, love is also the enemy of *productivity,* and if you can't eat crackers in bed while conducting *business,* how will you have time to sleep on the crumbs?

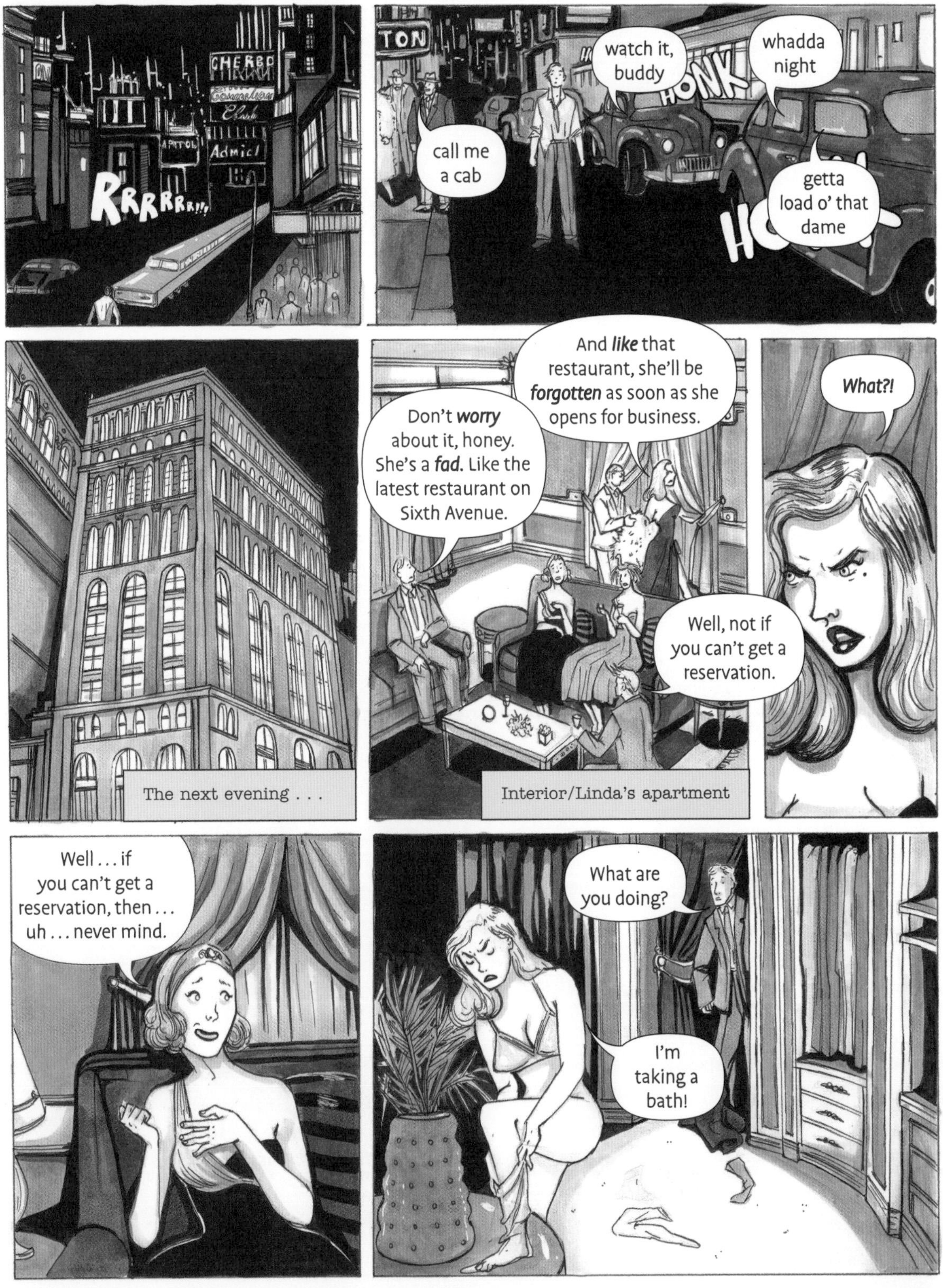
RRRRRR!!!
watch it, buddy
HONK
whadda night
call me a cab
getta load o' that dame
And like that restaurant, she'll be forgotten as soon as she opens for business.
Don't worry about it, honey. She's a fad. Like the latest restaurant on Sixth Avenue.
What?!
Well, not if you can't get a reservation.
The next evening . . .
Interior/Linda's apartment
Well . . . if you can't get a reservation, then . . . uh . . . never mind.
What are you doing?
I'm taking a bath!

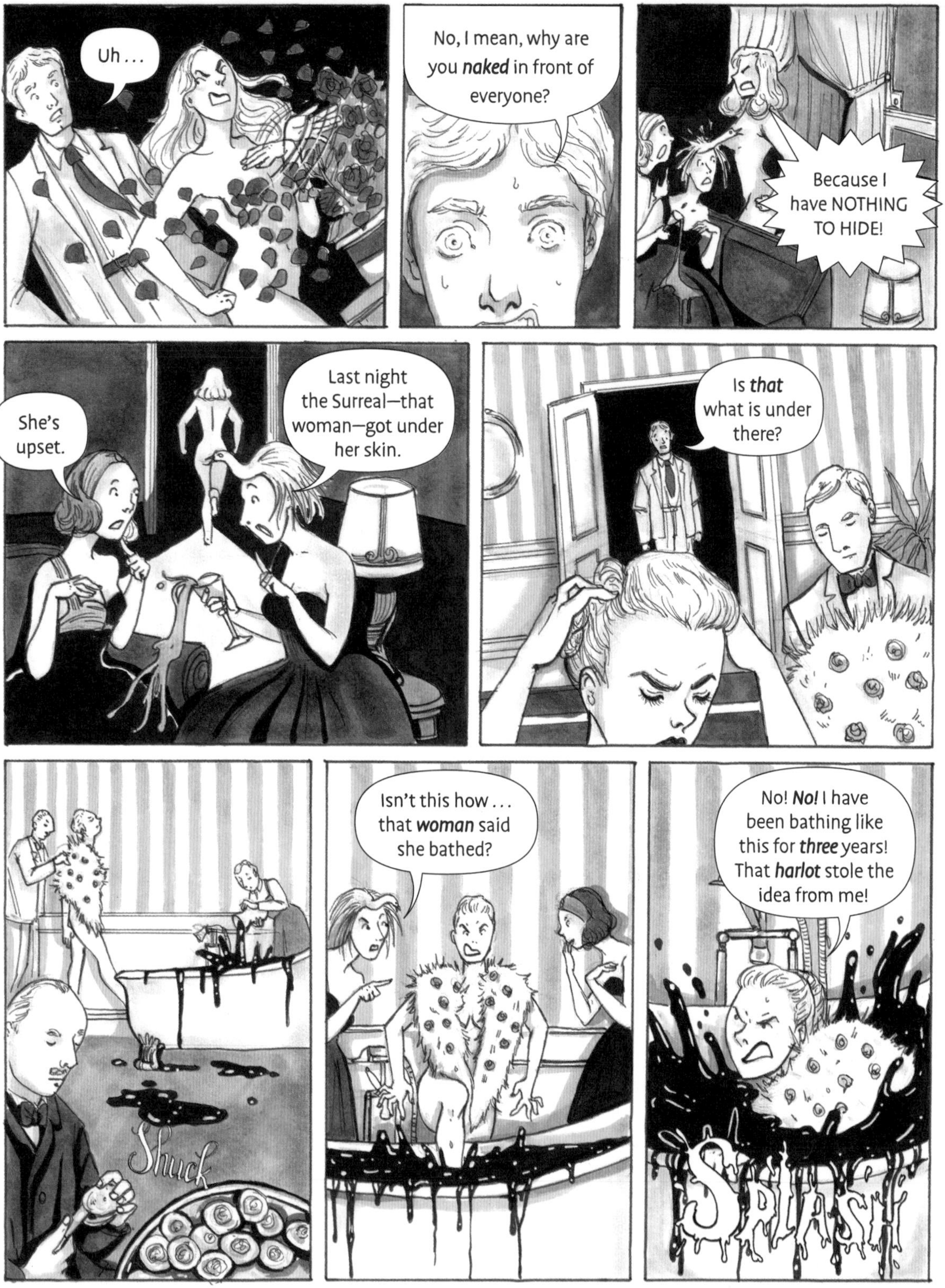
Uh . . .
No, I mean, why are you *naked* in front of everyone?
Because I have NOTHING TO HIDE!
She's upset.
Last night the Surreal—that woman—got under her skin.
Is *that* what is under there?
Shuck
Isn't this how . . . that *woman* said she bathed?
No! *No!* I have been bathing like this for *three* years! That *harlot* stole the idea from me!
SPLASH

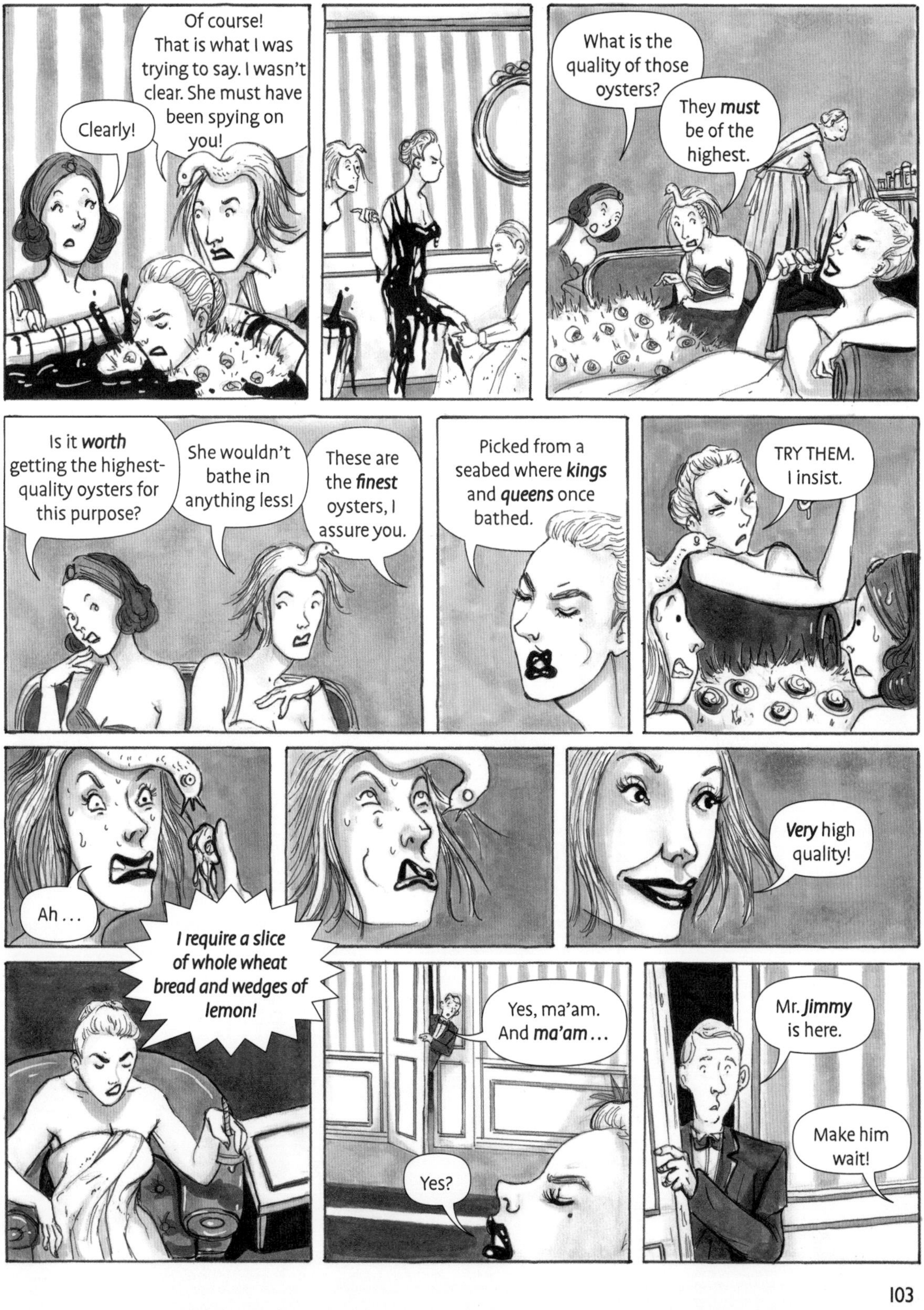
Clearly!
Of course! That is what I was trying to say. I wasn't clear. She must have been spying on you!
What is the quality of those oysters?
They *must* be of the highest.
Is it *worth* getting the highest-quality oysters for this purpose?
She wouldn't bathe in anything less!
These are the *finest* oysters, I assure you.
Picked from a seabed where *kings* and *queens* once bathed.
TRY THEM. I insist.
Ah . . .
Very high quality!
I require a slice of whole wheat bread and wedges of lemon!
Yes, ma'am. And *ma'am* . . .
Yes?
Mr. *Jimmy* is here.
Make him wait!

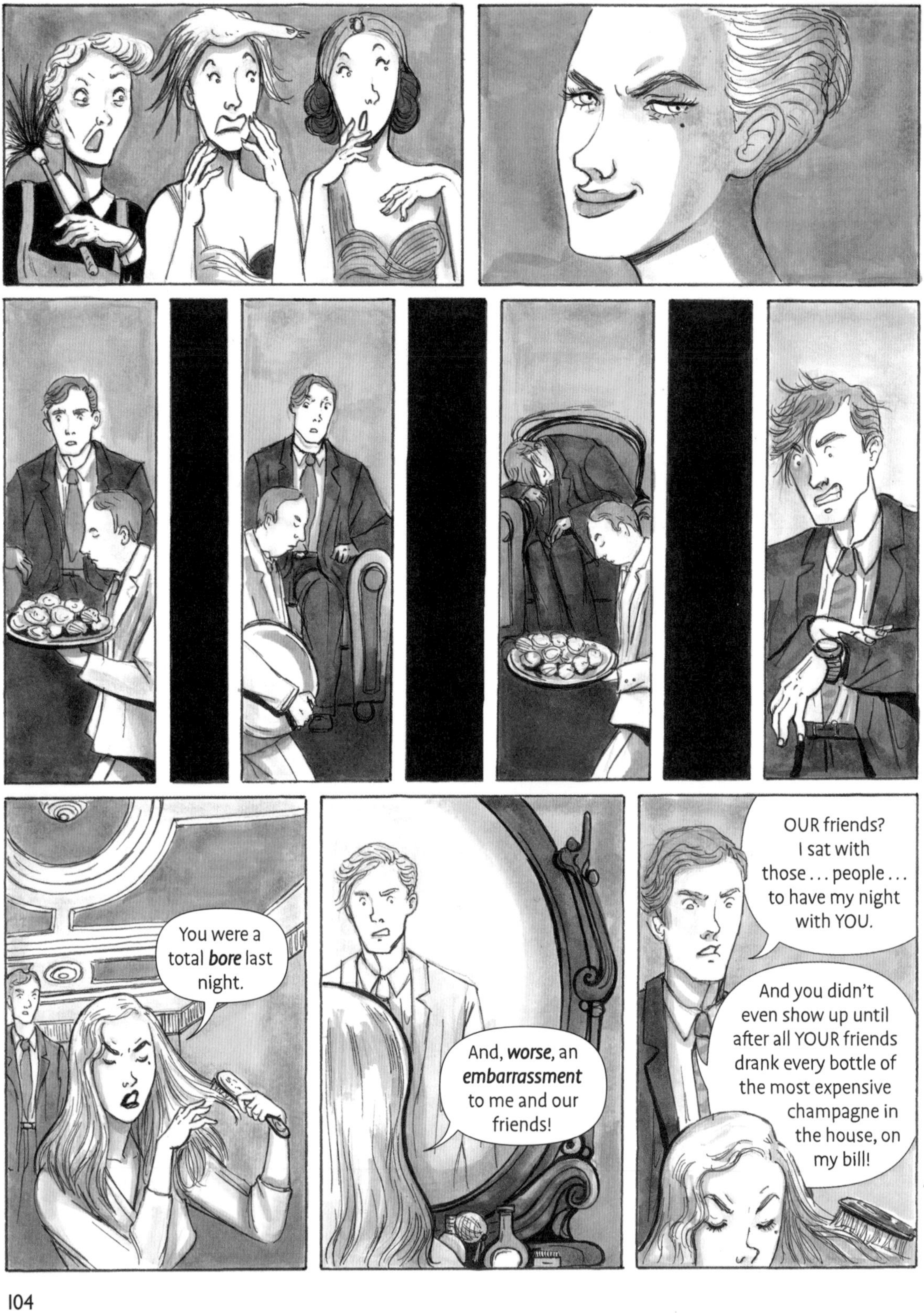
You were a total bore last night.
And, worse, an embarrassment to me and our friends!
OUR friends? I sat with those . . . people . . . to have my night with YOU.
And you didn't even show up until after all YOUR friends drank every bottle of the most expensive champagne in the house, on my bill!

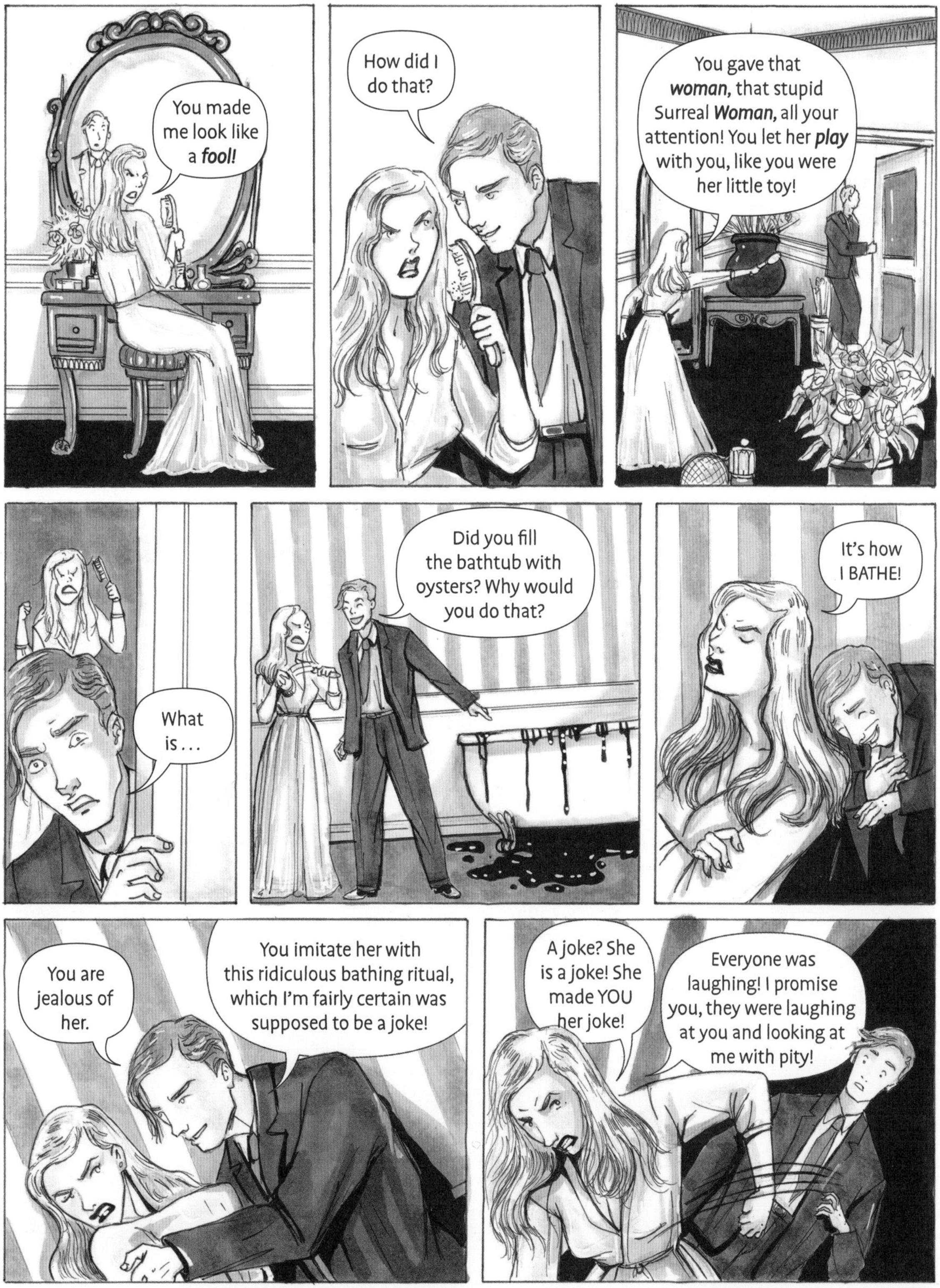
You made me look like a ***fool!***
How did I do that?
You gave that ***woman,*** that stupid Surreal ***Woman,*** all your attention! You let her ***play*** with you, like you were her little toy!
What is . . .
Did you fill the bathtub with oysters? Why would you do that?
It's how I BATHE!
You are jealous of her.
You imitate her with this ridiculous bathing ritual, which I'm fairly certain was supposed to be a joke!
A joke? She is a joke! She made YOU her joke!
Everyone was laughing! I promise you, they were laughing at you and looking at me with pity!

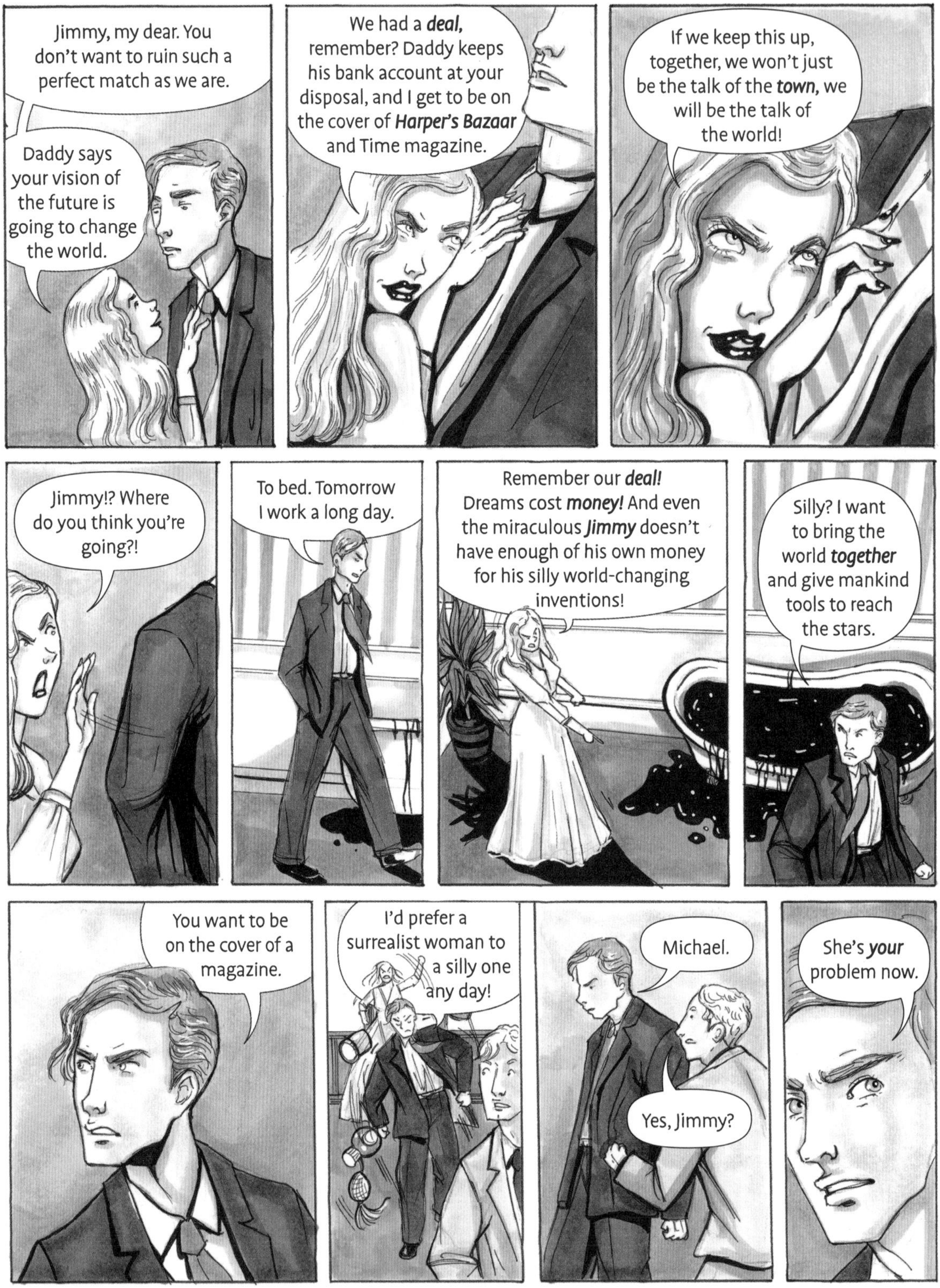
Jimmy, my dear. You don't want to ruin such a perfect match as we are.
Daddy says your vision of the future is going to change the world.
We had a *deal,* remember? Daddy keeps his bank account at your disposal, and I get to be on the cover of *Harper's Bazaar* and Time magazine.
If we keep this up, together, we won't just be the talk of the *town,* we will be the talk of the world!
Jimmy!? Where do you think you're going?!
To bed. Tomorrow I work a long day.
Remember our *deal!* Dreams cost *money!* And even the miraculous *Jimmy* doesn't have enough of his own money for his silly world-changing inventions!
Silly? I want to bring the world *together* and give mankind tools to reach the stars.
You want to be on the cover of a magazine.
I'd prefer a surrealist woman to a silly one any day!
Michael.
Yes, Jimmy?
She's *your* problem now.

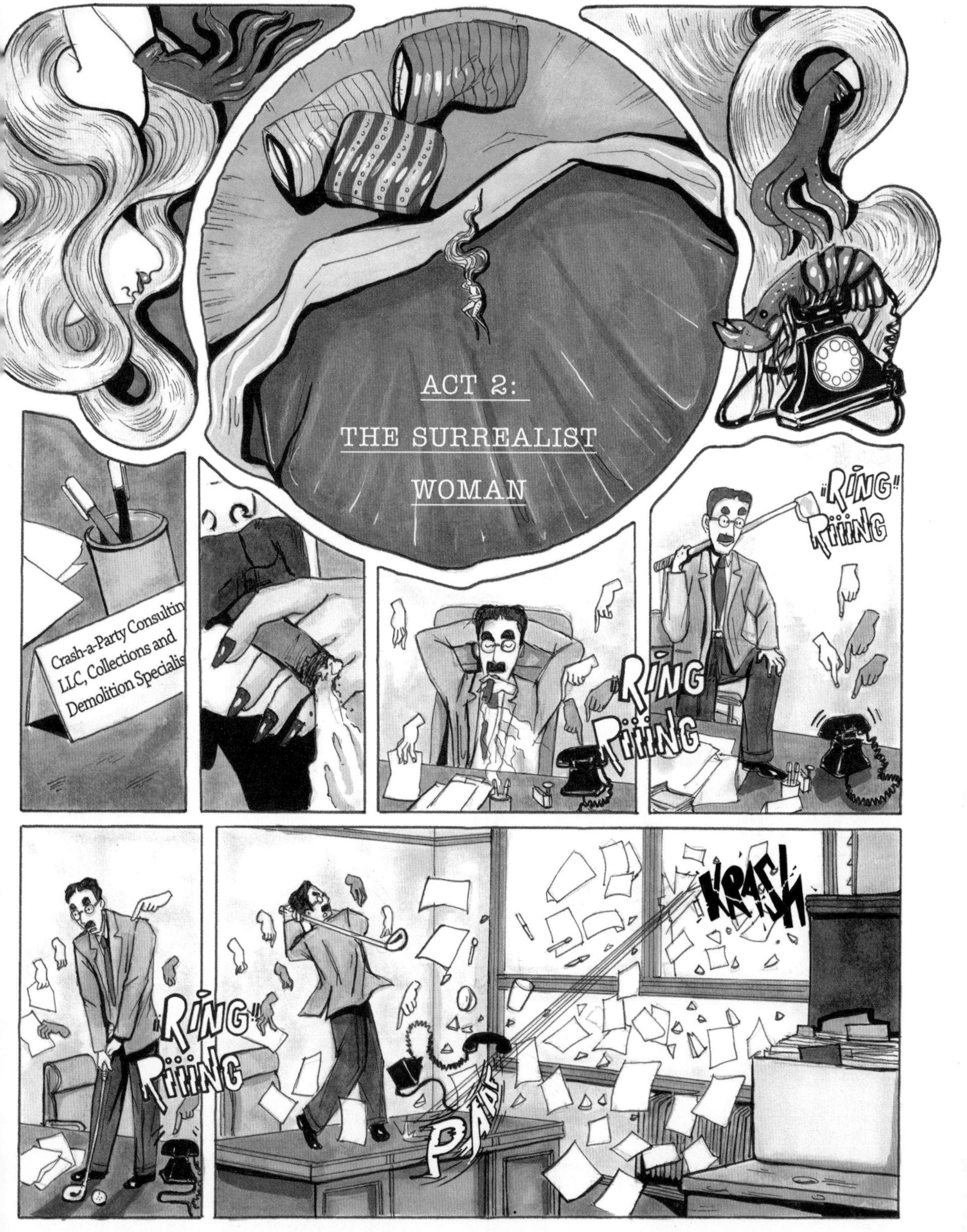

ACT 2:
THE SURREALIST
WOMAN
Crash-a-Party Consultin
LLC, Collections and
Demolition Specialis
RING
RIIING
"RING"
RIIING
"RING"
RIIING
KRASH

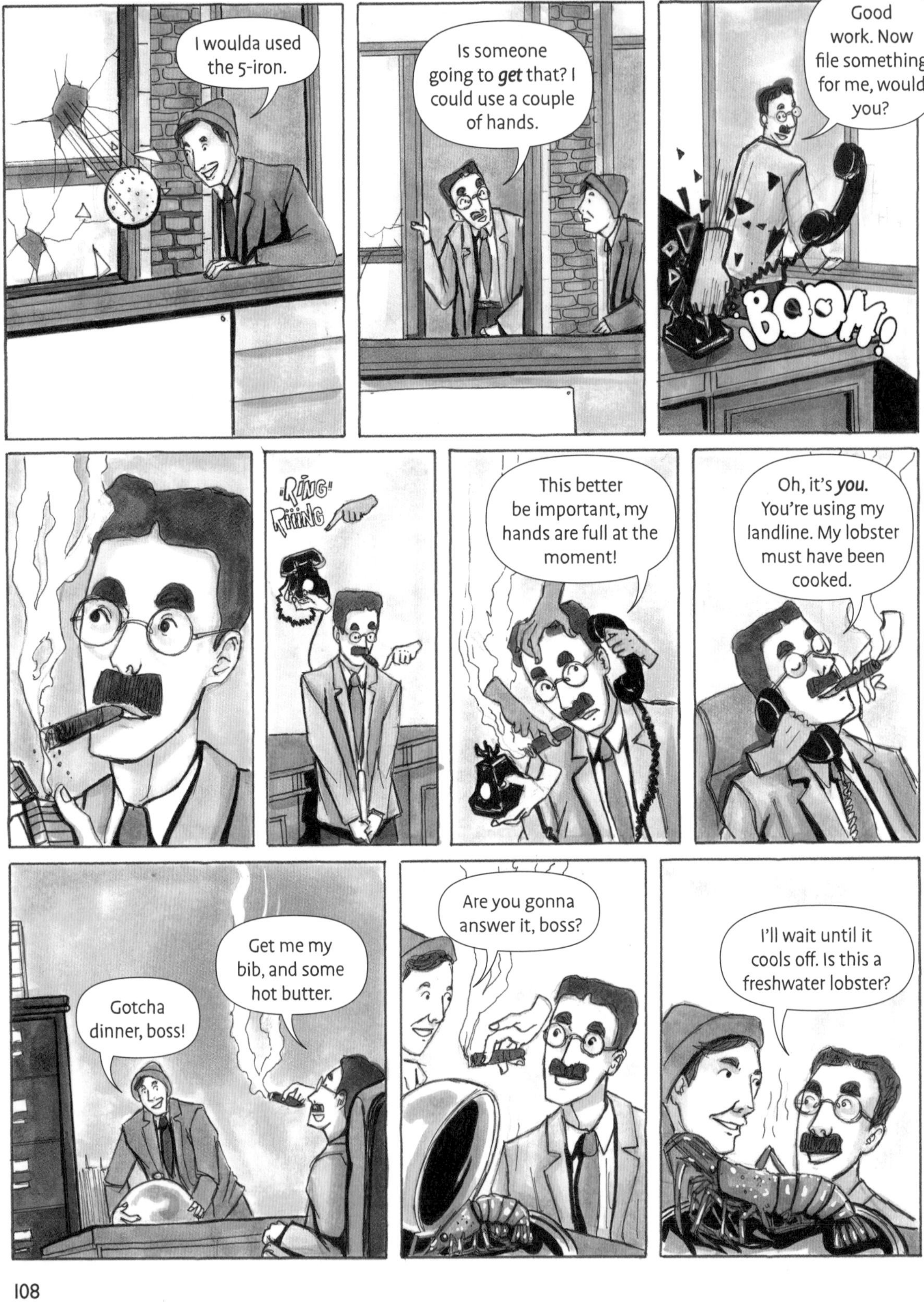
I woulda used the 5-iron.
Is someone going to *get* that? I could use a couple of hands.
Good work. Now file something for me, would you?
BOOM!
RING RIIING
This better be important, my hands are full at the moment!
Oh, it's *you.* You're using my landline. My lobster must have been cooked.
Get me my bib, and some hot butter.
Gotcha dinner, boss!
Are you gonna answer it, boss?
I'll wait until it cools off. Is this a freshwater lobster?

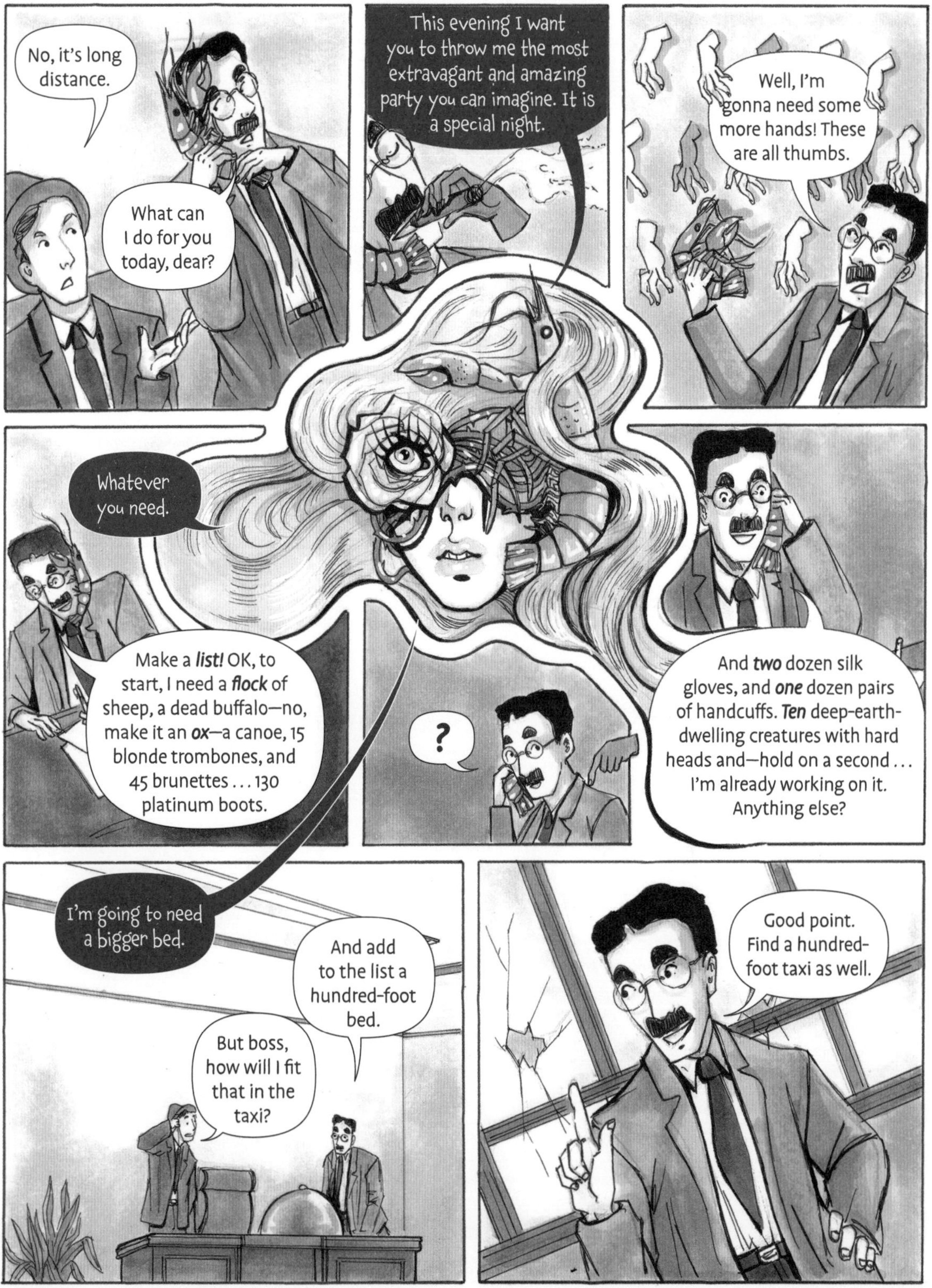

No, it's long distance.
What can I do for you today, dear?
This evening I want you to throw me the most extravagant and amazing party you can imagine. It is a special night.
Well, I'm gonna need some more hands! These are all thumbs.
Whatever you need.
Make a *list!* OK, to start, I need a *flock* of sheep, a dead buffalo—no, make it an *ox*—a canoe, 15 blonde trombones, and 45 brunettes . . . 130 platinum boots.
?
And *two* dozen silk gloves, and *one* dozen pairs of handcuffs. *Ten* deep-earth-dwelling creatures with hard heads and—hold on a second . . . I'm already working on it. Anything else?
I'm going to need a bigger bed.
And add to the list a hundred-foot bed.
But boss, how will I fit that in the taxi?
Good point. Find a hundred-foot taxi as well.

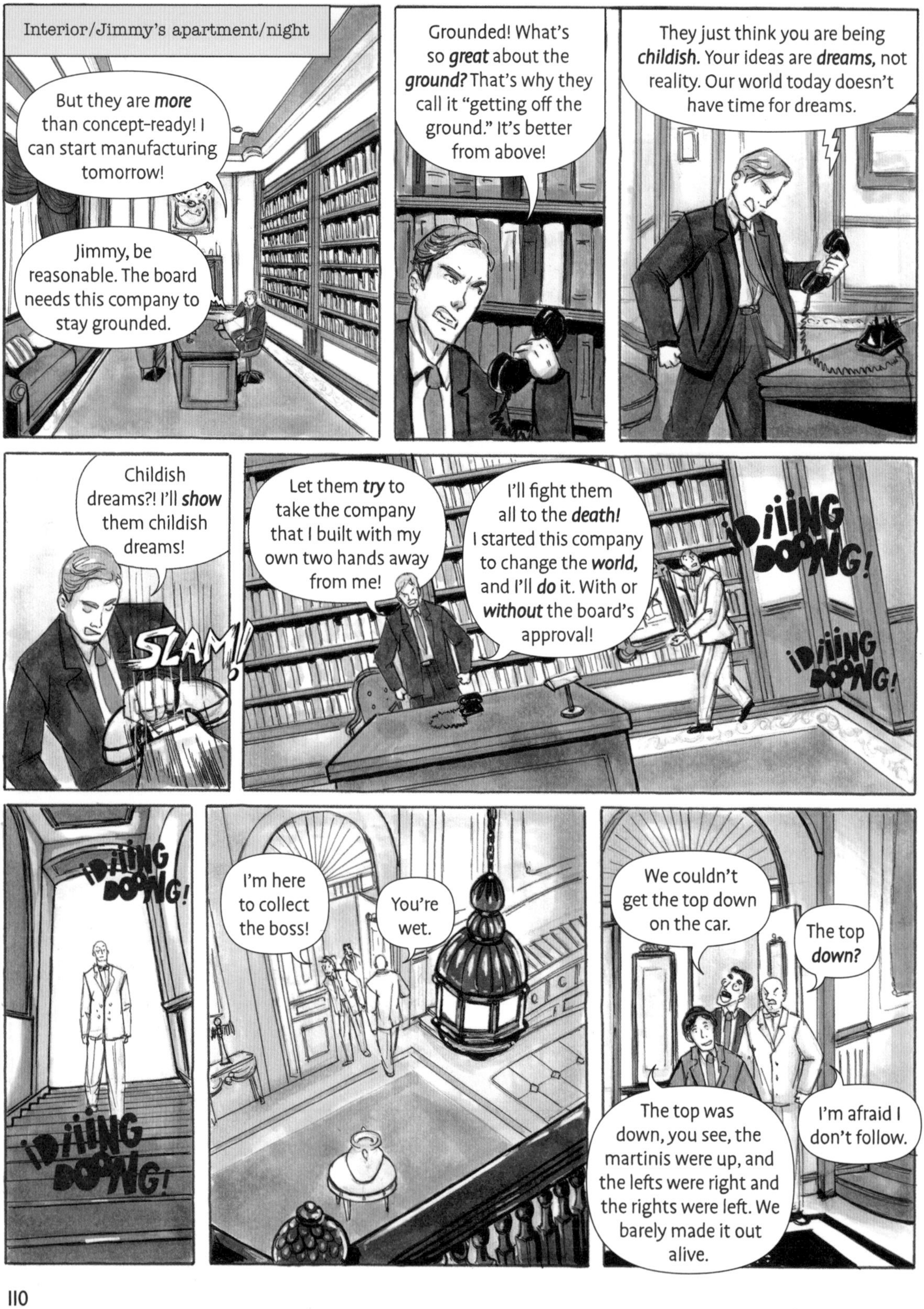
Interior/Jimmy's apartment/night
But they are *more* than concept-ready! I can start manufacturing tomorrow!
Jimmy, be reasonable. The board needs this company to stay grounded.
Grounded! What's so *great* about the *ground?* That's why they call it "getting off the ground." It's better from above!
They just think you are being *childish.* Your ideas are *dreams,* not reality. Our world today doesn't have time for dreams.
Childish dreams?! I'll *show* them childish dreams!
SLAM!
Let them *try* to take the company that I built with my own two hands away from me!
I'll fight them all to the *death!* I started this company to change the *world,* and I'll *do* it. With or *without* the board's approval!
¡DIIING DOONG!
¡DIIING DOONG!
¡DIIING DOONG!
¡DIIING DOONG!
I'm here to collect the boss!
You're wet.
We couldn't get the top down on the car.
The top *down?*
The top was down, you see, the martinis were up, and the lefts were right and the rights were left. We barely made it out alive.
I'm afraid I don't follow.

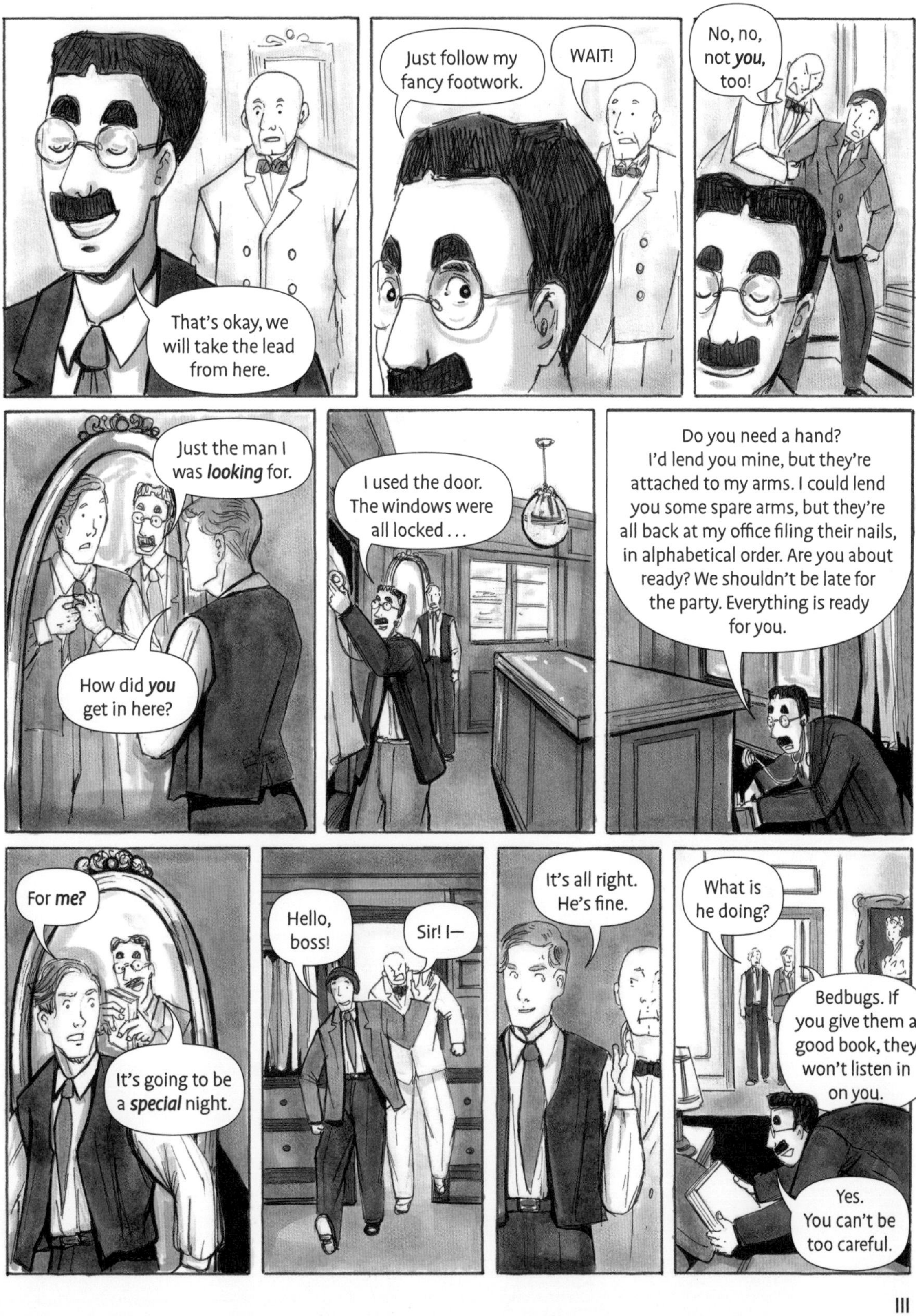
That's okay, we will take the lead from here.
Just follow my fancy footwork.
WAIT!
No, no, not *you,* too!
Just the man I was *looking* for.
How did *you* get in here?
I used the door. The windows were all locked . . .
Do you need a hand? I'd lend you mine, but they're attached to my arms. I could lend you some spare arms, but they're all back at my office filing their nails, in alphabetical order. Are you about ready? We shouldn't be late for the party. Everything is ready for you.
For *me?*
It's going to be a *special* night.
Hello, boss!
Sir! I—
It's all right. He's fine.
What is he doing?
Bedbugs. If you give them a good book, they won't listen in on you.
Yes. You can't be too careful.

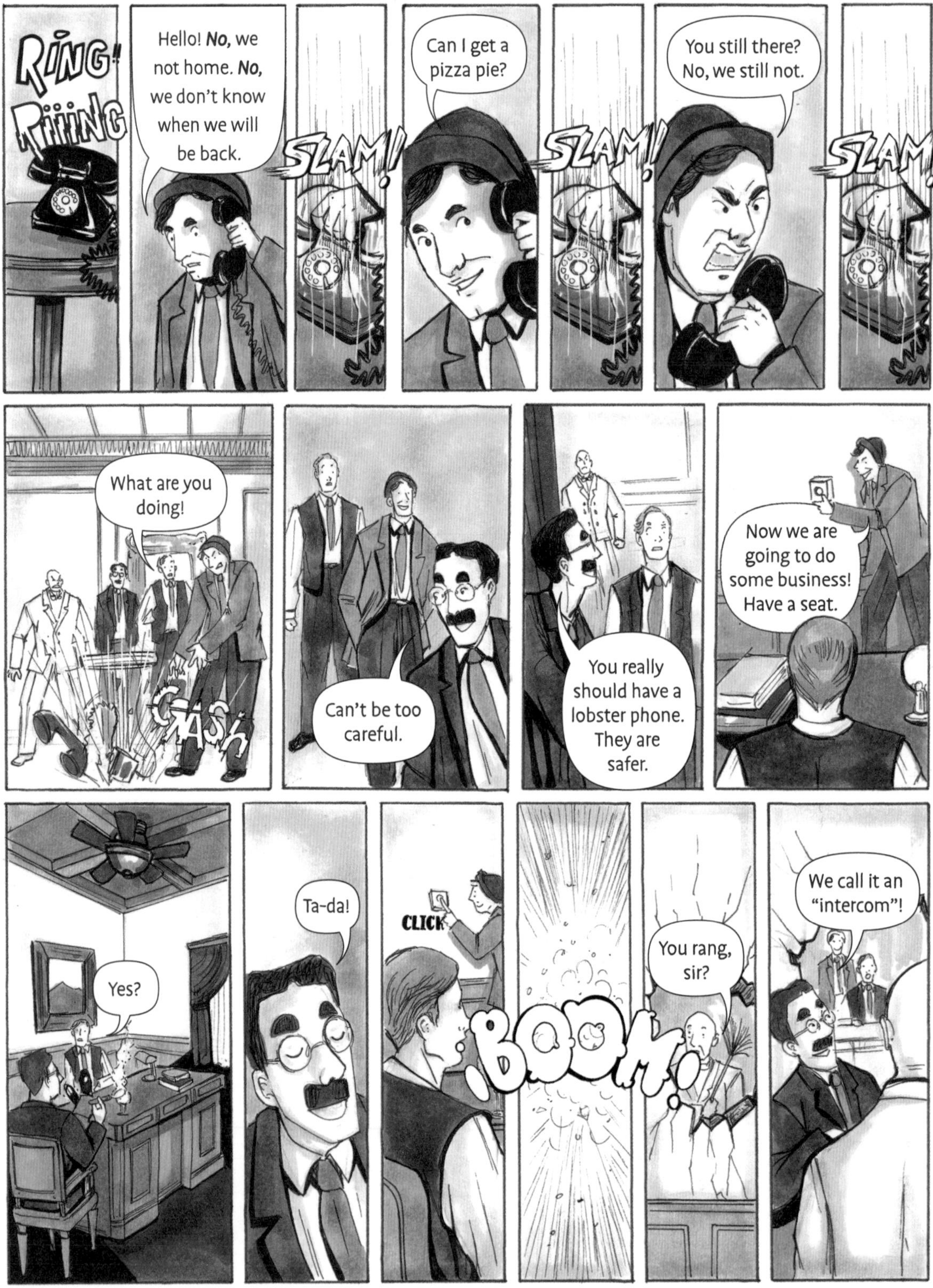
RING!!
RIIING
Hello! No, we not home. No, we don't know when we will be back.
SLAM!
Can I get a pizza pie?
SLAM!
You still there? No, we still not.
SLAM!
What are you doing!
CRASH
Can't be too careful.
You really should have a lobster phone. They are safer.
Now we are going to do some business! Have a seat.
Yes?
Ta-da!
CLICK
BOOM!
You rang, sir?
We call it an "intercom"!

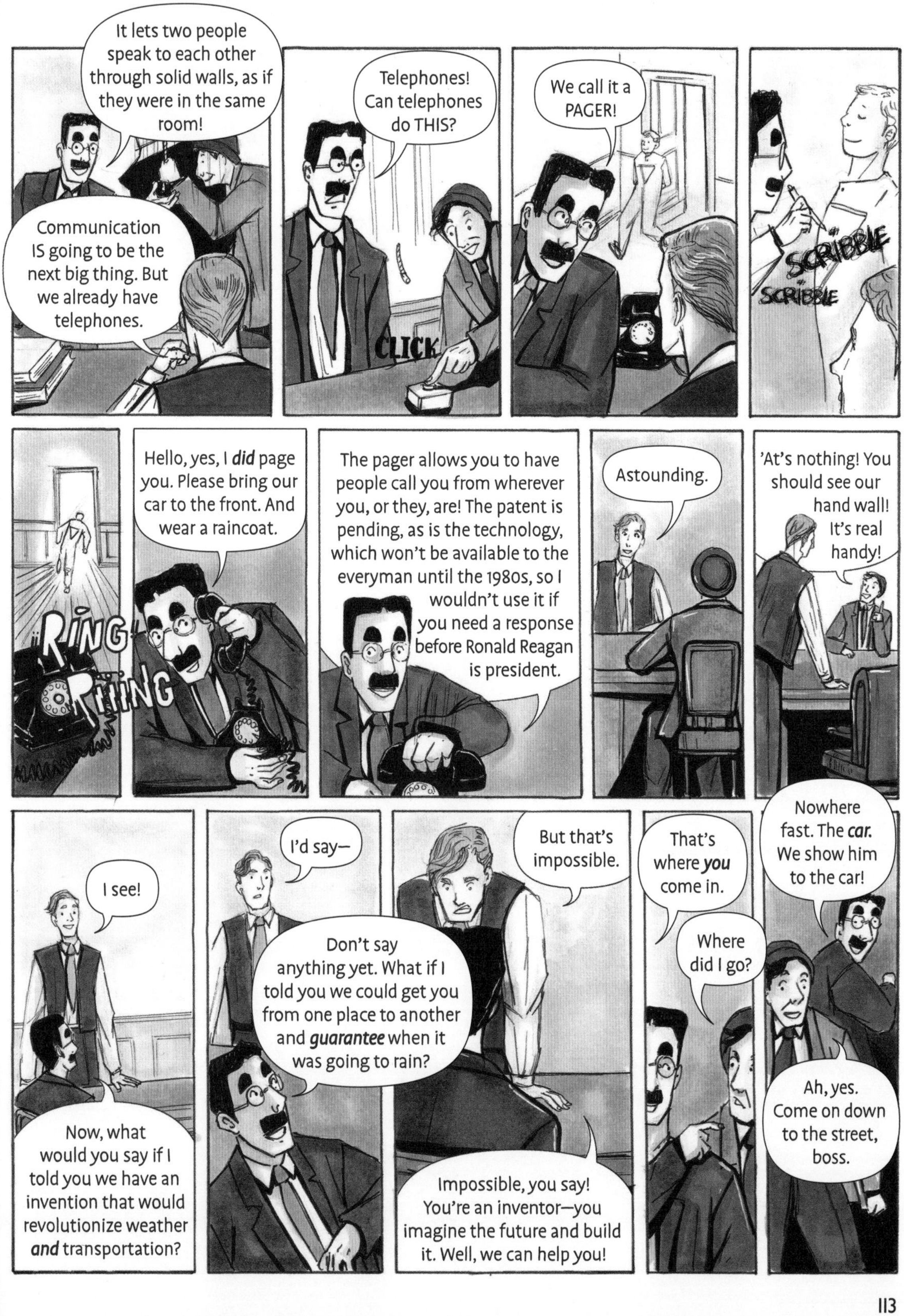

It lets two people speak to each other through solid walls, as if they were in the same room!
Communication IS going to be the next big thing. But we already have telephones.
Telephones! Can telephones do THIS?
CLICK
We call it a PAGER!
SCRIBBLE
SCRIBBLE
RING
RIIING
Hello, yes, I *did* page you. Please bring our car to the front. And wear a raincoat.
The pager allows you to have people call you from wherever you, or they, are! The patent is pending, as is the technology, which won't be available to the everyman until the 1980s, so I wouldn't use it if you need a response before Ronald Reagan is president.
Astounding.
'At's nothing! You should see our hand wall! It's real handy!
I see!
Now, what would you say if I told you we have an invention that would revolutionize weather *and* transportation?
I'd say—
Don't say anything yet. What if I told you we could get you from one place to another and *guarantee* when it was going to rain?
But that's impossible.
Impossible, you say! You're an inventor—you imagine the future and build it. Well, we can help you!
That's where *you* come in.
Where did I go?
Nowhere fast. The *car.* We show him to the car!
Ah, yes. Come on down to the street, boss.

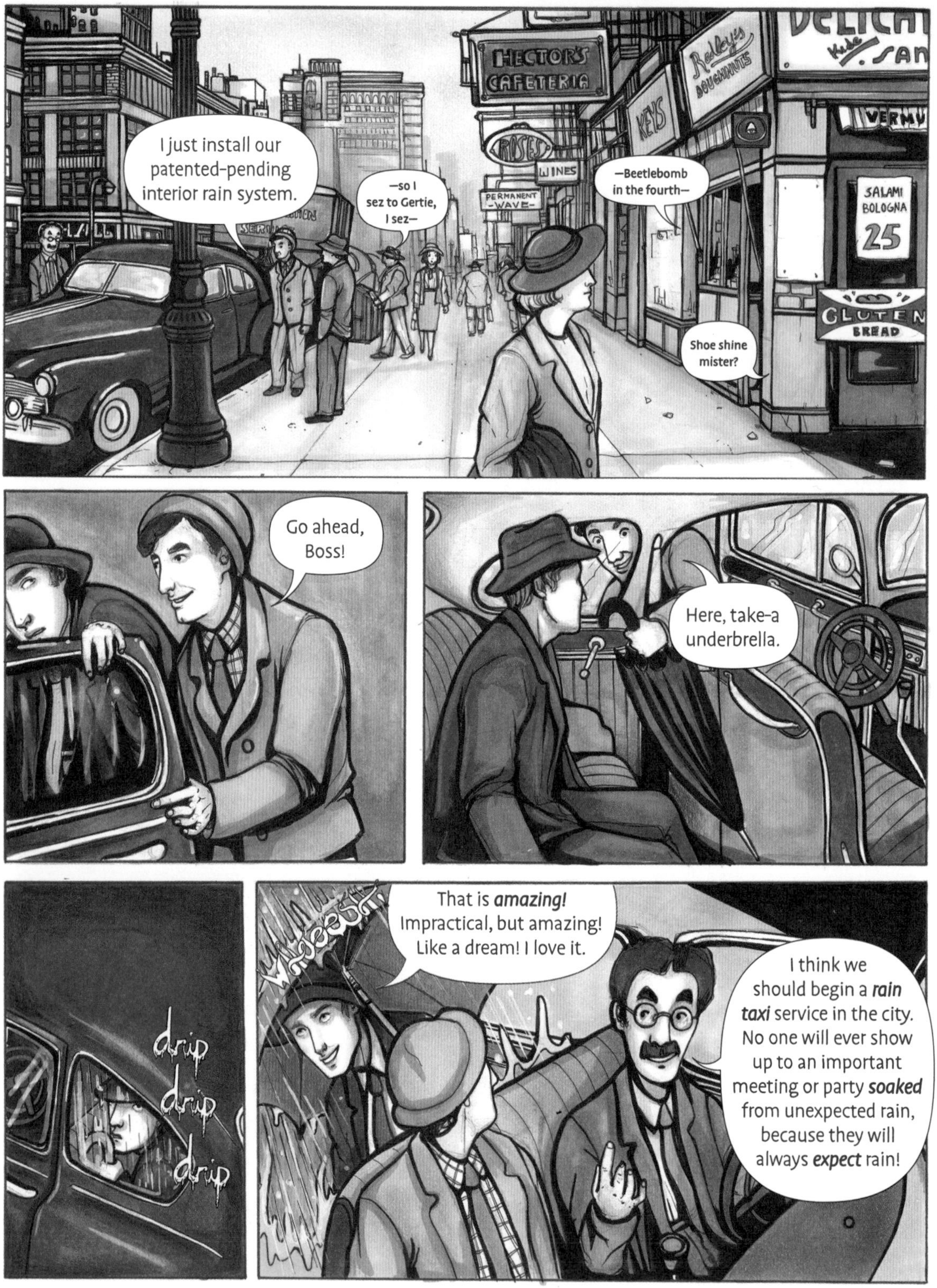
I just install our patented-pending interior rain system.
—so I sez to Gertie, I sez—
—Beetlebomb in the fourth—
Shoe shine mister?
Go ahead, Boss!
Here, take-a underbrella.
drip drip drip
That is *amazing!* Impractical, but amazing! Like a dream! I love it.
I think we should begin a ***rain taxi*** service in the city. No one will ever show up to an important meeting or party ***soaked*** from unexpected rain, because they will always ***expect*** rain!

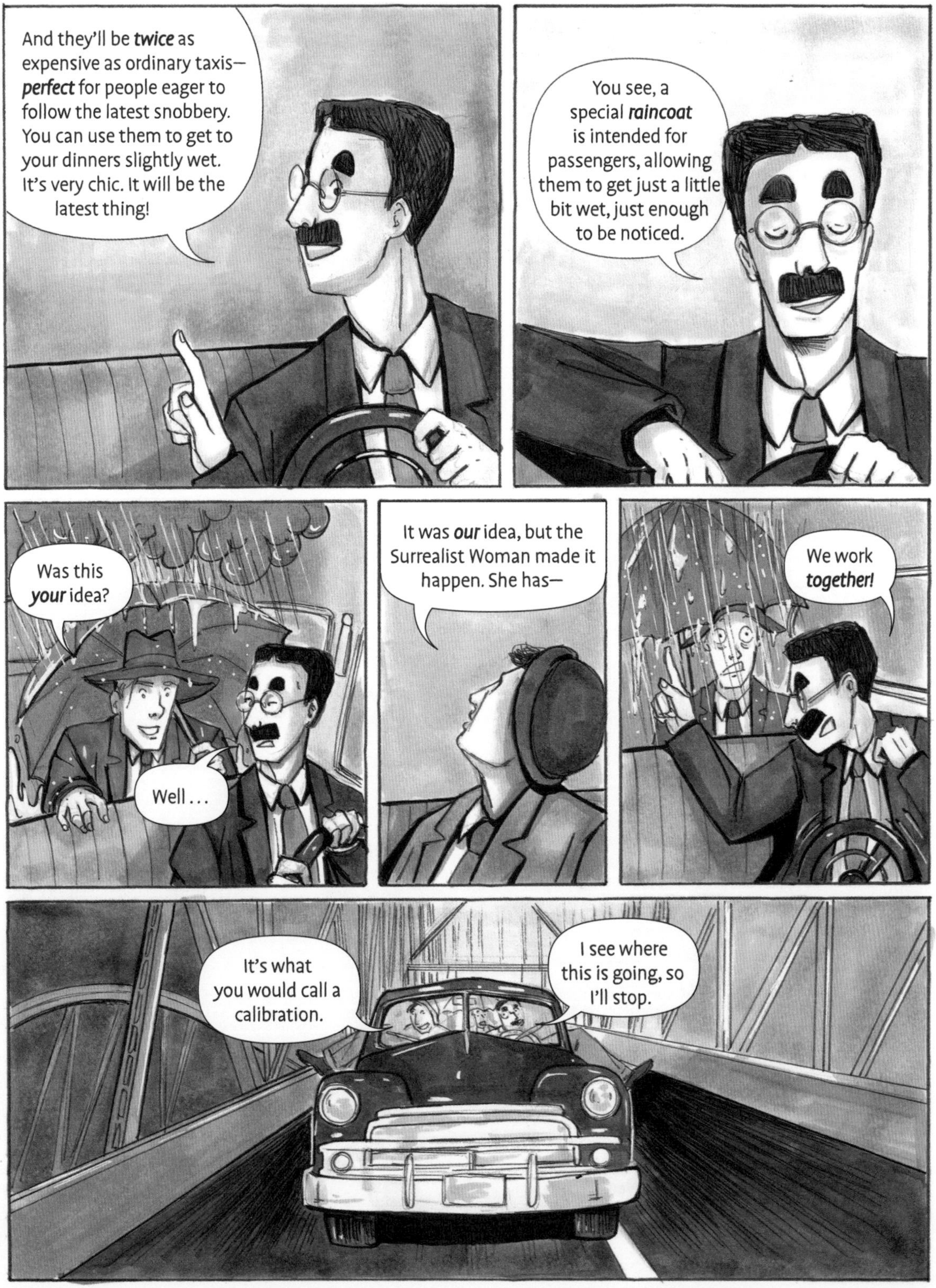
And they'll be *twice* as expensive as ordinary taxis— *perfect* for people eager to follow the latest snobbery. You can use them to get to your dinners slightly wet. It's very chic. It will be the latest thing!
You see, a special *raincoat* is intended for passengers, allowing them to get just a little bit wet, just enough to be noticed.
Was this *your* idea?
Well . . .
It was *our* idea, but the Surrealist Woman made it happen. She has—
We work *together!*
It's what you would call a calibration.
I see where this is going, so I'll stop.

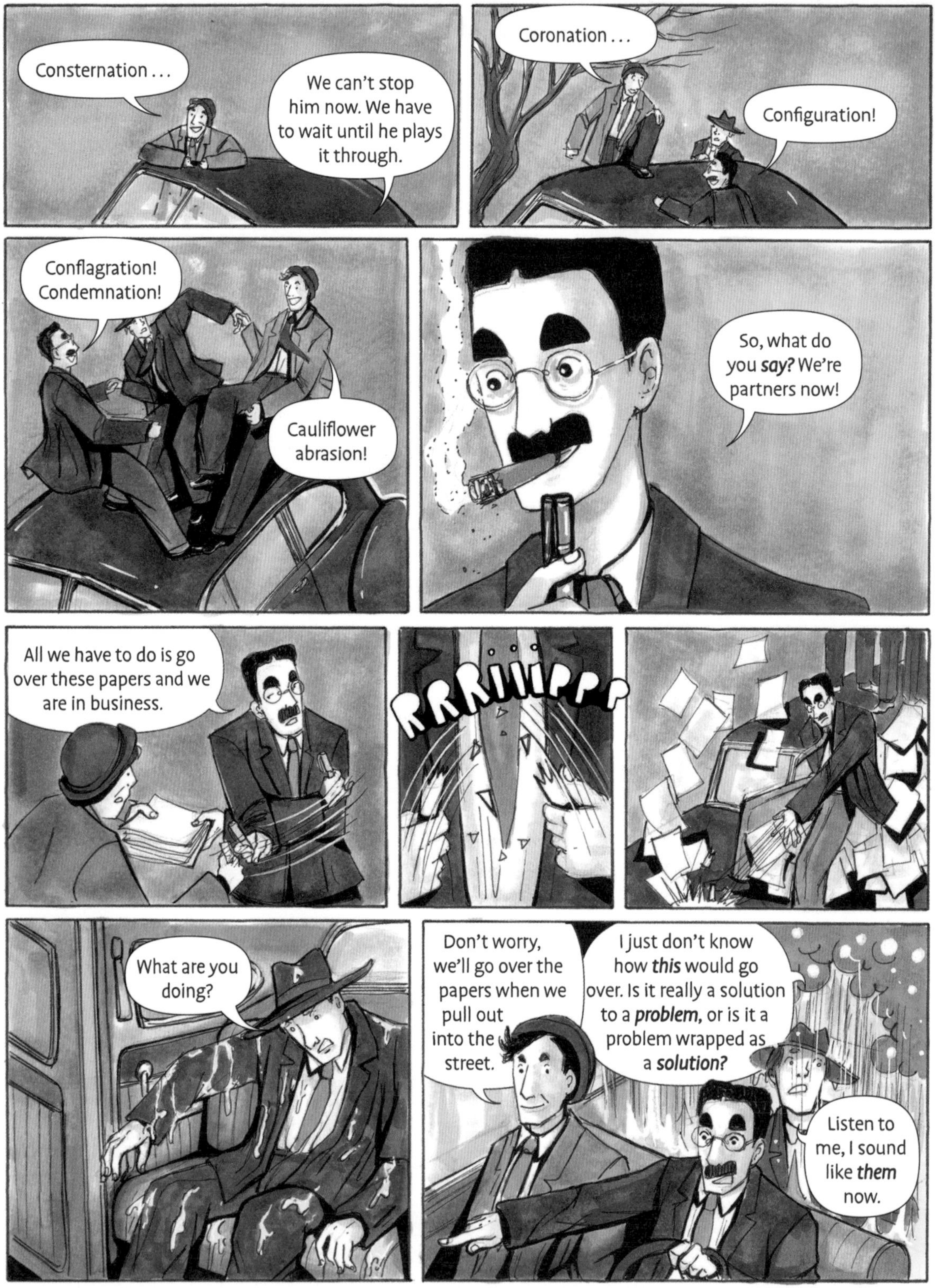
Consternation . . .
We can't stop him now. We have to wait until he plays it through.
Coronation . . .
Configuration!
Conflagration! Condemnation!
Cauliflower abrasion!
So, what do you *say?* We're partners now!
All we have to do is go over these papers and we are in business.
RRRIIIIPPP
What are you doing?
Don't worry, we'll go over the papers when we pull out into the street.
I just don't know how *this* would go over. Is it really a solution to a *problem,* or is it a problem wrapped as a *solution?*
Listen to me, I sound like *them* now.

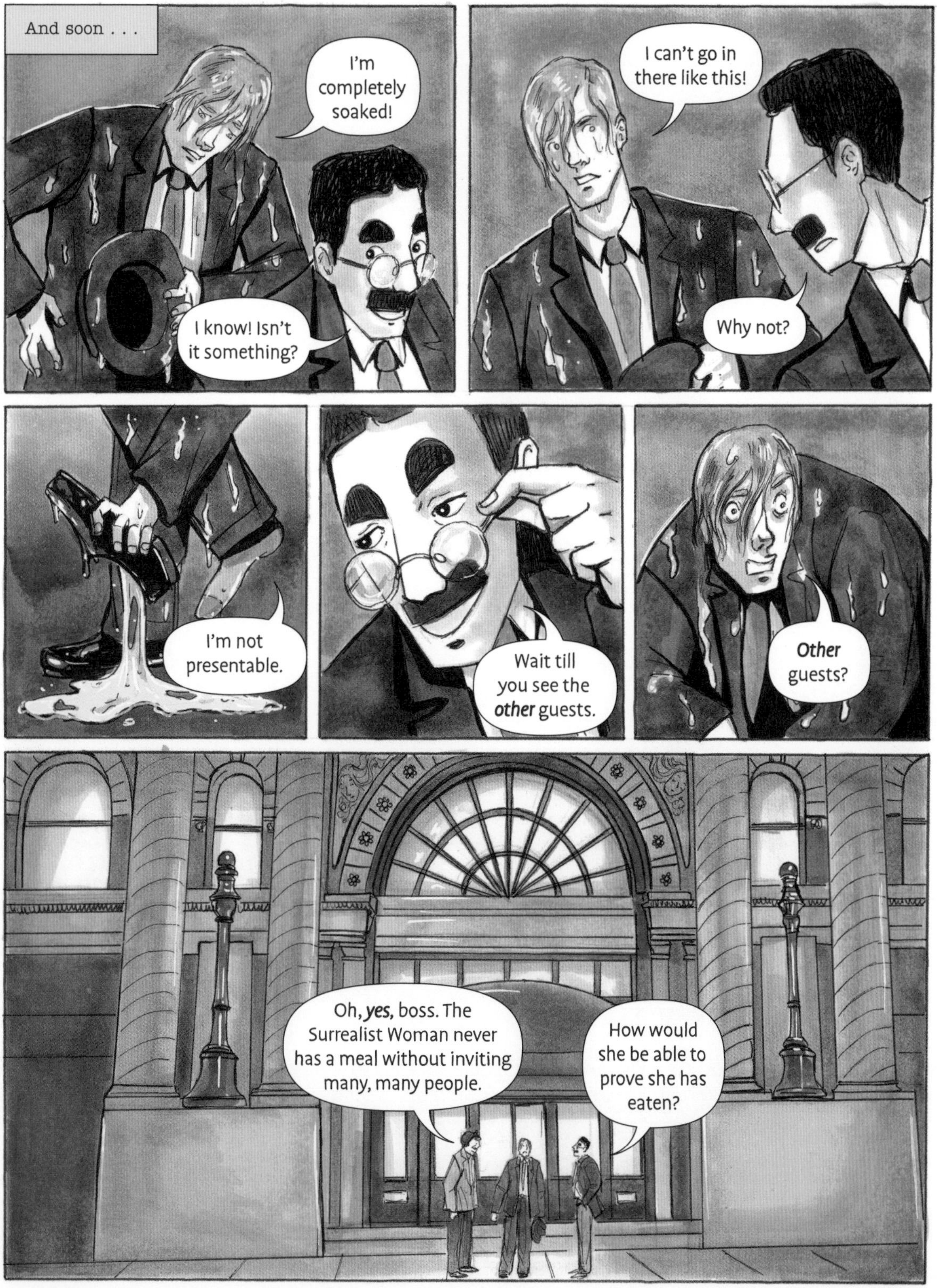
And soon . . .
I'm completely soaked!
I know! Isn't it something?
I can't go in there like this!
Why not?
I'm not presentable.
Wait till you see the *other* guests.
Other guests?
Oh, ***yes,*** boss. The Surrealist Woman never has a meal without inviting many, many people.
How would she be able to prove she has eaten?

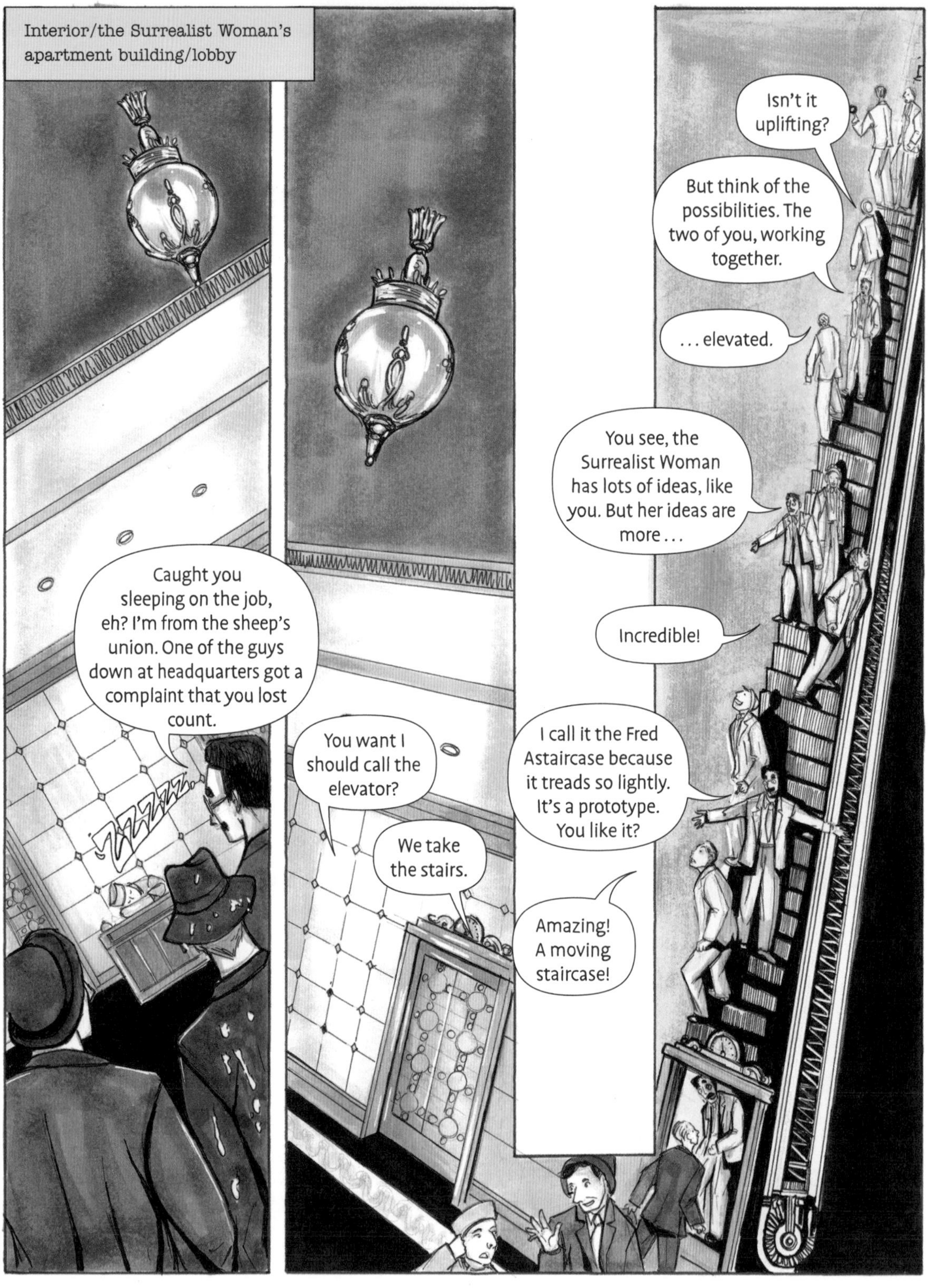
Interior/the Surrealist Woman's apartment building/lobby
Caught you sleeping on the job, eh? I'm from the sheep's union. One of the guys down at headquarters got a complaint that you lost count.
ZZZZZZZ.
You want I should call the elevator?
We take the stairs.
Isn't it uplifting?
But think of the possibilities. The two of you, working together.
. . . elevated.
You see, the Surrealist Woman has lots of ideas, like you. But her ideas are more . . .
Incredible!
I call it the Fred Astaircase because it treads so lightly. It's a prototype. You like it?
Amazing! A moving staircase!

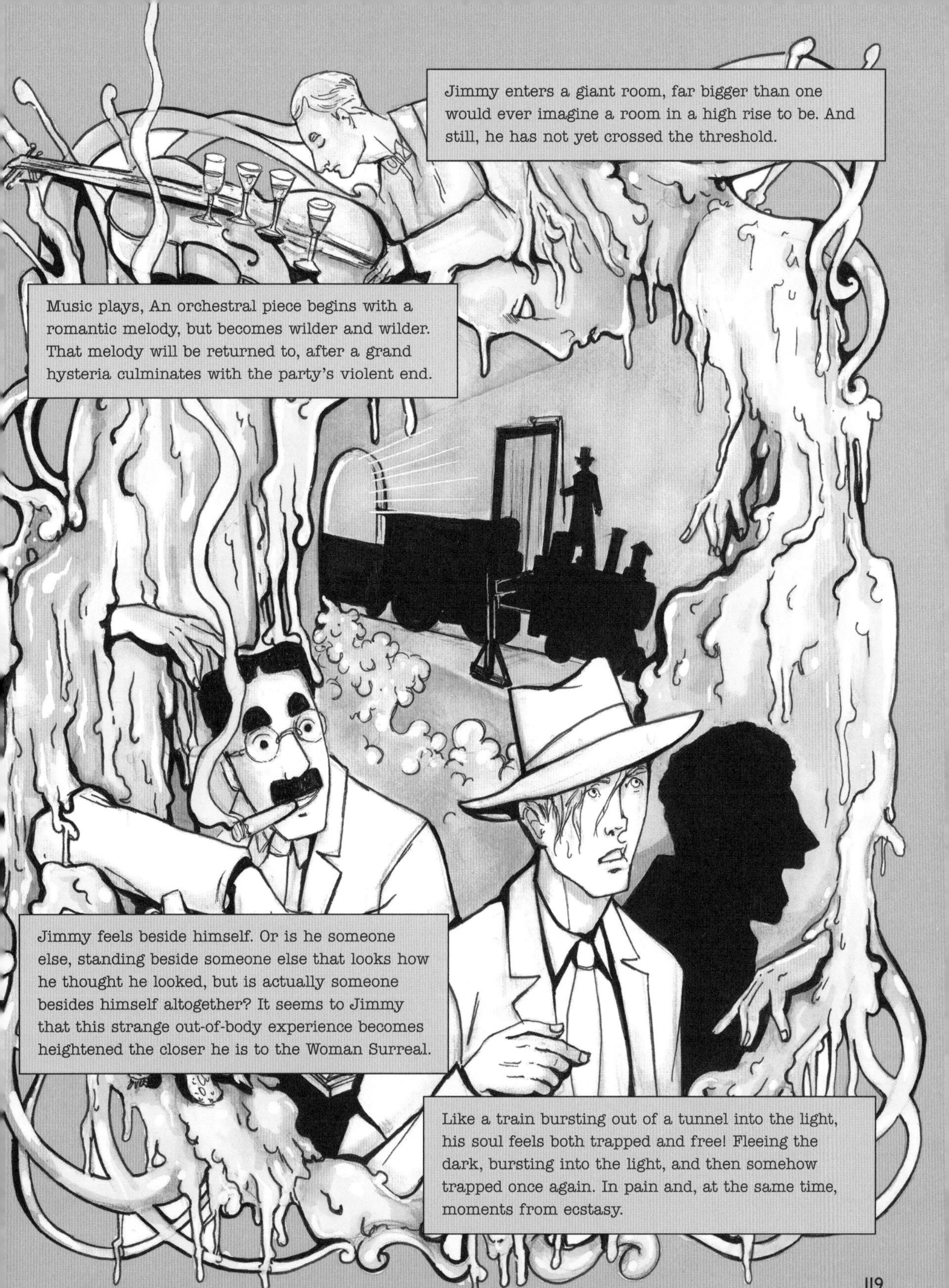
Jimmy enters a giant room, far bigger than one would ever imagine a room in a high rise to be. And still, he has not yet crossed the threshold.
Music plays, An orchestral piece begins with a romantic melody, but becomes wilder and wilder. That melody will be returned to, after a grand hysteria culminates with the party's violent end.
Jimmy feels beside himself. Or is he someone else, standing beside someone else that looks how he thought he looked, but is actually someone besides himself altogether? It seems to Jimmy that this strange out-of-body experience becomes heightened the closer he is to the Woman Surreal.
Like a train bursting out of a tunnel into the light, his soul feels both trapped and free! Fleeing the dark, bursting into the light, and then somehow trapped once again. In pain and, at the same time, moments from ecstasy.

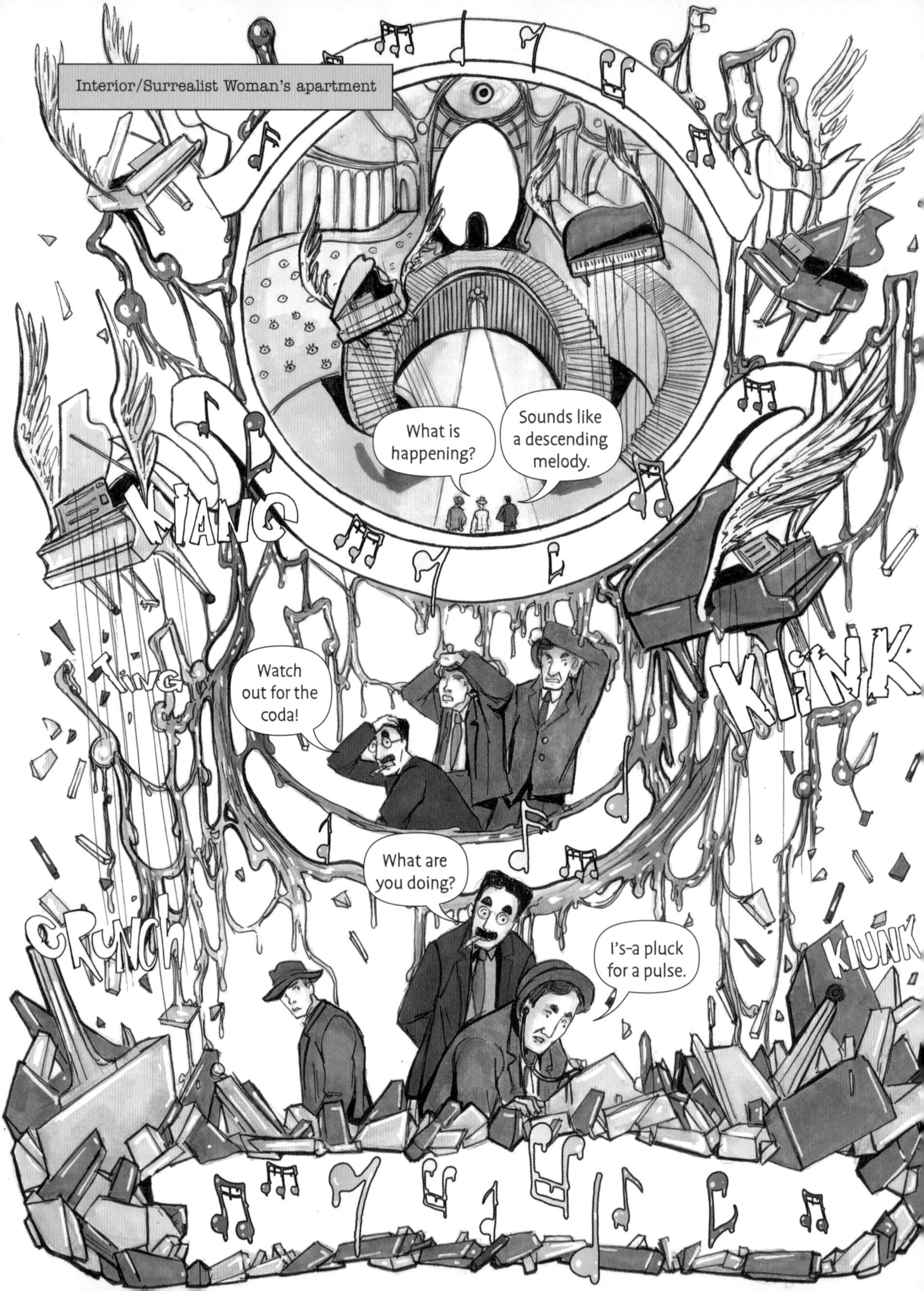
Interior/Surrealist Woman's apartment
What is happening?
Sounds like a descending melody.
KLANG
Watch out for the coda!
TING
KLINK
What are you doing?
CRUNCH
I's-a pluck for a pulse.
KLUNK

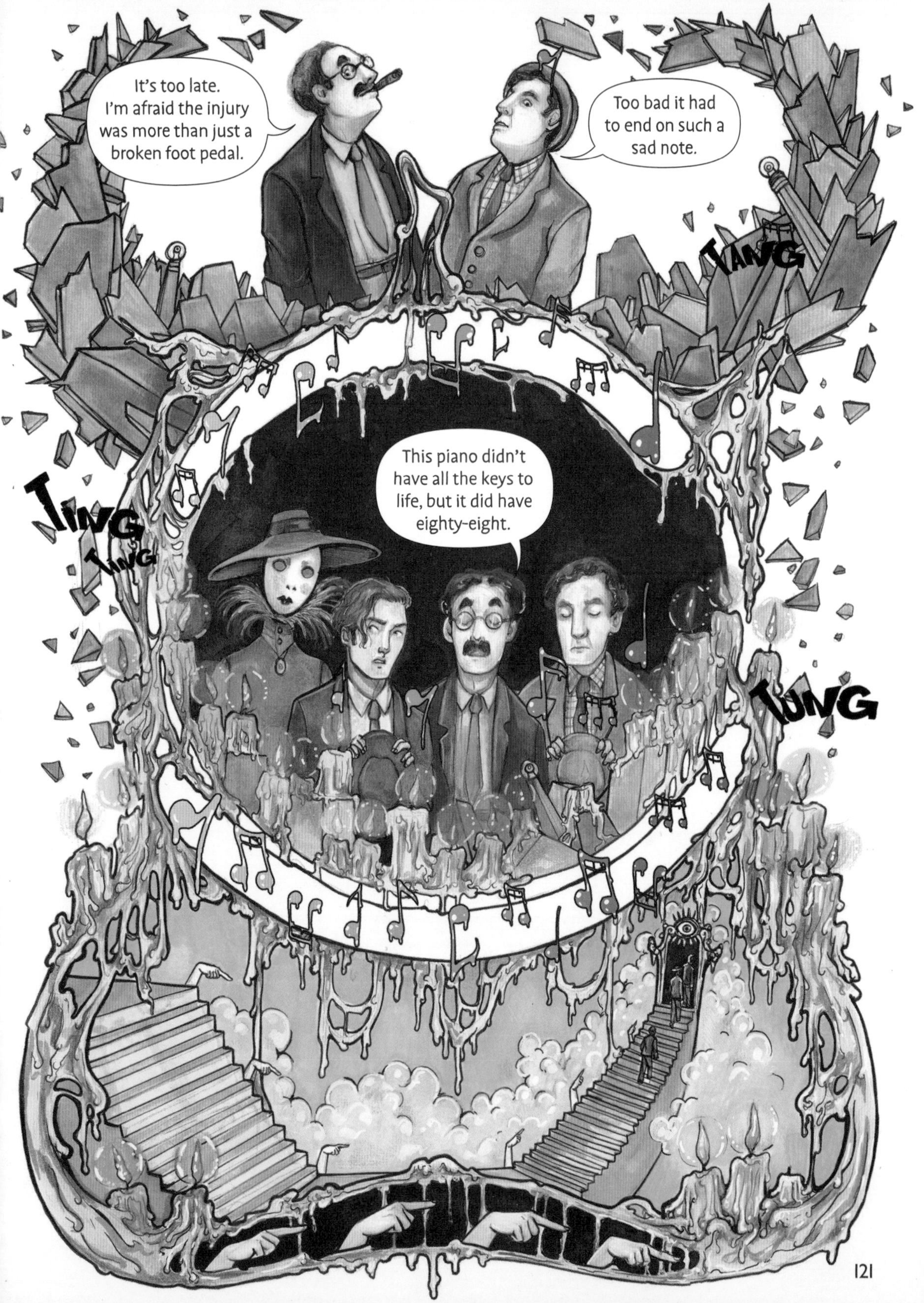
It's too late. I'm afraid the injury was more than just a broken foot pedal.
Too bad it had to end on such a sad note.
TANG
This piano didn't have all the keys to life, but it did have eighty-eight.
TING
TING
TUNG

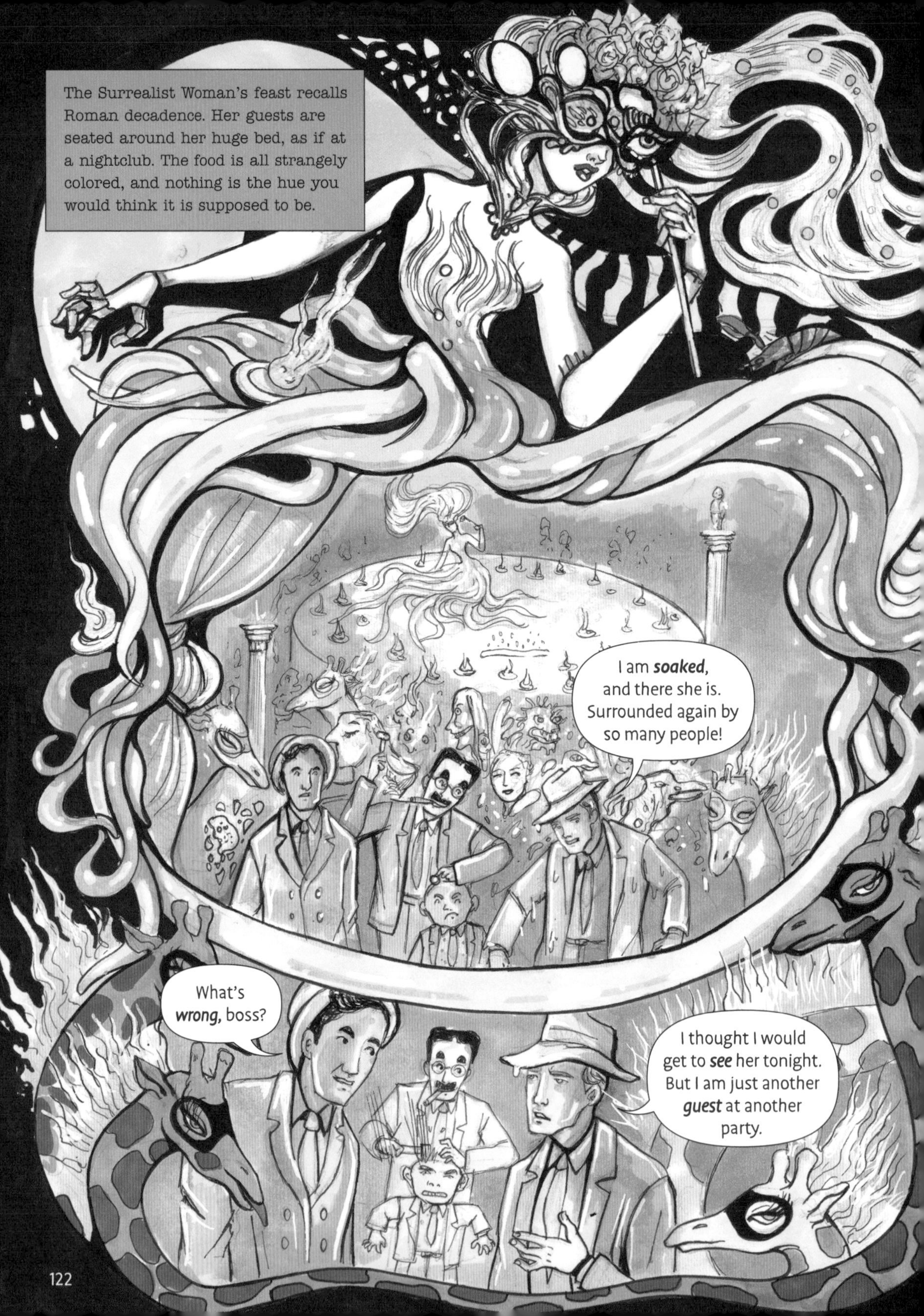
The Surrealist Woman's feast recalls Roman decadence. Her guests are seated around her huge bed, as if at a nightclub. The food is all strangely colored, and nothing is the hue you would think it is supposed to be.
I am *soaked*, and there she is. Surrounded again by so many people!
What's *wrong*, boss?
I thought I would get to *see* her tonight. But I am just another *guest* at another party.

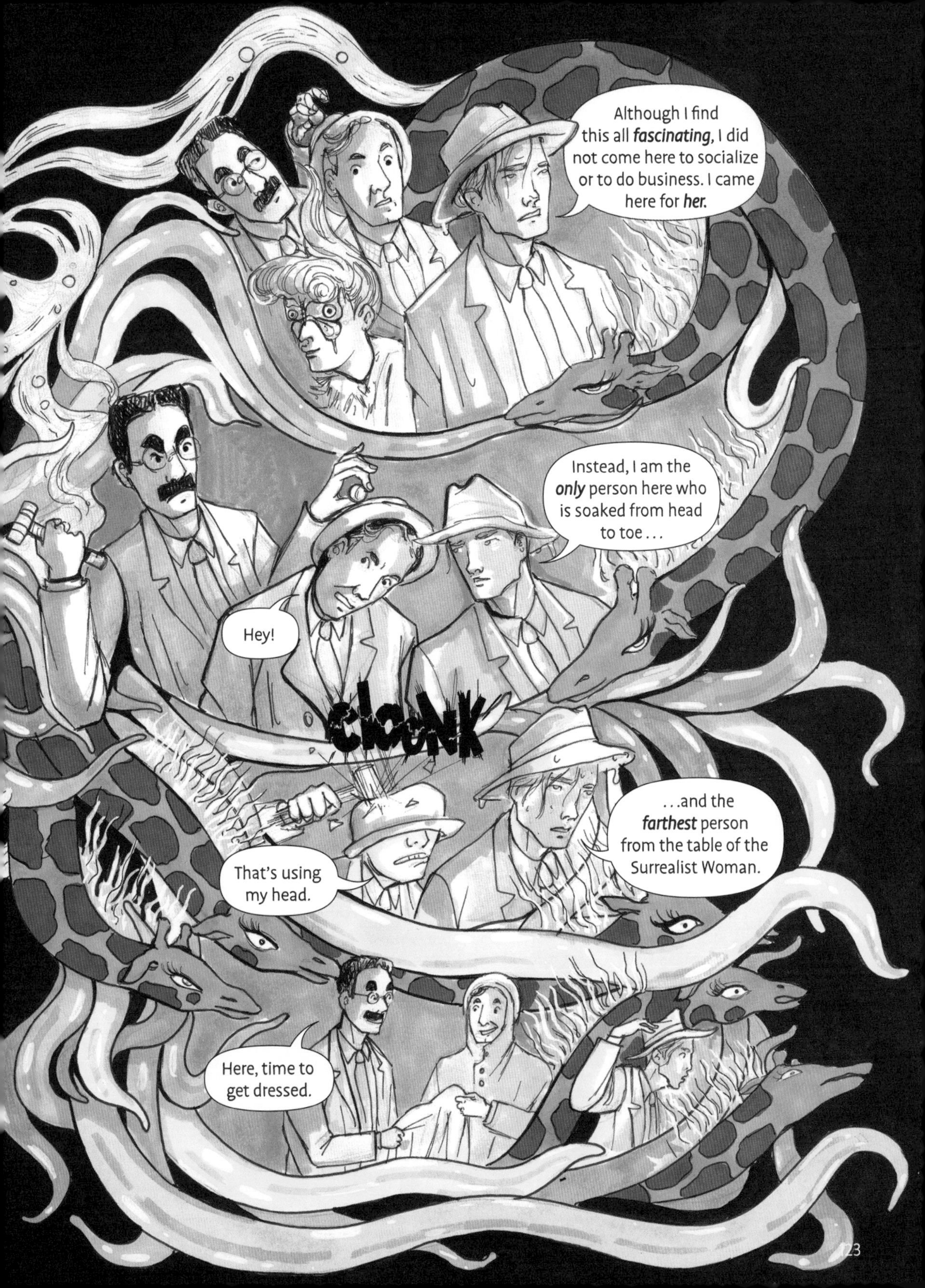
Although I find this all *fascinating*, I did not come here to socialize or to do business. I came here for *her*.
Instead, I am the *only* person here who is soaked from head to toe . . .
Hey!
CLOONK
. . .and the *farthest* person from the table of the Surrealist Woman.
That's using my head.
Here, time to get dressed.

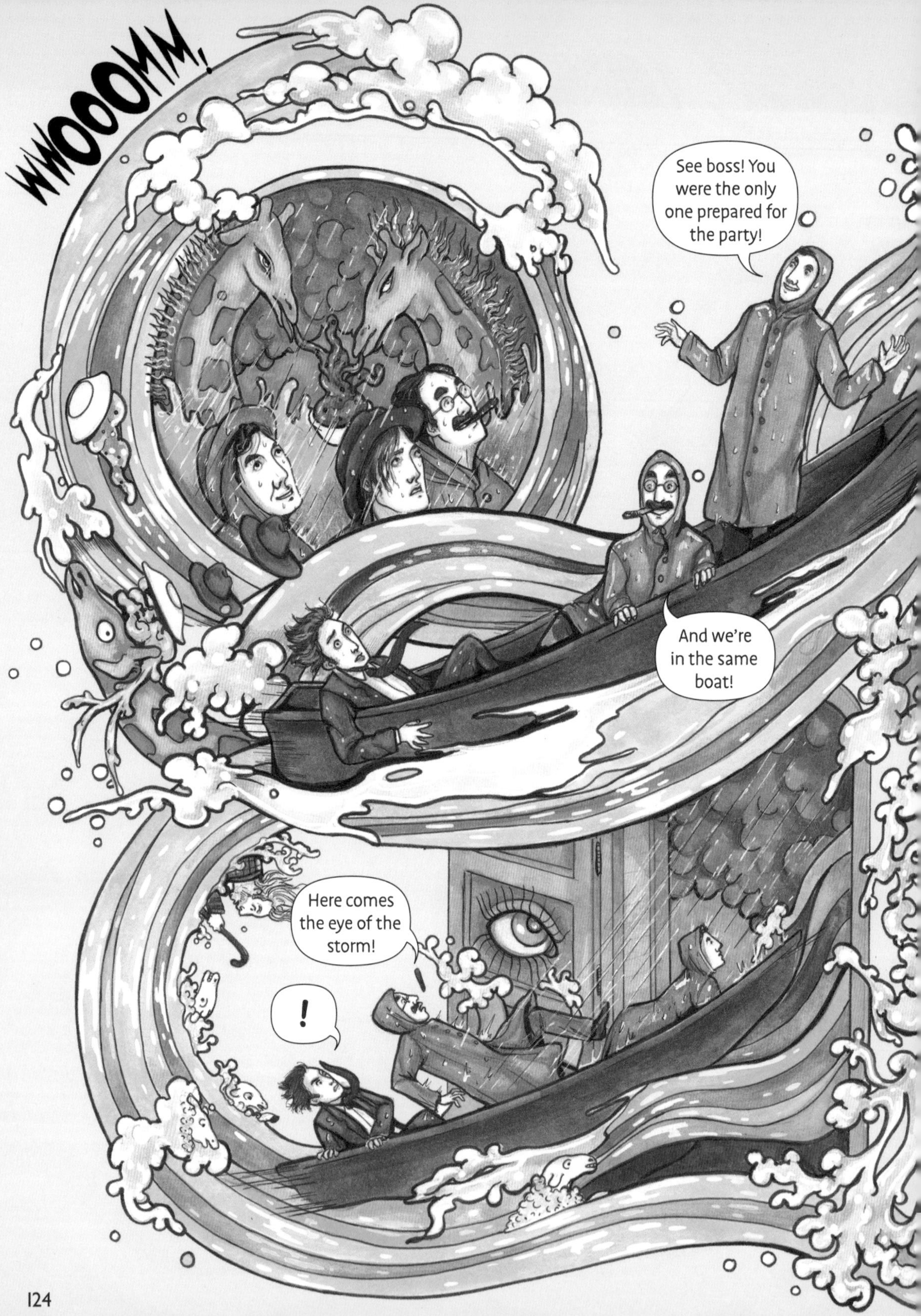
WWOOOMM!
See boss! You were the only one prepared for the party!
And we're in the same boat!
Here comes the eye of the storm!
!

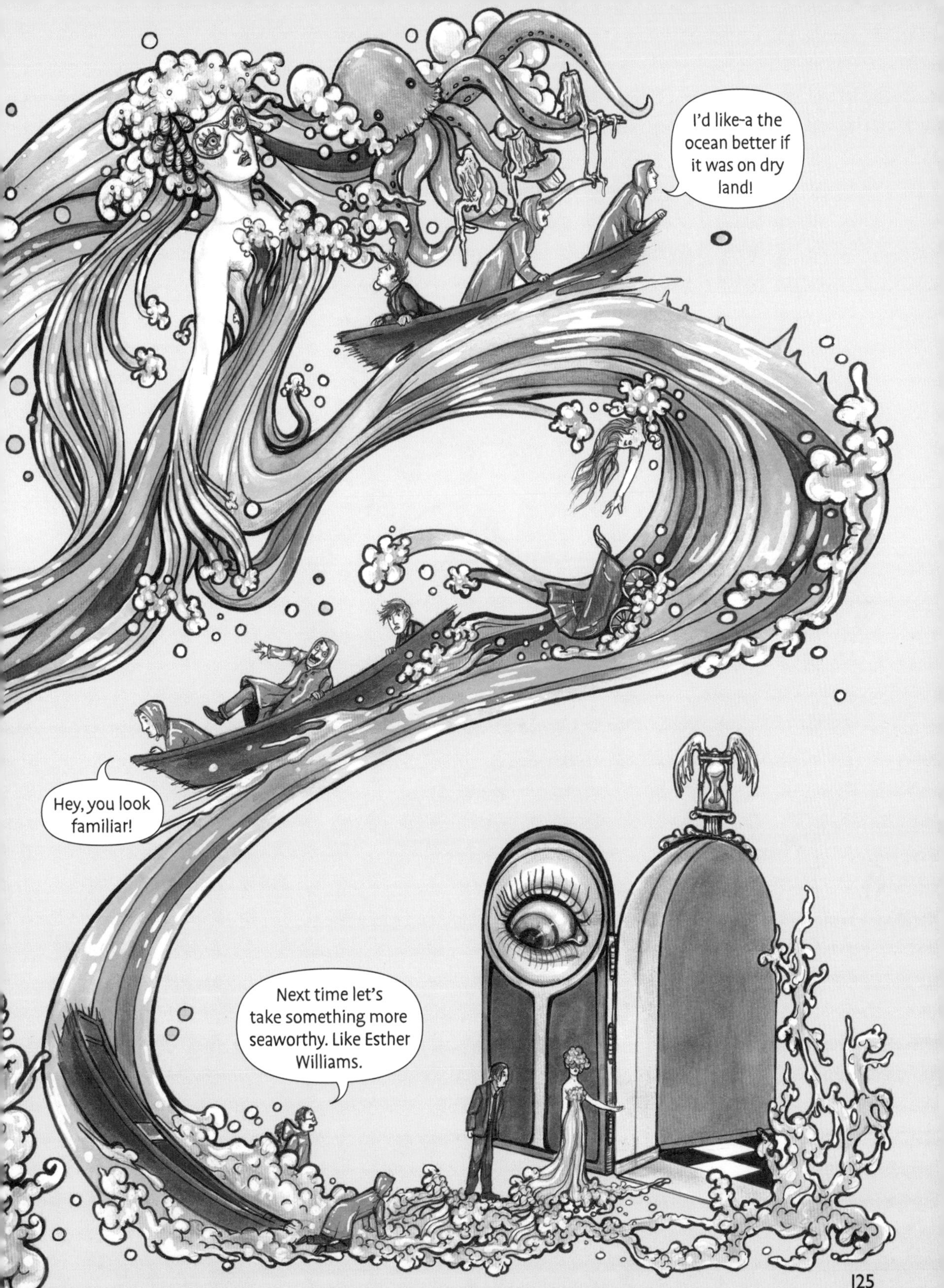
I'd like-a the ocean better if it was on dry land!
Hey, you look familiar!
Next time let's take something more seaworthy. Like Esther Williams.

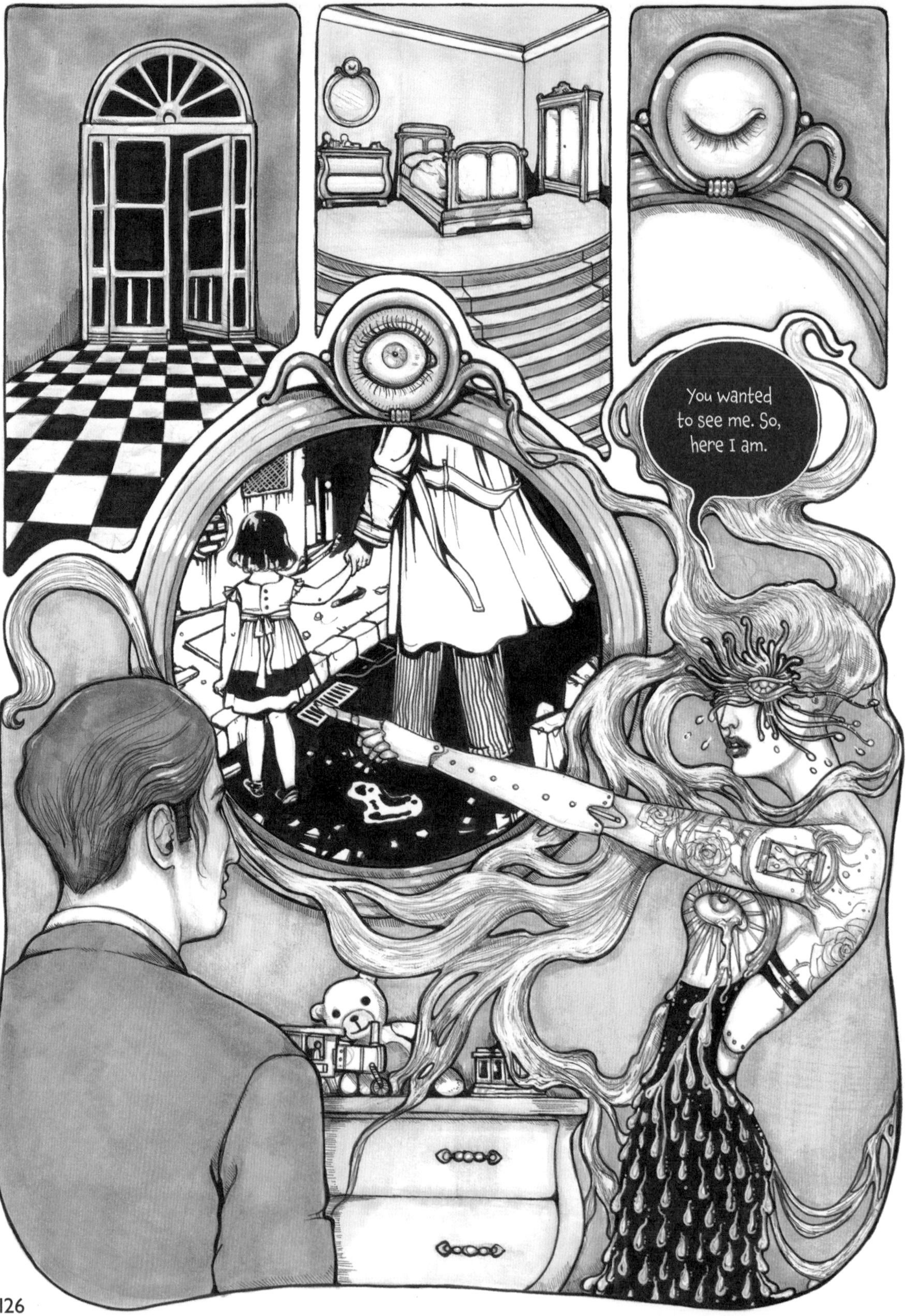
You wanted to see me. So, here I am.

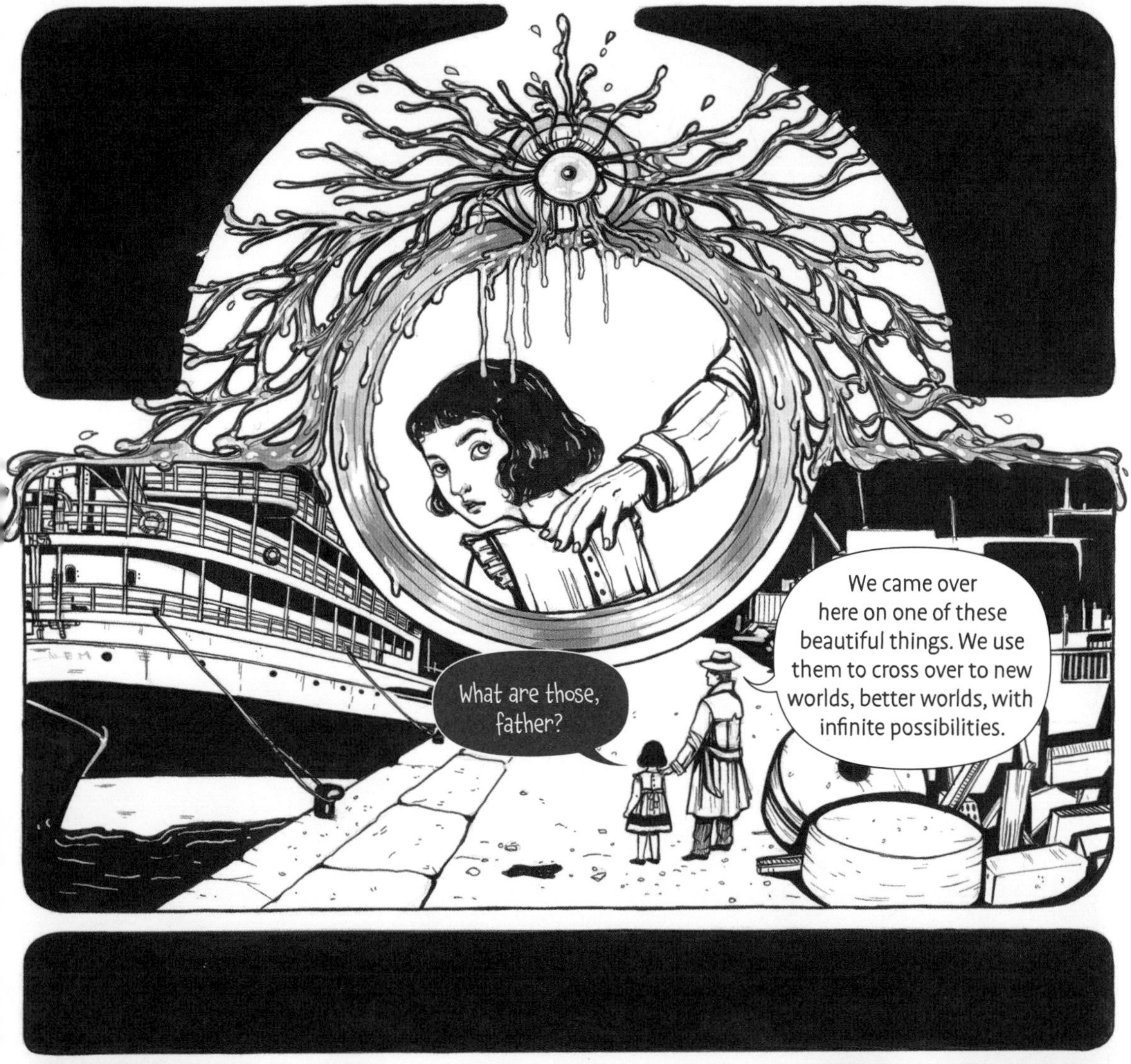
What are those, father?
We came over here on one of these beautiful things. We use them to cross over to new worlds, better worlds, with infinite possibilities.

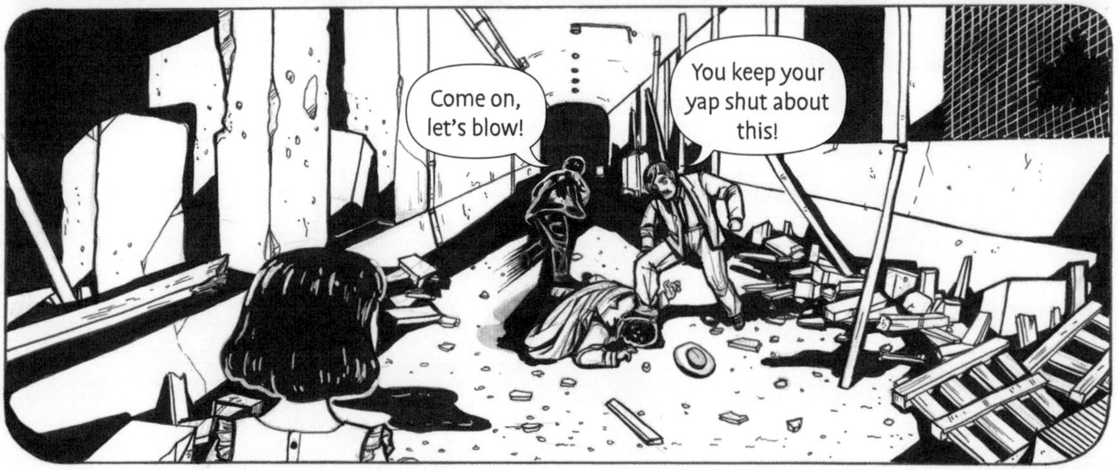
Come on, let's blow!
You keep your yap shut about this!

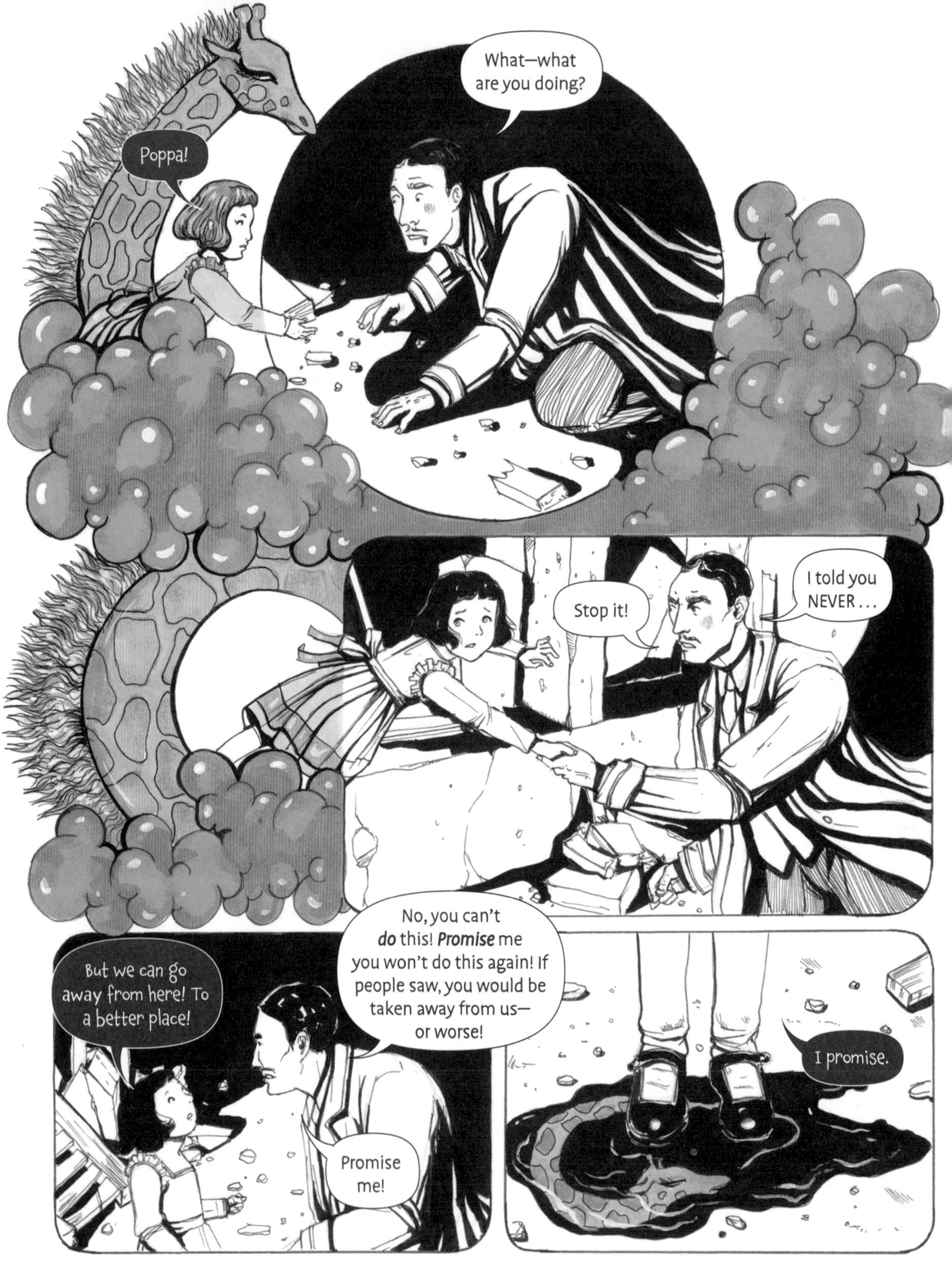
What—what are you doing?
Poppa!
Stop it!
I told you NEVER . . .
But we can go away from here! To a better place!
No, you can't *do* this! *Promise* me you won't do this again! If people saw, you would be taken away from us—or worse!
Promise me!
I promise.

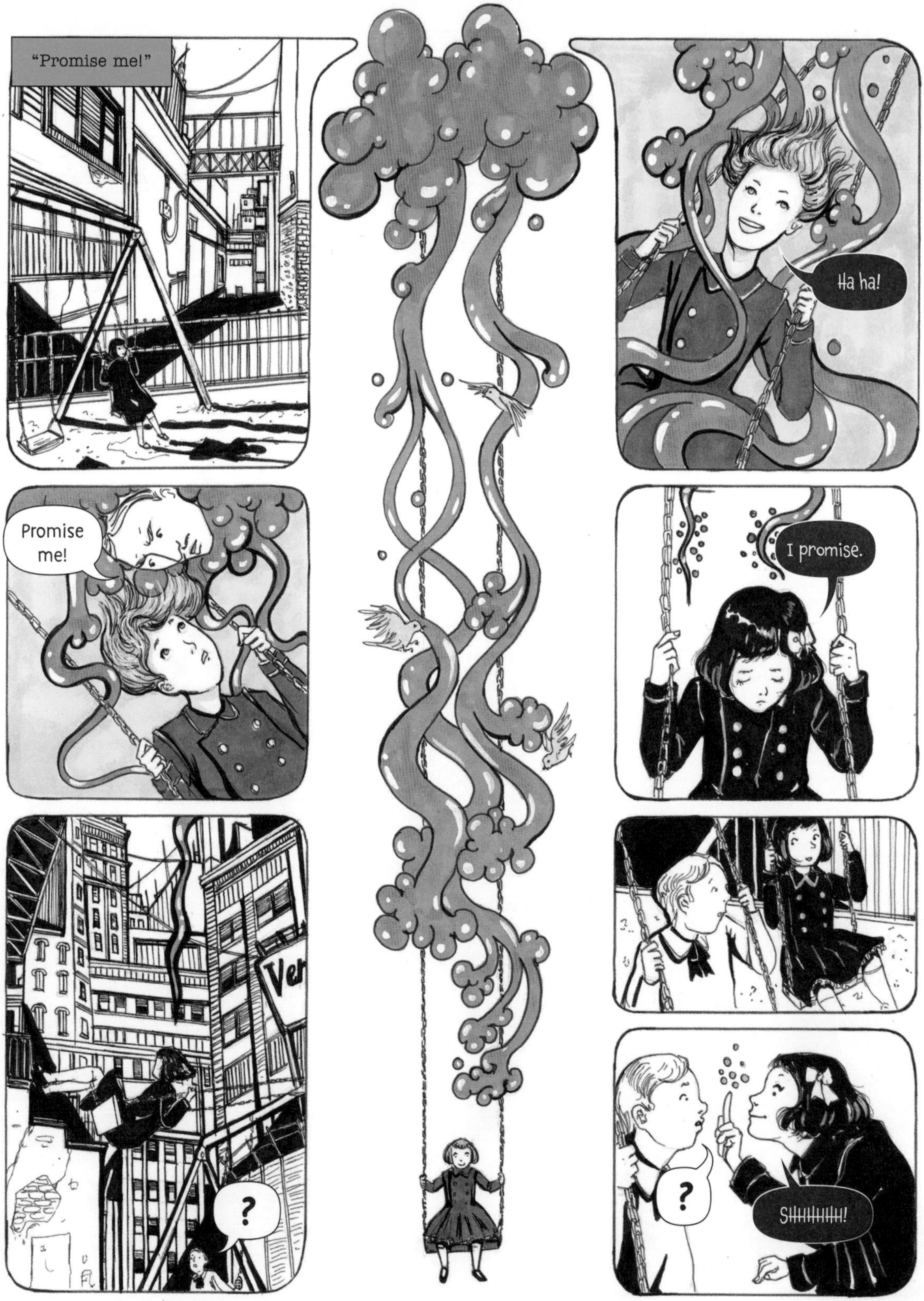
"Promise me!"
Promise me!
?
Ha ha!
I promise.
?
SHHHHHH!

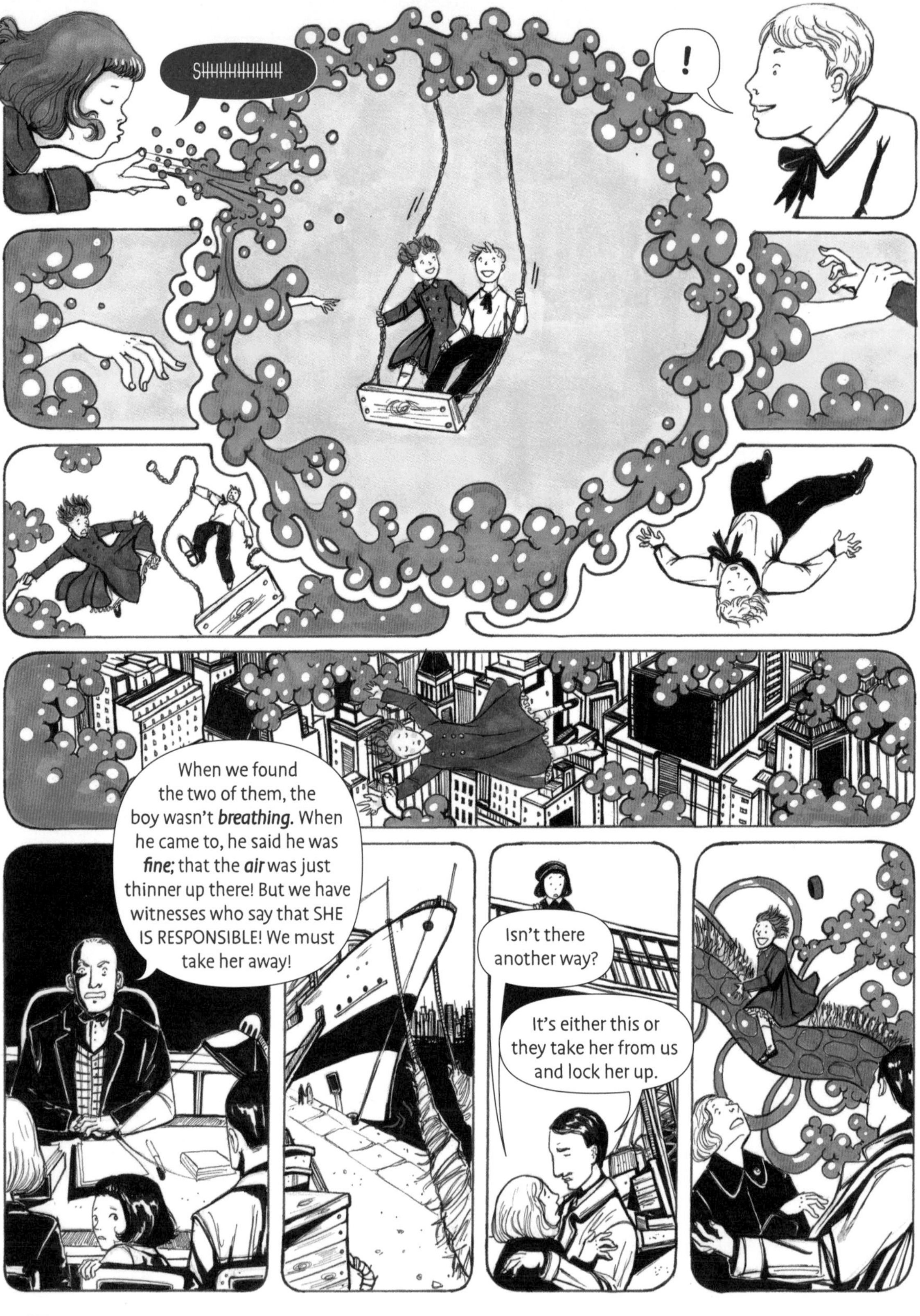
SHHHHHHHHH
!
When we found the two of them, the boy wasn't ***breathing.*** When he came to, he said he was ***fine;*** that the ***air*** was just thinner up there! But we have witnesses who say that SHE IS RESPONSIBLE! We must take her away!
Isn't there another way?
It's either this or they take her from us and lock her up.

INTERMISSION

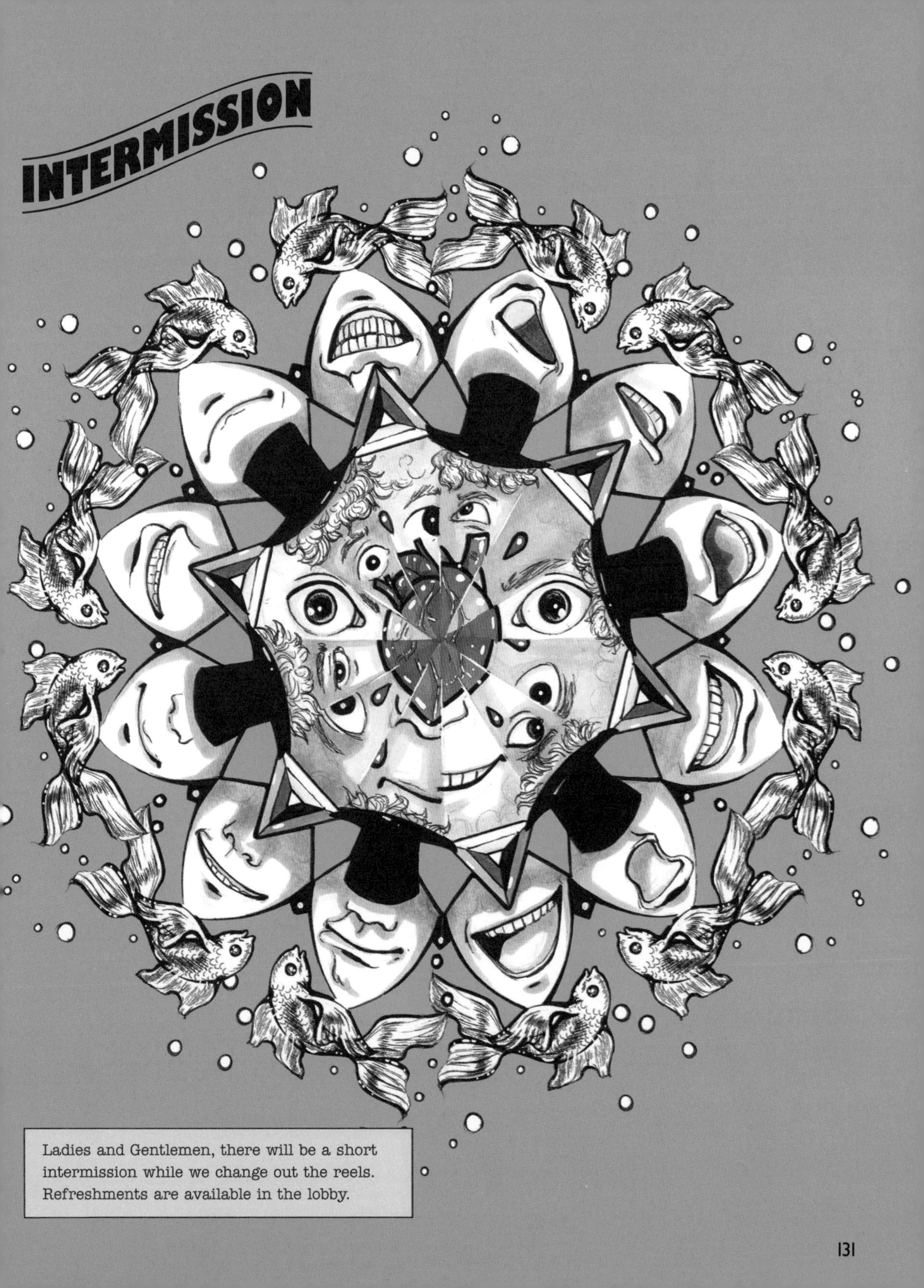

Ladies and Gentlemen, there will be a short intermission while we change out the reels. Refreshments are available in the lobby.

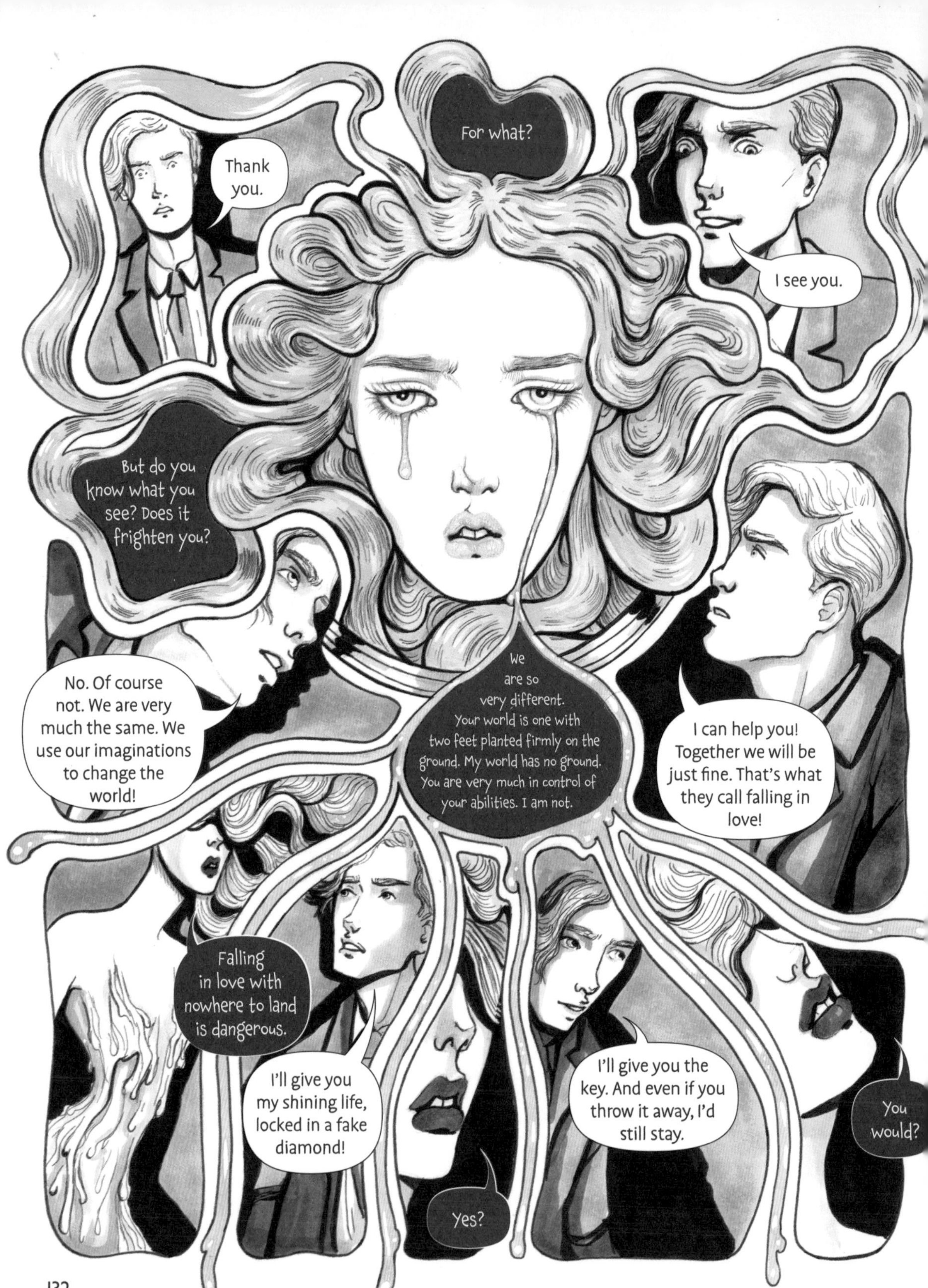
Thank you.
For what?
I see you.
But do you know what you see? Does it frighten you?
No. Of course not. We are very much the same. We use our imaginations to change the world!
We are so very different. Your world is one with two feet planted firmly on the ground. My world has no ground. You are very much in control of your abilities. I am not.
I can help you! Together we will be just fine. That's what they call falling in love!
Falling in love with nowhere to land is dangerous.
I'll give you my shining life, locked in a fake diamond!
Yes?
I'll give you the key. And even if you throw it away, I'd still stay.
You would?

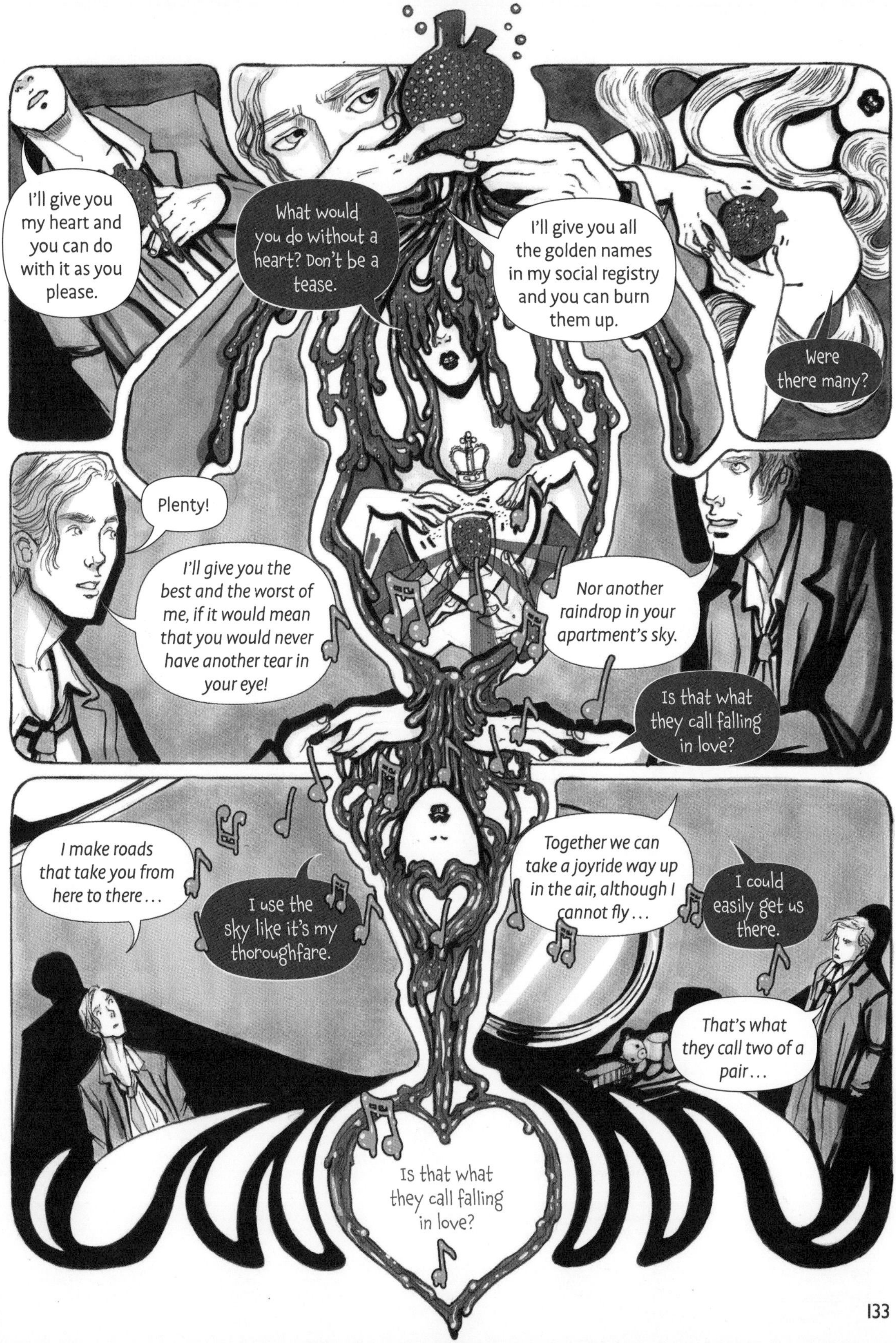
I'll give you my heart and you can do with it as you please.
What would you do without a heart? Don't be a tease.
I'll give you all the golden names in my social registry and you can burn them up.
Were there many?
Plenty!
I'll give you the best and the worst of me, if it would mean that you would never have another tear in your eye!
Nor another raindrop in your apartment's sky.
Is that what they call falling in love?
I make roads that take you from here to there...
I use the sky like it's my thoroughfare.
Together we can take a joyride way up in the air, although I cannot fly...
I could easily get us there.
That's what they call two of a pair...
Is that what they call falling in love?

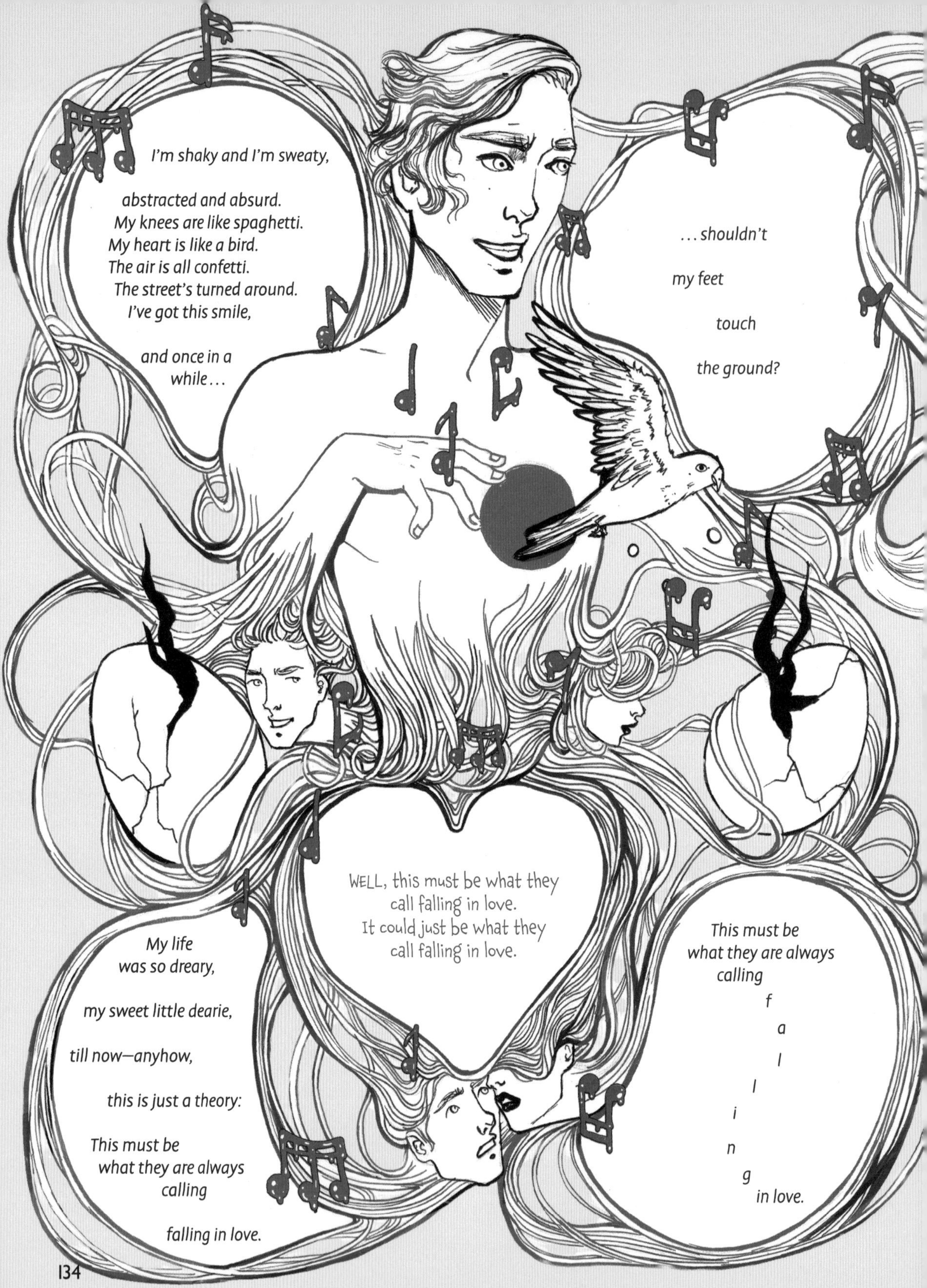
I'm shaky and I'm sweaty,
abstracted and absurd.
My knees are like spaghetti.
My heart is like a bird.
The air is all confetti.
The street's turned around.
I've got this smile,
and once in a while . . .
. . . shouldn't
my feet
touch
the ground?
WELL, this must be what they call falling in love.
It could just be what they call falling in love.
My life was so dreary,
my sweet little dearie,
till now—anyhow,
this is just a theory:
This must be what they are always calling
falling in love.
This must be what they are always calling
f a l l i n g in love.

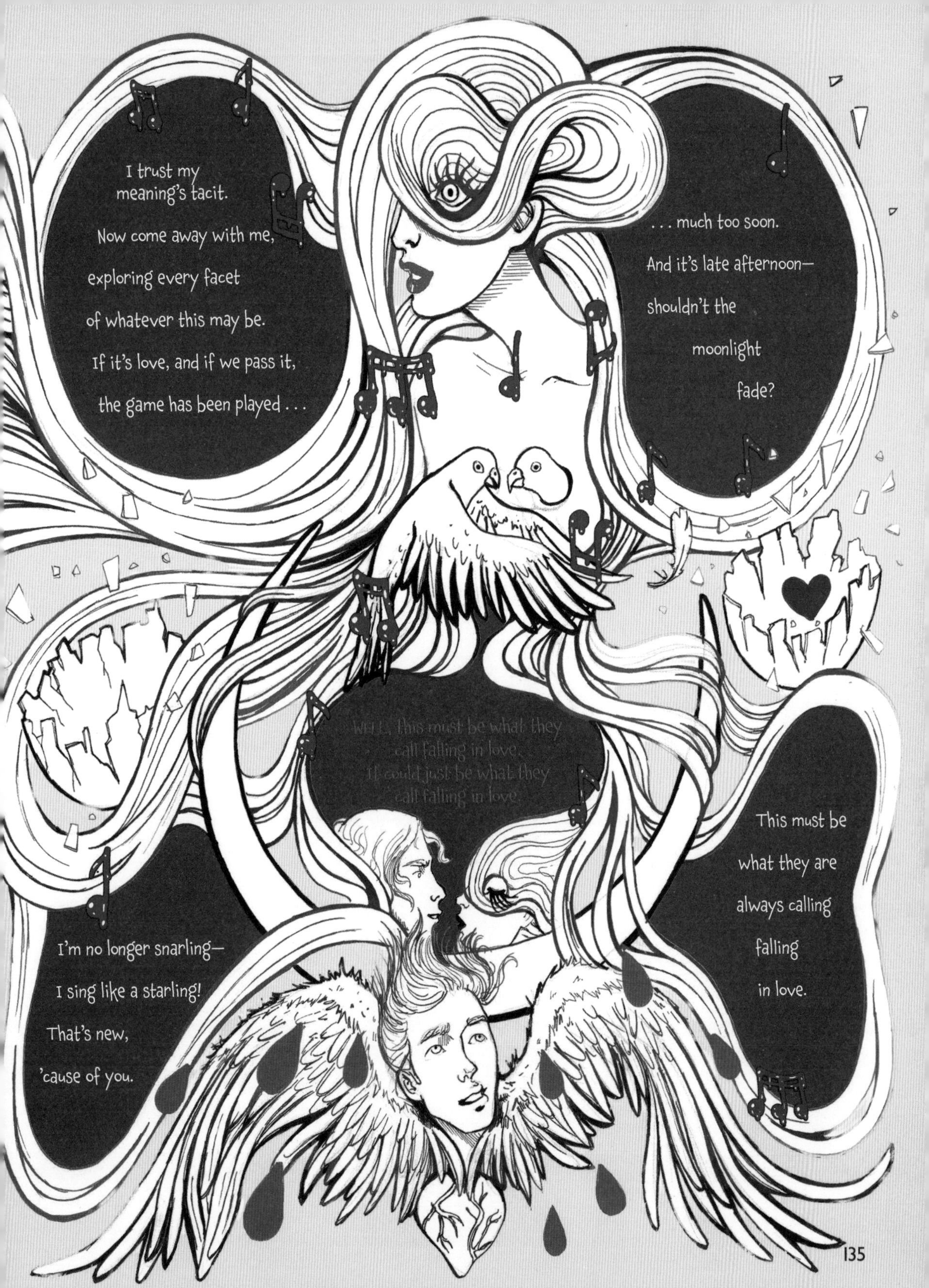
I trust my
meaning's tacit.
Now come away with me,
exploring every facet
of whatever this may be.
If it's love, and if we pass it,
the game has been played . . .
. . . much too soon.
And it's late afternoon—
shouldn't the
moonlight
fade?
WELL, this must be what they
call falling in love.
It could just be what they
call falling in love.
This must be
what they are
always calling
falling
in love.
I'm no longer snarling—
I sing like a starling!
That's new,
'cause of you.

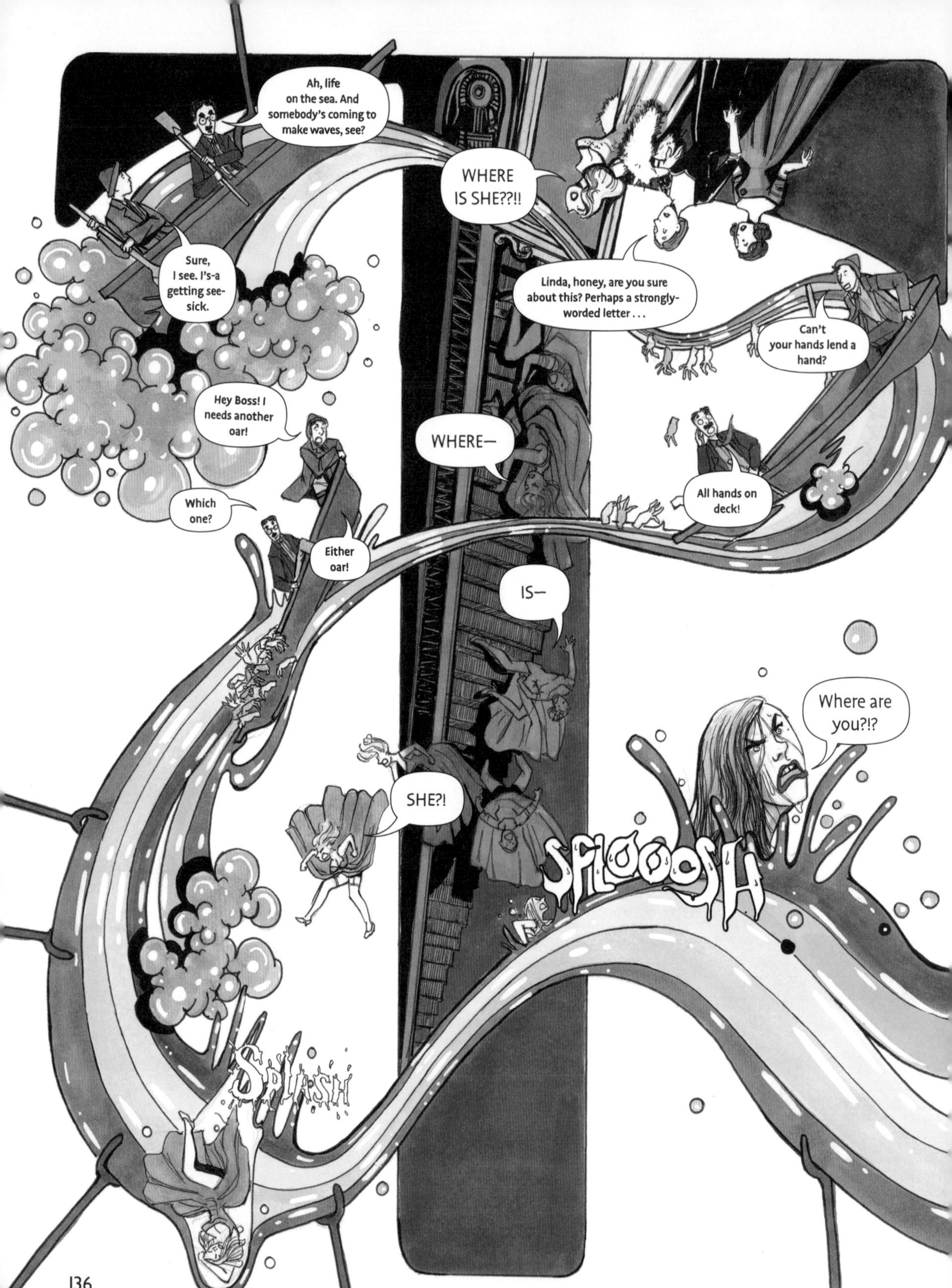
Ah, life on the sea. And somebody's coming to make waves, see?
Sure, I see. I's-a getting see-sick.
WHERE IS SHE??!!
Linda, honey, are you sure about this? Perhaps a strongly-worded letter . . .
Can't your hands lend a hand?
Hey Boss! I needs another oar!
WHERE—
Which one?
Either oar!
All hands on deck!
IS—
SHE?!
Where are you?!?
SPLOOOSH
SPLASH

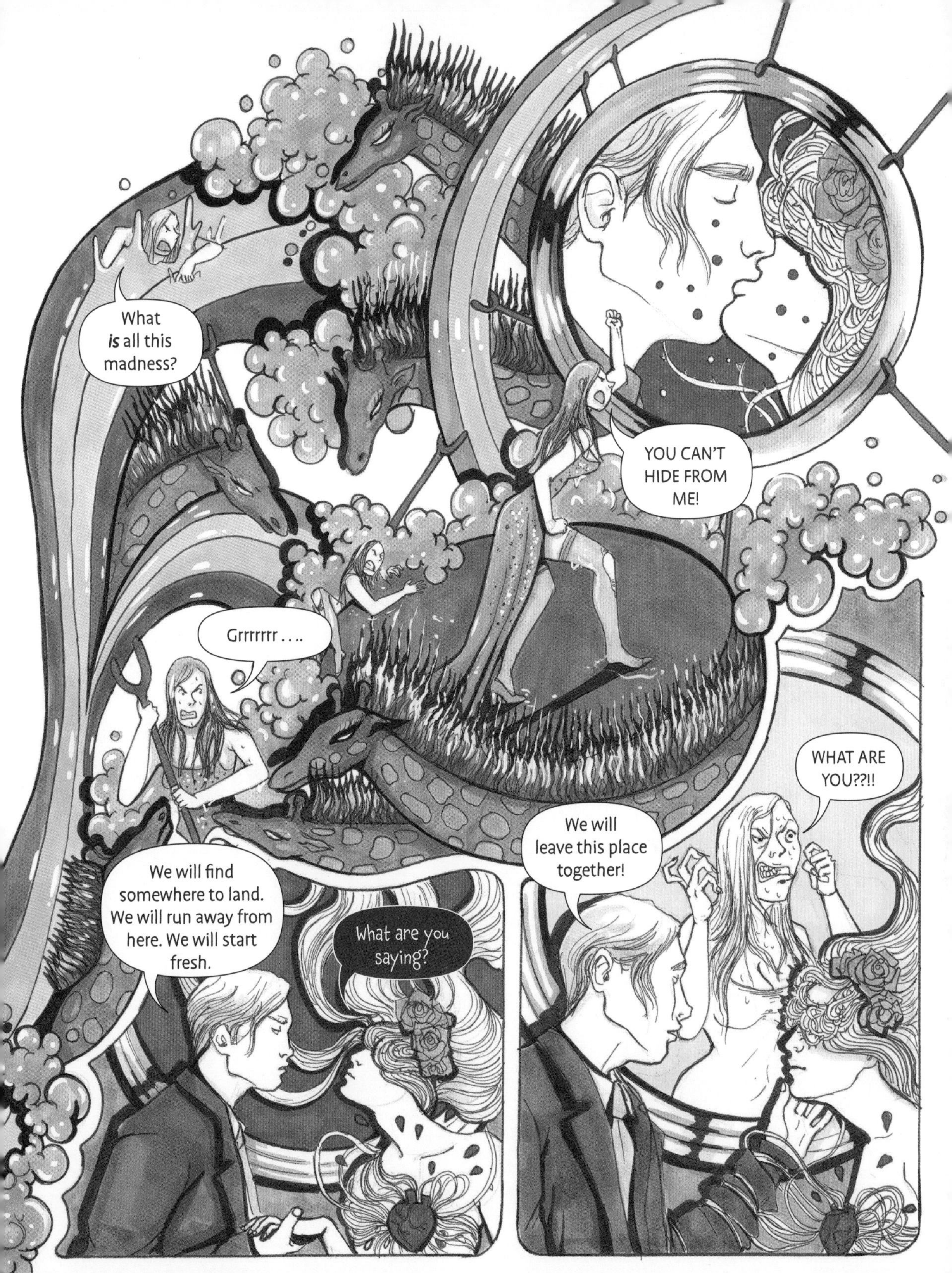
What *is* all this madness?
YOU CAN'T HIDE FROM ME!
Grrrrrrr . . ..
WHAT ARE YOU??!!
We will leave this place together!
We will find somewhere to land. We will run away from here. We will start fresh.
What are you saying?

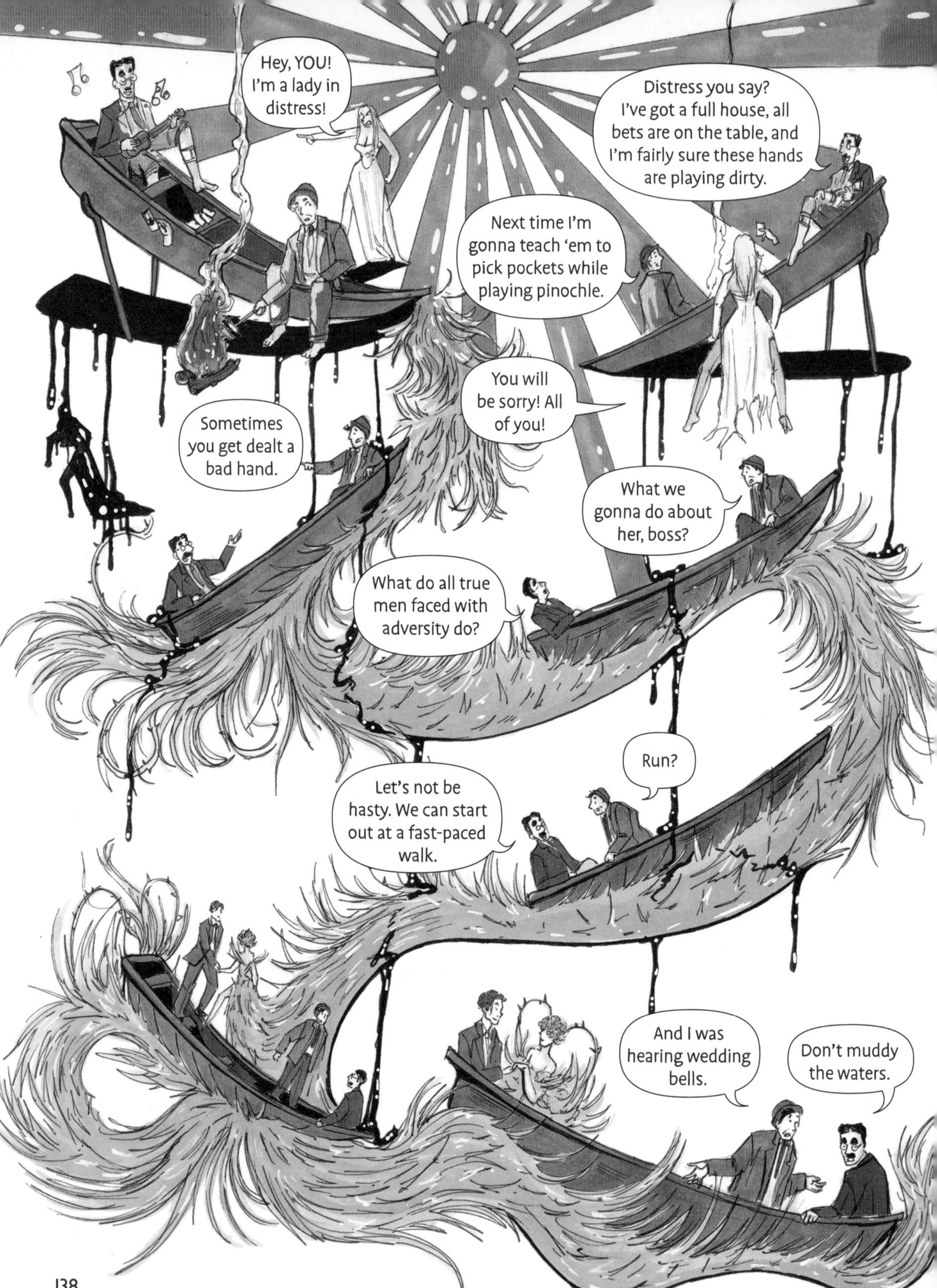
Hey, YOU! I'm a lady in distress!
Distress you say? I've got a full house, all bets are on the table, and I'm fairly sure these hands are playing dirty.
Next time I'm gonna teach 'em to pick pockets while playing pinochle.
You will be sorry! All of you!
Sometimes you get dealt a bad hand.
What we gonna do about her, boss?
What do all true men faced with adversity do?
Run?
Let's not be hasty. We can start out at a fast-paced walk.
And I was hearing wedding bells.
Don't muddy the waters.

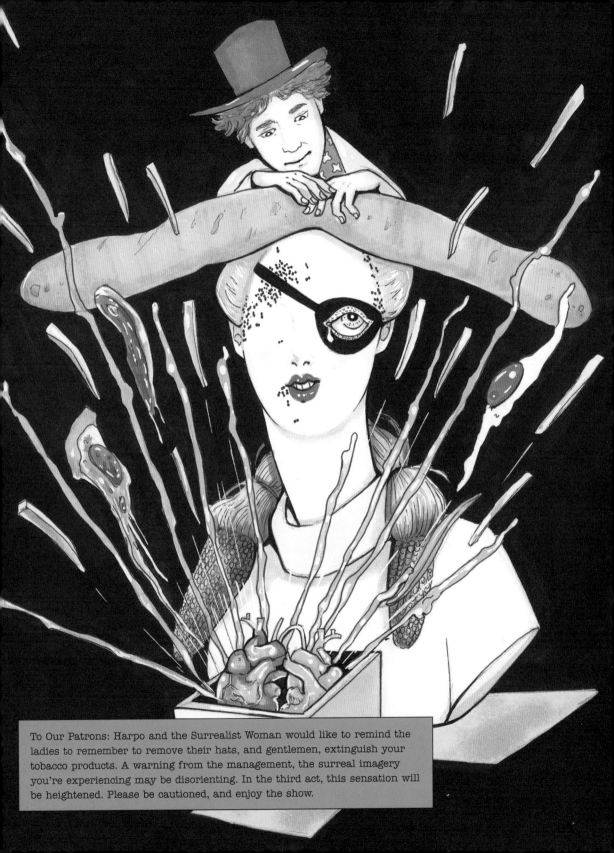

To Our Patrons: Harpo and the Surrealist Woman would like to remind the ladies to remember to remove their hats, and gentlemen, extinguish your tobacco products. A warning from the management, the surreal imagery you're experiencing may be disorienting. In the third act, this sensation will be heightened. Please be cautioned, and enjoy the show.

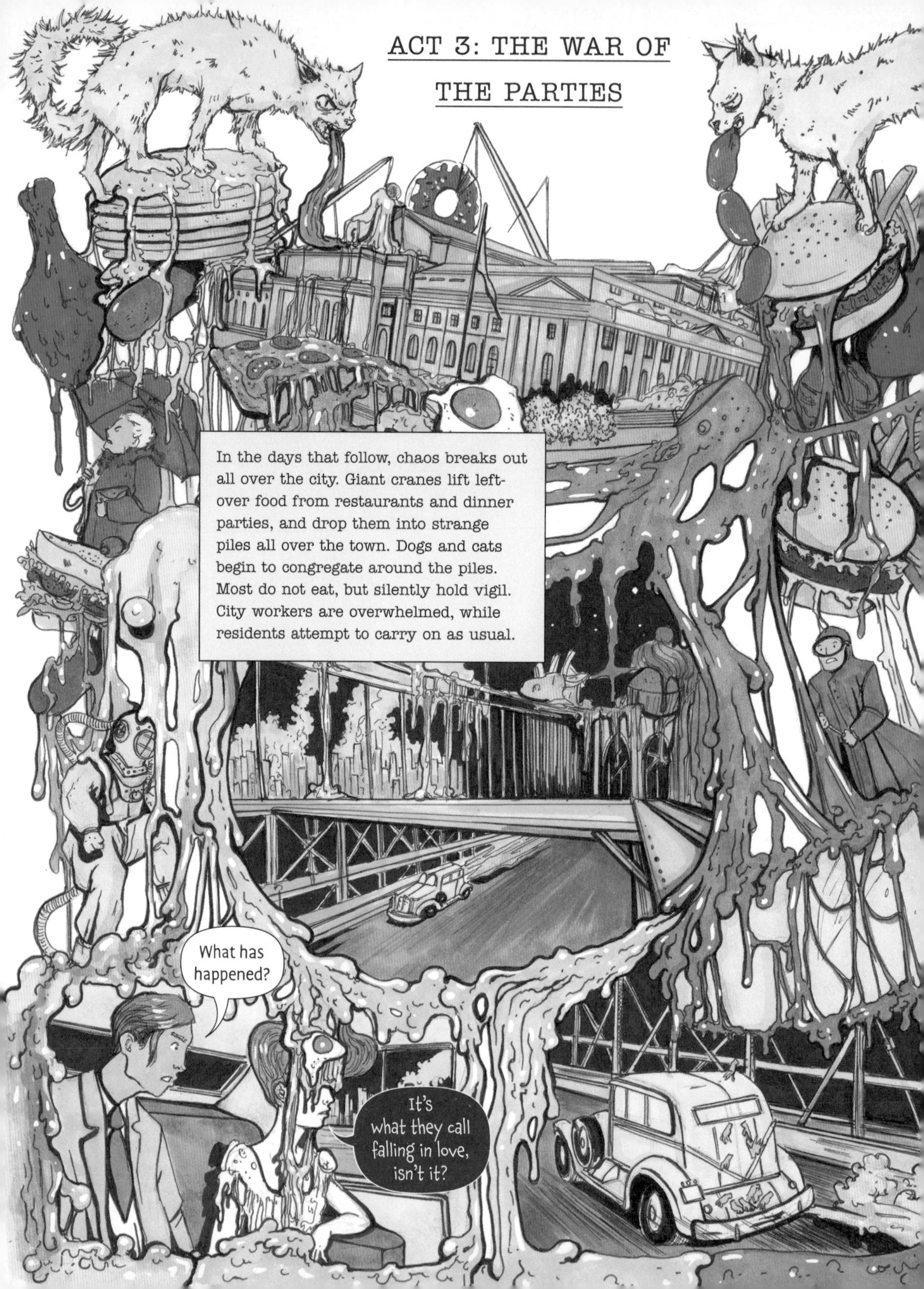
ACT 3: THE WAR OF THE PARTIES
In the days that follow, chaos breaks out all over the city. Giant cranes lift left-over food from restaurants and dinner parties, and drop them into strange piles all over the town. Dogs and cats begin to congregate around the piles. Most do not eat, but silently hold vigil. City workers are overwhelmed, while residents attempt to carry on as usual.
What has happened?
It's what they call falling in love, isn't it?

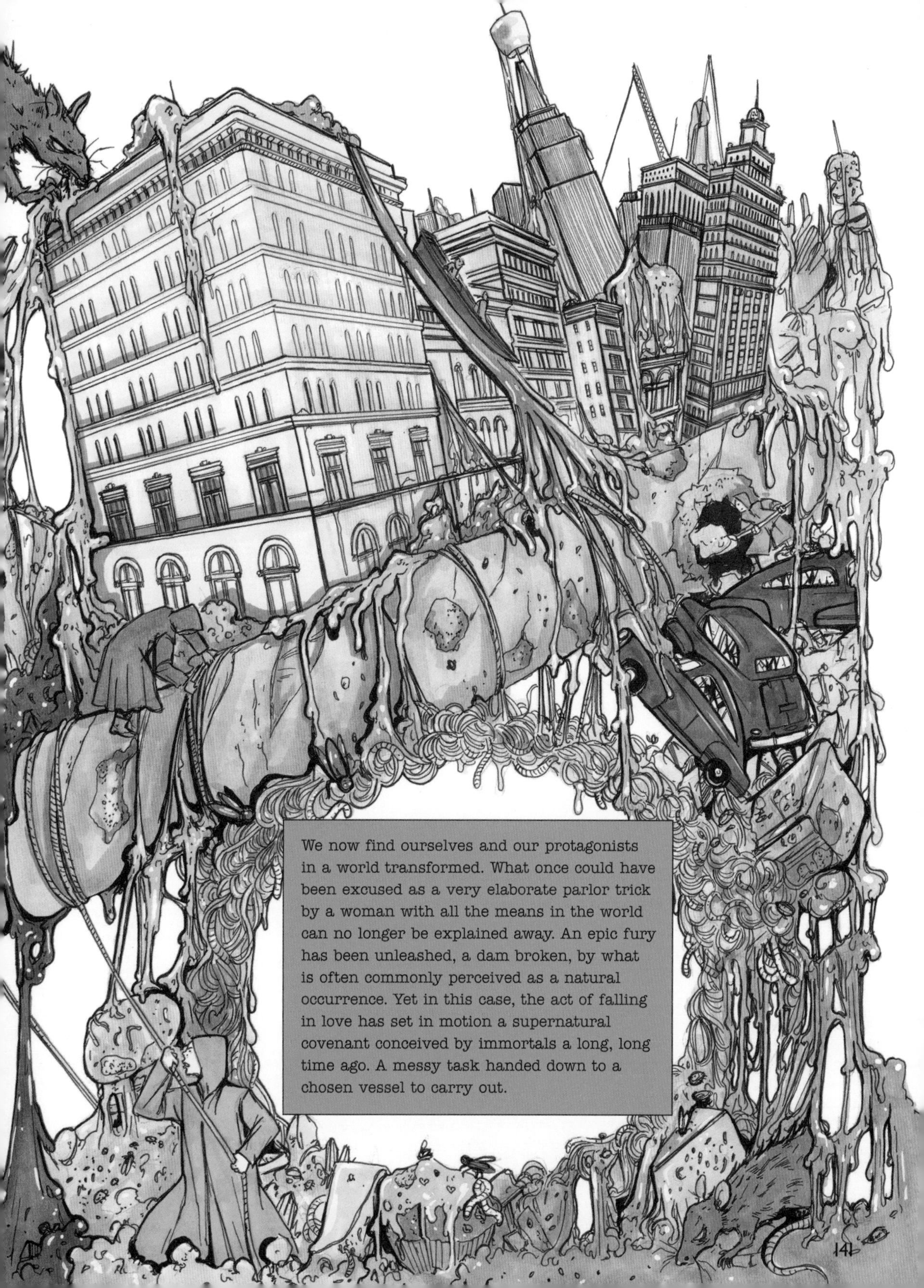
We now find ourselves and our protagonists in a world transformed. What once could have been excused as a very elaborate parlor trick by a woman with all the means in the world can no longer be explained away. An epic fury has been unleashed, a dam broken, by what is often commonly perceived as a natural occurrence. Yet in this case, the act of falling in love has set in motion a supernatural covenant conceived by immortals a long, long time ago. A messy task handed down to a chosen vessel to carry out.

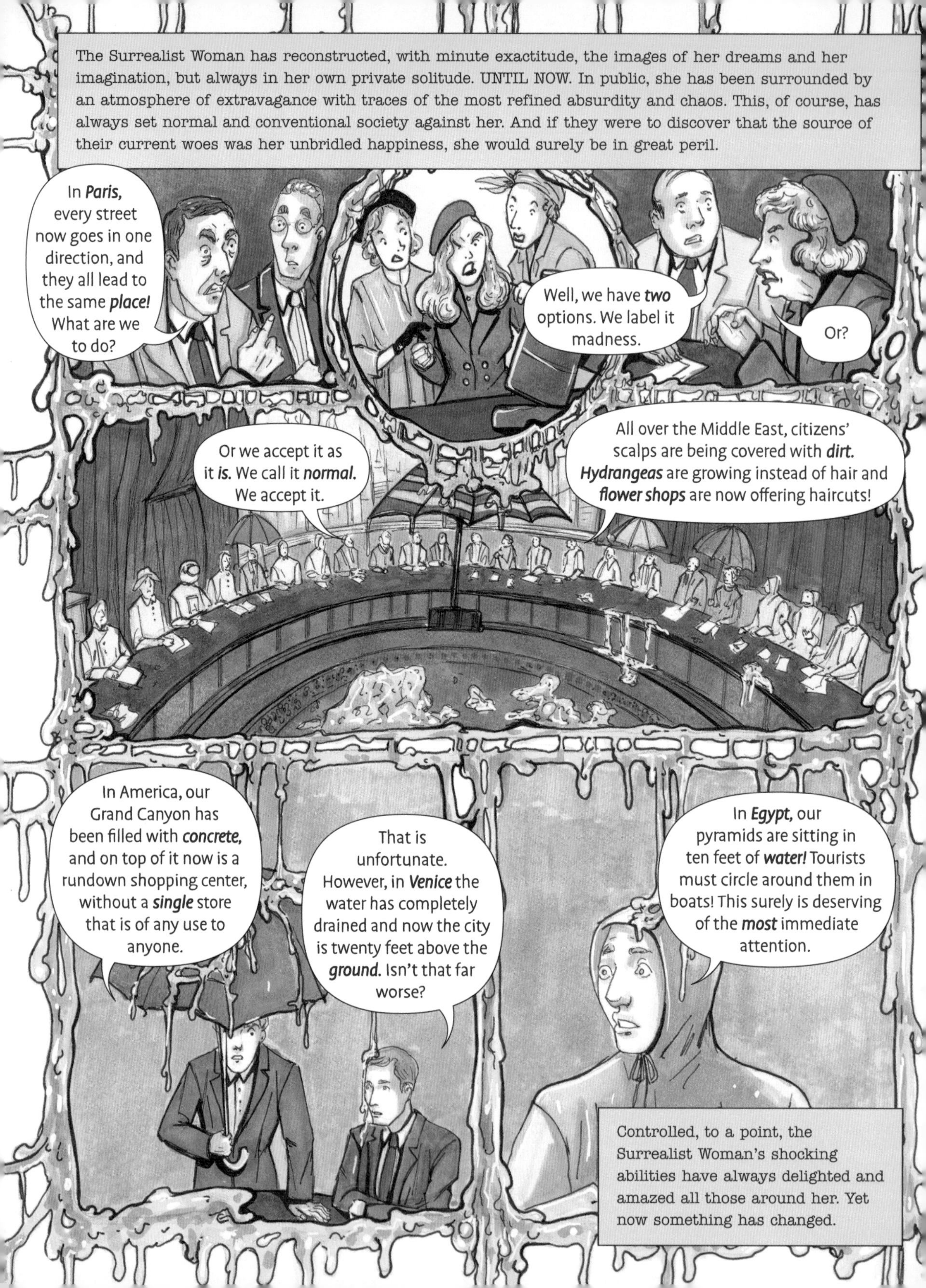
The Surrealist Woman has reconstructed, with minute exactitude, the images of her dreams and her imagination, but always in her own private solitude. UNTIL NOW. In public, she has been surrounded by an atmosphere of extravagance with traces of the most refined absurdity and chaos. This, of course, has always set normal and conventional society against her. And if they were to discover that the source of their current woes was her unbridled happiness, she would surely be in great peril.
In *Paris,* every street now goes in one direction, and they all lead to the same *place!* What are we to do?
Well, we have *two* options. We label it madness.
Or?
Or we accept it as it *is.* We call it *normal.* We accept it.
All over the Middle East, citizens' scalps are being covered with *dirt. Hydrangeas* are growing instead of hair and *flower shops* are now offering haircuts!
In America, our Grand Canyon has been filled with *concrete,* and on top of it now is a rundown shopping center, without a *single* store that is of any use to anyone.
That is unfortunate. However, in *Venice* the water has completely drained and now the city is twenty feet above the *ground.* Isn't that far worse?
In *Egypt,* our pyramids are sitting in ten feet of *water!* Tourists must circle around them in boats! This surely is deserving of the *most* immediate attention.
Controlled, to a point, the Surrealist Woman's shocking abilities have always delighted and amazed all those around her. Yet now something has changed.

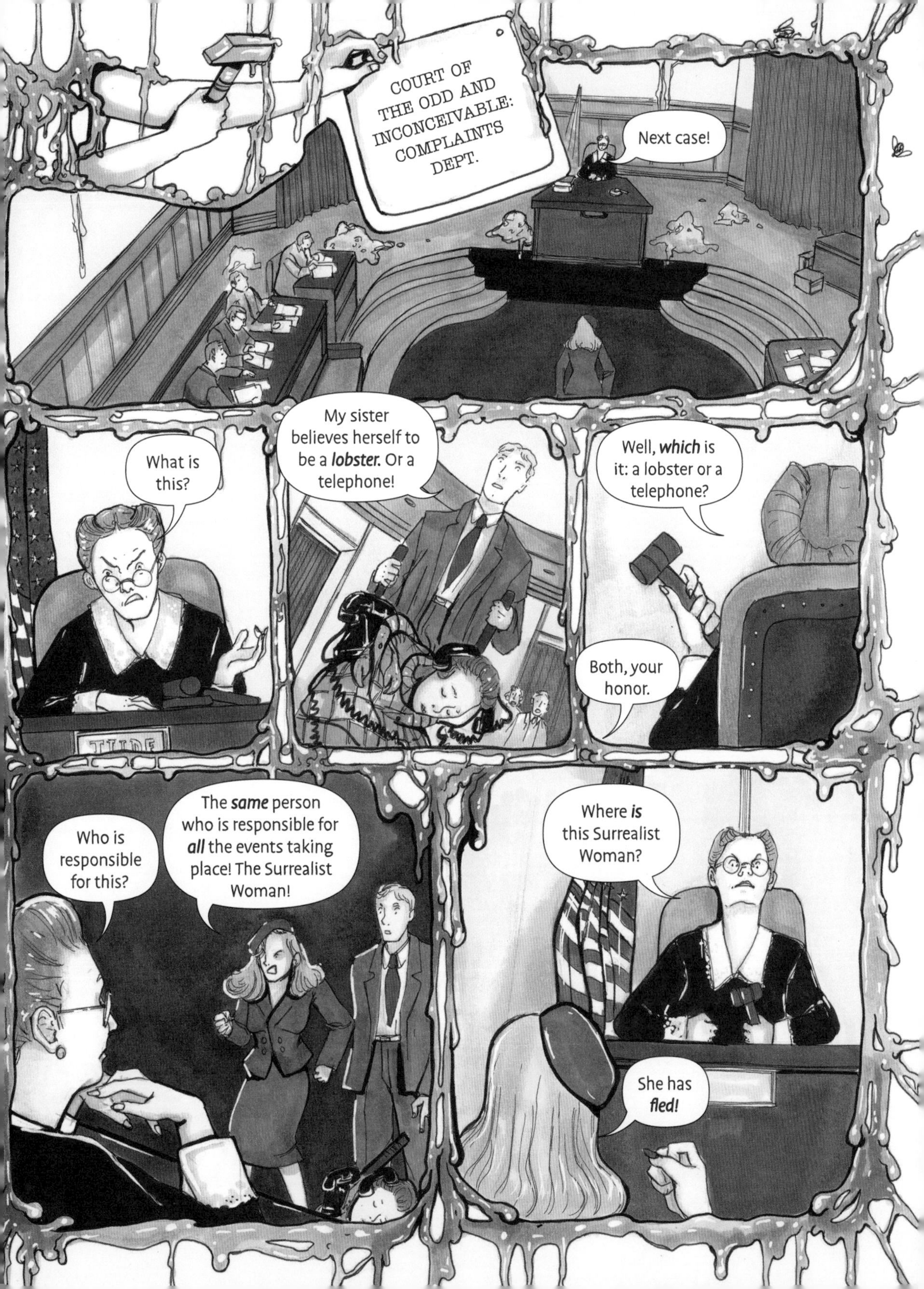
COURT OF THE ODD AND INCONCEIVABLE: COMPLAINTS DEPT.
Next case!
What is this?
My sister believes herself to be a *lobster.* Or a telephone!
Well, *which* is it: a lobster or a telephone?
Both, your honor.
Who is responsible for this?
The *same* person who is responsible for *all* the events taking place! The Surrealist Woman!
Where *is* this Surrealist Woman?
She has *fled!*

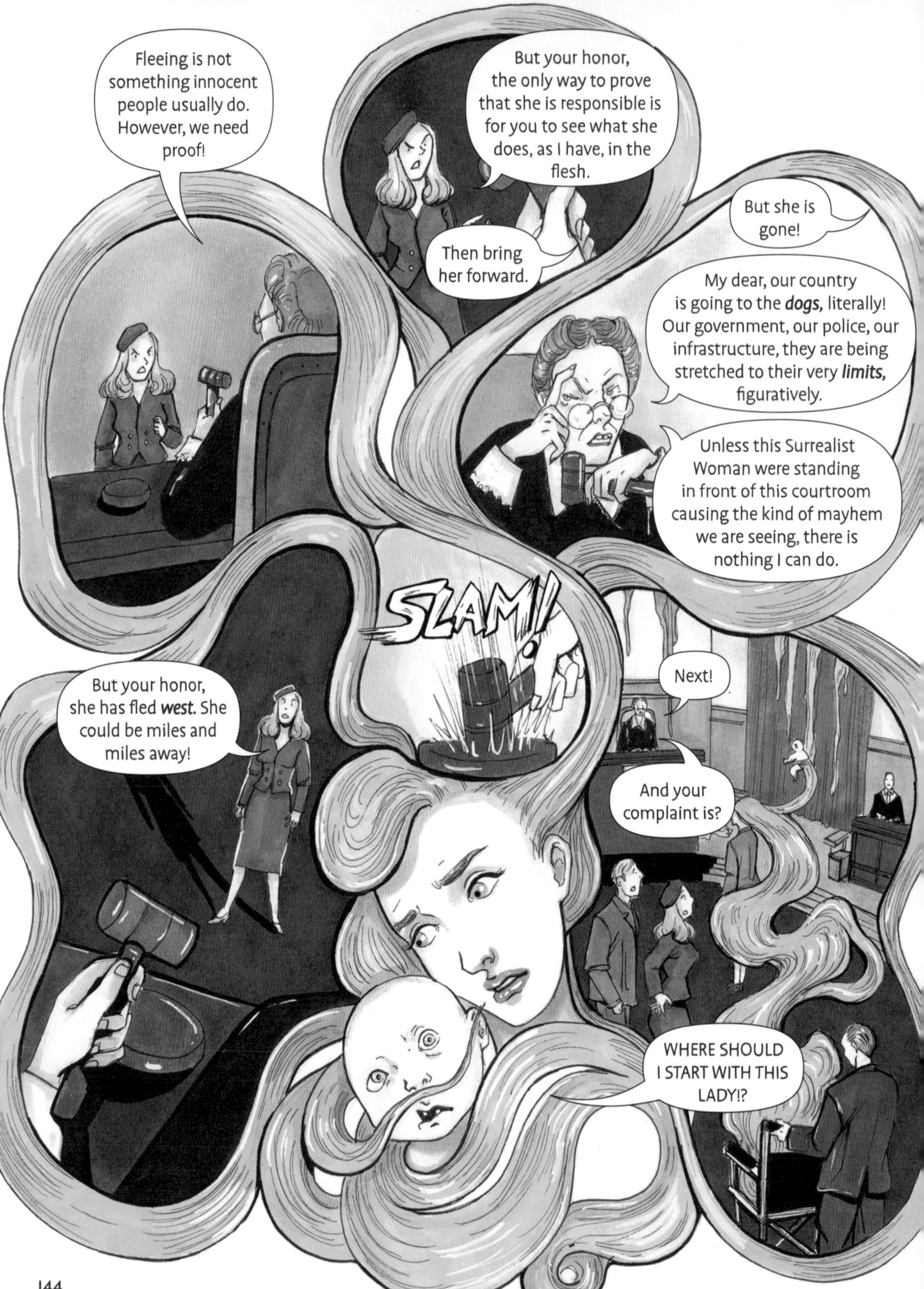
Fleeing is not something innocent people usually do. However, we need proof!
But your honor, the only way to prove that she is responsible is for you to see what she does, as I have, in the flesh.
Then bring her forward.
But she is gone!
My dear, our country is going to the **dogs,** literally! Our government, our police, our infrastructure, they are being stretched to their very **limits,** figuratively.
Unless this Surrealist Woman were standing in front of this courtroom causing the kind of mayhem we are seeing, there is nothing I can do.
SLAM!!
But your honor, she has fled **west.** She could be miles and miles away!
Next!
And your complaint is?
WHERE SHOULD I START WITH THIS LADY!?

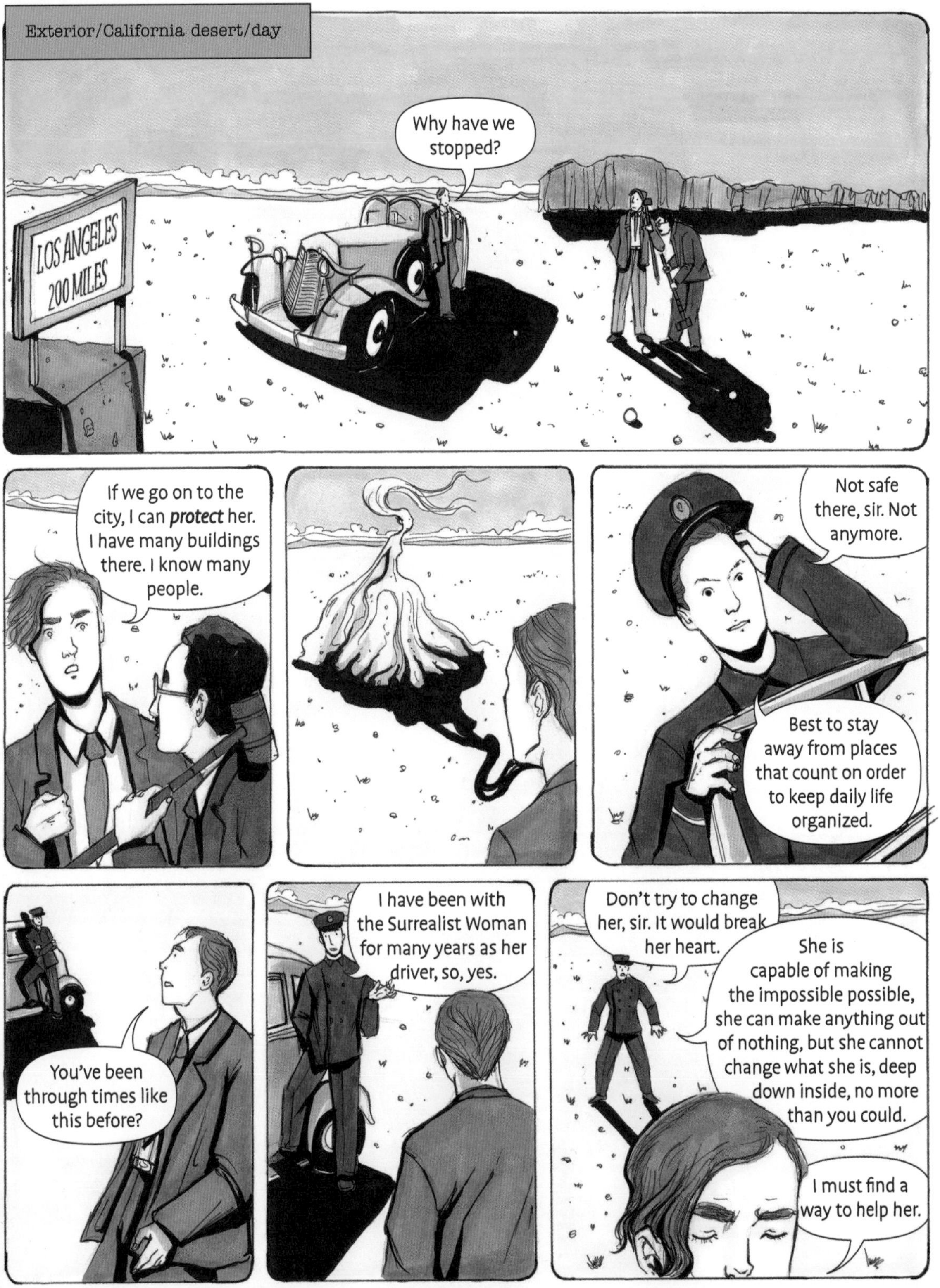
Exterior/California desert/day
LOS ANGELES 200 MILES
Why have we stopped?
If we go on to the city, I can *protect* her. I have many buildings there. I know many people.
Not safe there, sir. Not anymore.
Best to stay away from places that count on order to keep daily life organized.
You've been through times like this before?
I have been with the Surrealist Woman for many years as her driver, so, yes.
Don't try to change her, sir. It would break her heart.
She is capable of making the impossible possible, she can make anything out of nothing, but she cannot change what she is, deep down inside, no more than you could.
I must find a way to help her.

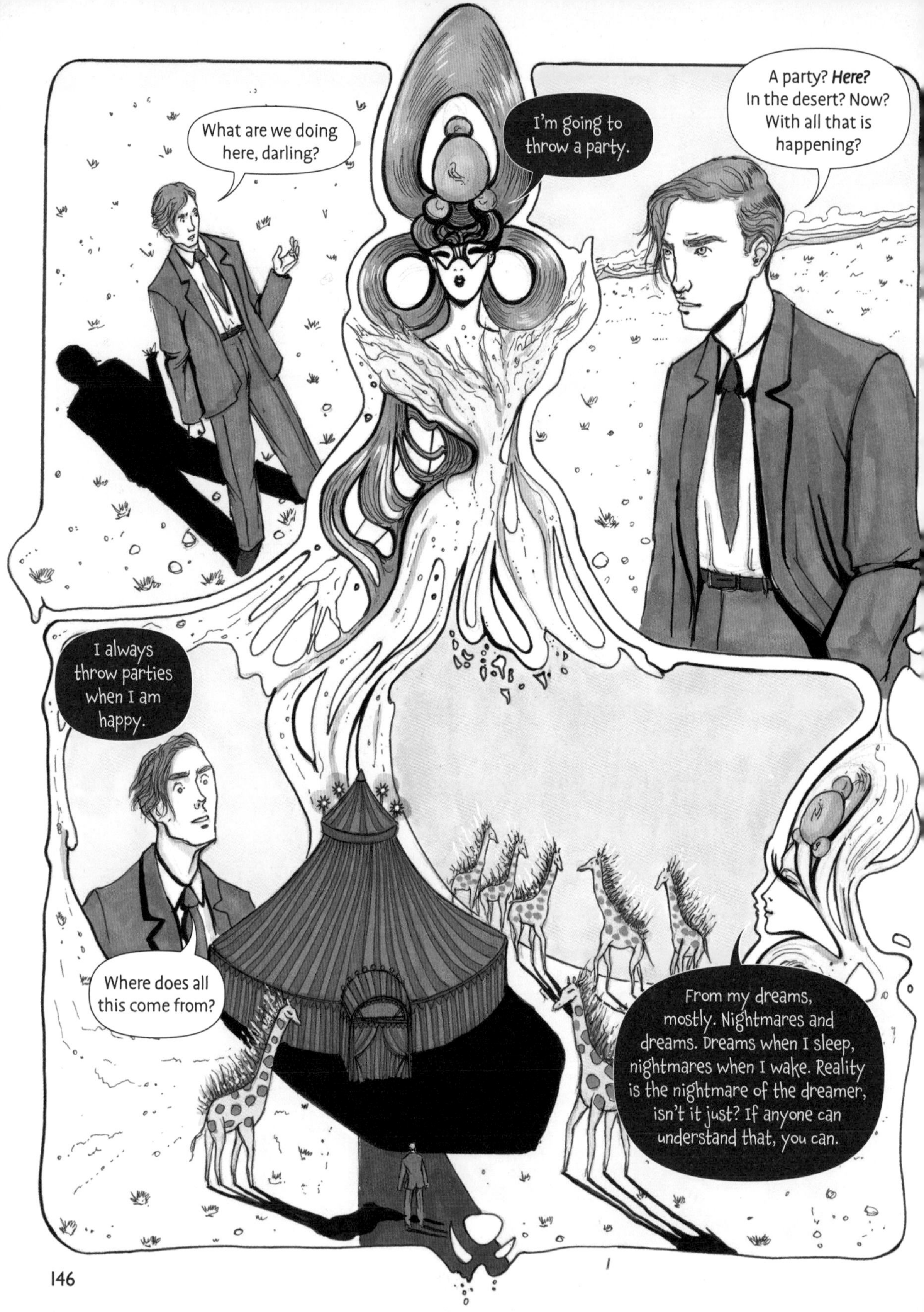
What are we doing here, darling?
I'm going to throw a party.
A party? **Here?** In the desert? Now? With all that is happening?
I always throw parties when I am happy.
Where does all this come from?
From my dreams, mostly. Nightmares and dreams. Dreams when I sleep, nightmares when I wake. Reality is the nightmare of the dreamer, isn't it just? If anyone can understand that, you can.

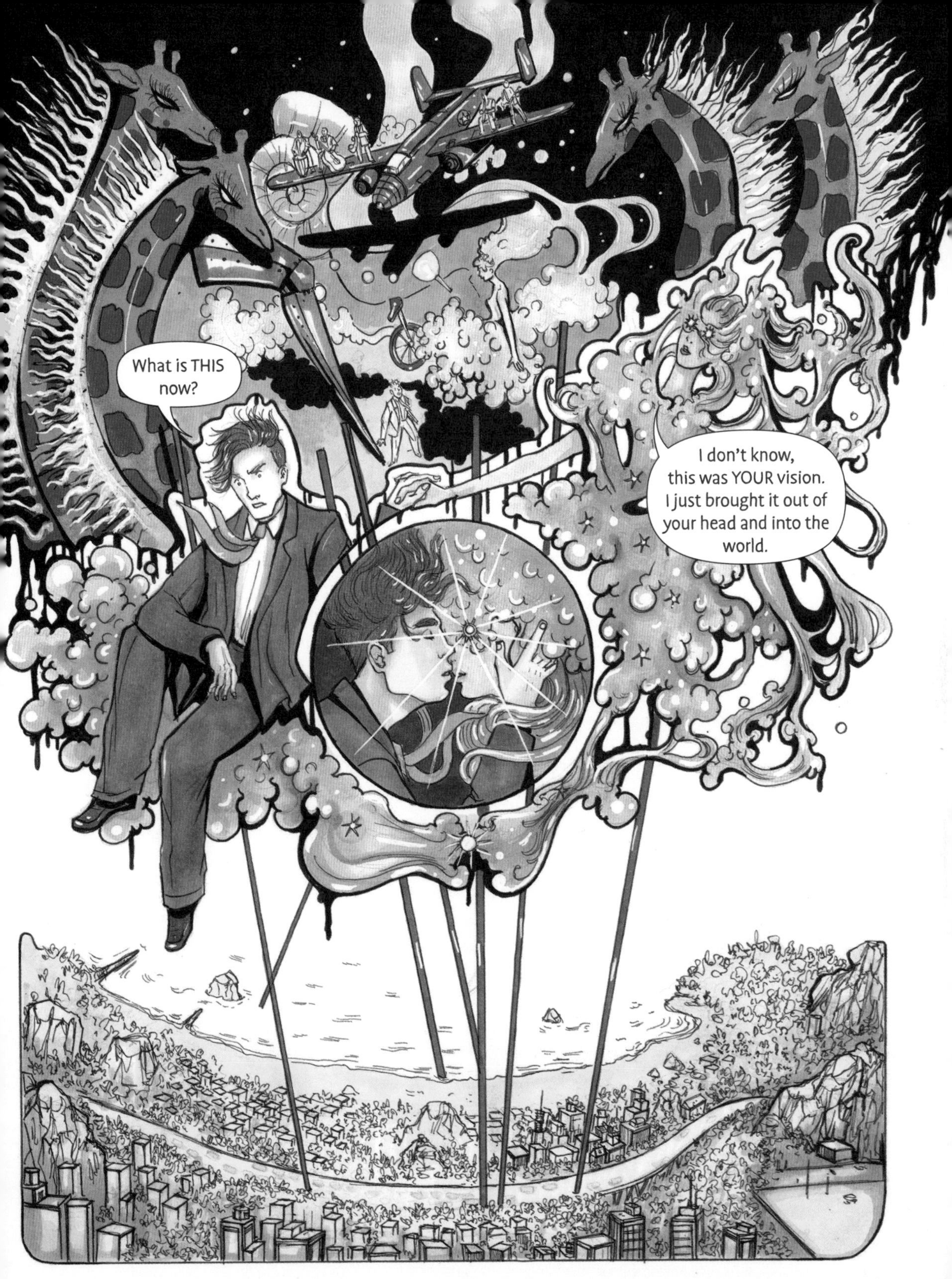
What is THIS now?
I don't know, this was YOUR vision. I just brought it out of your head and into the world.

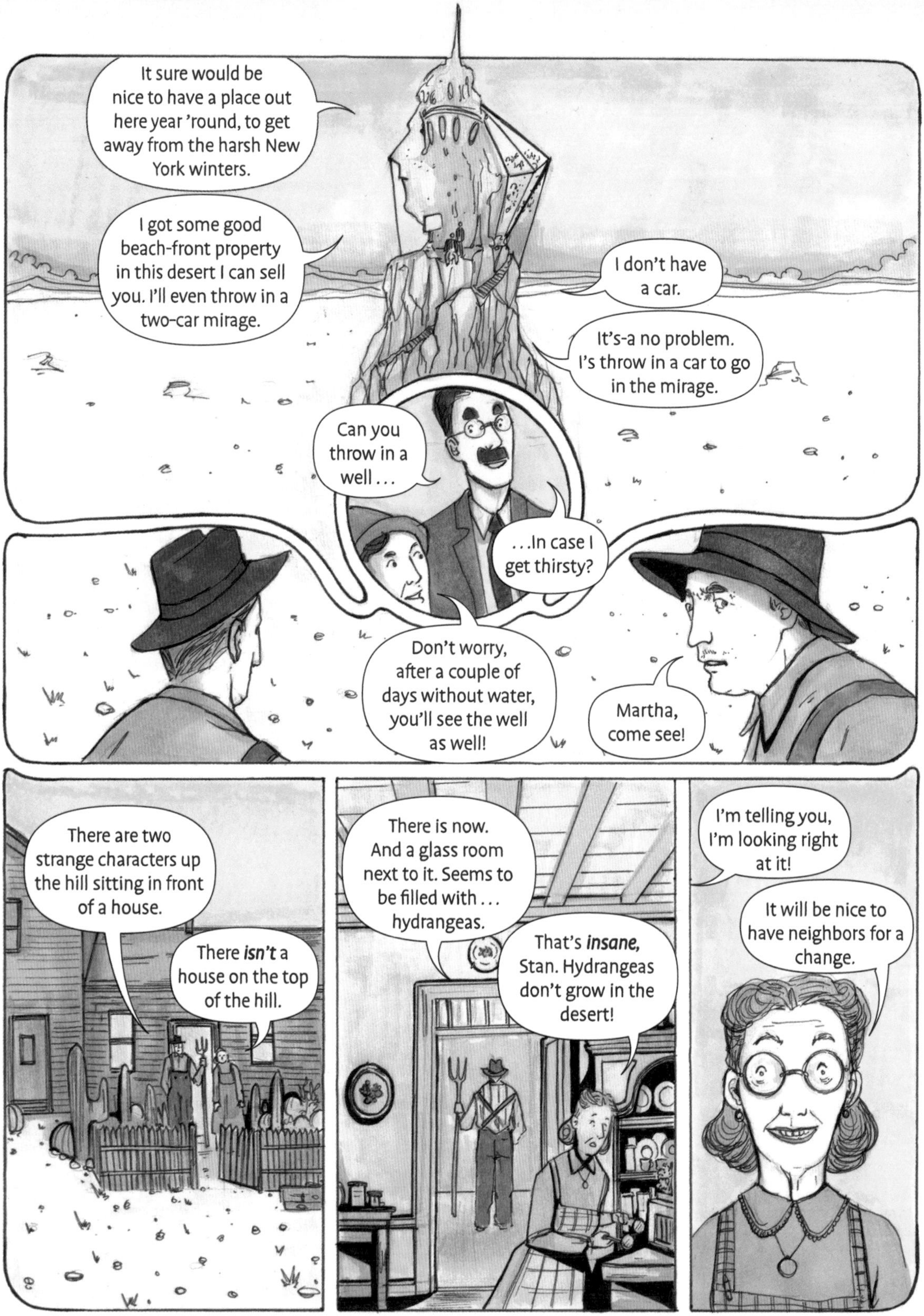
It sure would be nice to have a place out here year 'round, to get away from the harsh New York winters.
I got some good beach-front property in this desert I can sell you. I'll even throw in a two-car mirage.
I don't have a car.
It's-a no problem. I's throw in a car to go in the mirage.
Can you throw in a well . . .
. . .In case I get thirsty?
Don't worry, after a couple of days without water, you'll see the well as well!
Martha, come see!
There are two strange characters up the hill sitting in front of a house.
There *isn't* a house on the top of the hill.
There is now. And a glass room next to it. Seems to be filled with . . . hydrangeas.
That's ***insane,*** Stan. Hydrangeas don't grow in the desert!
I'm telling you, I'm looking right at it!
It will be nice to have neighbors for a change.

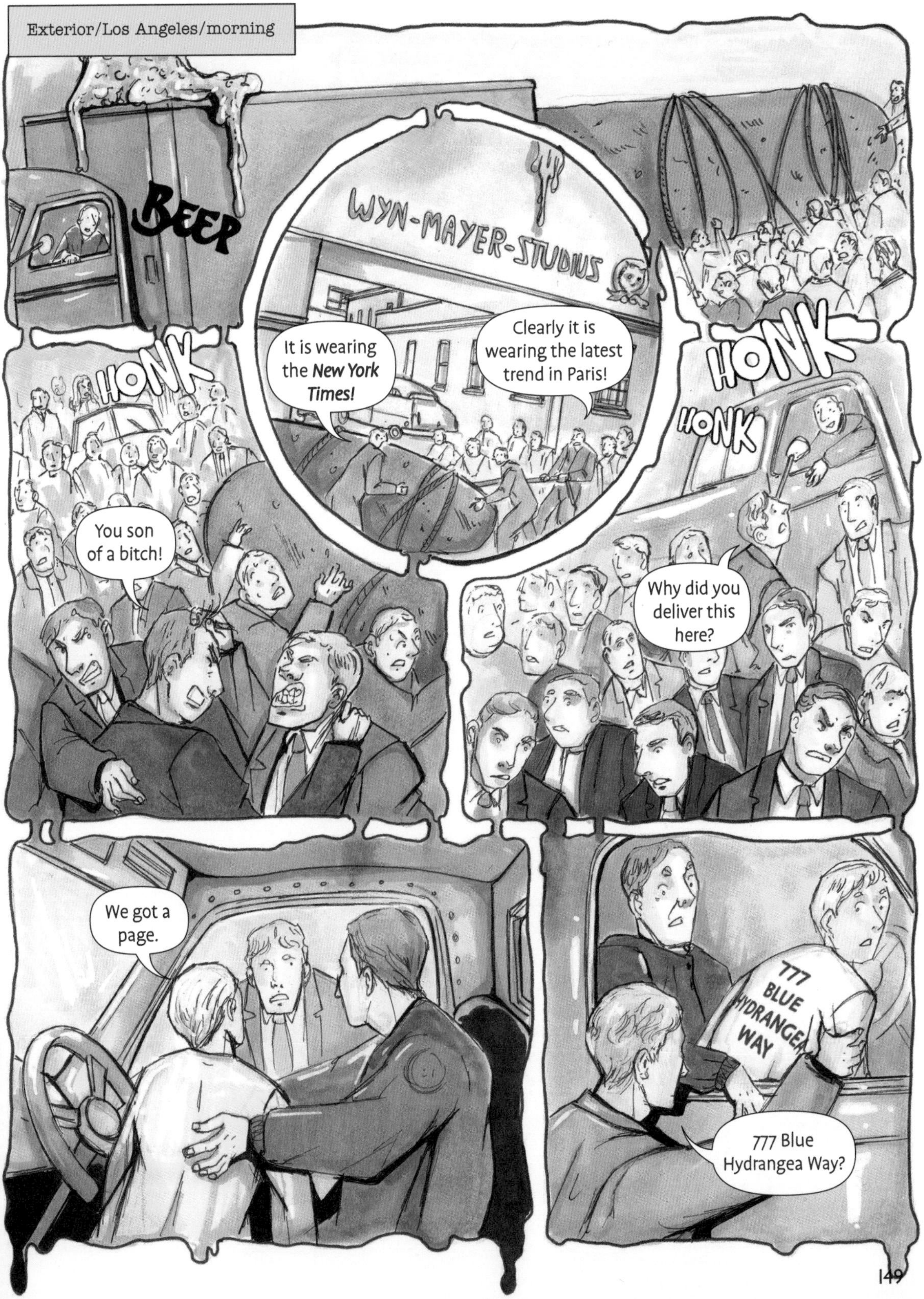
Exterior/Los Angeles/morning
BEEP
WYN-MAYER-STUDIUS
It is wearing the *New York Times!*
Clearly it is wearing the latest trend in Paris!
HONK
HONK
HONK
You son of a bitch!
Why did you deliver this here?
We got a page.
777 BLUE HYDRANGEA WAY
777 Blue Hydrangea Way?

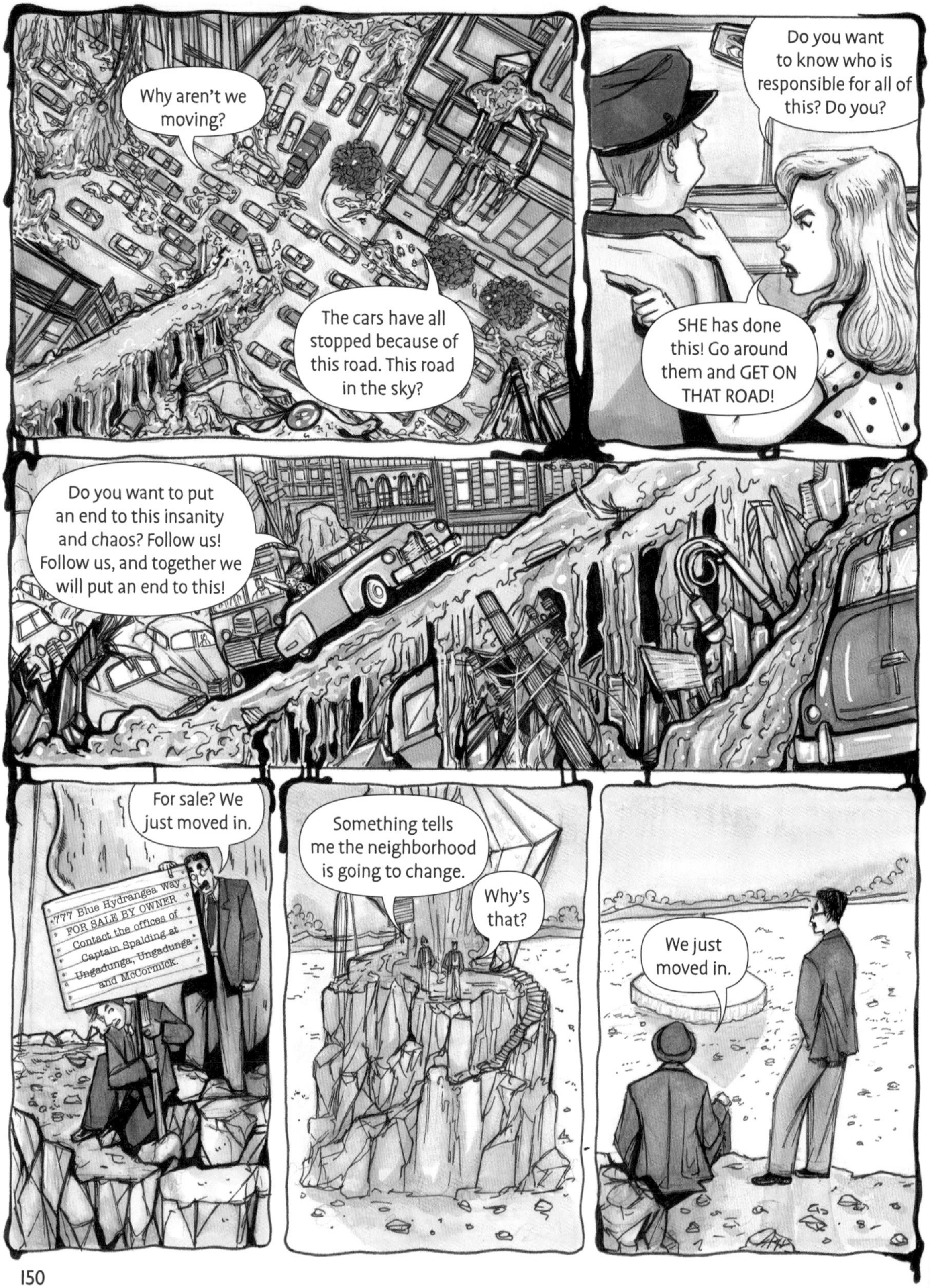
Why aren't we moving?
The cars have all stopped because of this road. This road in the sky?
Do you want to know who is responsible for all of this? Do you?
SHE has done this! Go around them and GET ON THAT ROAD!
Do you want to put an end to this insanity and chaos? Follow us! Follow us, and together we will put an end to this!
For sale? We just moved in.
777 Blue Hydrangea Way
FOR SALE BY OWNER
Contact the offices of
Captain Spalding at
Ungadunga, Ungadunga
and McCormick.
Something tells me the neighborhood is going to change.
Why's that?
We just moved in.

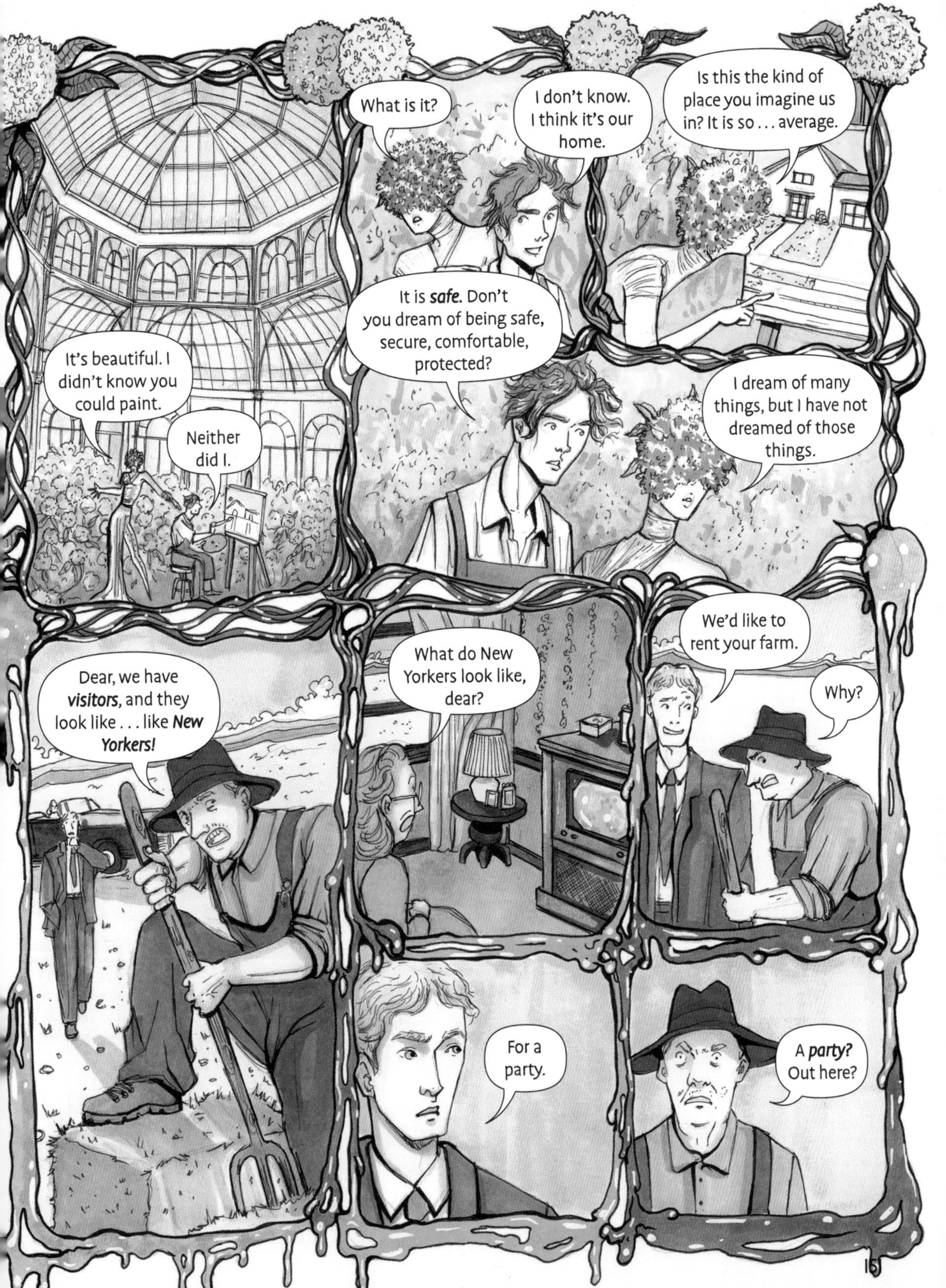
It's beautiful. I didn't know you could paint.
Neither did I.
What is it?
I don't know. I think it's our home.
Is this the kind of place you imagine us in? It is so . . . average.
It is **safe.** Don't you dream of being safe, secure, comfortable, protected?
I dream of many things, but I have not dreamed of those things.
Dear, we have **visitors**, and they look like . . . like **New Yorkers!**
What do New Yorkers look like, dear?
We'd like to rent your farm.
Why?
For a party.
A **party?** Out here?

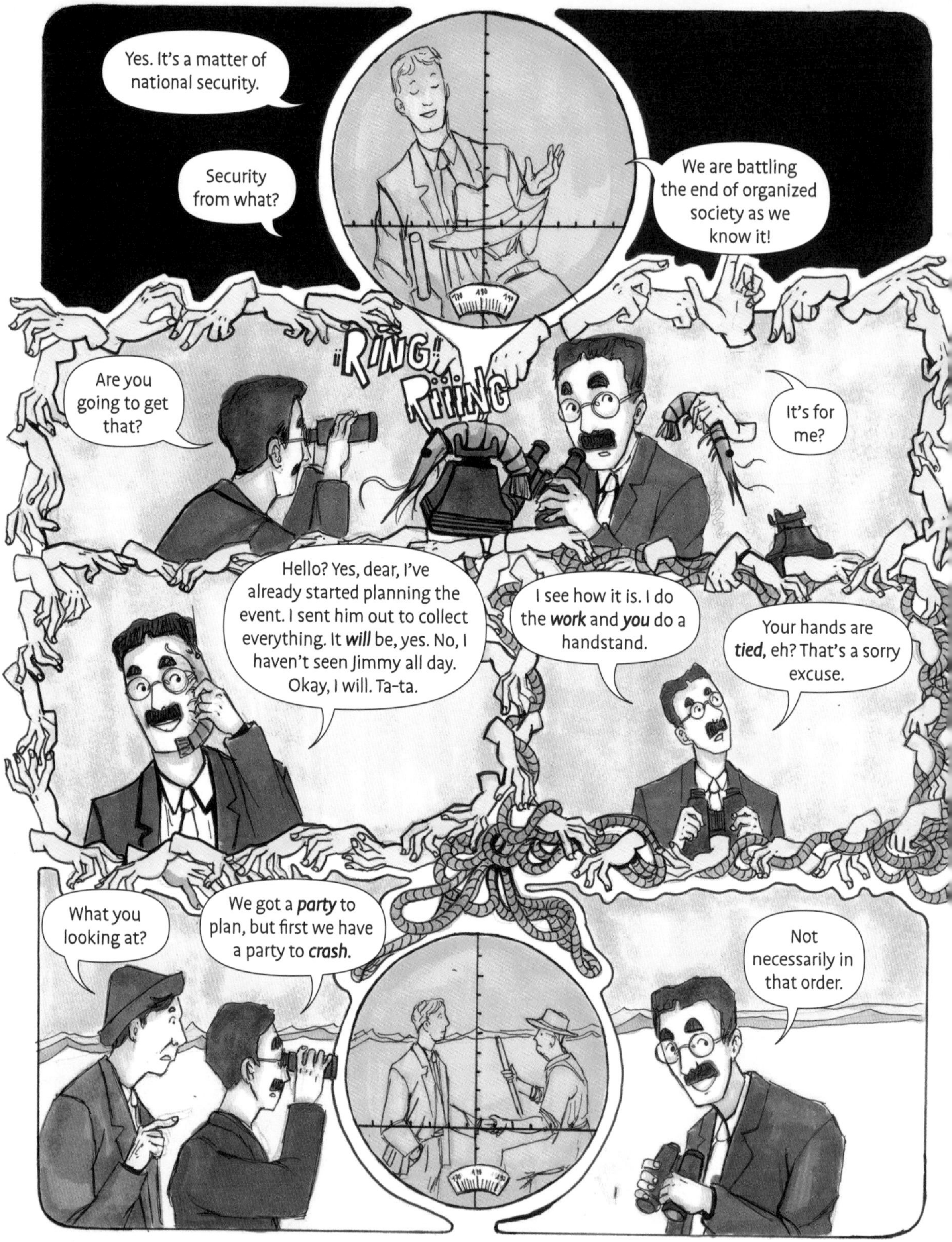
Yes. It's a matter of national security.
Security from what?
We are battling the end of organized society as we know it!
¡RING!
RIIING
Are you going to get that?
It's for me?
Hello? Yes, dear, I've already started planning the event. I sent him out to collect everything. It *will* be, yes. No, I haven't seen Jimmy all day. Okay, I will. Ta-ta.
I see how it is. I do the ***work*** and ***you*** do a handstand.
Your hands are ***tied***, eh? That's a sorry excuse.
What you looking at?
We got a ***party*** to plan, but first we have a party to ***crash***.
Not necessarily in that order.

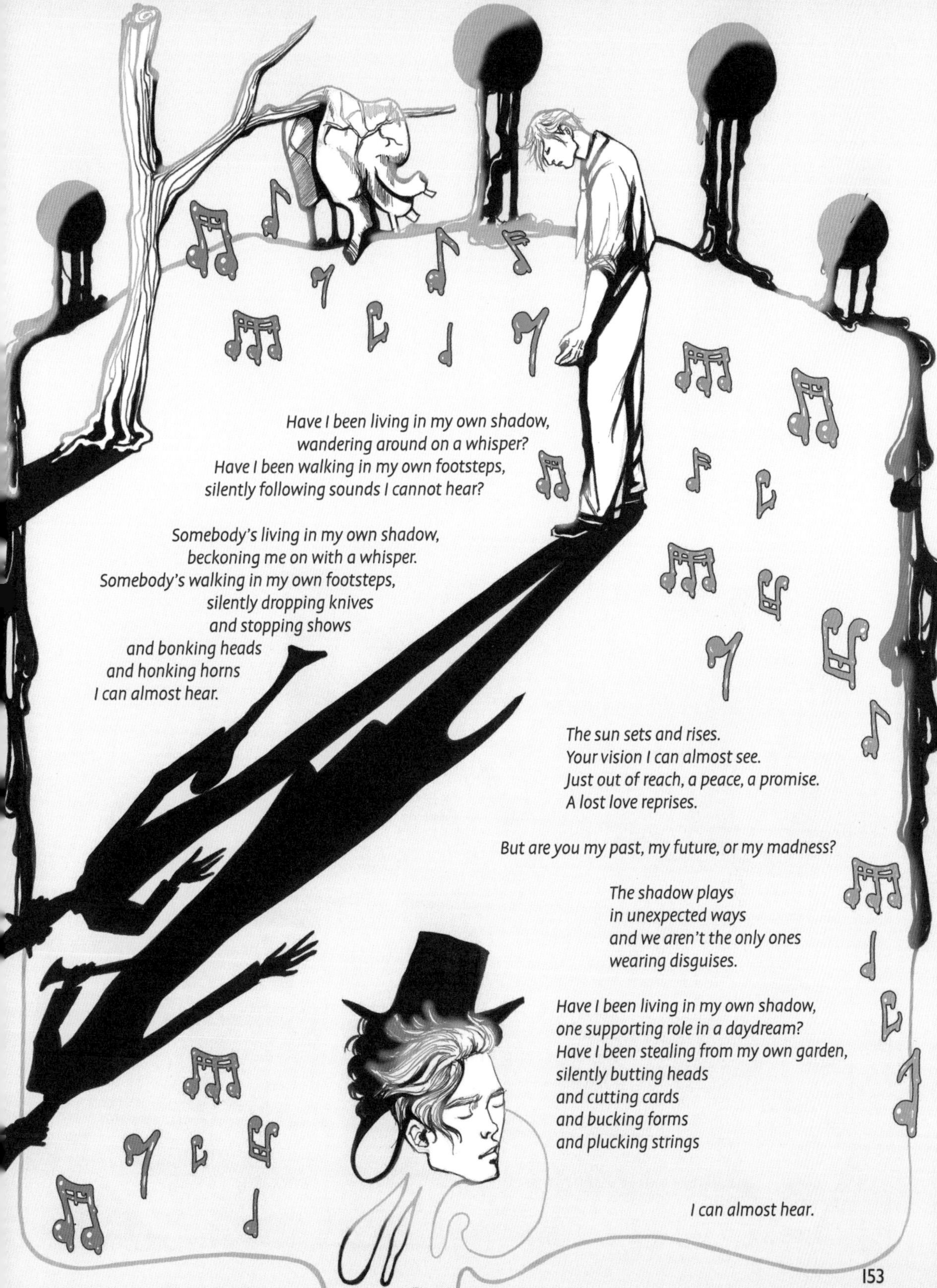

Have I been living in my own shadow,
wandering around on a whisper?
Have I been walking in my own footsteps,
silently following sounds I cannot hear?

Somebody's living in my own shadow,
beckoning me on with a whisper.
Somebody's walking in my own footsteps,
silently dropping knives
and stopping shows
and bonking heads
and honking horns
I can almost hear.

The sun sets and rises.
Your vision I can almost see.
Just out of reach, a peace, a promise.
A lost love reprises.

But are you my past, my future, or my madness?

The shadow plays
in unexpected ways
and we aren't the only ones
wearing disguises.

Have I been living in my own shadow,
one supporting role in a daydream?
Have I been stealing from my own garden,
silently butting heads
and cutting cards
and bucking forms
and plucking strings

I can almost hear.

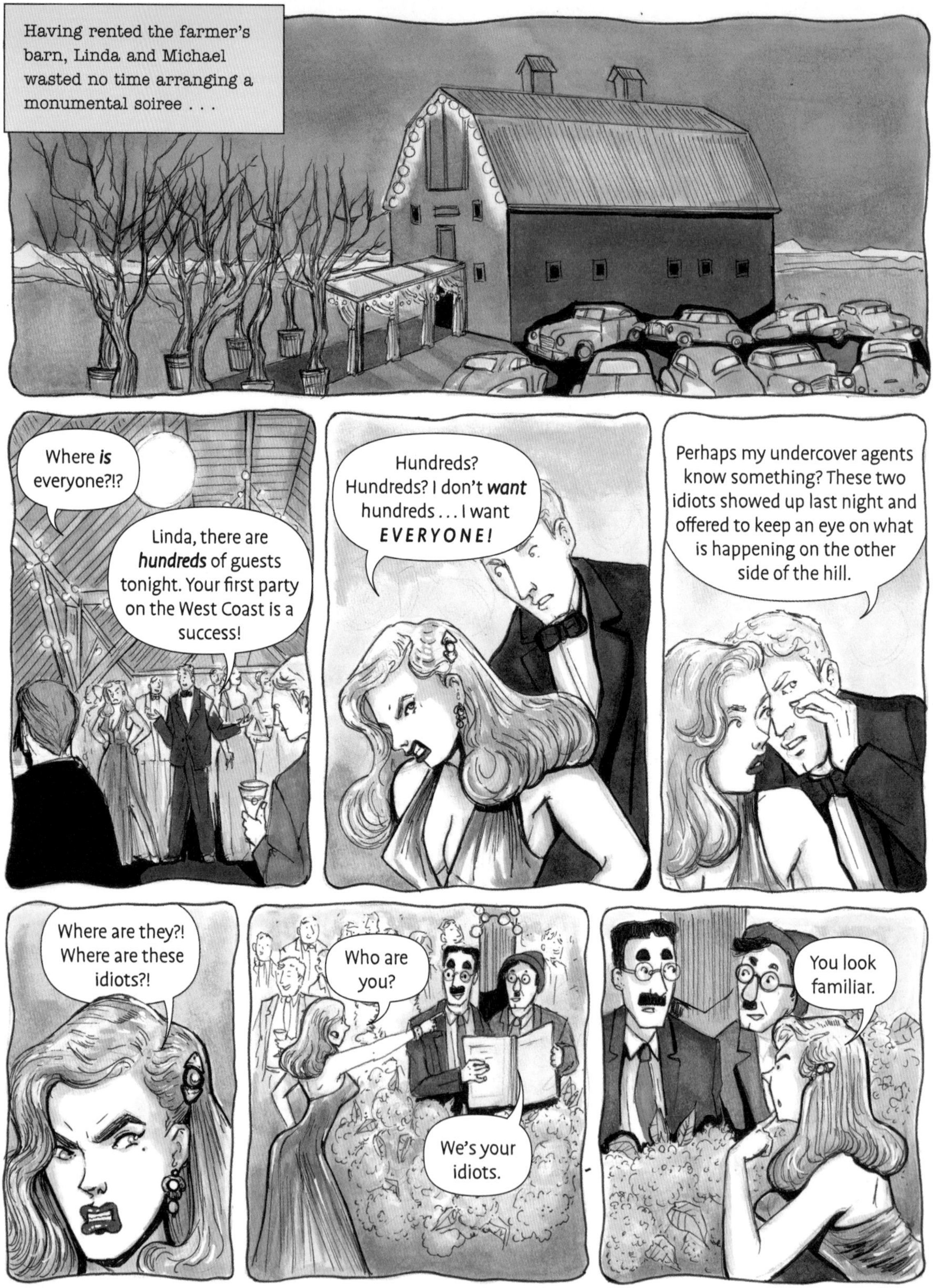

Having rented the farmer's barn, Linda and Michael wasted no time arranging a monumental soiree . . .
Where *is* everyone?!?
Linda, there are ***hundreds*** of guests tonight. Your first party on the West Coast is a success!
Hundreds? Hundreds? I don't ***want*** hundreds . . . I want ***EVERYONE!***
Perhaps my undercover agents know something? These two idiots showed up last night and offered to keep an eye on what is happening on the other side of the hill.
Where are they?! Where are these idiots?!
Who are you?
We's your idiots.
You look familiar.

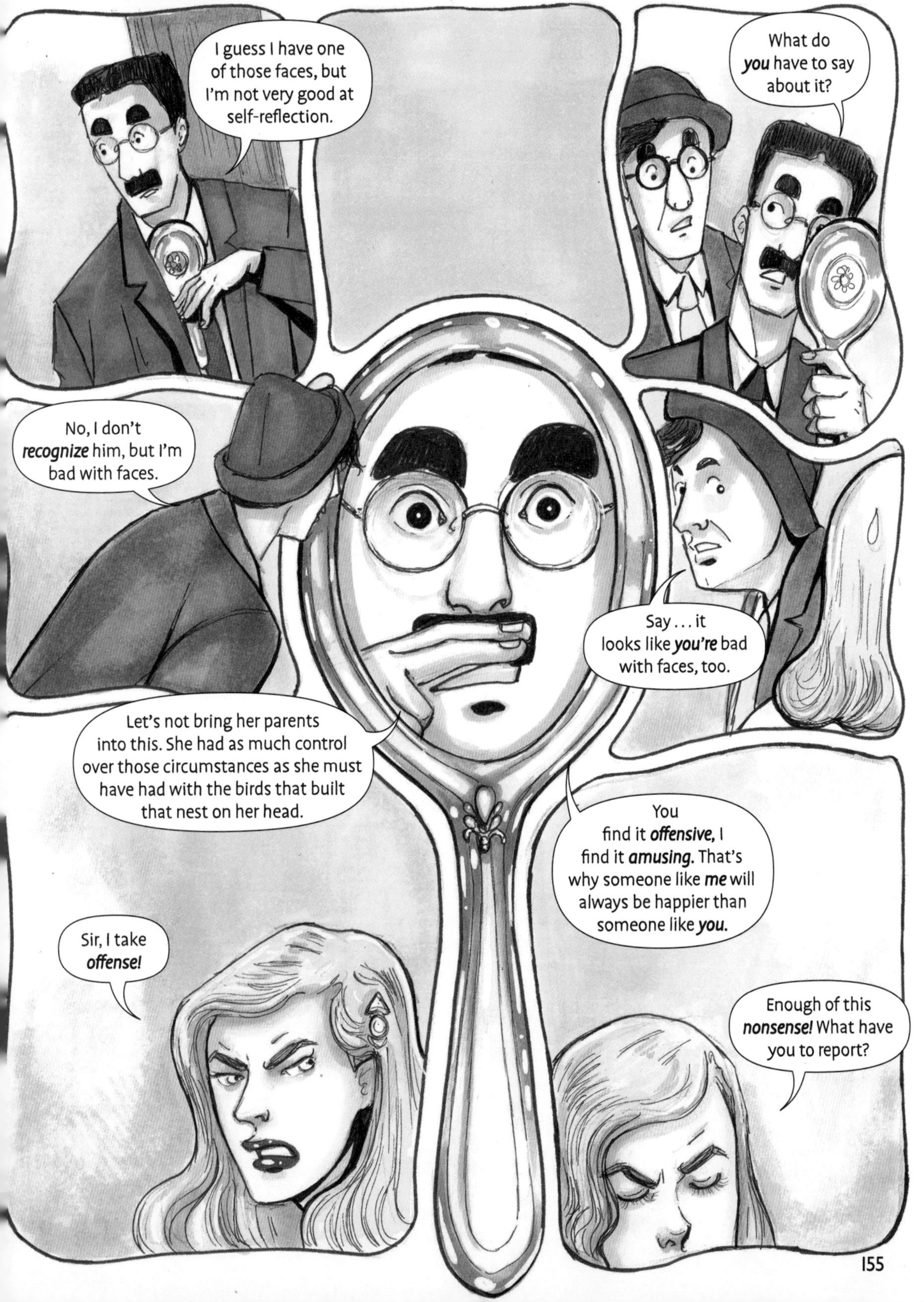
I guess I have one of those faces, but I'm not very good at self-reflection.
What do *you* have to say about it?
No, I don't *recognize* him, but I'm bad with faces.
Say . . . it looks like *you're* bad with faces, too.
Let's not bring her parents into this. She had as much control over those circumstances as she must have had with the birds that built that nest on her head.
You find it *offensive,* I find it *amusing.* That's why someone like *me* will always be happier than someone like *you.*
Sir, I take *offense!*
Enough of this *nonsense!* What have you to report?

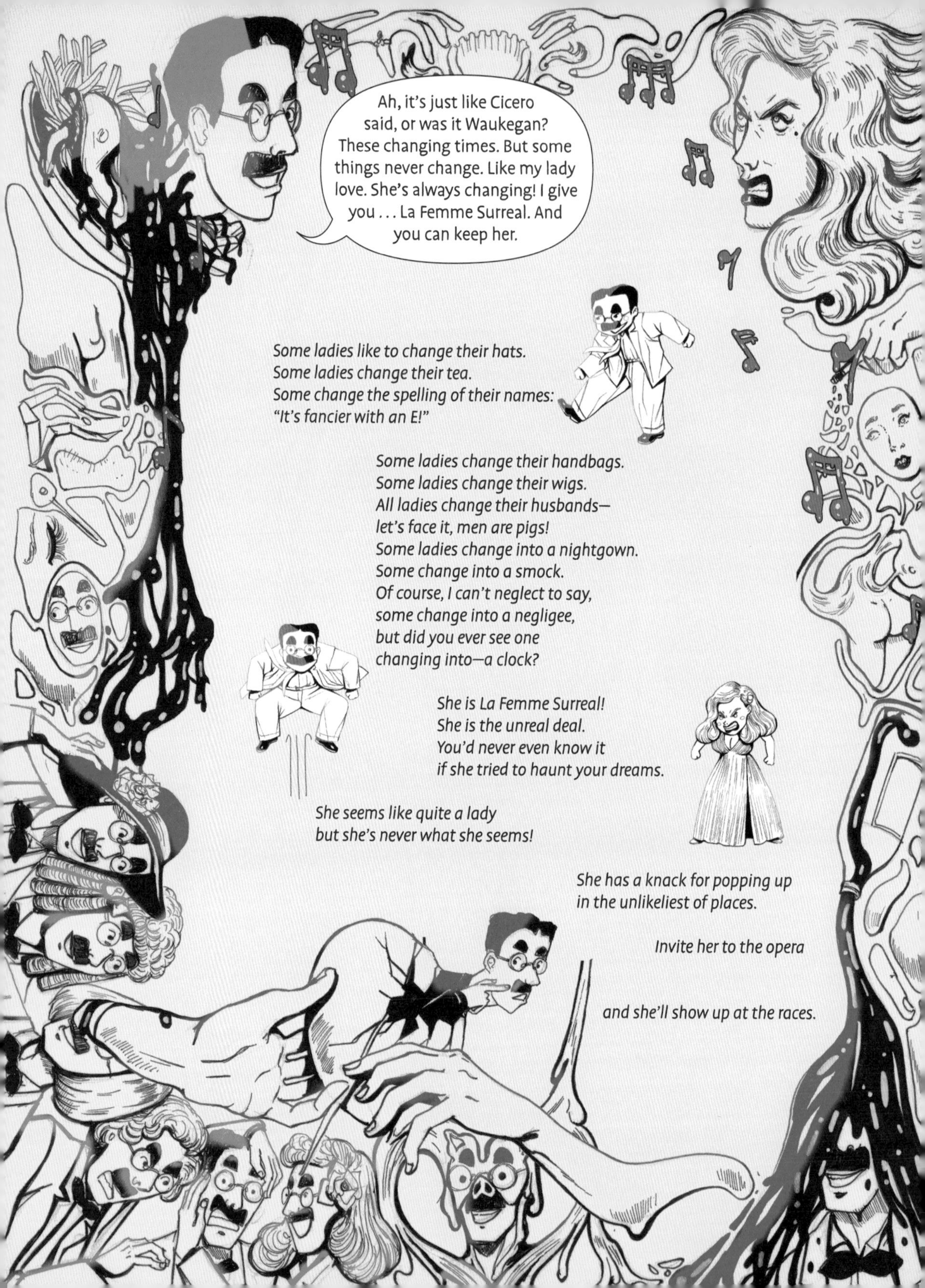
Ah, it's just like Cicero said, or was it Waukegan? These changing times. But some things never change. Like my lady love. She's always changing! I give you . . . La Femme Surreal. And you can keep her.
Some ladies like to change their hats.
Some ladies change their tea.
Some change the spelling of their names:
"It's fancier with an E!"
Some ladies change their handbags.
Some ladies change their wigs.
All ladies change their husbands—
let's face it, men are pigs!
Some ladies change into a nightgown.
Some change into a smock.
Of course, I can't neglect to say,
some change into a negligee,
but did you ever see one
changing into—a clock?
She is La Femme Surreal!
She is the unreal deal.
You'd never even know it
if she tried to haunt your dreams.
She seems like quite a lady
but she's never what she seems!
She has a knack for popping up
in the unlikeliest of places.
Invite her to the opera
and she'll show up at the races.

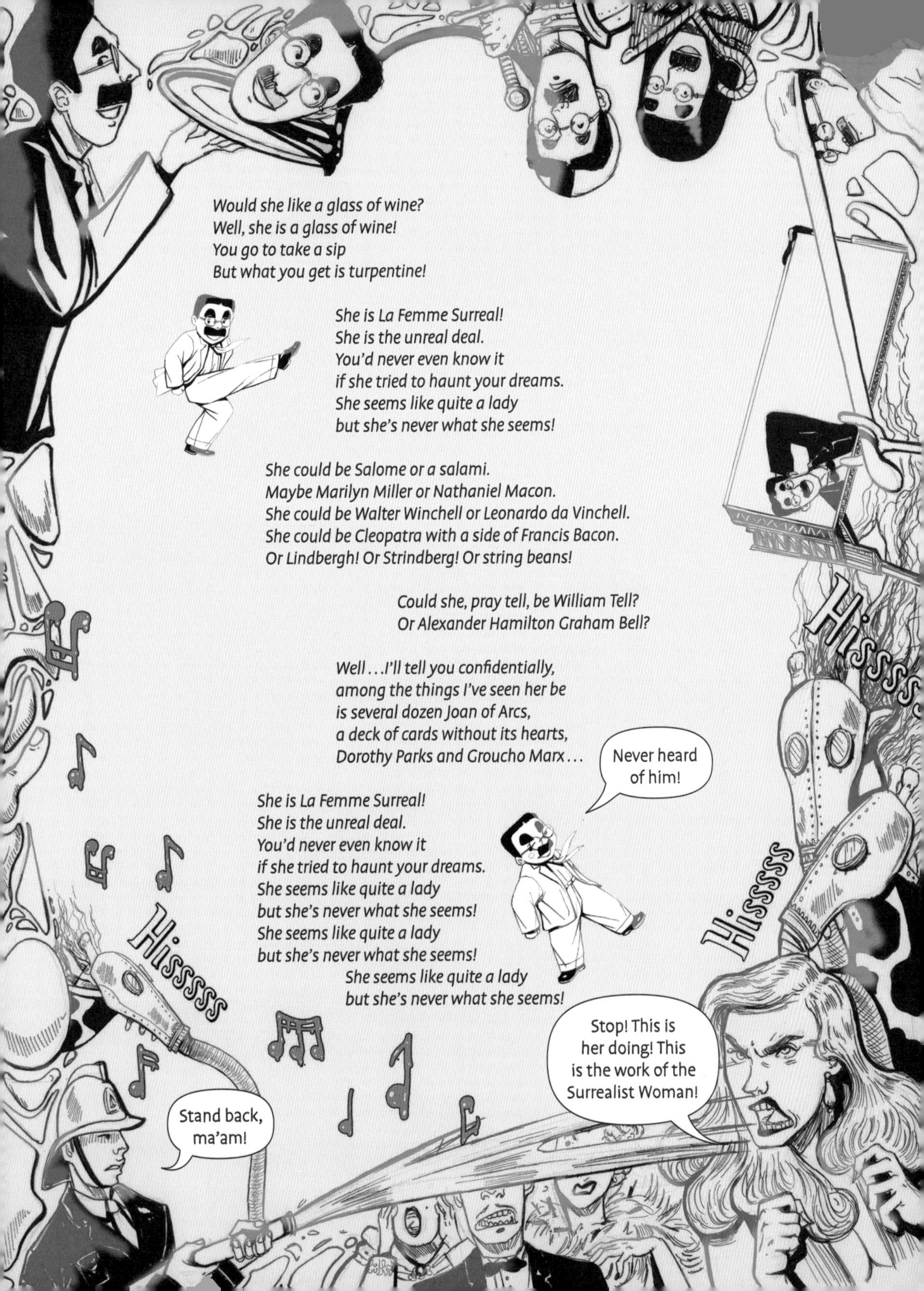
Would she like a glass of wine?
Well, she is a glass of wine!
You go to take a sip
But what you get is turpentine!
She is La Femme Surreal!
She is the unreal deal.
You'd never even know it
if she tried to haunt your dreams.
She seems like quite a lady
but she's never what she seems!
She could be Salome or a salami.
Maybe Marilyn Miller or Nathaniel Macon.
She could be Walter Winchell or Leonardo da Vinchell.
She could be Cleopatra with a side of Francis Bacon.
Or Lindbergh! Or Strindberg! Or string beans!
Could she, pray tell, be William Tell?
Or Alexander Hamilton Graham Bell?
Hisssss
Well . . . I'll tell you confidentially,
among the things I've seen her be
is several dozen Joan of Arcs,
a deck of cards without its hearts,
Dorothy Parks and Groucho Marx . . .
Never heard of him!
She is La Femme Surreal!
She is the unreal deal.
You'd never even know it
if she tried to haunt your dreams.
She seems like quite a lady
but she's never what she seems!
She seems like quite a lady
but she's never what she seems!
She seems like quite a lady
but she's never what she seems!
Hissssss
Hisssss
Stop! This is her doing! This is the work of the Surrealist Woman!
Stand back, ma'am!

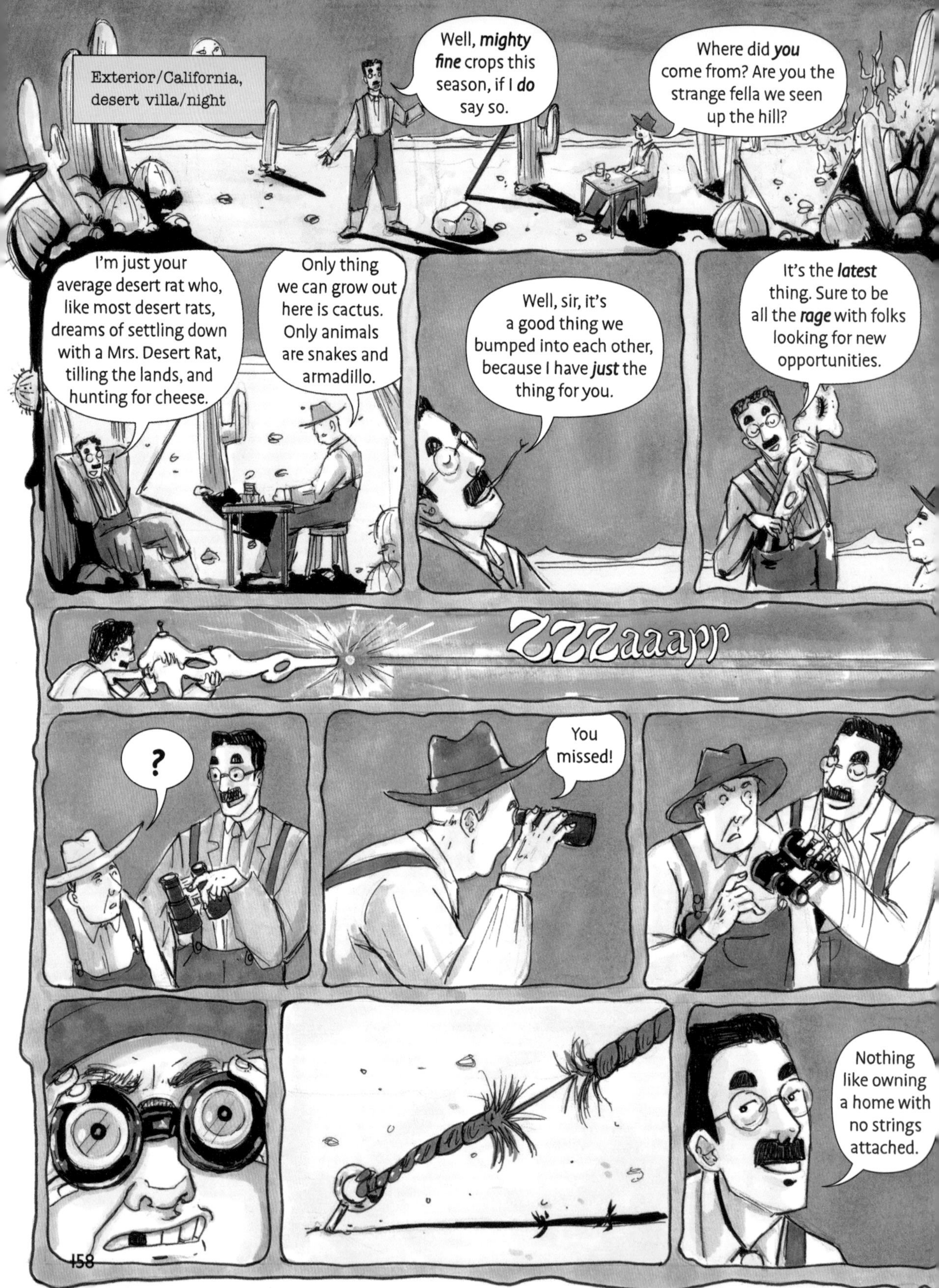

Exterior/California, desert villa/night
Well, ***mighty fine*** crops this season, if I ***do*** say so.
Where did ***you*** come from? Are you the strange fella we seen up the hill?
I'm just your average desert rat who, like most desert rats, dreams of settling down with a Mrs. Desert Rat, tilling the lands, and hunting for cheese.
Only thing we can grow out here is cactus. Only animals are snakes and armadillo.
Well, sir, it's a good thing we bumped into each other, because I have ***just*** the thing for you.
It's the ***latest*** thing. Sure to be all the ***rage*** with folks looking for new opportunities.
ZZZaaapp
?
You missed!
Nothing like owning a home with no strings attached.

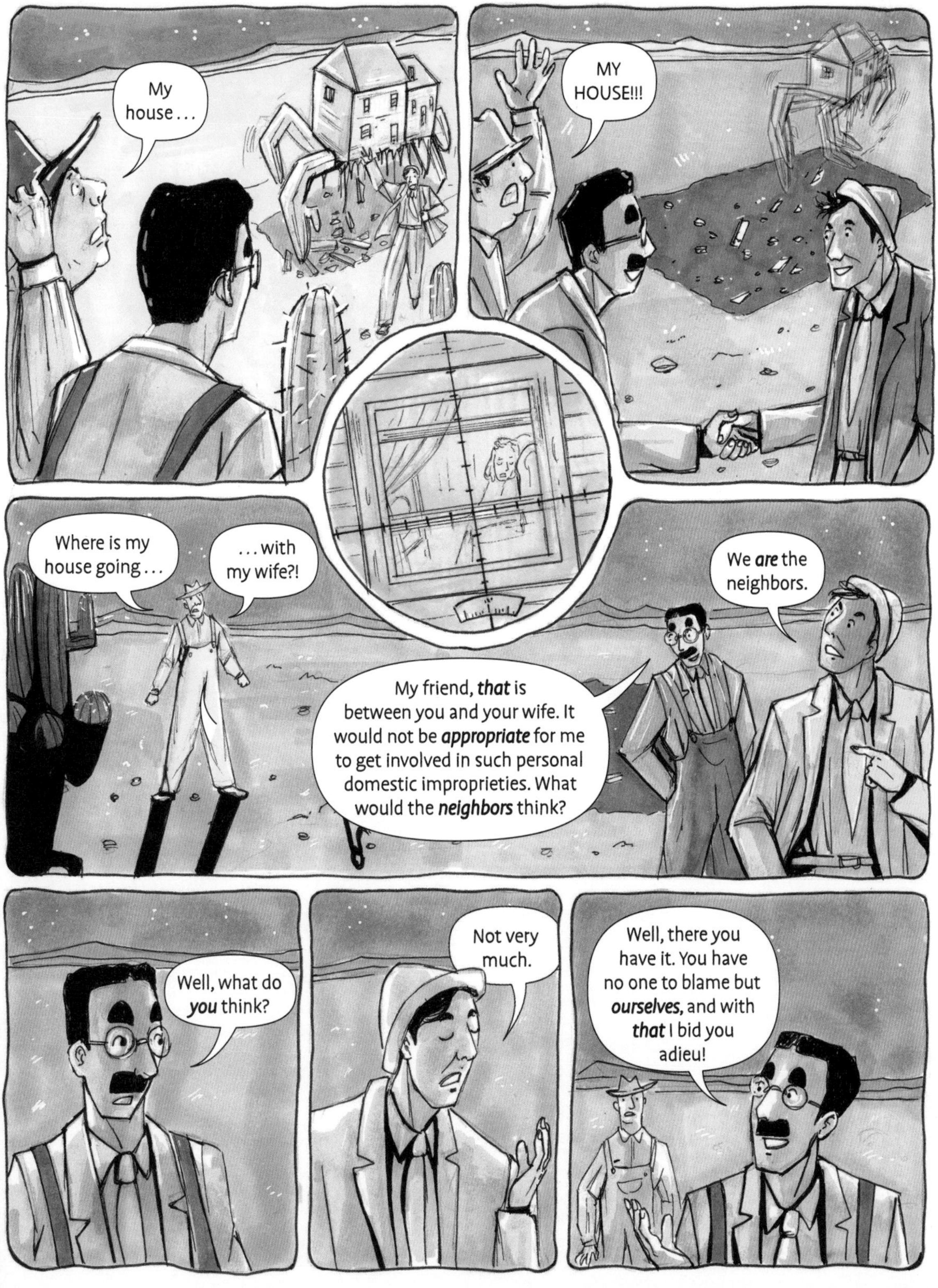
My house...
MY HOUSE!!!
Where is my house going...
...with my wife?!
We *are* the neighbors.
My friend, *that* is between you and your wife. It would not be *appropriate* for me to get involved in such personal domestic improprieties. What would the *neighbors* think?
Well, what do *you* think?
Not very much.
Well, there you have it. You have no one to blame but *ourselves,* and with *that* I bid you adieu!

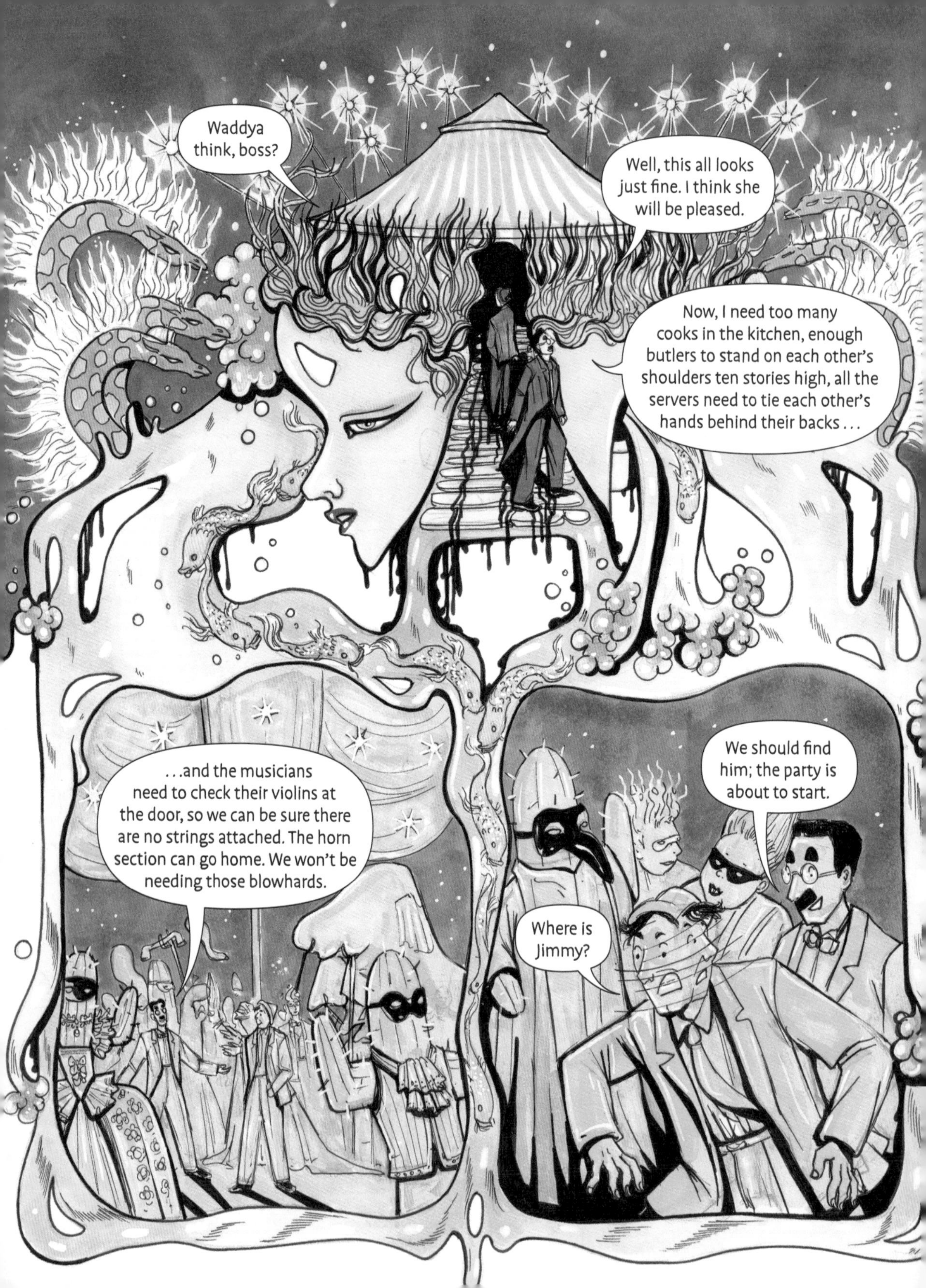
Waddya think, boss?
Well, this all looks just fine. I think she will be pleased.
Now, I need too many cooks in the kitchen, enough butlers to stand on each other's shoulders ten stories high, all the servers need to tie each other's hands behind their backs . . .
. . .and the musicians need to check their violins at the door, so we can be sure there are no strings attached. The horn section can go home. We won't be needing those blowhards.
We should find him; the party is about to start.
Where is Jimmy?

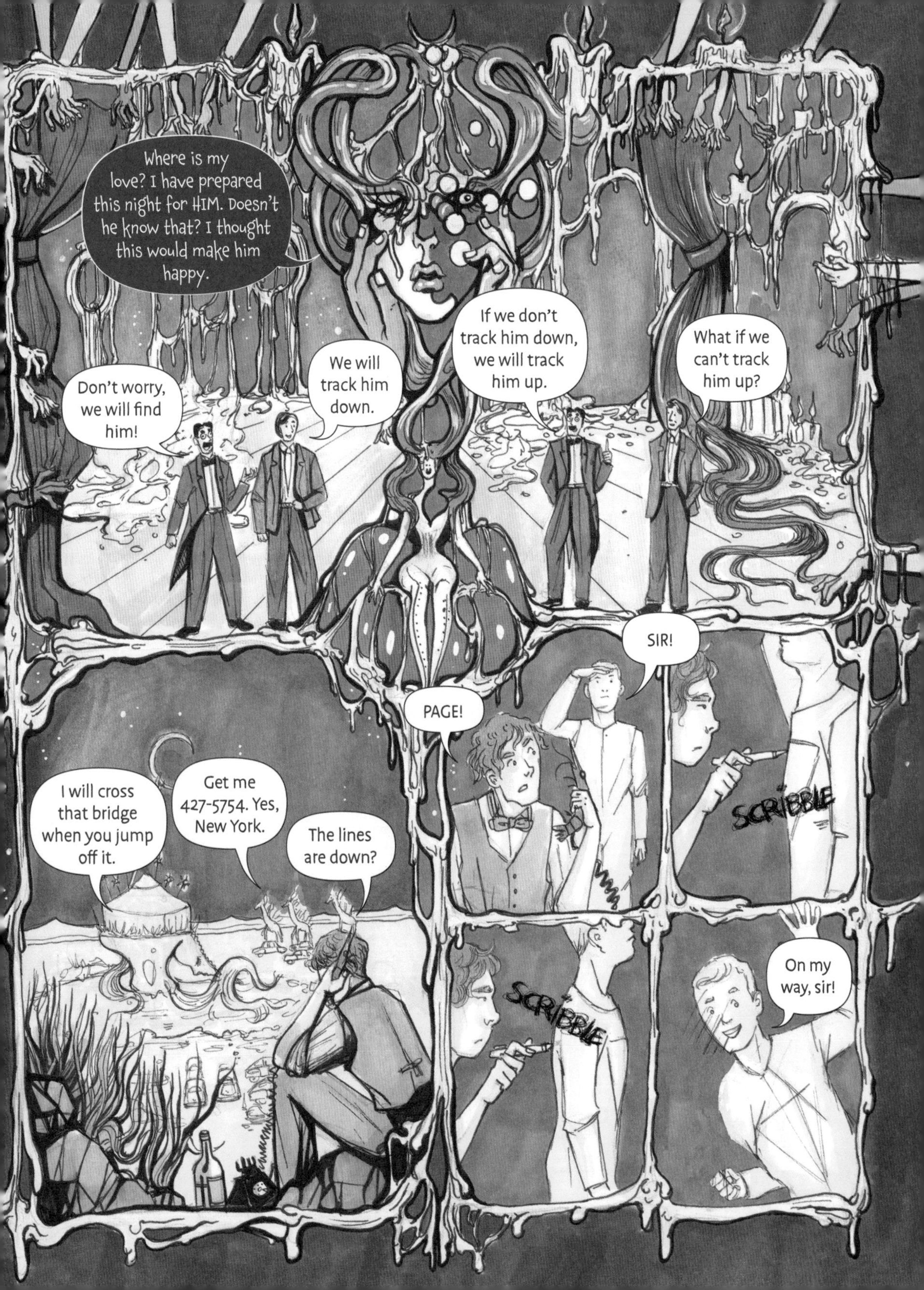
Where is my love? I have prepared this night for HIM. Doesn't he know that? I thought this would make him happy.
Don't worry, we will find him!
We will track him down.
If we don't track him down, we will track him up.
What if we can't track him up?
I will cross that bridge when you jump off it.
Get me 427-5754. Yes, New York.
The lines are down?
PAGE!
SIR!
SCRIBBLE
SCRIBBLE
On my way, sir!

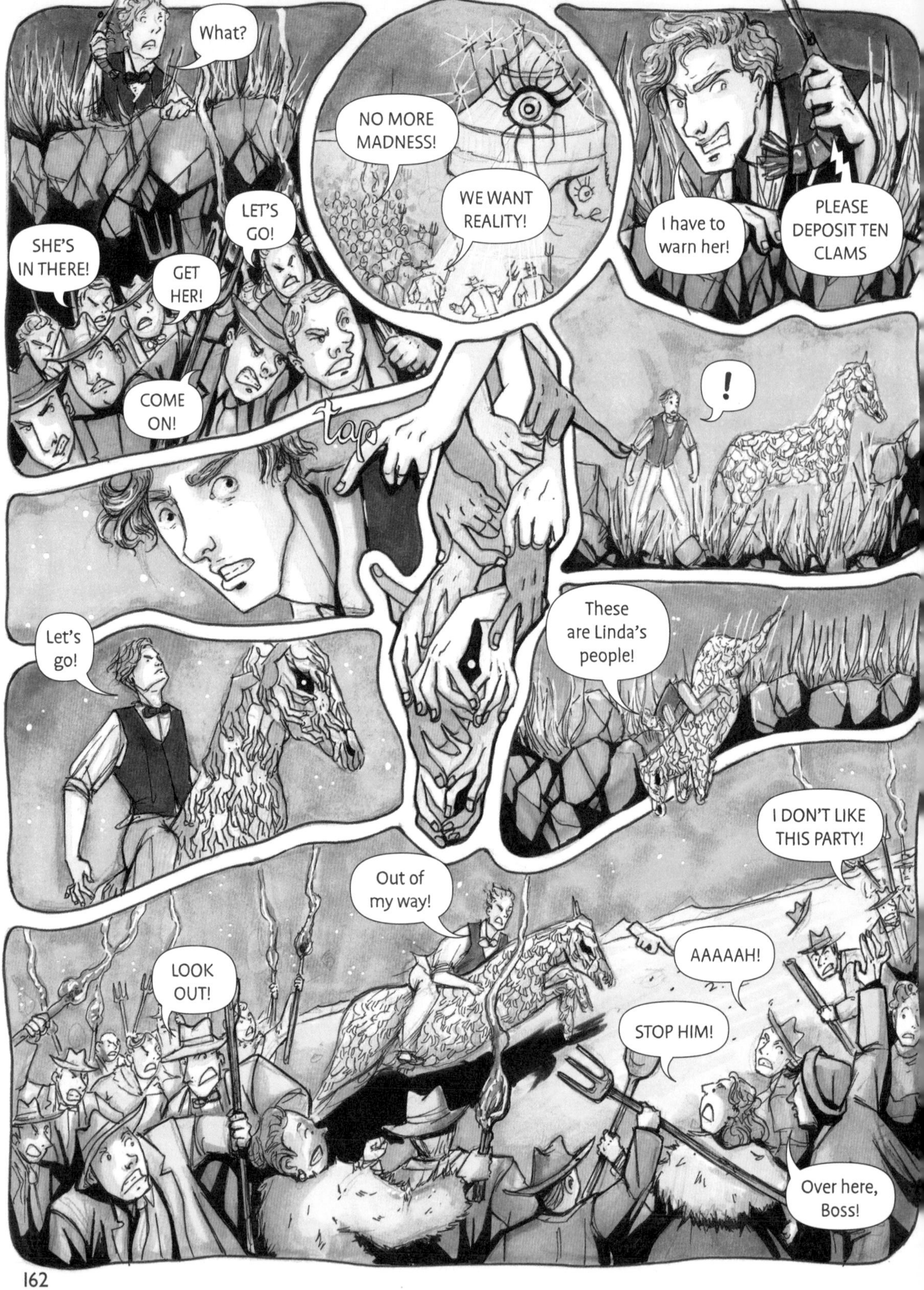
What?
NO MORE MADNESS!
WE WANT REALITY!
I have to warn her!
PLEASE DEPOSIT TEN CLAMS
LET'S GO!
SHE'S IN THERE!
GET HER!
COME ON!
tap
!
Let's go!
These are Linda's people!
I DON'T LIKE THIS PARTY!
Out of my way!
LOOK OUT!
AAAAAH!
STOP HIM!
Over here, Boss!

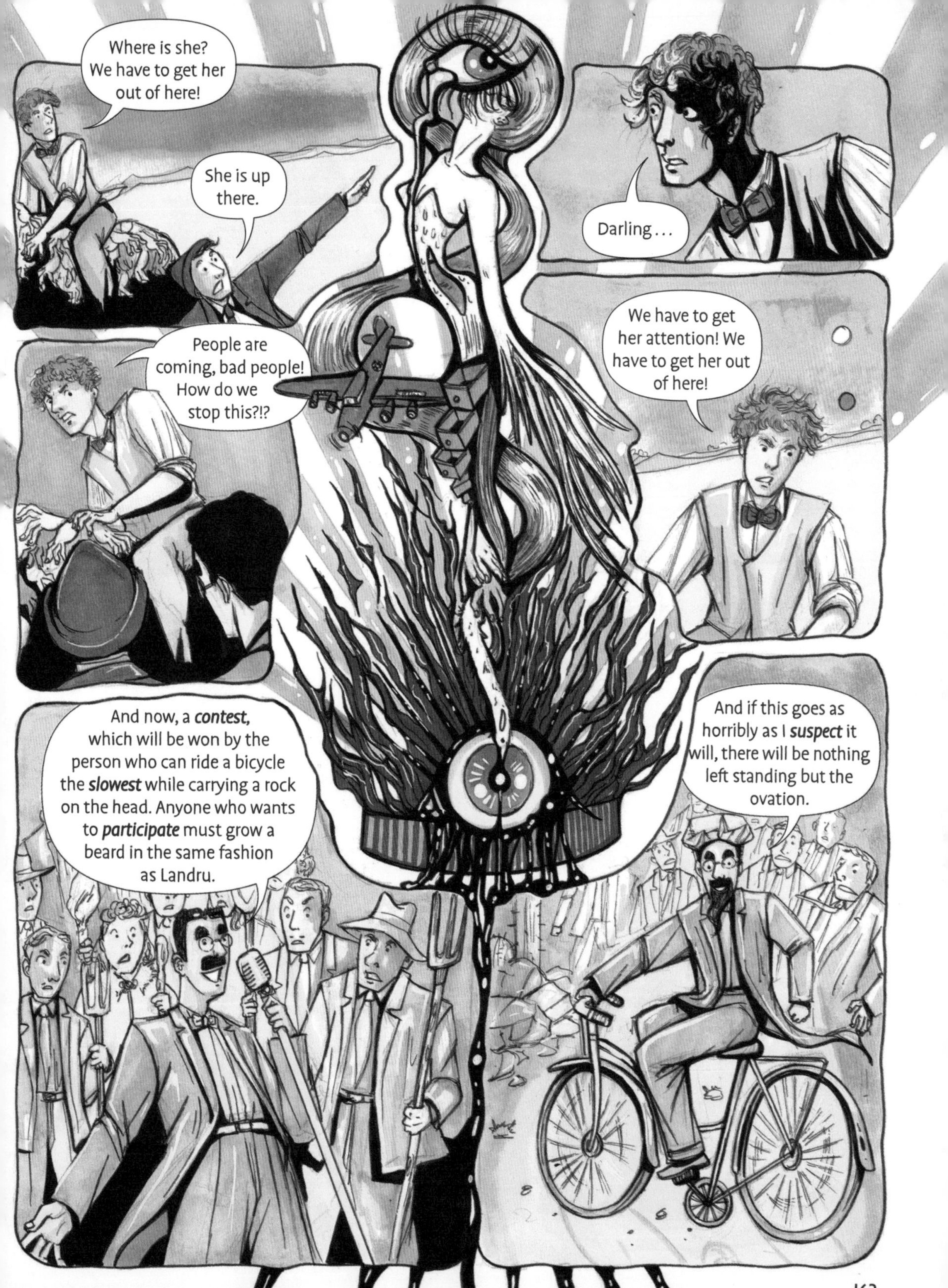
Where is she? We have to get her out of here!
She is up there.
Darling . . .
People are coming, bad people! How do we stop this?!?
We have to get her attention! We have to get her out of here!
And now, a ***contest,*** which will be won by the person who can ride a bicycle the ***slowest*** while carrying a rock on the head. Anyone who wants to ***participate*** must grow a beard in the same fashion as Landru.
And if this goes as horribly as I ***suspect*** it will, there will be nothing left standing but the ovation.

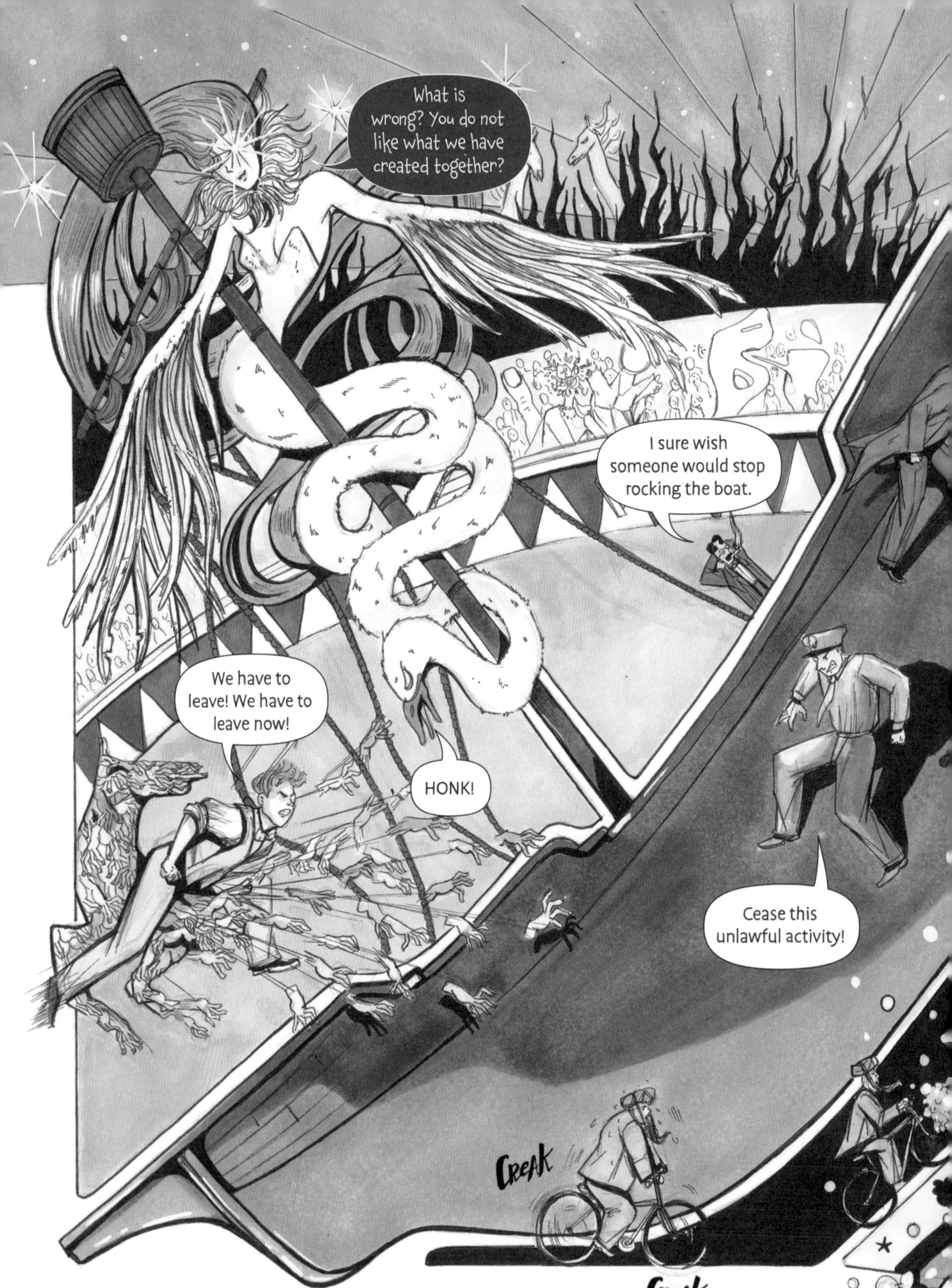
What is wrong? You do not like what we have created together?
I sure wish someone would stop rocking the boat.
We have to leave! We have to leave now!
HONK!
Cease this unlawful activity!
CREAK
CREAK

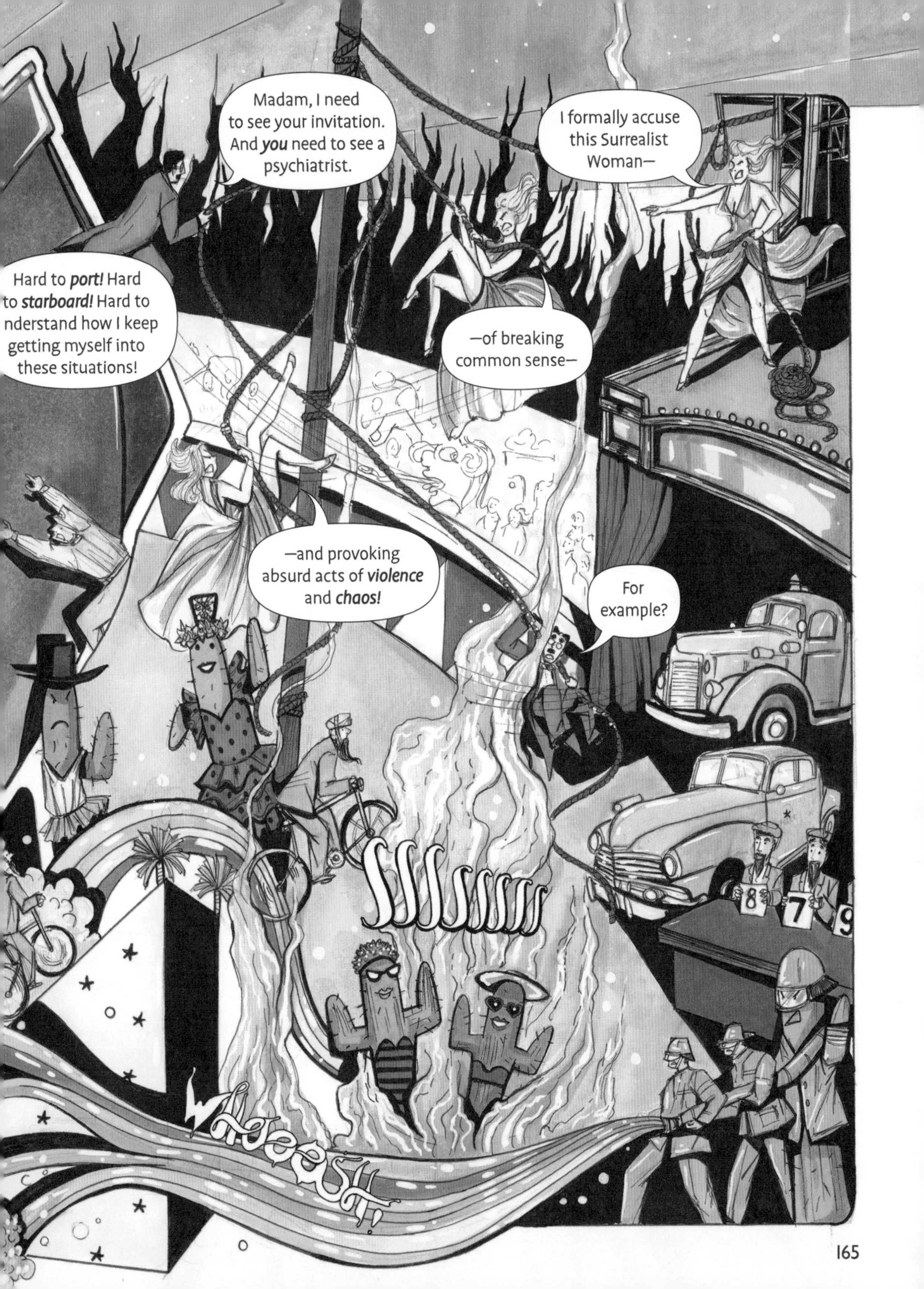
Madam, I need to see your invitation. And *you* need to see a psychiatrist.
I formally accuse this Surrealist Woman—
Hard to *port!* Hard to *starboard!* Hard to nderstand how I keep getting myself into these situations!
—of breaking common sense—
—and provoking absurd acts of *violence* and *chaos!*
For example?
SSSSSSSS
8
7
9
WHOOOSH!

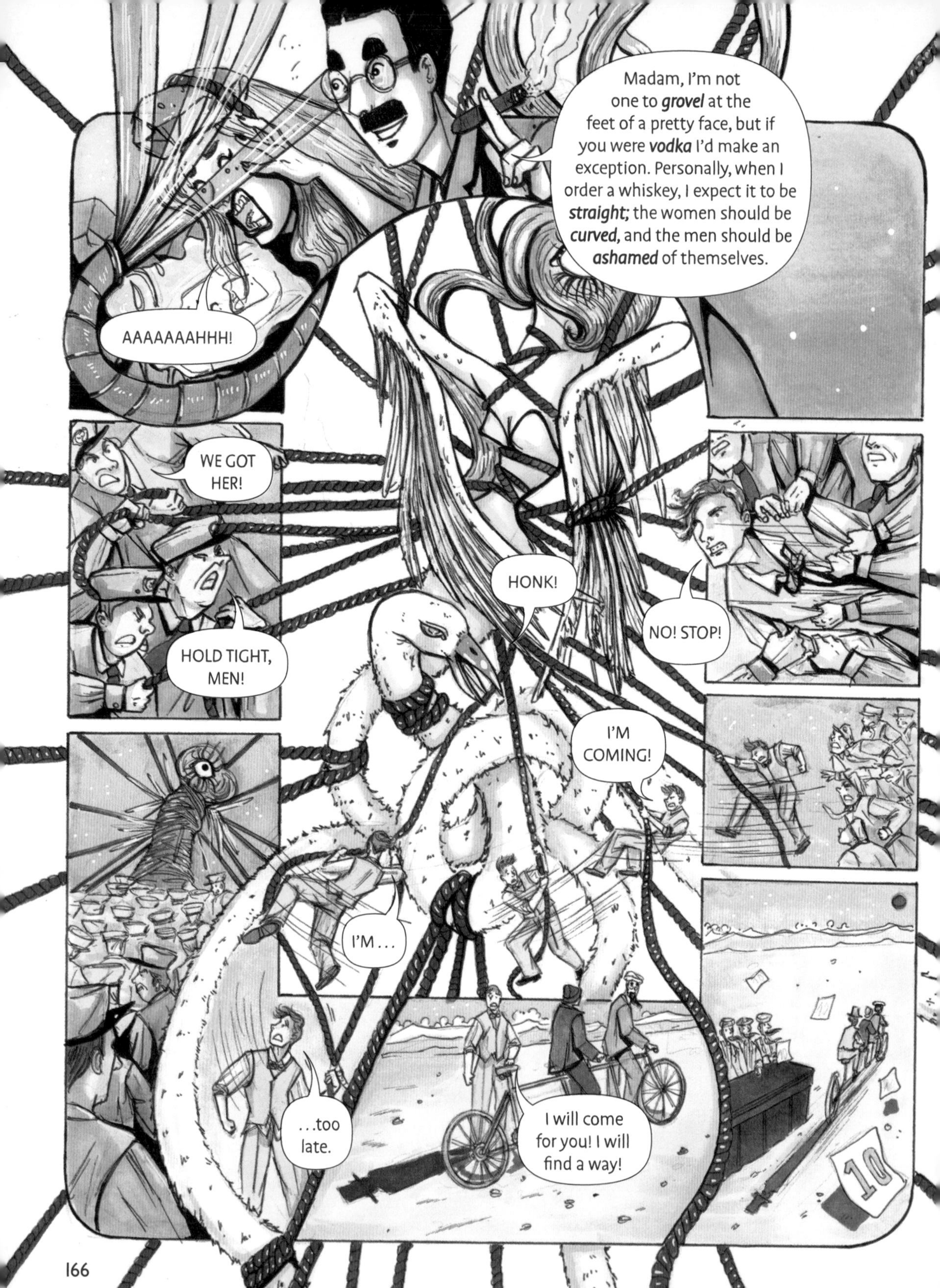
Madam, I'm not one to *grovel* at the feet of a pretty face, but if you were *vodka* I'd make an exception. Personally, when I order a whiskey, I expect it to be *straight;* the women should be *curved,* and the men should be *ashamed* of themselves.
AAAAAAAHHH!
WE GOT HER!
HOLD TIGHT, MEN!
HONK!
NO! STOP!
I'M COMING!
I'M . . .
. . .too late.
I will come for you! I will find a way!
10

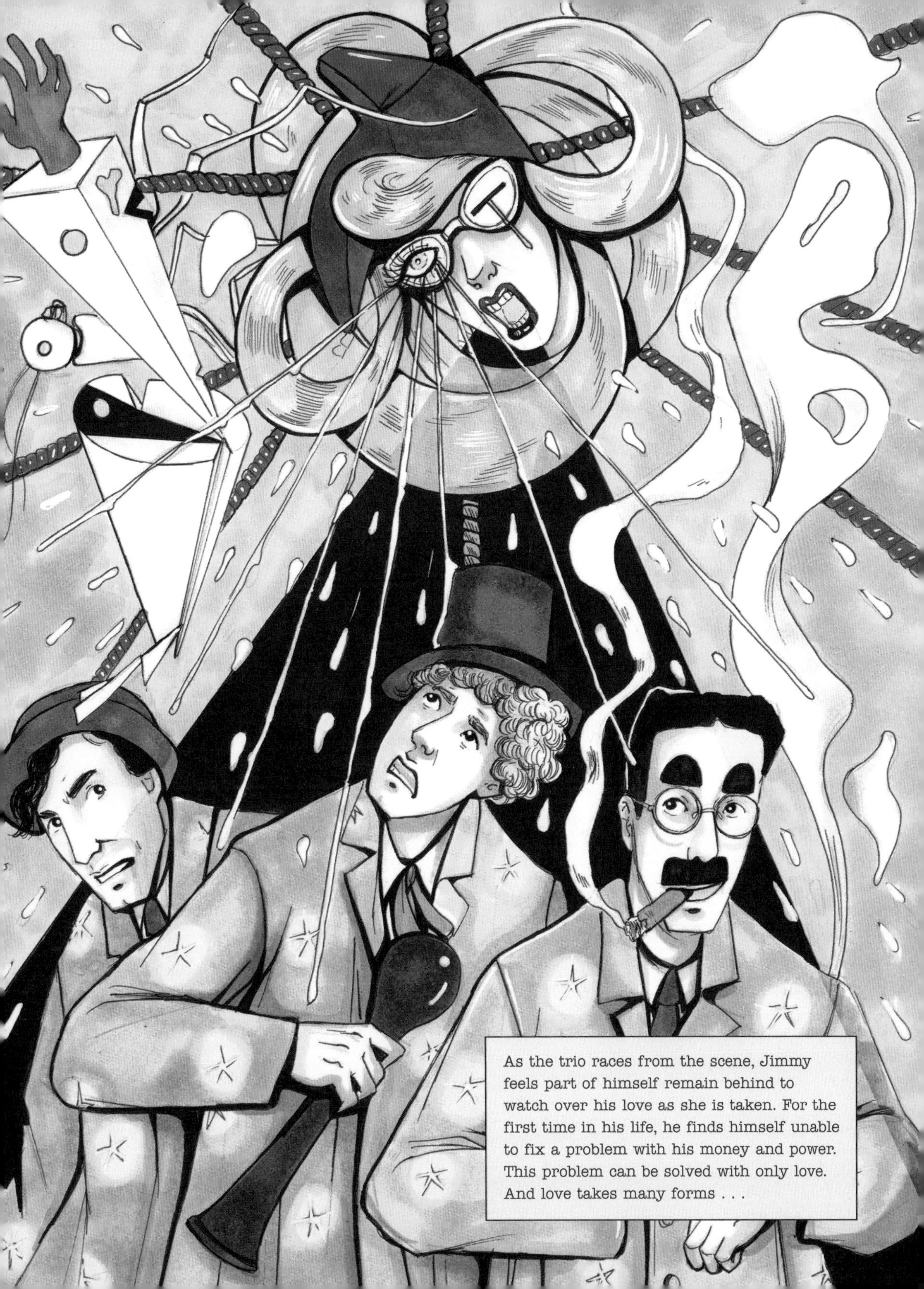
As the trio races from the scene, Jimmy feels part of himself remain behind to watch over his love as she is taken. For the first time in his life, he finds himself unable to fix a problem with his money and power. This problem can be solved with only love. And love takes many forms . . .

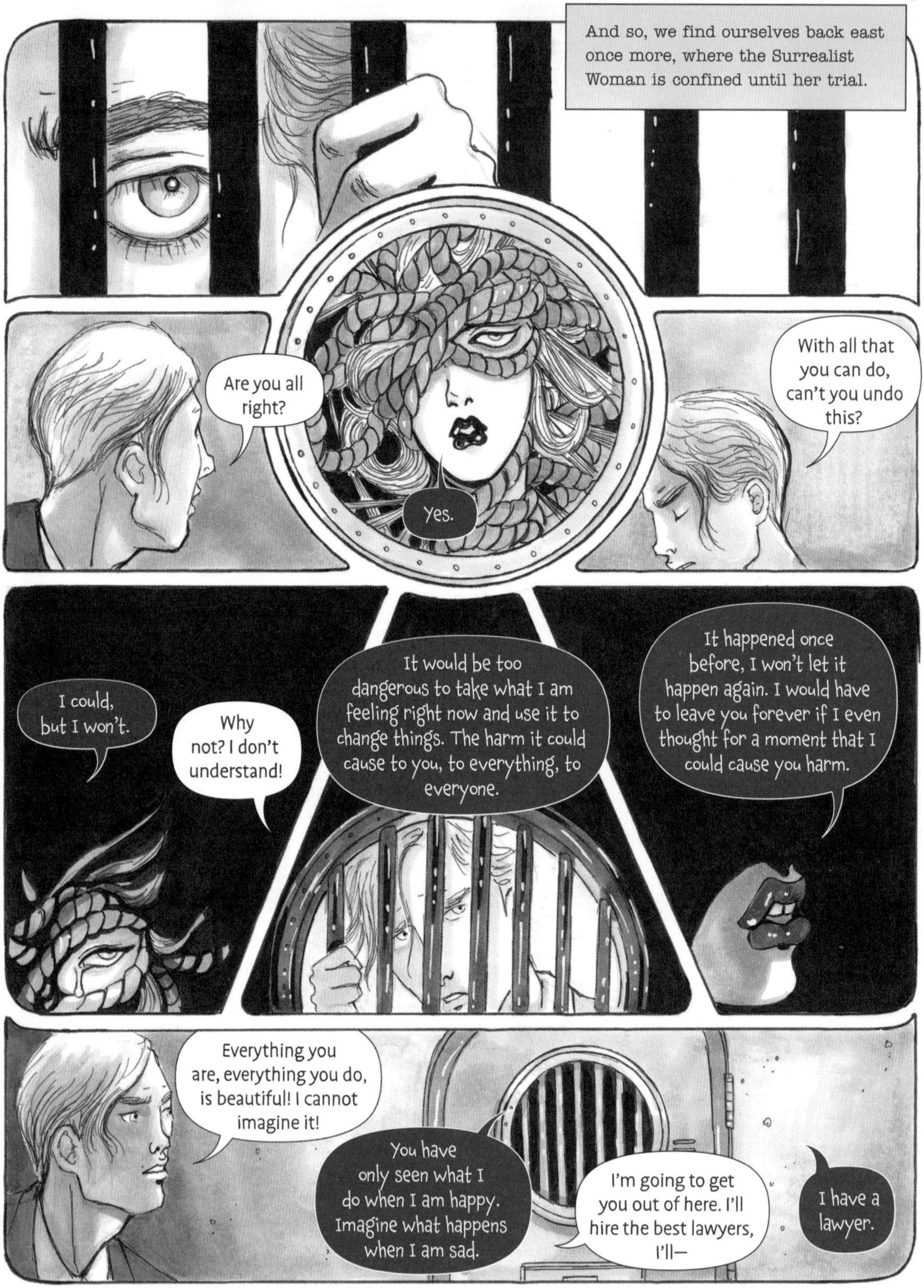

And so, we find ourselves back east once more, where the Surrealist Woman is confined until her trial.
Are you all right?
Yes.
With all that you can do, can't you undo this?
I could, but I won't.
Why not? I don't understand!
It would be too dangerous to take what I am feeling right now and use it to change things. The harm it could cause to you, to everything, to everyone.
It happened once before, I won't let it happen again. I would have to leave you forever if I even thought for a moment that I could cause you harm.
Everything you are, everything you do, is beautiful! I cannot imagine it!
You have only seen what I do when I am happy. Imagine what happens when I am sad.
I'm going to get you out of here. I'll hire the best lawyers, I'll—
I have a lawyer.

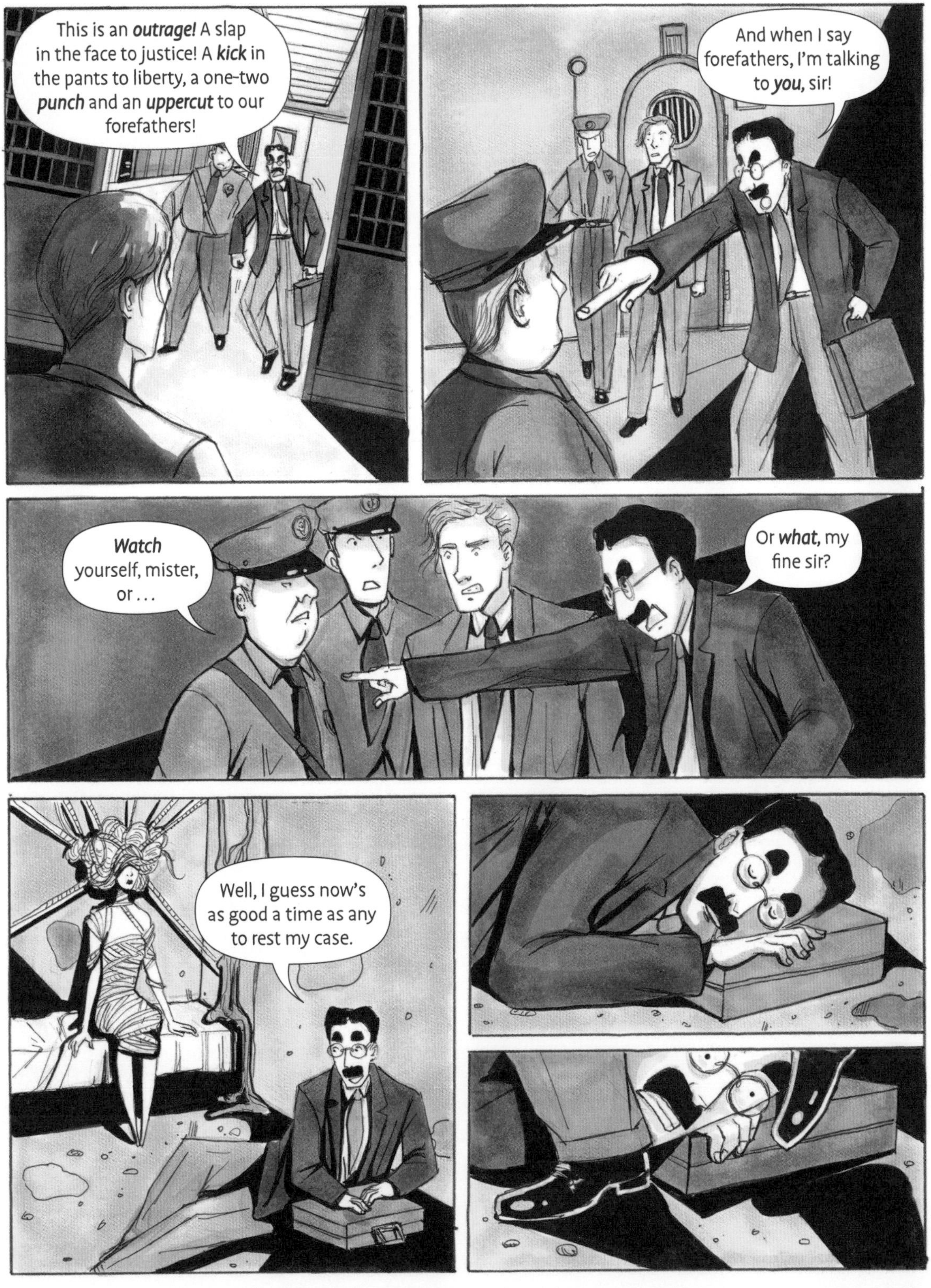
This is an *outrage!* A slap in the face to justice! A *kick* in the pants to liberty, a one-two *punch* and an *uppercut* to our forefathers!
And when I say forefathers, I'm talking to *you,* sir!
Watch yourself, mister, or . . .
Or *what,* my fine sir?
Well, I guess now's as good a time as any to rest my case.

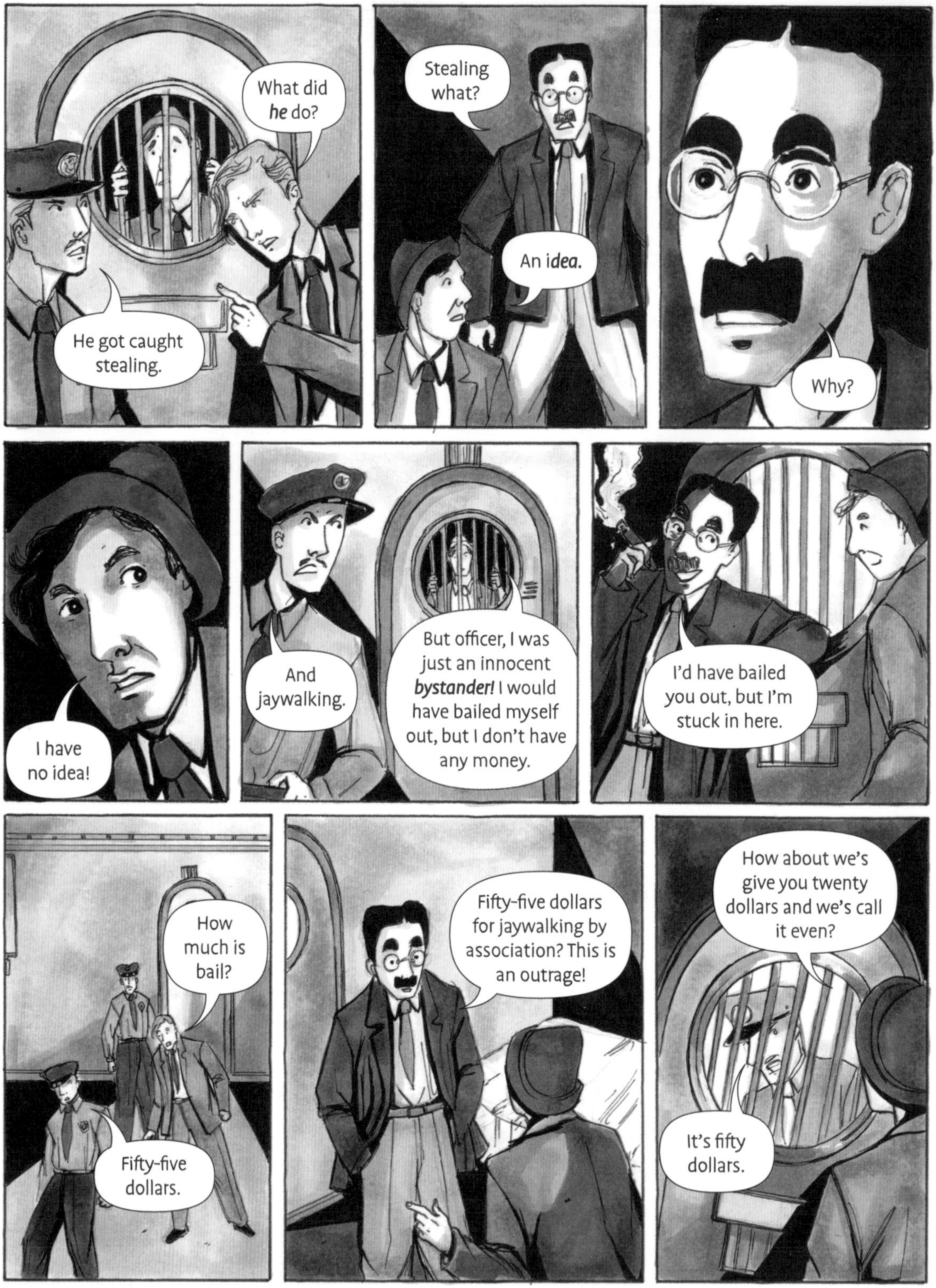
What did *he* do?
He got caught stealing.
Stealing what?
An *idea.*
Why?
I have no idea!
And jaywalking.
But officer, I was just an innocent ***bystander!*** I would have bailed myself out, but I don't have any money.
I'd have bailed you out, but I'm stuck in here.
How much is bail?
Fifty-five dollars.
Fifty-five dollars for jaywalking by association? This is an outrage!
How about we's give you twenty dollars and we's call it even?
It's fifty dollars.

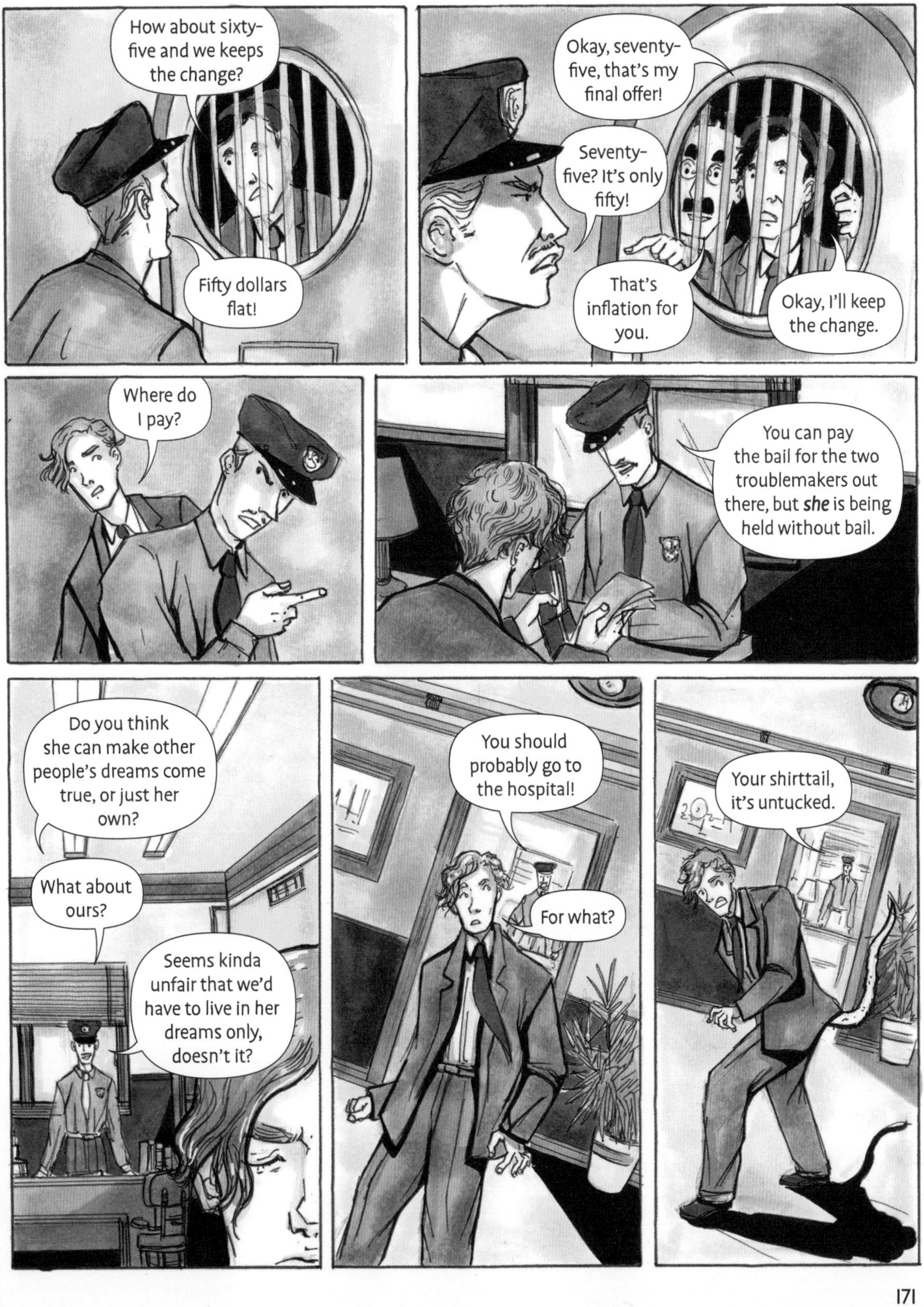
How about sixty-five and we keeps the change?
Fifty dollars flat!
Okay, seventy-five, that's my final offer!
Seventy-five? It's only fifty!
That's inflation for you.
Okay, I'll keep the change.
Where do I pay?
You can pay the bail for the two troublemakers out there, but *she* is being held without bail.
Do you think she can make other people's dreams come true, or just her own?
What about ours?
Seems kinda unfair that we'd have to live in her dreams only, doesn't it?
You should probably go to the hospital!
For what?
Your shirttail, it's untucked.

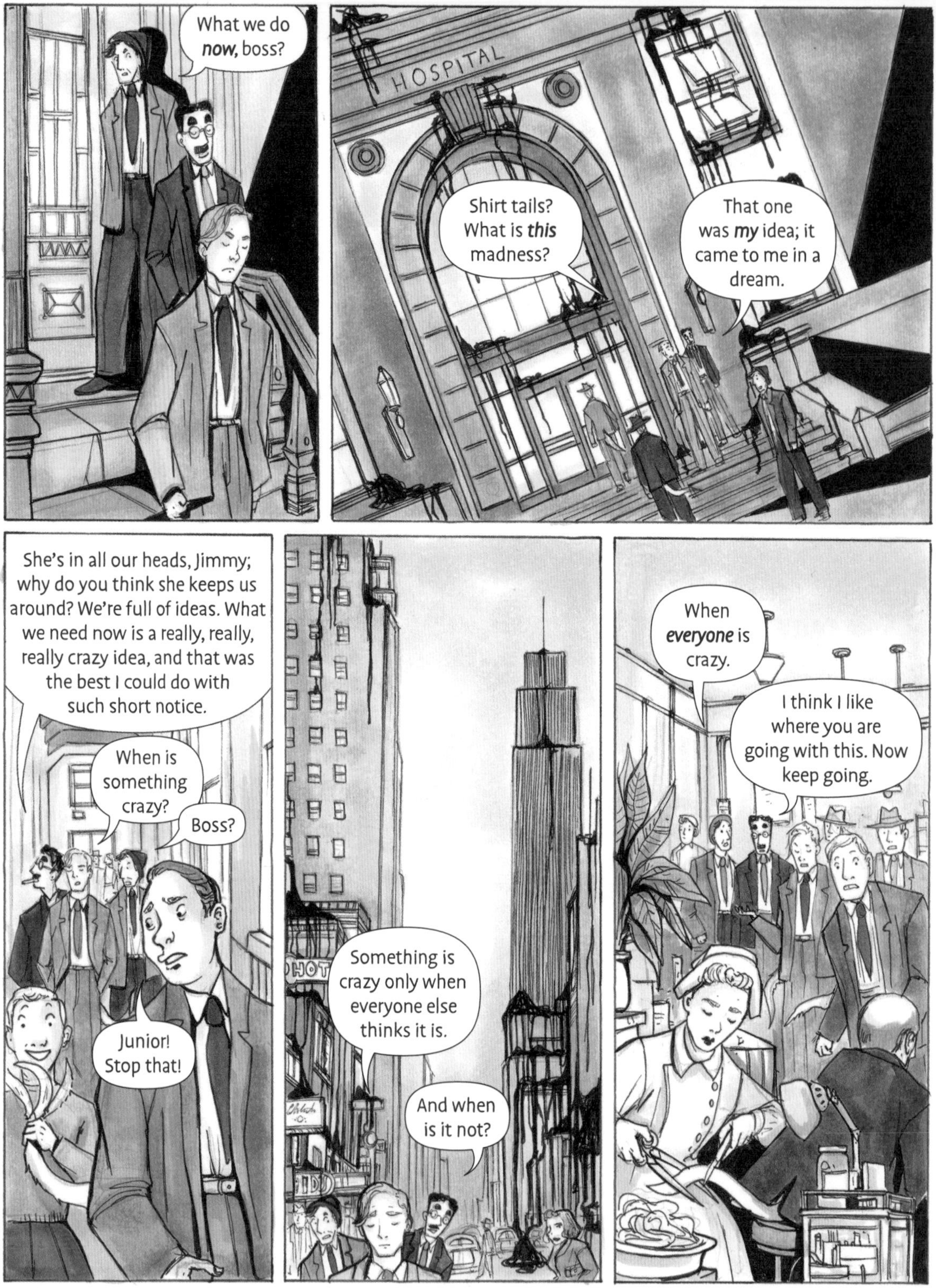
What we do *now,* boss?
HOSPITAL
Shirt tails? What is *this* madness?
That one was *my* idea; it came to me in a dream.
She's in all our heads, Jimmy; why do you think she keeps us around? We're full of ideas. What we need now is a really, really, really crazy idea, and that was the best I could do with such short notice.
When is something crazy?
Boss?
Junior! Stop that!
Something is crazy only when everyone else thinks it is.
And when is it not?
When *everyone* is crazy.
I think I like where you are going with this. Now keep going.

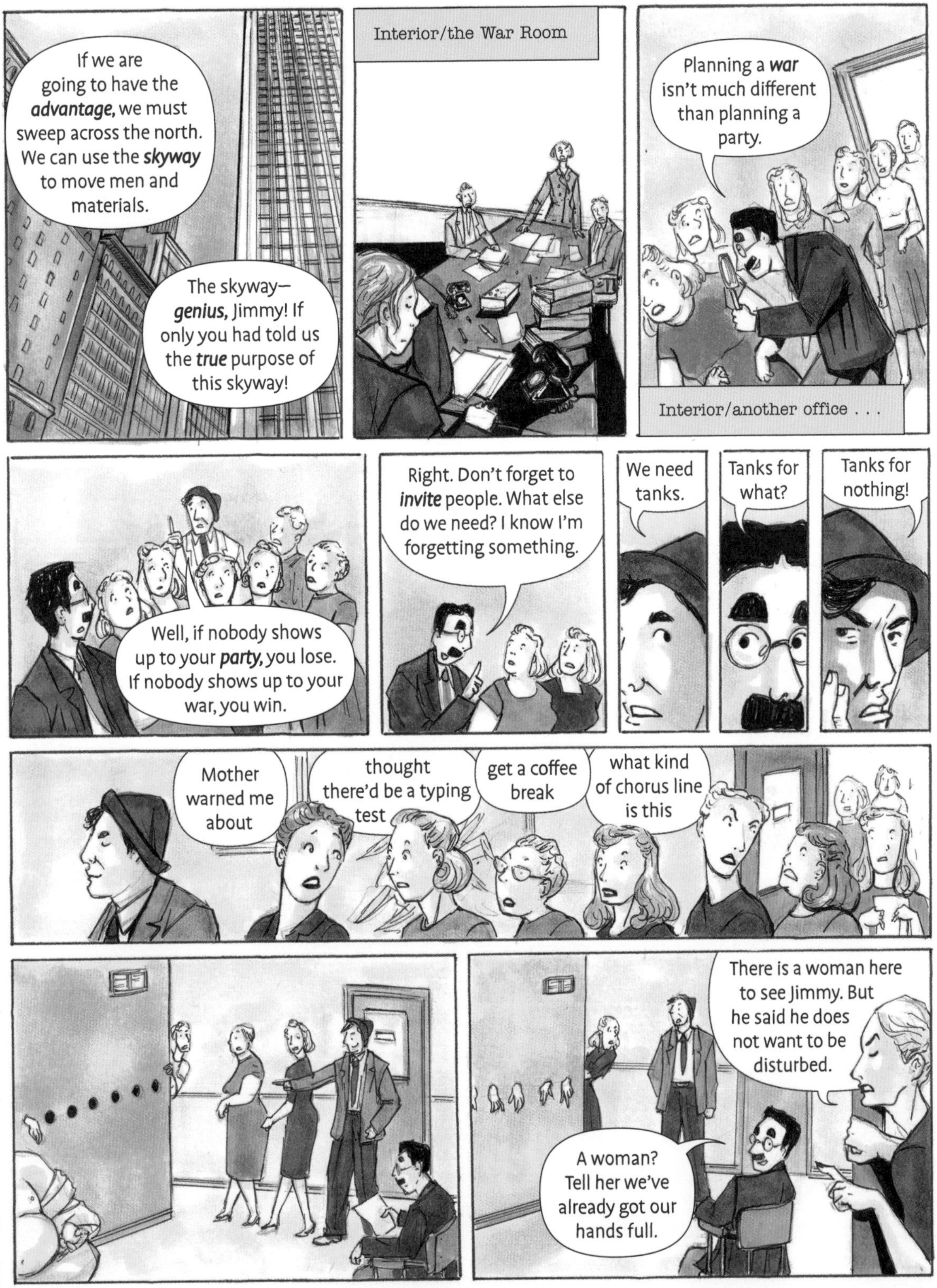
If we are going to have the advantage, we must sweep across the north. We can use the skyway to move men and materials.
The skyway—genius, Jimmy! If only you had told us the true purpose of this skyway!
Interior/the War Room
Planning a war isn't much different than planning a party.
Interior/another office . . .
Well, if nobody shows up to your party, you lose. If nobody shows up to your war, you win.
Right. Don't forget to invite people. What else do we need? I know I'm forgetting something.
We need tanks.
Tanks for what?
Tanks for nothing!
Mother warned me about
thought there'd be a typing test
get a coffee break
what kind of chorus line is this
There is a woman here to see Jimmy. But he said he does not want to be disturbed.
A woman? Tell her we've already got our hands full.

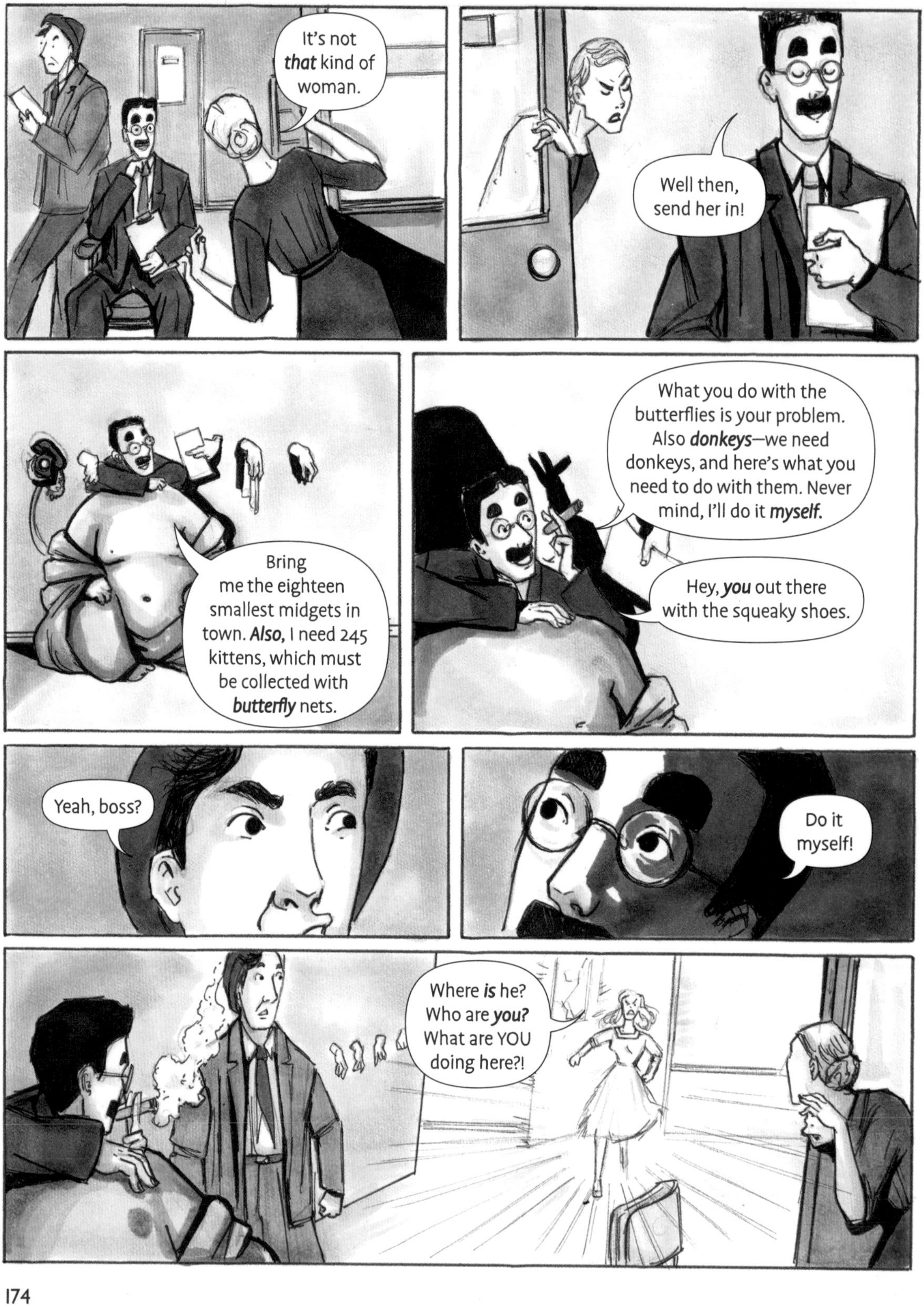
It's not *that* kind of woman.
Well then, send her in!
Bring me the eighteen smallest midgets in town. *Also,* I need 245 kittens, which must be collected with *butterfly* nets.
What you do with the butterflies is your problem. Also *donkeys*—we need donkeys, and here's what you need to do with them. Never mind, I'll do it *myself.*
Hey, *you* out there with the squeaky shoes.
Yeah, boss?
Do it myself!
Where *is* he? Who are *you?* What are YOU doing here?!

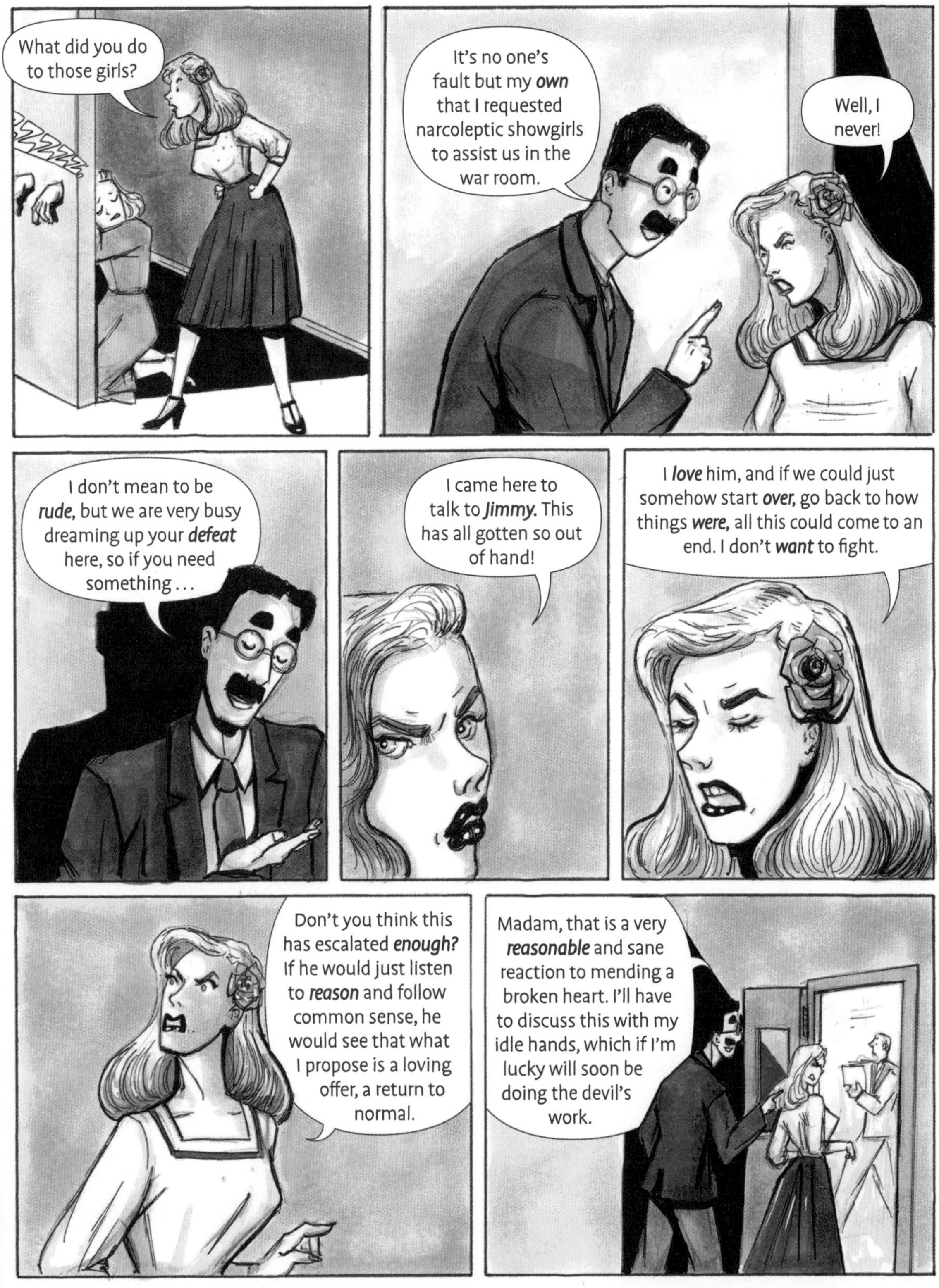
What did you do to those girls?
ZZZZZ
It's no one's fault but my *own* that I requested narcoleptic showgirls to assist us in the war room.
Well, I never!
I don't mean to be *rude*, but we are very busy dreaming up your *defeat* here, so if you need something . . .
I came here to talk to *Jimmy*. This has all gotten so out of hand!
I *love* him, and if we could just somehow start *over*, go back to how things *were*, all this could come to an end. I don't *want* to fight.
Don't you think this has escalated *enough?* If he would just listen to *reason* and follow common sense, he would see that what I propose is a loving offer, a return to normal.
Madam, that is a very *reasonable* and sane reaction to mending a broken heart. I'll have to discuss this with my idle hands, which if I'm lucky will soon be doing the devil's work.

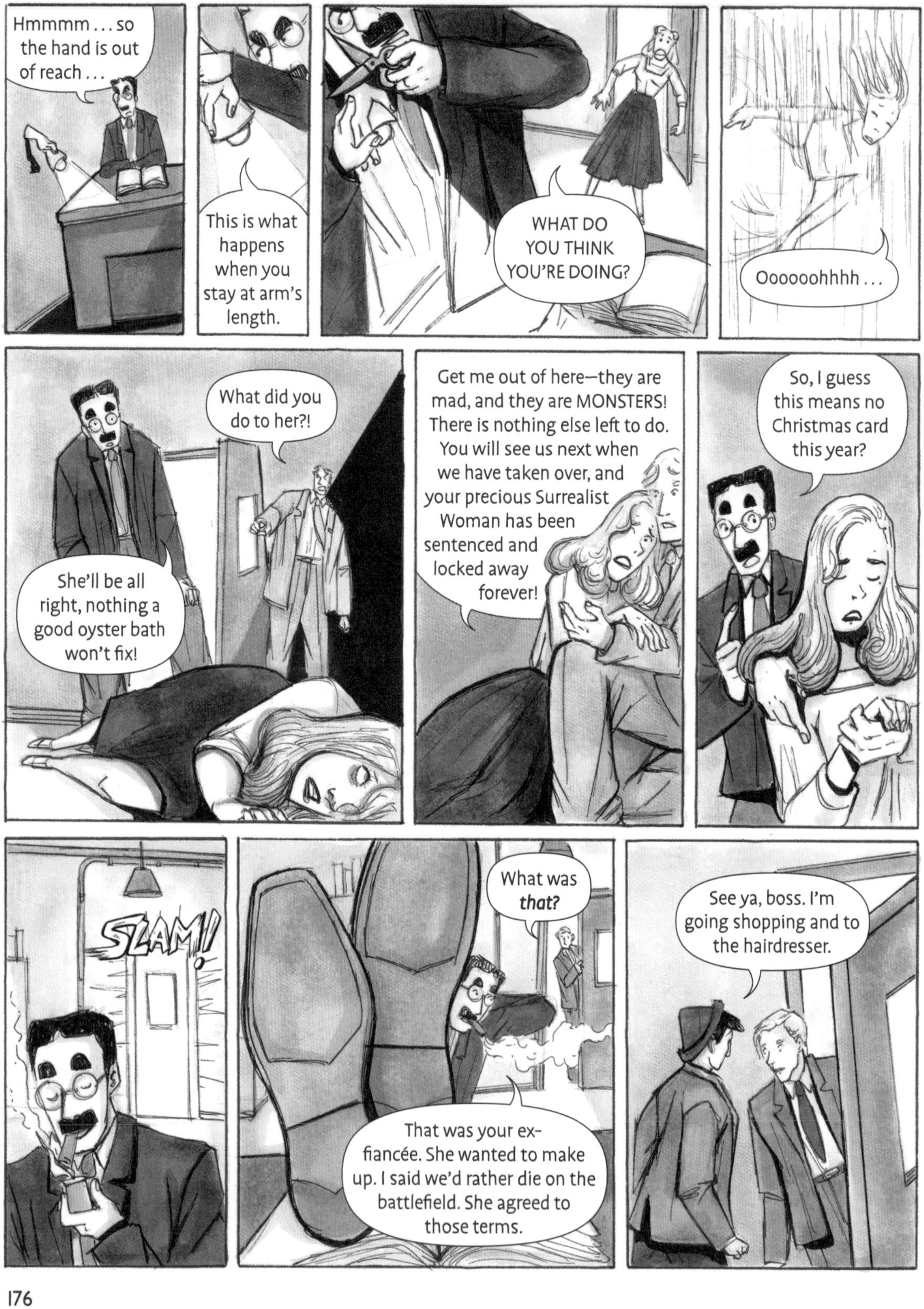

Hmmmm . . . so the hand is out of reach . . .
This is what happens when you stay at arm's length.
WHAT DO YOU THINK YOU'RE DOING?
Oooooohhhh . . .
What did you do to her?!
She'll be all right, nothing a good oyster bath won't fix!
Get me out of here—they are mad, and they are MONSTERS! There is nothing else left to do. You will see us next when we have taken over, and your precious Surrealist Woman has been sentenced and locked away forever!
So, I guess this means no Christmas card this year?
SLAM!
What was *that?*
That was your ex-fiancée. She wanted to make up. I said we'd rather die on the battlefield. She agreed to those terms.
See ya, boss. I'm going shopping and to the hairdresser.

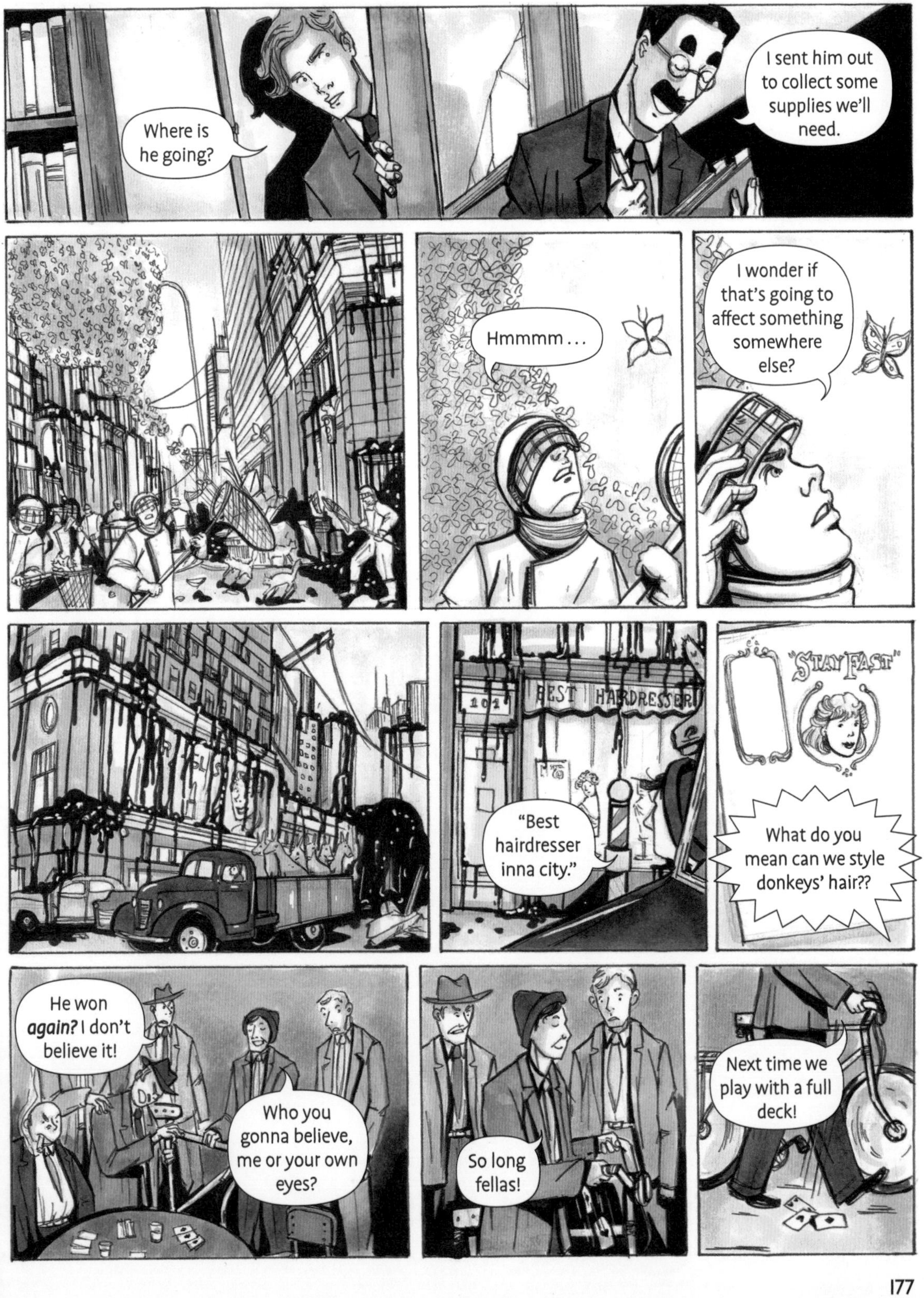
Where is he going?
I sent him out to collect some supplies we'll need.
Hmmmm . . .
I wonder if that's going to affect something somewhere else?
BEST HAIRDRESSER
101
"Best hairdresser inna city."
"STAY FAST"
What do you mean can we style donkeys' hair??
He won *again?* I don't believe it!
Who you gonna believe, me or your own eyes?
So long fellas!
Next time we play with a full deck!

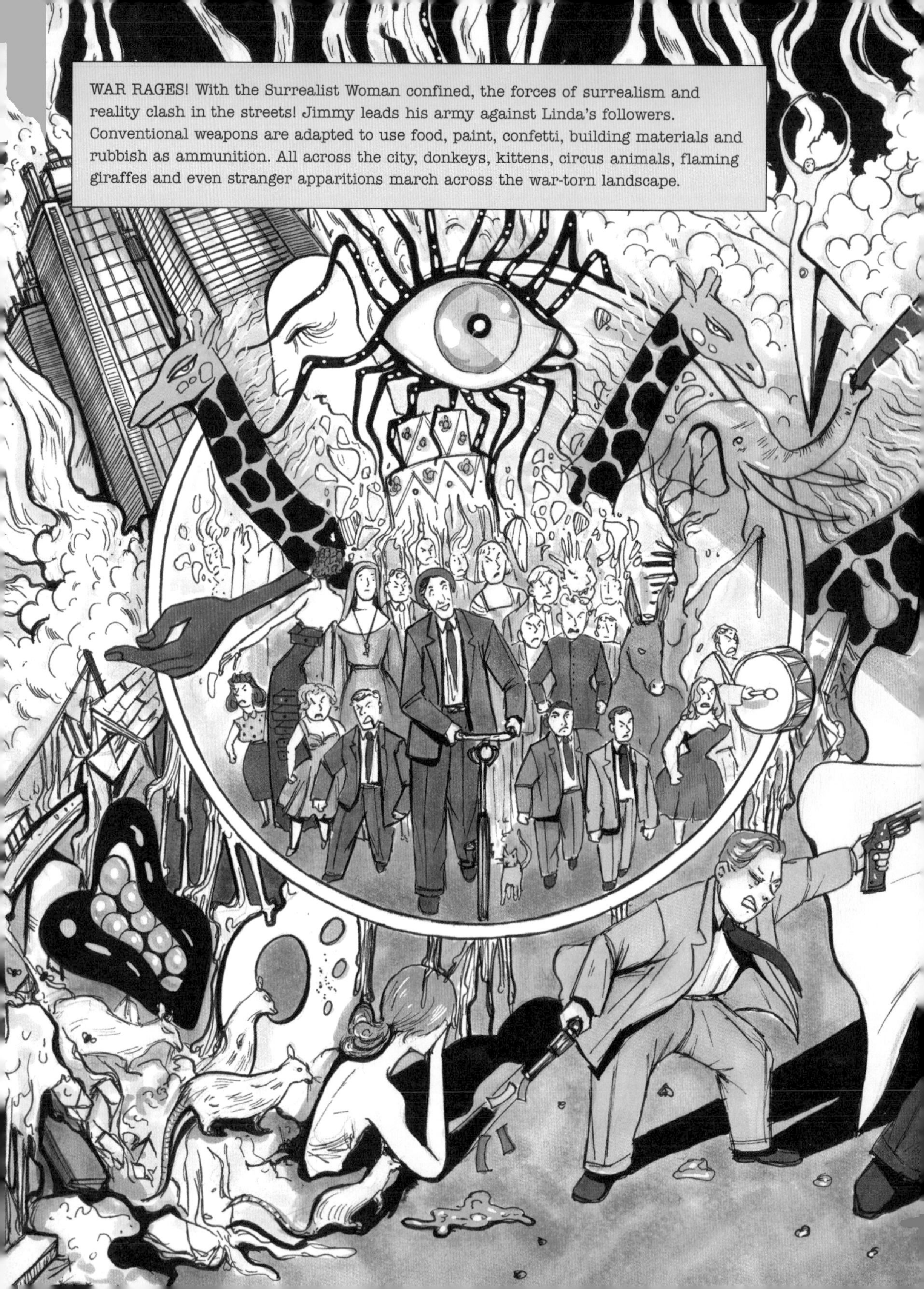
WAR RAGES! With the Surrealist Woman confined, the forces of surrealism and reality clash in the streets! Jimmy leads his army against Linda's followers. Conventional weapons are adapted to use food, paint, confetti, building materials and rubbish as ammunition. All across the city, donkeys, kittens, circus animals, flaming giraffes and even stranger apparitions march across the war-torn landscape.

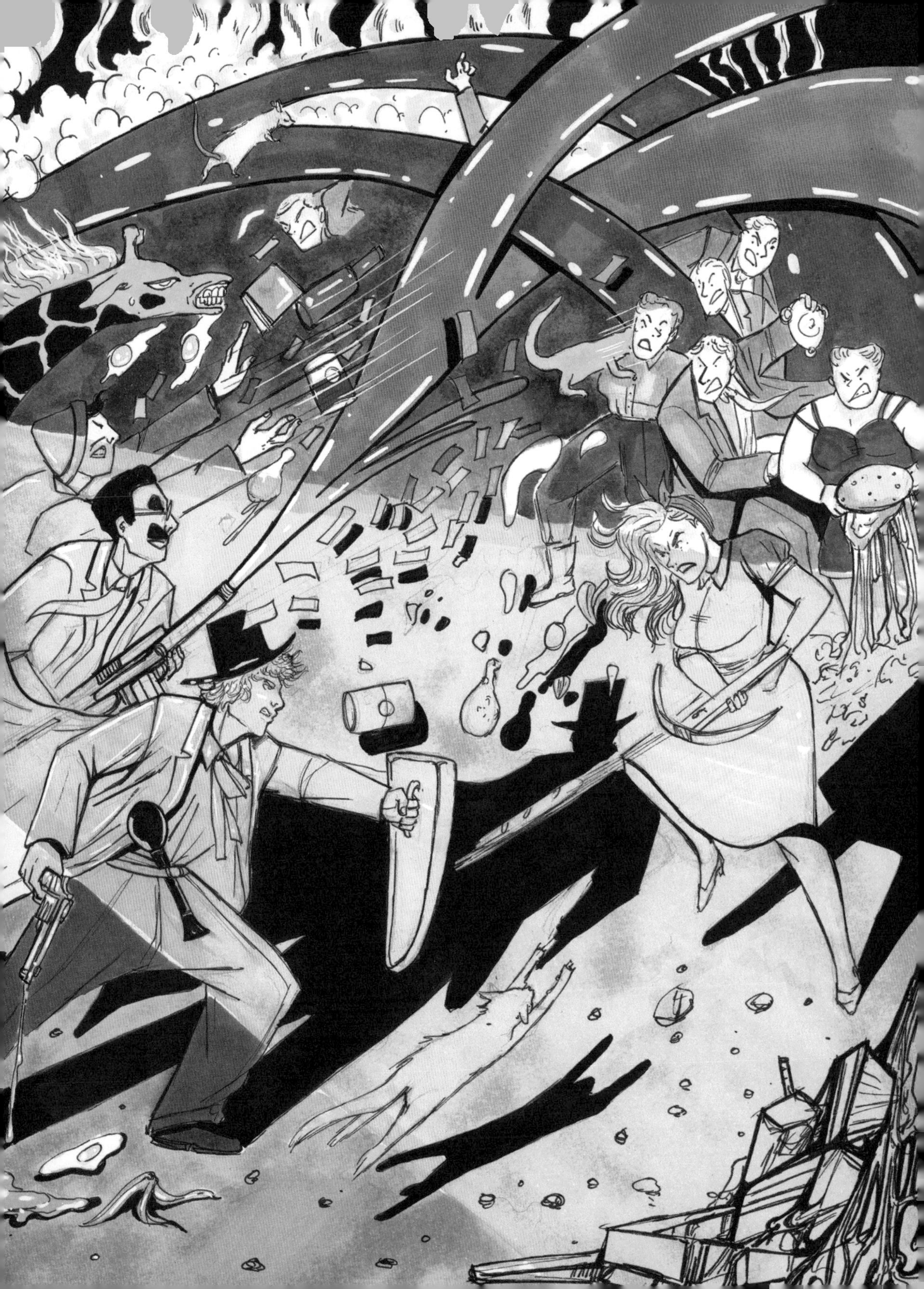

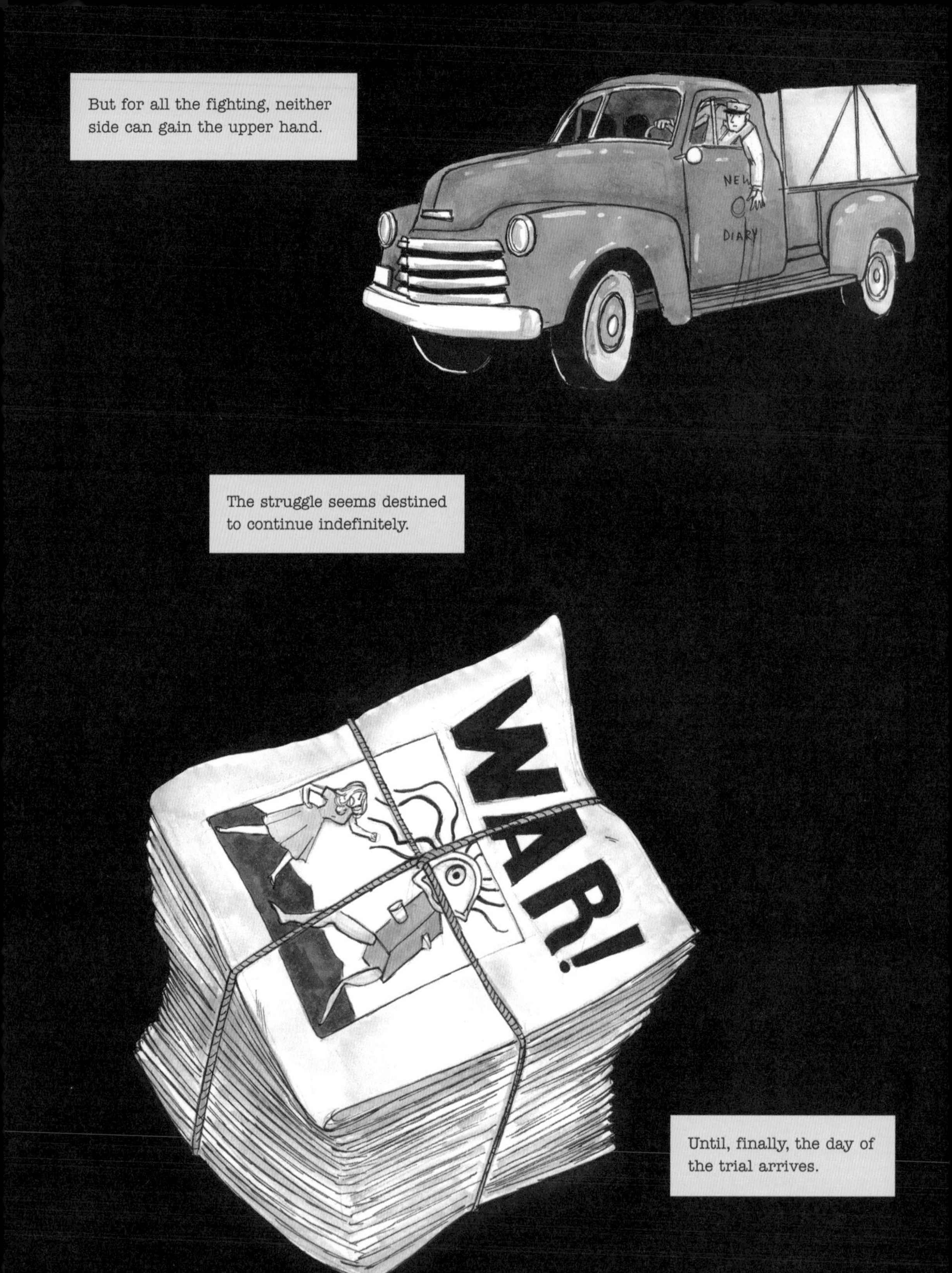
But for all the fighting, neither side can gain the upper hand.
NEW
DIARY
The struggle seems destined to continue indefinitely.
WAR!
Until, finally, the day of the trial arrives.

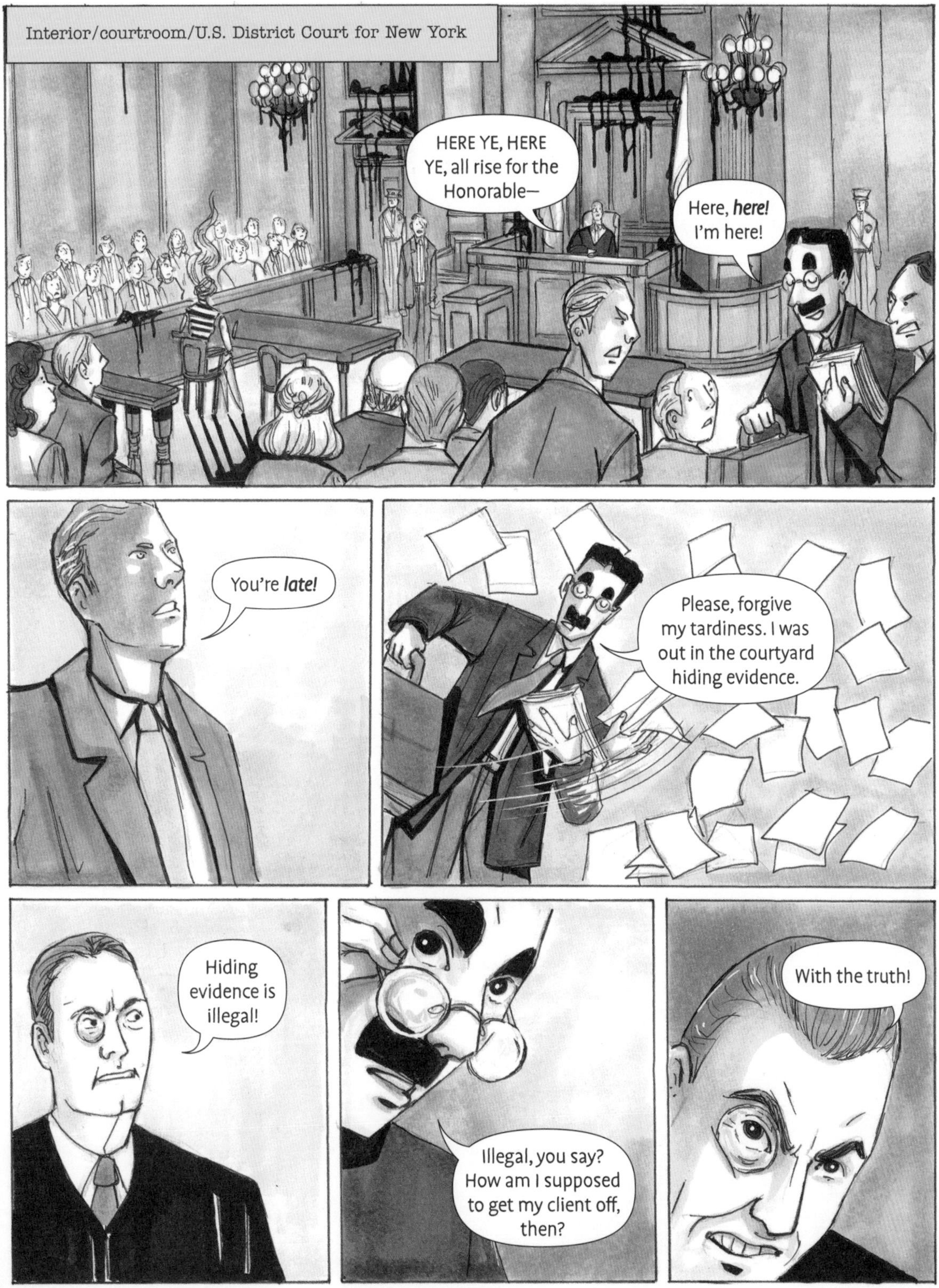
Interior/courtroom/U.S. District Court for New York
HERE YE, HERE YE, all rise for the Honorable—
Here, *here!* I'm here!
You're *late!*
Please, forgive my tardiness. I was out in the courtyard hiding evidence.
Hiding evidence is illegal!
Illegal, you say? How am I supposed to get my client off, then?
With the truth!

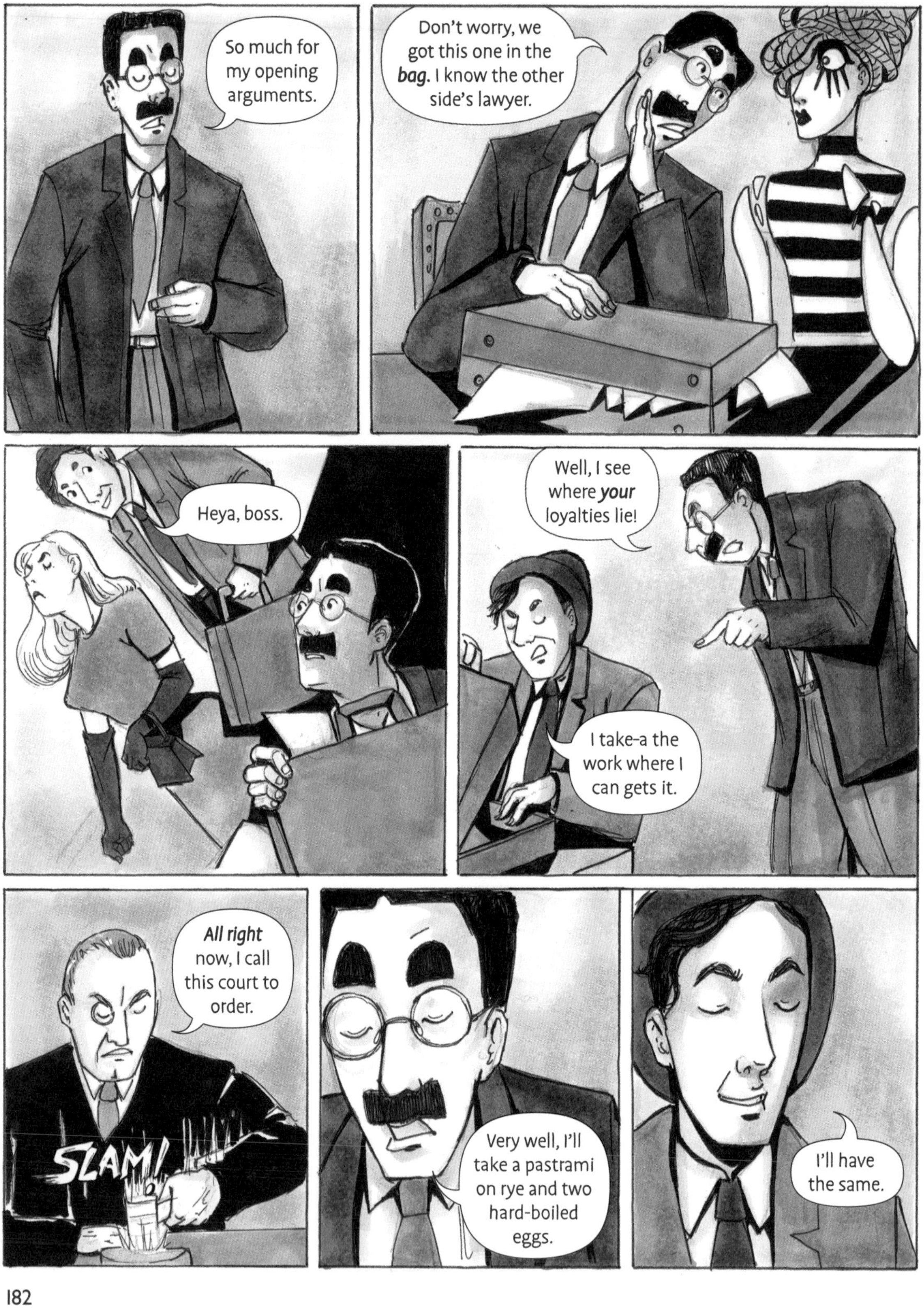
So much for my opening arguments.
Don't worry, we got this one in the bag. I know the other side's lawyer.
Heya, boss.
Well, I see where your loyalties lie!
I take-a the work where I can gets it.
All right now, I call this court to order.
SLAM!
Very well, I'll take a pastrami on rye and two hard-boiled eggs.
I'll have the same.

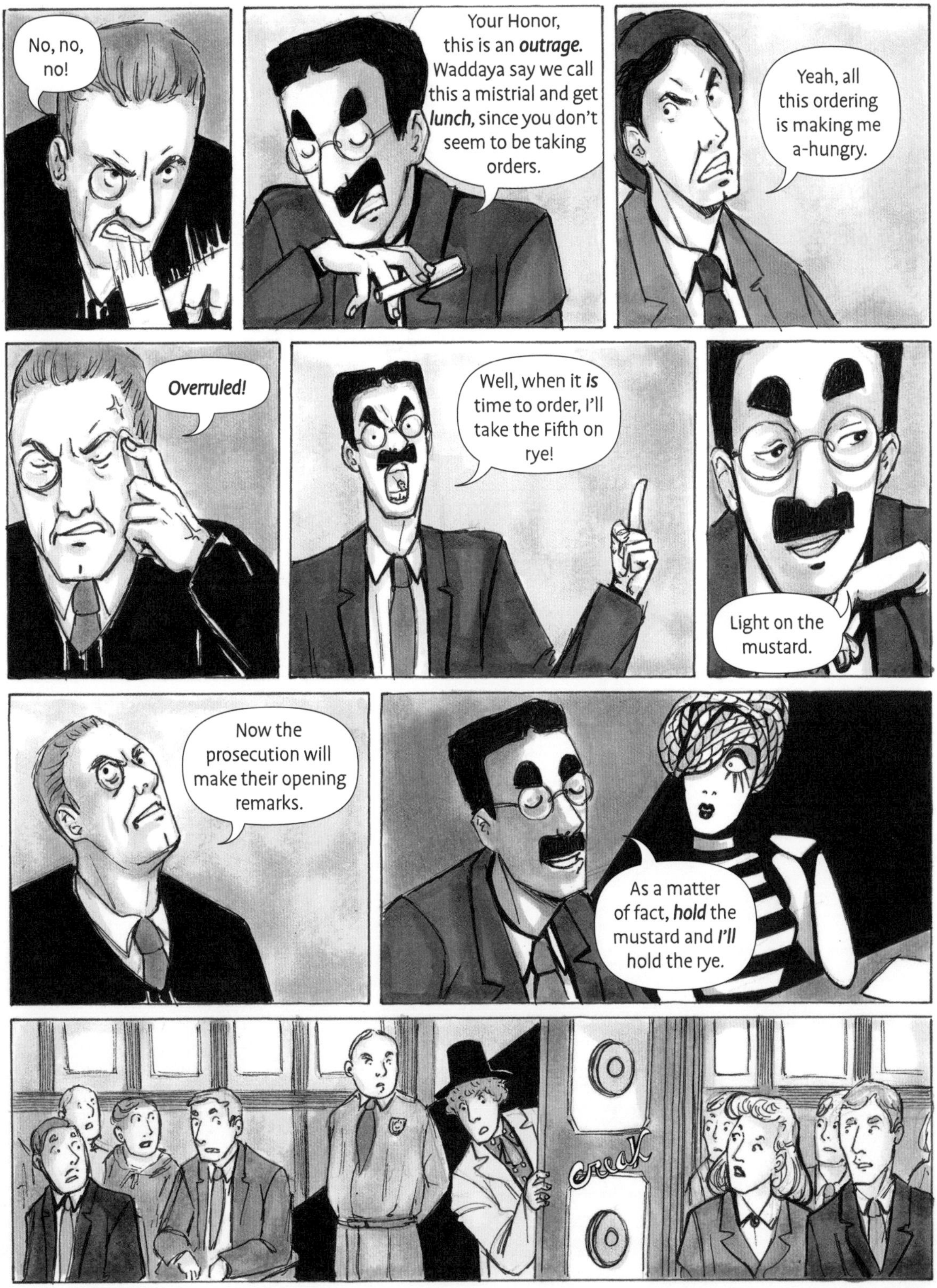
No, no, no!
Your Honor, this is an ***outrage.*** Waddaya say we call this a mistrial and get ***lunch,*** since you don't seem to be taking orders.
Yeah, all this ordering is making me a-hungry.
Overruled!
Well, when it ***is*** time to order, I'll take the Fifth on rye!
Light on the mustard.
Now the prosecution will make their opening remarks.
As a matter of fact, ***hold*** the mustard and ***I'll*** hold the rye.
creak

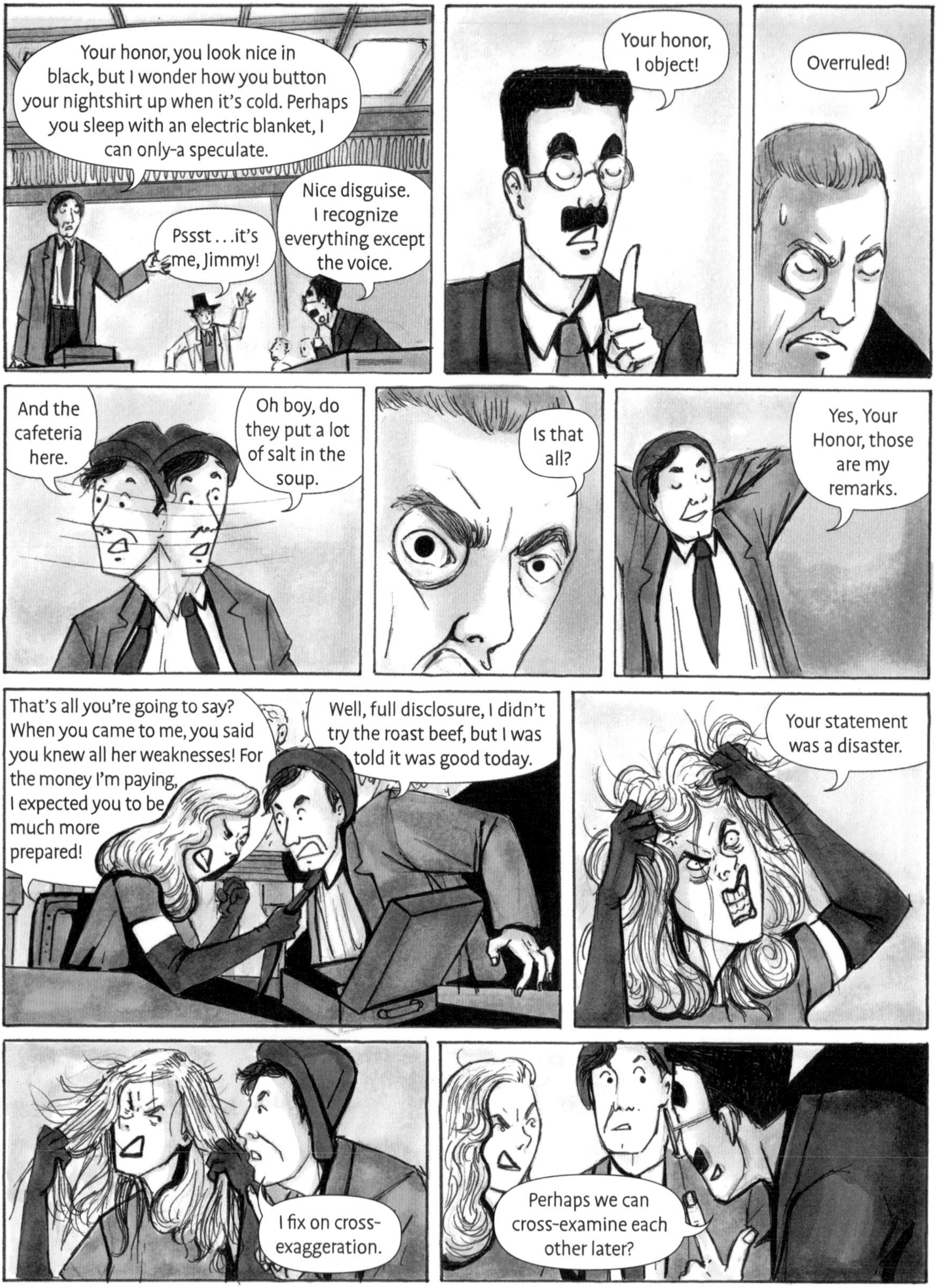
Your honor, you look nice in black, but I wonder how you button your nightshirt up when it's cold. Perhaps you sleep with an electric blanket, I can only-a speculate.
Pssst . . . it's me, Jimmy!
Nice disguise. I recognize everything except the voice.
Your honor, I object!
Overruled!
And the cafeteria here.
Oh boy, do they put a lot of salt in the soup.
Is that all?
Yes, Your Honor, those are my remarks.
That's all you're going to say? When you came to me, you said you knew all her weaknesses! For the money I'm paying, I expected you to be much more prepared!
Well, full disclosure, I didn't try the roast beef, but I was told it was good today.
Your statement was a disaster.
I fix on cross-exaggeration.
Perhaps we can cross-examine each other later?

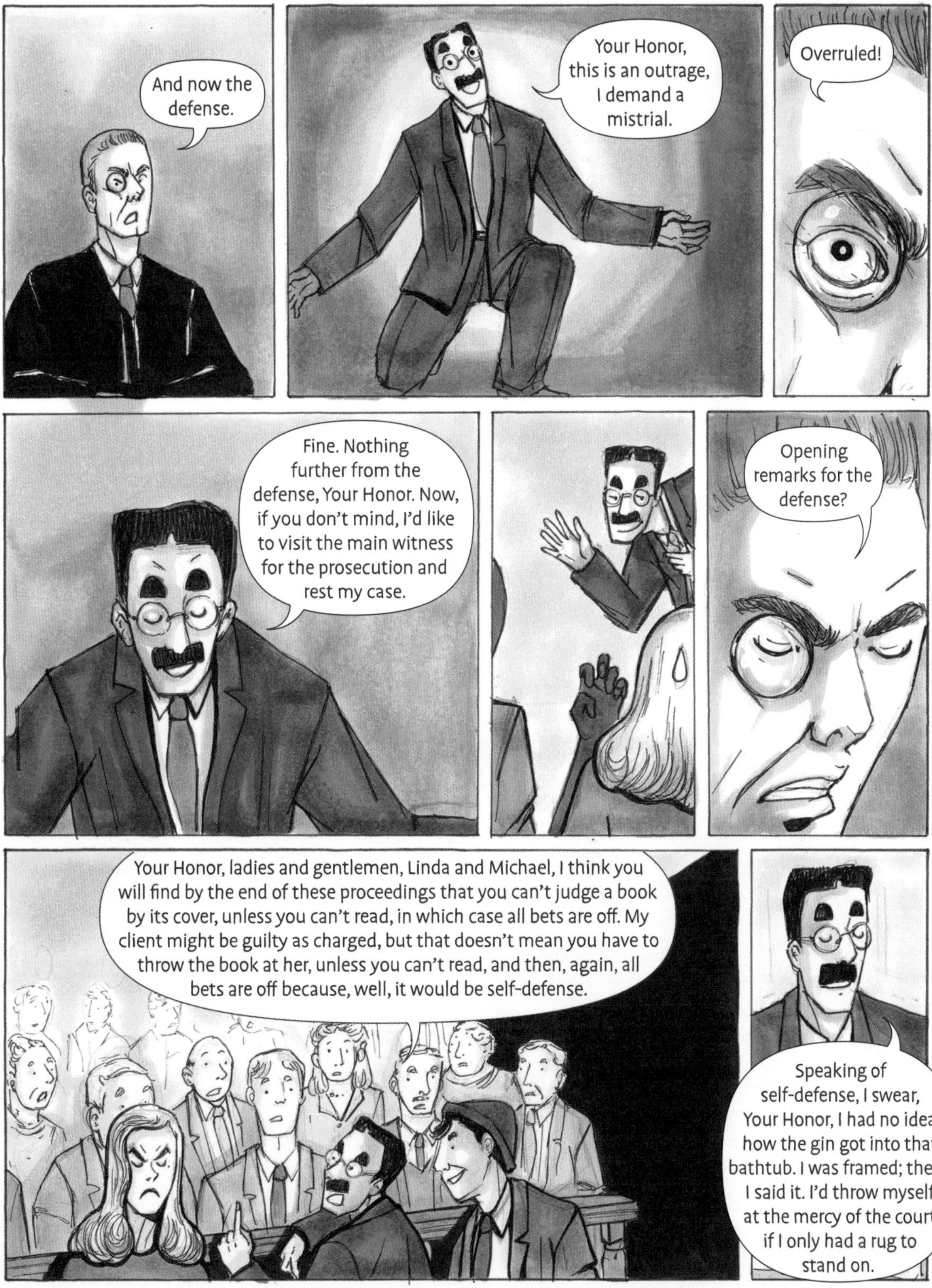
And now the defense.
Your Honor, this is an outrage, I demand a mistrial.
Overruled!
Fine. Nothing further from the defense, Your Honor. Now, if you don't mind, I'd like to visit the main witness for the prosecution and rest my case.
Opening remarks for the defense?
Your Honor, ladies and gentlemen, Linda and Michael, I think you will find by the end of these proceedings that you can't judge a book by its cover, unless you can't read, in which case all bets are off. My client might be guilty as charged, but that doesn't mean you have to throw the book at her, unless you can't read, and then, again, all bets are off because, well, it would be self-defense.
Speaking of self-defense, I swear, Your Honor, I had no idea how the gin got into that bathtub. I was framed; there, I said it. I'd throw myself at the mercy of the court if I only had a rug to stand on.

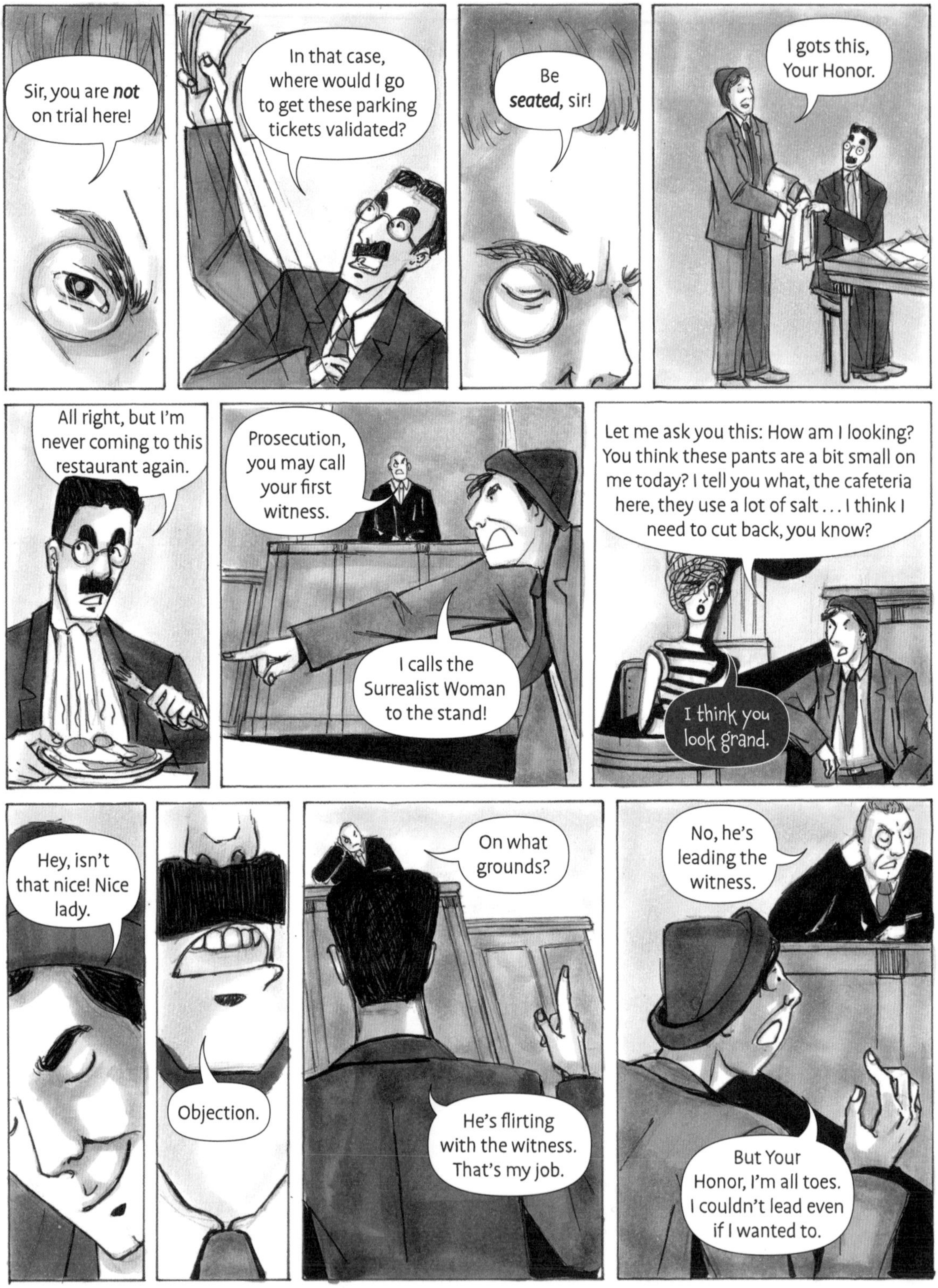
Sir, you are ***not*** on trial here!
In that case, where would I go to get these parking tickets validated?
Be ***seated***, sir!
I gots this, Your Honor.
All right, but I'm never coming to this restaurant again.
Prosecution, you may call your first witness.
I calls the Surrealist Woman to the stand!
Let me ask you this: How am I looking? You think these pants are a bit small on me today? I tell you what, the cafeteria here, they use a lot of salt . . . I think I need to cut back, you know?
I think you look grand.
Hey, isn't that nice! Nice lady.
Objection.
On what grounds?
He's flirting with the witness. That's my job.
No, he's leading the witness.
But Your Honor, I'm all toes. I couldn't lead even if I wanted to.

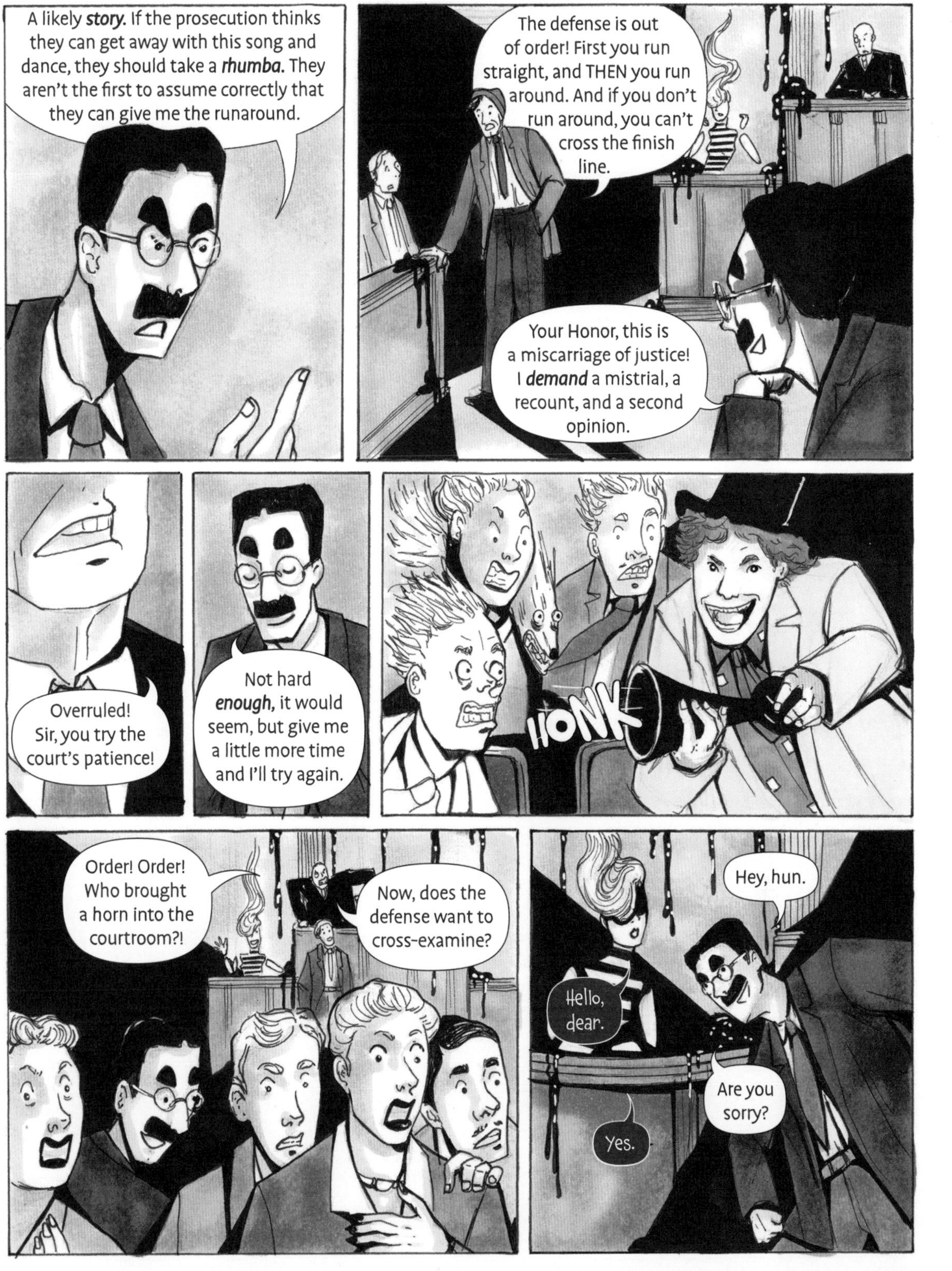
A likely *story.* If the prosecution thinks they can get away with this song and dance, they should take a *rhumba.* They aren't the first to assume correctly that they can give me the runaround.
The defense is out of order! First you run straight, and THEN you run around. And if you don't run around, you can't cross the finish line.
Your Honor, this is a miscarriage of justice! I *demand* a mistrial, a recount, and a second opinion.
Overruled! Sir, you try the court's patience!
Not hard *enough,* it would seem, but give me a little more time and I'll try again.
HONK
Order! Order! Who brought a horn into the courtroom?!
Now, does the defense want to cross-examine?
Hey, hun.
Hello, dear.
Are you sorry?
Yes.

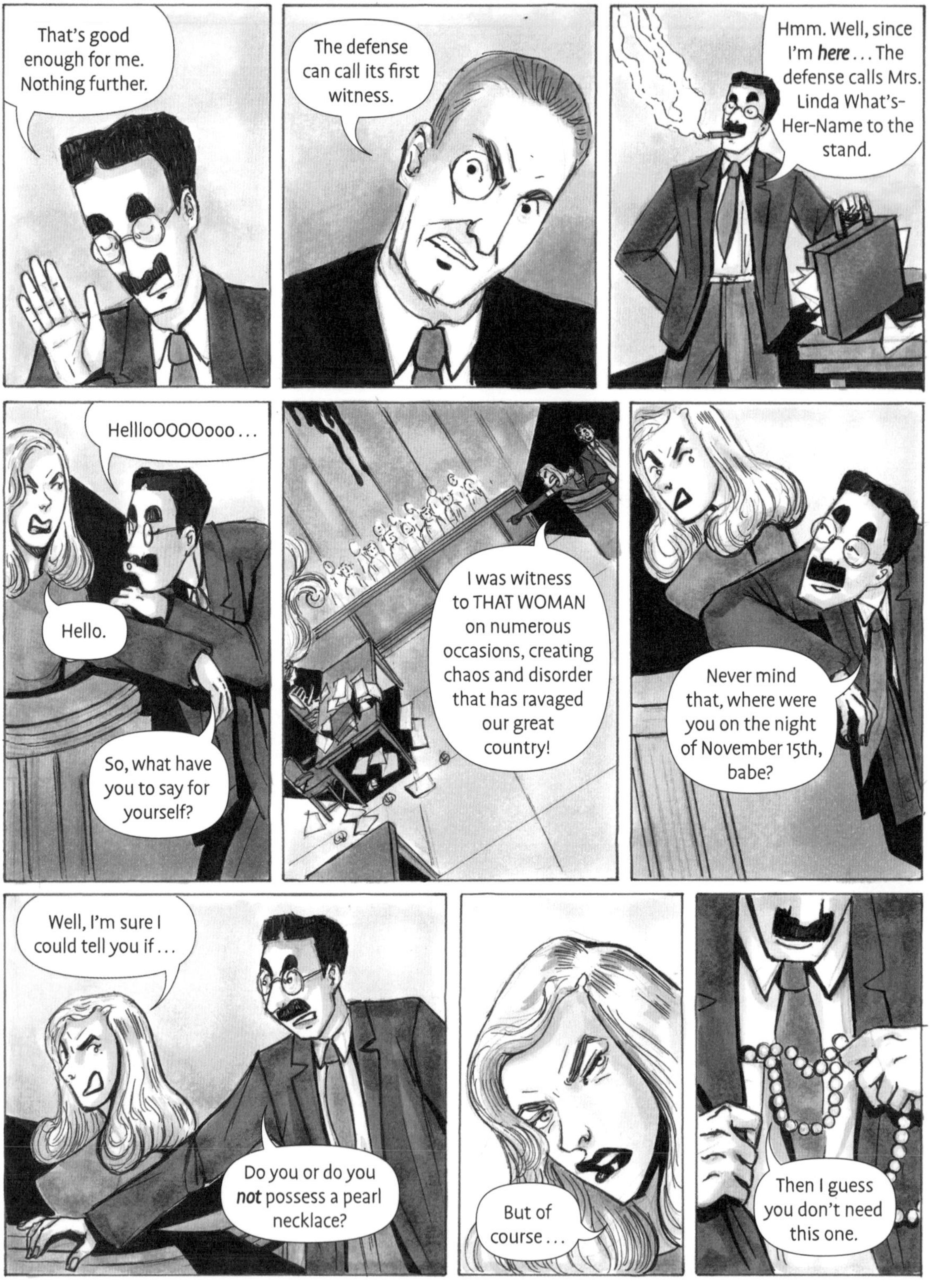
That's good enough for me. Nothing further.
The defense can call its first witness.
Hmm. Well, since I'm ***here***... The defense calls Mrs. Linda What's-Her-Name to the stand.
HellloOOOOooo...
Hello.
So, what have you to say for yourself?
I was witness to THAT WOMAN on numerous occasions, creating chaos and disorder that has ravaged our great country!
Never mind that, where were you on the night of November 15th, babe?
Well, I'm sure I could tell you if...
Do you or do you ***not*** possess a pearl necklace?
But of course...
Then I guess you don't need this one.

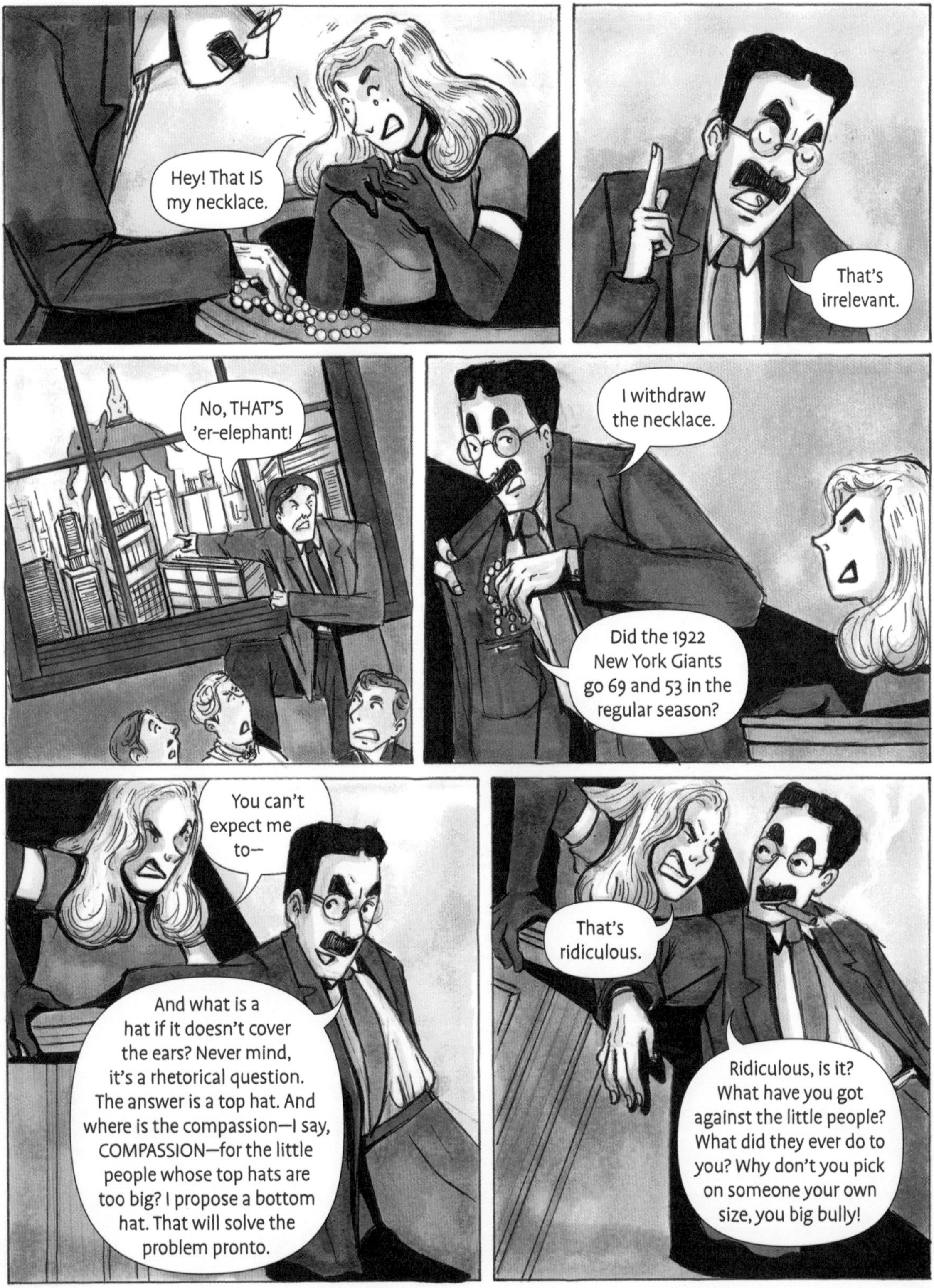

Hey! That IS my necklace.
That's irrelevant.
No, THAT'S 'er-elephant!
I withdraw the necklace.
Did the 1922 New York Giants go 69 and 53 in the regular season?
You can't expect me to—
And what is a hat if it doesn't cover the ears? Never mind, it's a rhetorical question. The answer is a top hat. And where is the compassion—I say, COMPASSION—for the little people whose top hats are too big? I propose a bottom hat. That will solve the problem pronto.
That's ridiculous.
Ridiculous, is it? What have you got against the little people? What did they ever do to you? Why don't you pick on someone your own size, you big bully!

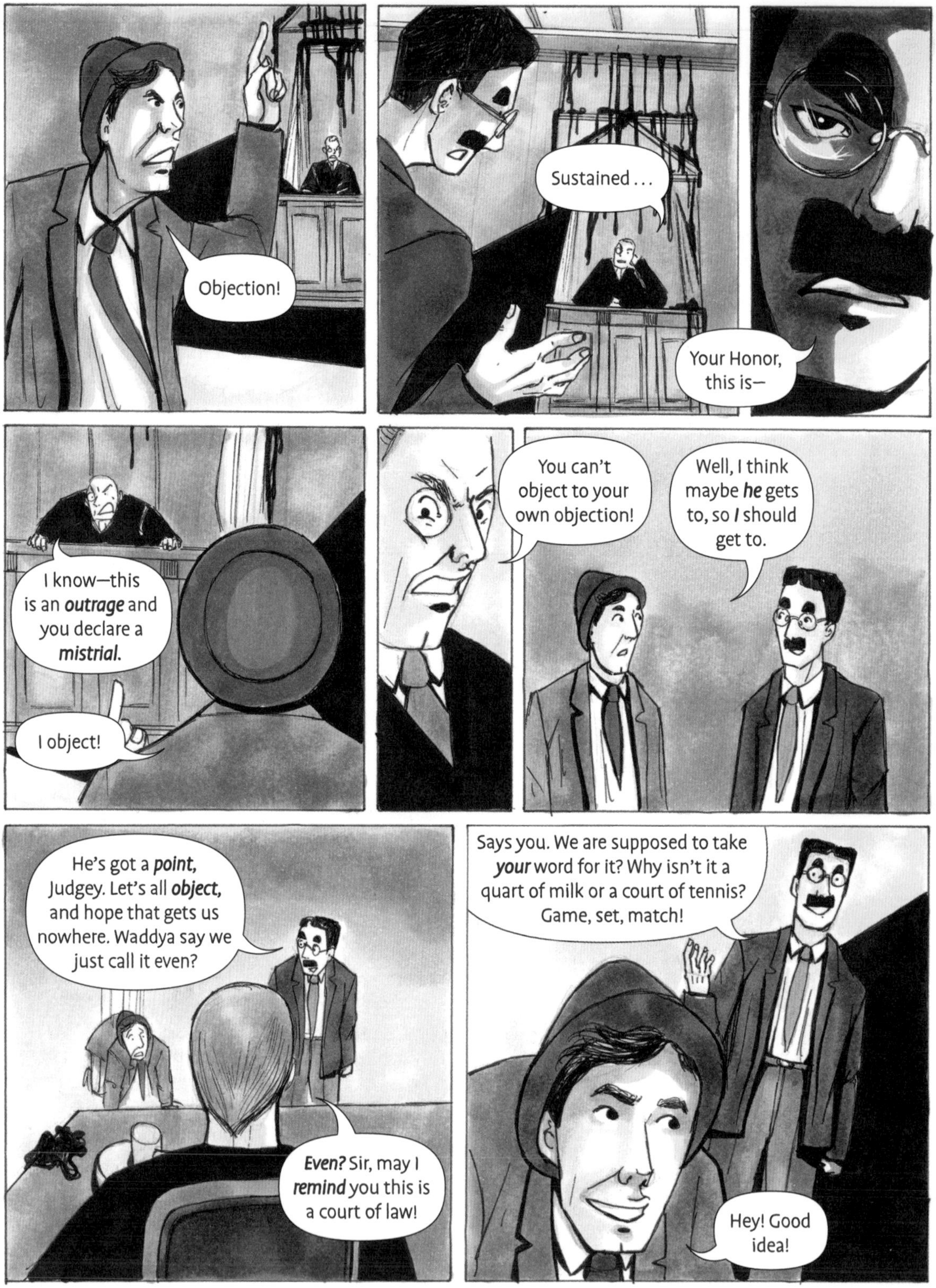
Objection!
Sustained . . .
Your Honor, this is—
I know—this is an *outrage* and you declare a *mistrial*.
I object!
You can't object to your own objection!
Well, I think maybe *he* gets to, so *I* should get to.
He's got a *point*, Judgey. Let's all *object*, and hope that gets us nowhere. Waddya say we just call it even?
Even? Sir, may I *remind* you this is a court of law!
Says you. We are supposed to take *your* word for it? Why isn't it a quart of milk or a court of tennis? Game, set, match!
Hey! Good idea!

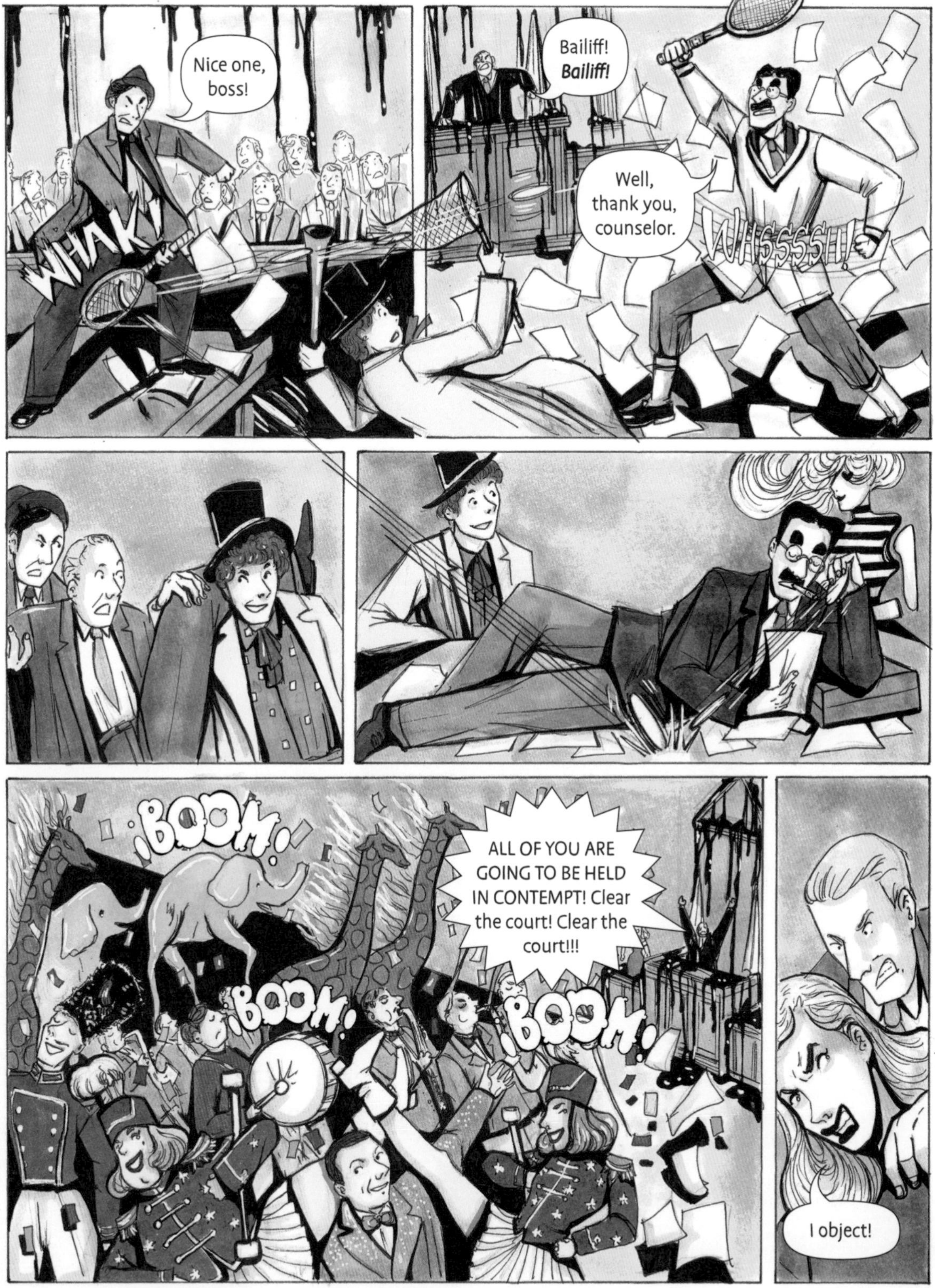
Nice one, boss!
WHAK!
Bailiff! *Bailiff!*
Well, thank you, counselor.
WHSSSSH!
BOOM!
ALL OF YOU ARE GOING TO BE HELD IN CONTEMPT! Clear the court! Clear the court!!!
BOOM!
BOOM!
I object!

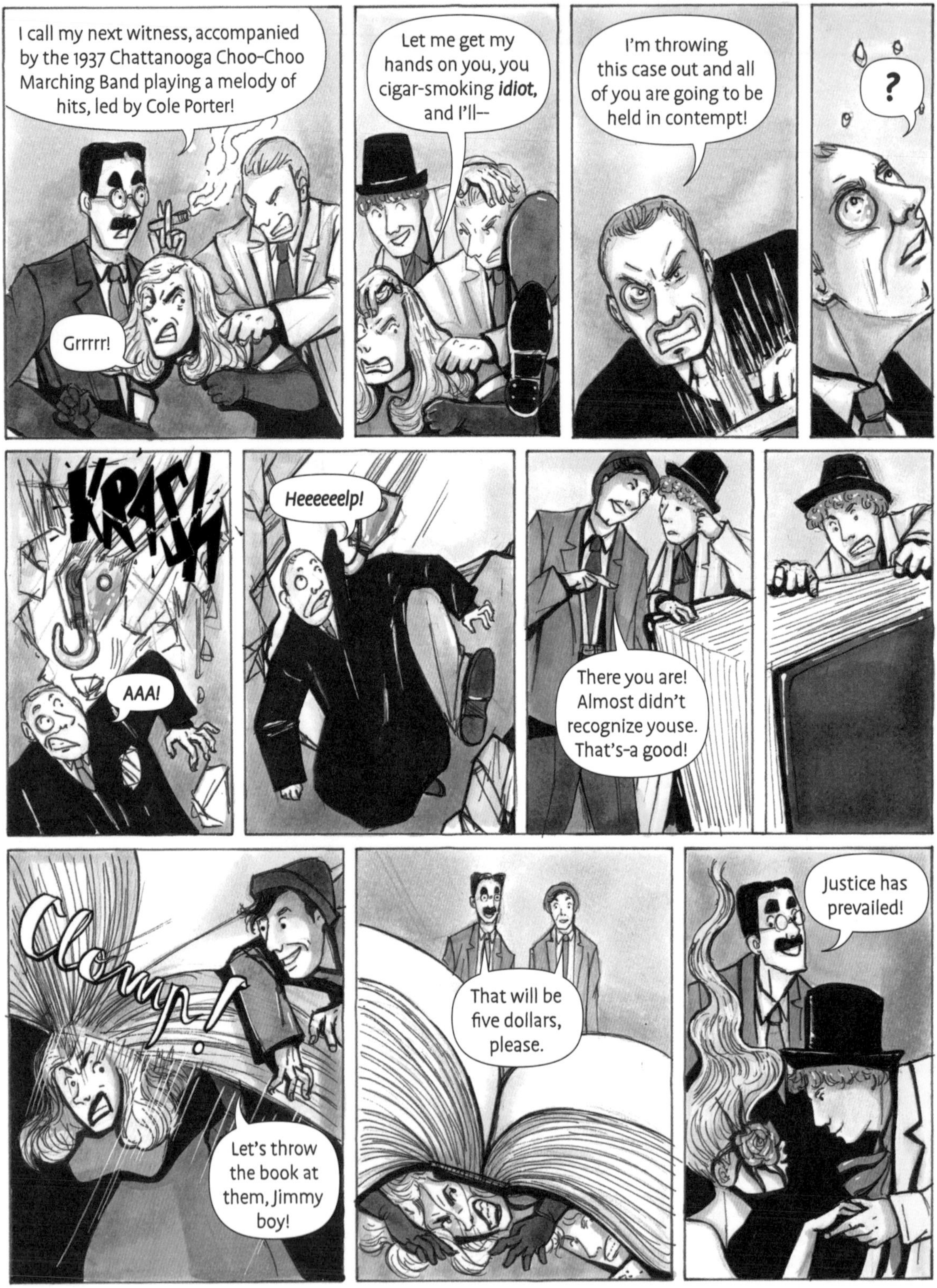

I call my next witness, accompanied by the 1937 Chattanooga Choo-Choo Marching Band playing a melody of hits, led by Cole Porter!
Grrrrr!
Let me get my hands on you, you cigar-smoking *idiot*, and I'll--
I'm throwing this case out and all of you are going to be held in contempt!
?
KRASH
AAA!
Heeeeeelp!
There you are! Almost didn't recognize youse. That's-a good!
Cloump!
Let's throw the book at them, Jimmy boy!
That will be five dollars, please.
Justice has prevailed!

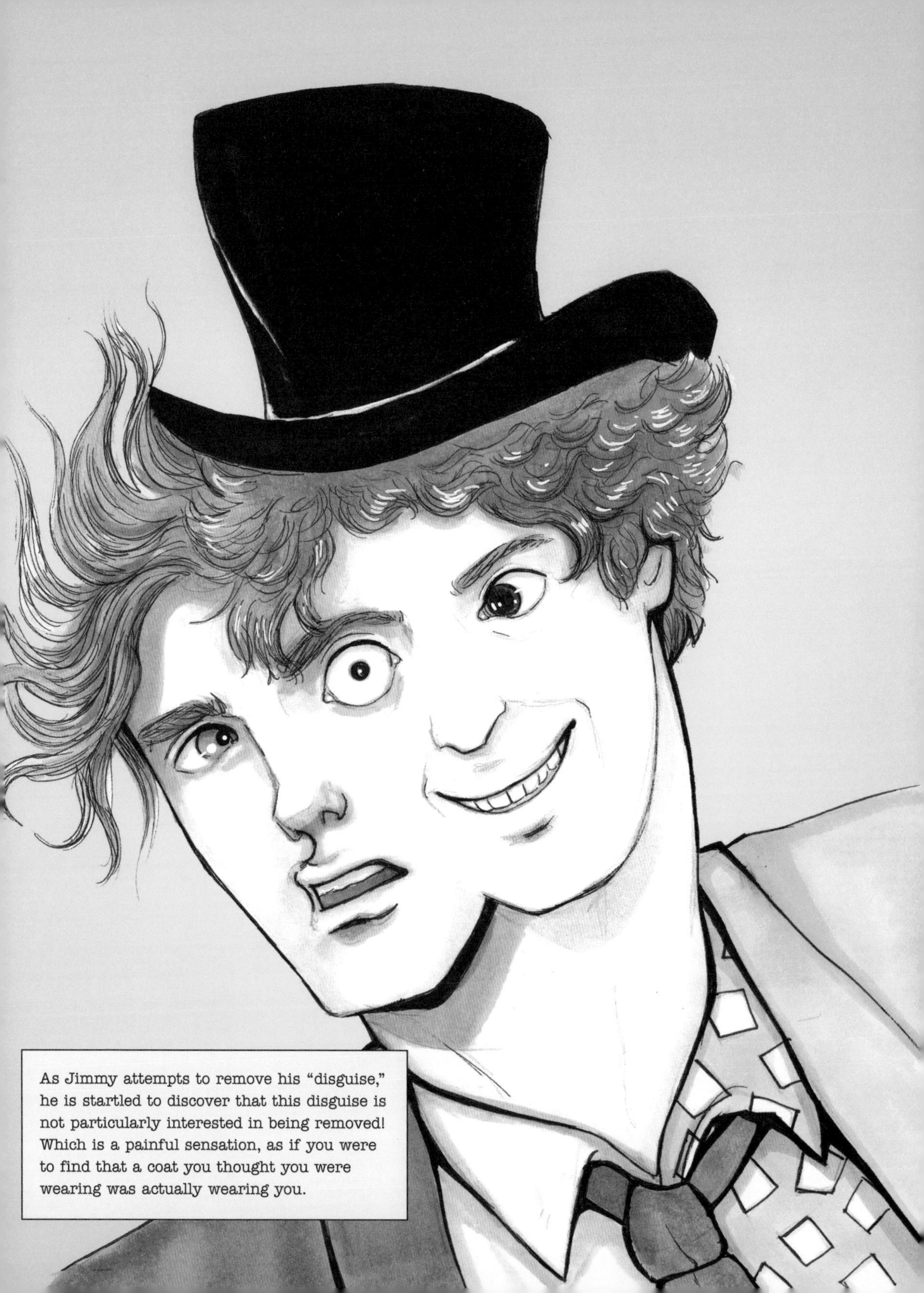
As Jimmy attempts to remove his "disguise," he is startled to discover that this disguise is not particularly interested in being removed! Which is a painful sensation, as if you were to find that a coat you thought you were wearing was actually wearing you.

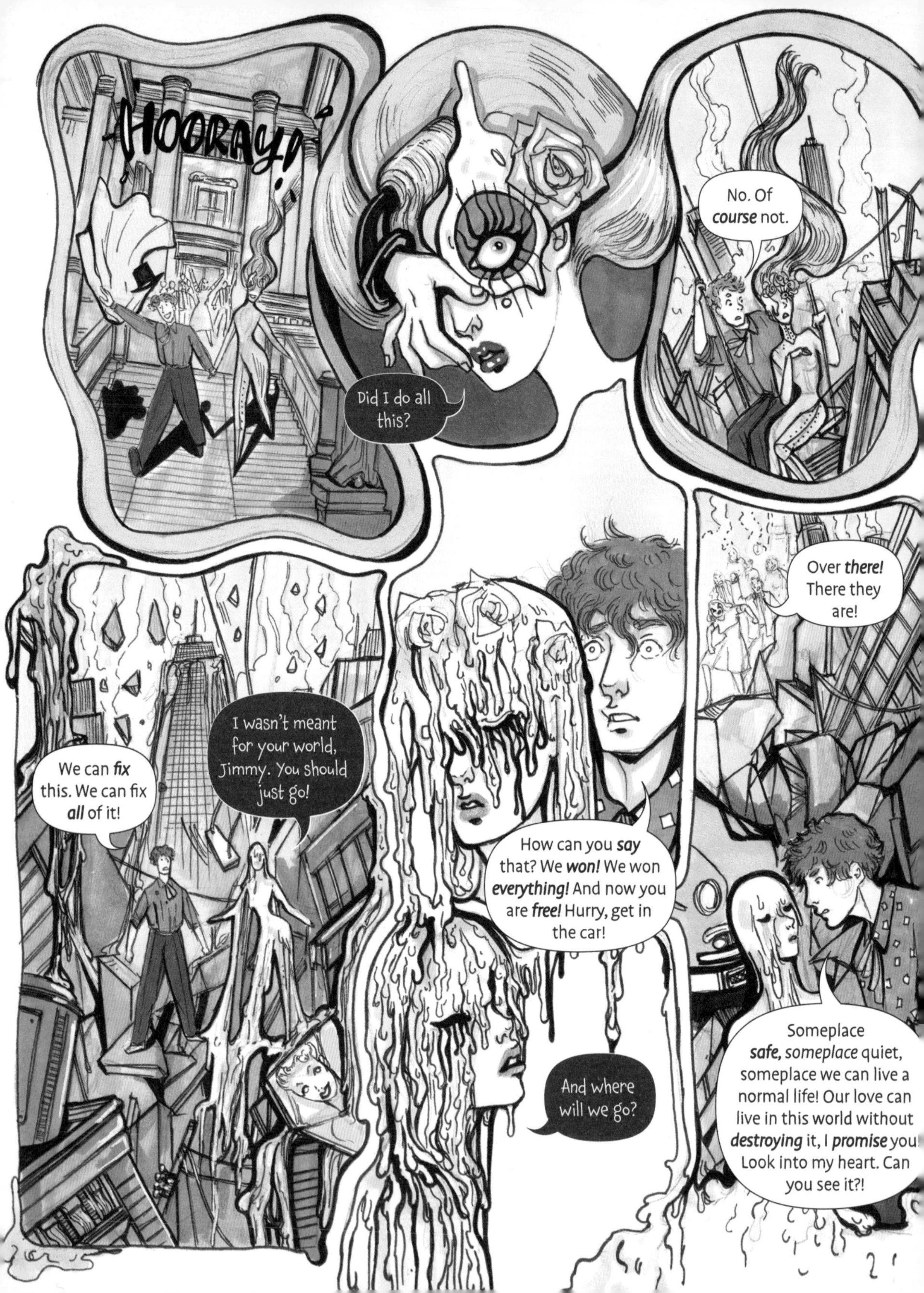
HOORAY!
Did I do all this?
No. Of **course** not.
Over **there!** There they are!
We can **fix** this. We can fix **all** of it!
I wasn't meant for your world, Jimmy. You should just go!
How can you **say** that? We **won!** We won **everything!** And now you are **free!** Hurry, get in the car!
And where will we go?
Someplace **safe,** *someplace* quiet, someplace we can live a normal life! Our love can live in this world without **destroying** it, I **promise** you! Look into my heart. Can you see it?!

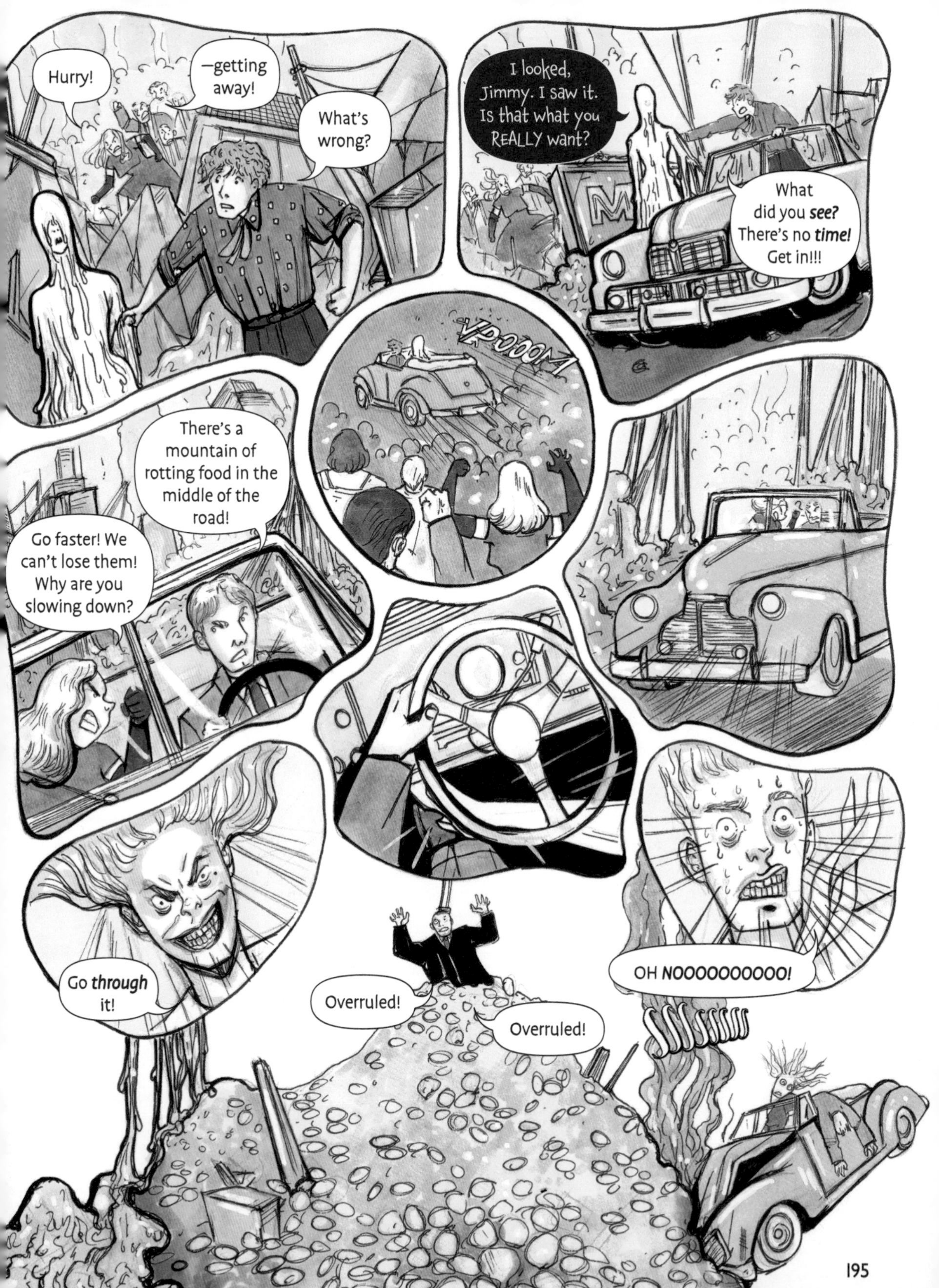
Hurry!
—getting away!
What's wrong?
I looked, Jimmy. I saw it. Is that what you REALLY want?
What did you *see?* There's no *time!* Get in!!!
VROOOM
There's a mountain of rotting food in the middle of the road!
Go faster! We can't lose them! Why are you slowing down?
Go *through* it!
Overruled!
Overruled!
OH *NOOOOOOOOOO!*
SSSSSSS

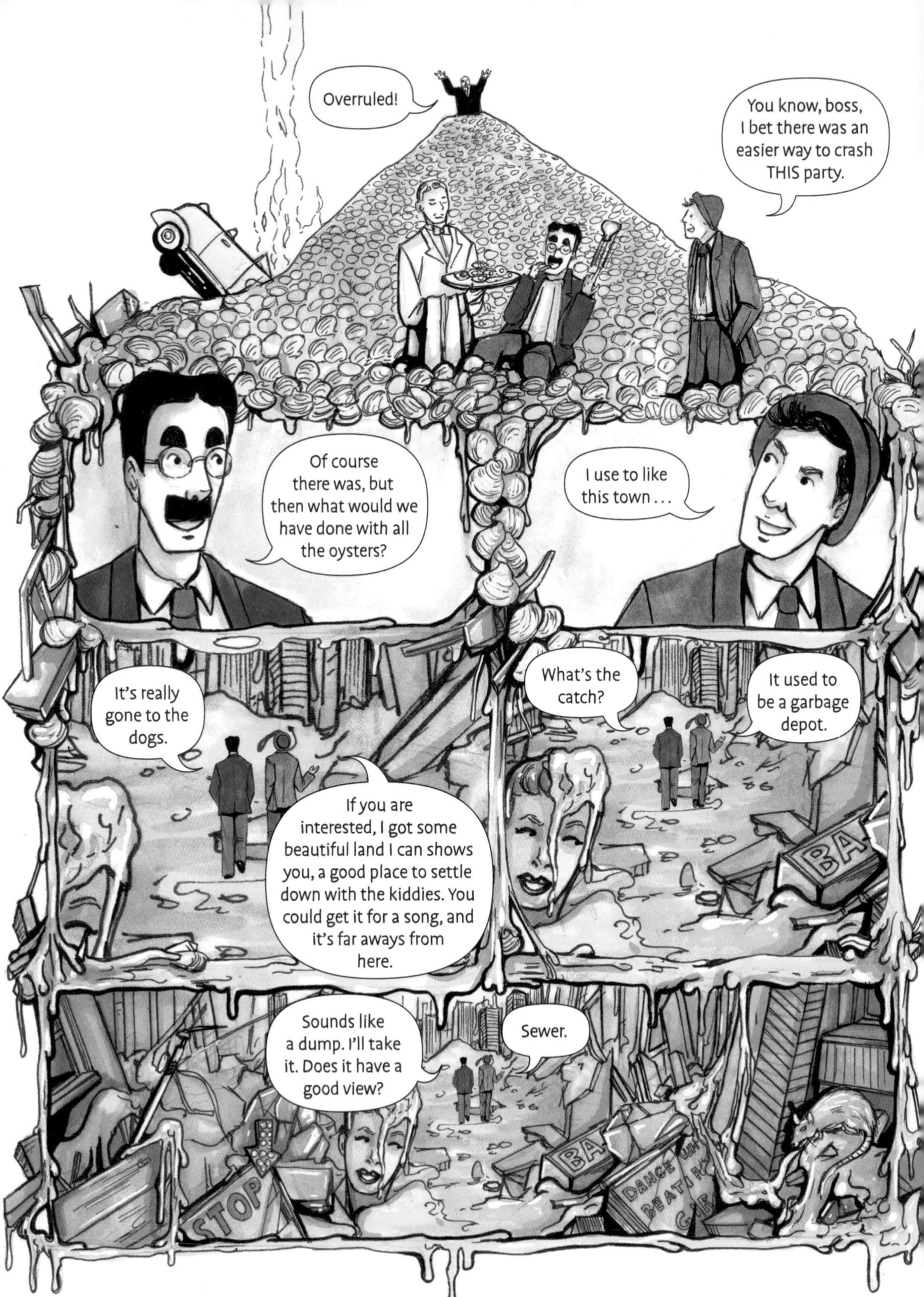
Overruled!
You know, boss, I bet there was an easier way to crash THIS party.
Of course there was, but then what would we have done with all the oysters?
I use to like this town . . .
It's really gone to the dogs.
If you are interested, I got some beautiful land I can shows you, a good place to settle down with the kiddies. You could get it for a song, and it's far aways from here.
What's the catch?
It used to be a garbage depot.
Sounds like a dump. I'll take it. Does it have a good view?
Sewer.
STOP

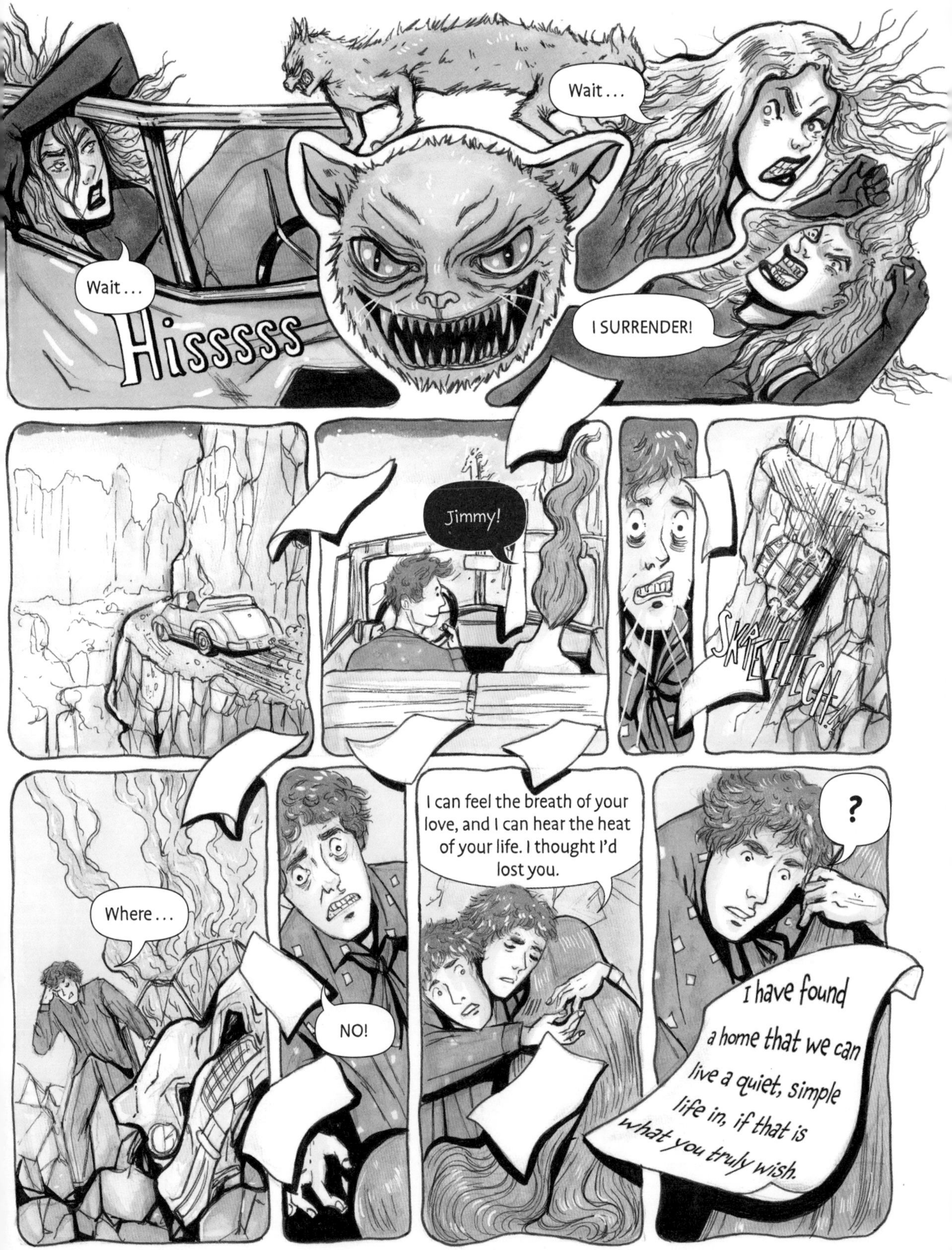
Wait...
Wait...
Hissssss
I SURRENDER!
Jimmy!
SKREEEECH!
Where...
NO!
I can feel the breath of your love, and I can hear the heat of your life. I thought I'd lost you.
?
I have found a home that we can live a quiet, simple life in, if that is what you truly wish.

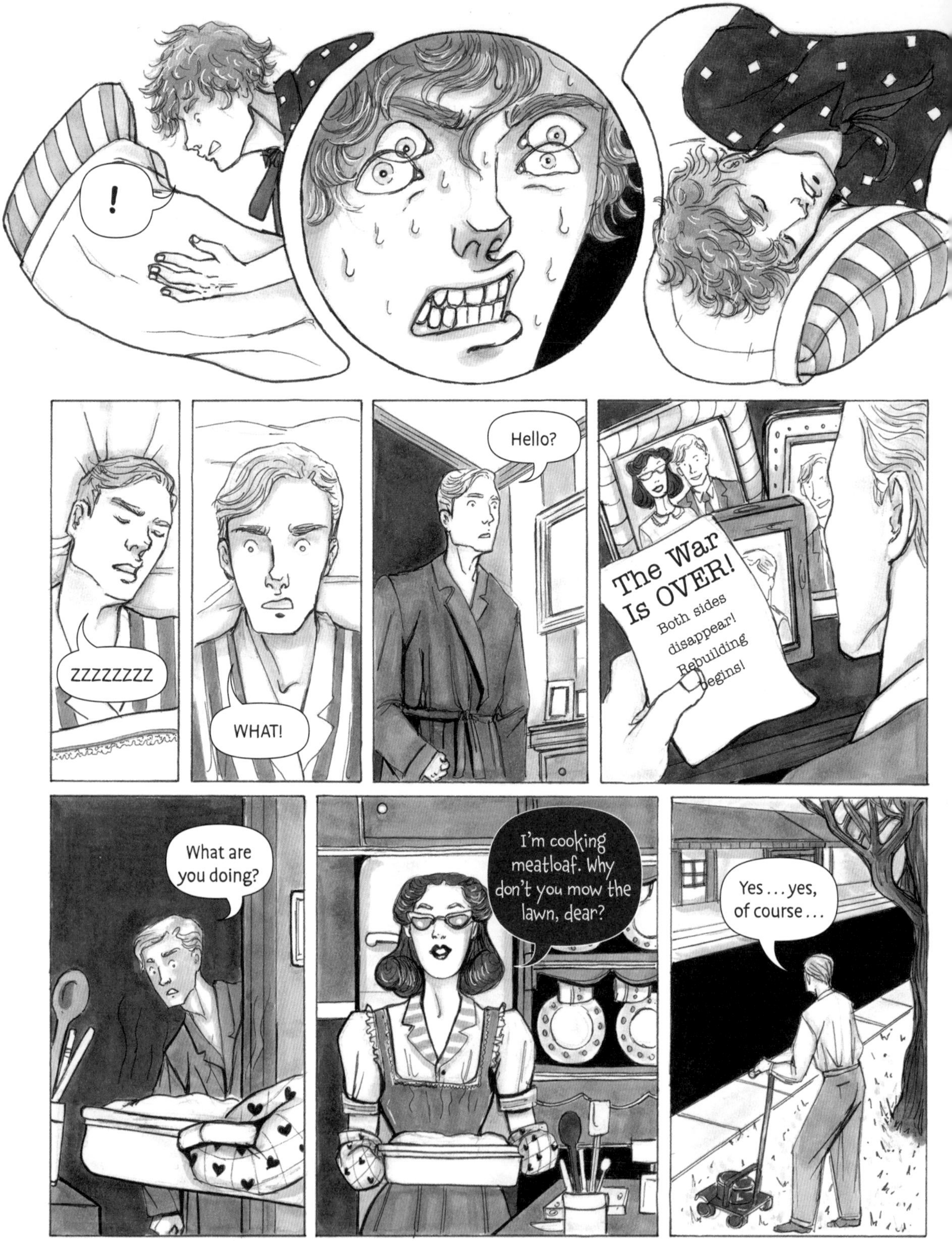
!
ZZZZZZZZ
WHAT!
Hello?
The War Is OVER!
Both sides disappear!
Rebuilding begins!
What are you doing?
I'm cooking meatloaf. Why don't you mow the lawn, dear?
Yes . . . yes, of course . . .

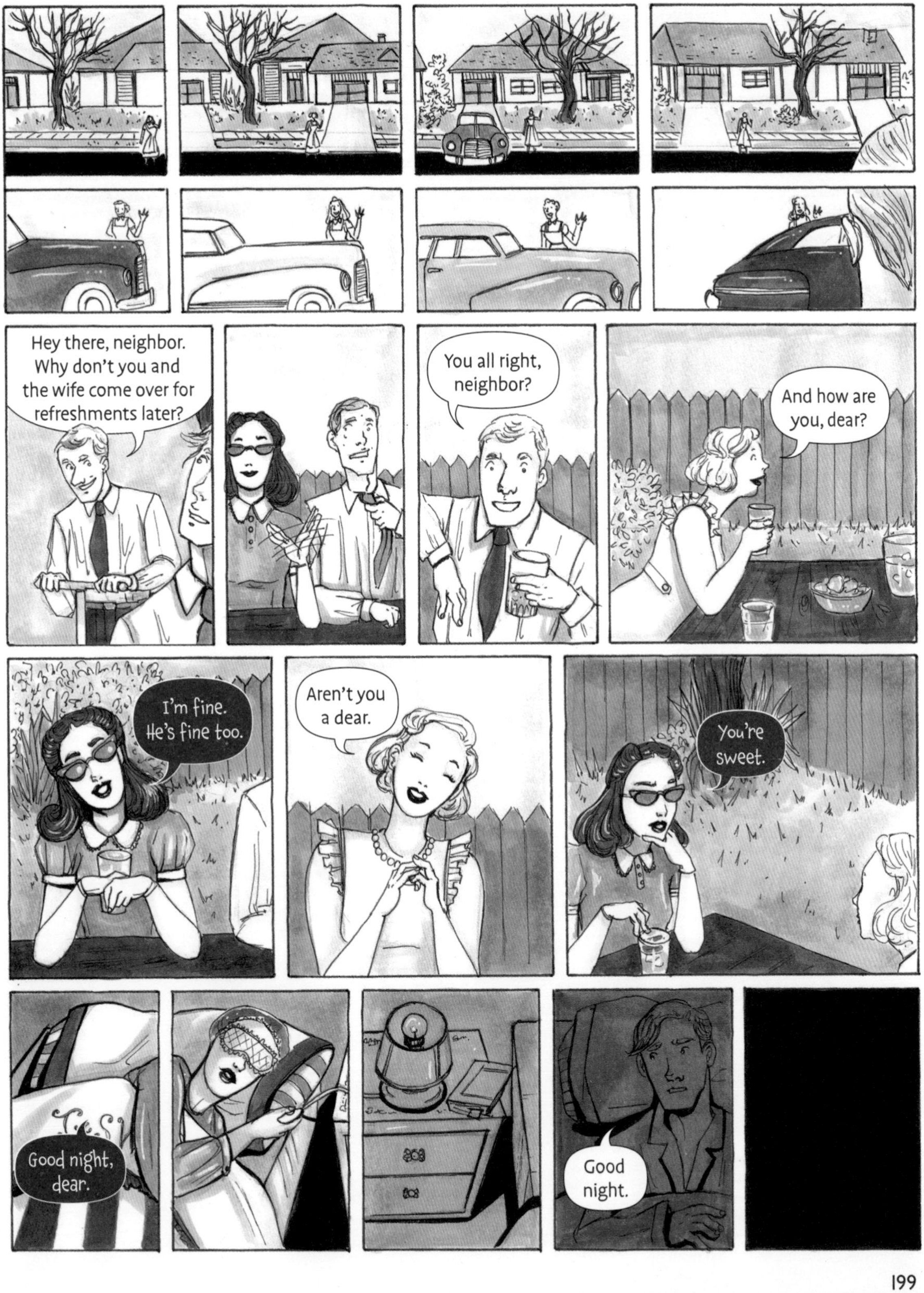
Hey there, neighbor. Why don't you and the wife come over for refreshments later?
You all right, neighbor?
And how are you, dear?
I'm fine. He's fine too.
Aren't you a dear.
You're sweet.
Good night, dear.
Good night.

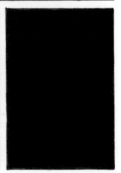

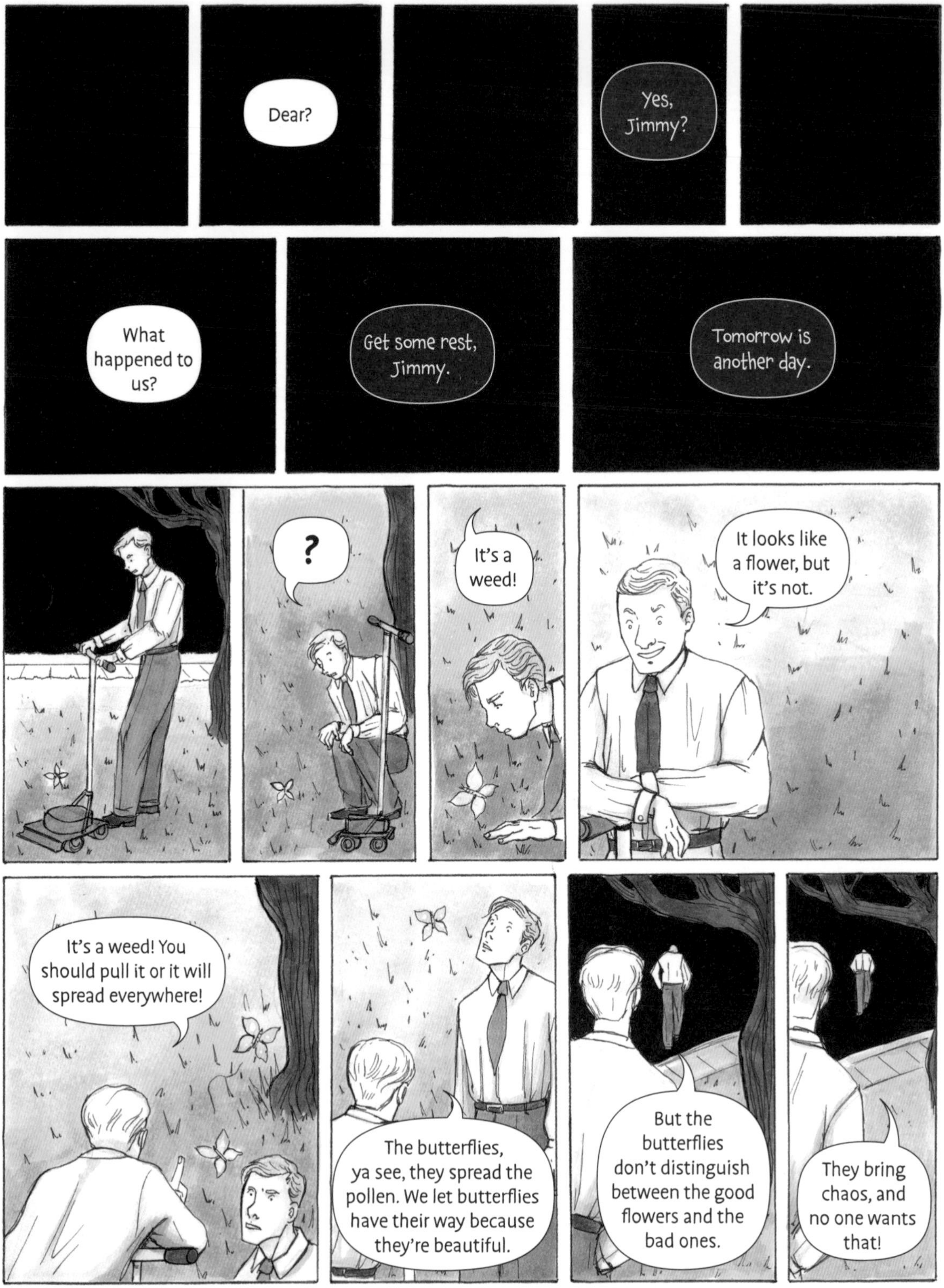
Dear?
Yes, Jimmy?
What happened to us?
Get some rest, Jimmy.
Tomorrow is another day.
?
It's a weed!
It looks like a flower, but it's not.
It's a weed! You should pull it or it will spread everywhere!
The butterflies, ya see, they spread the pollen. We let butterflies have their way because they're beautiful.
But the butterflies don't distinguish between the good flowers and the bad ones.
They bring chaos, and no one wants that!

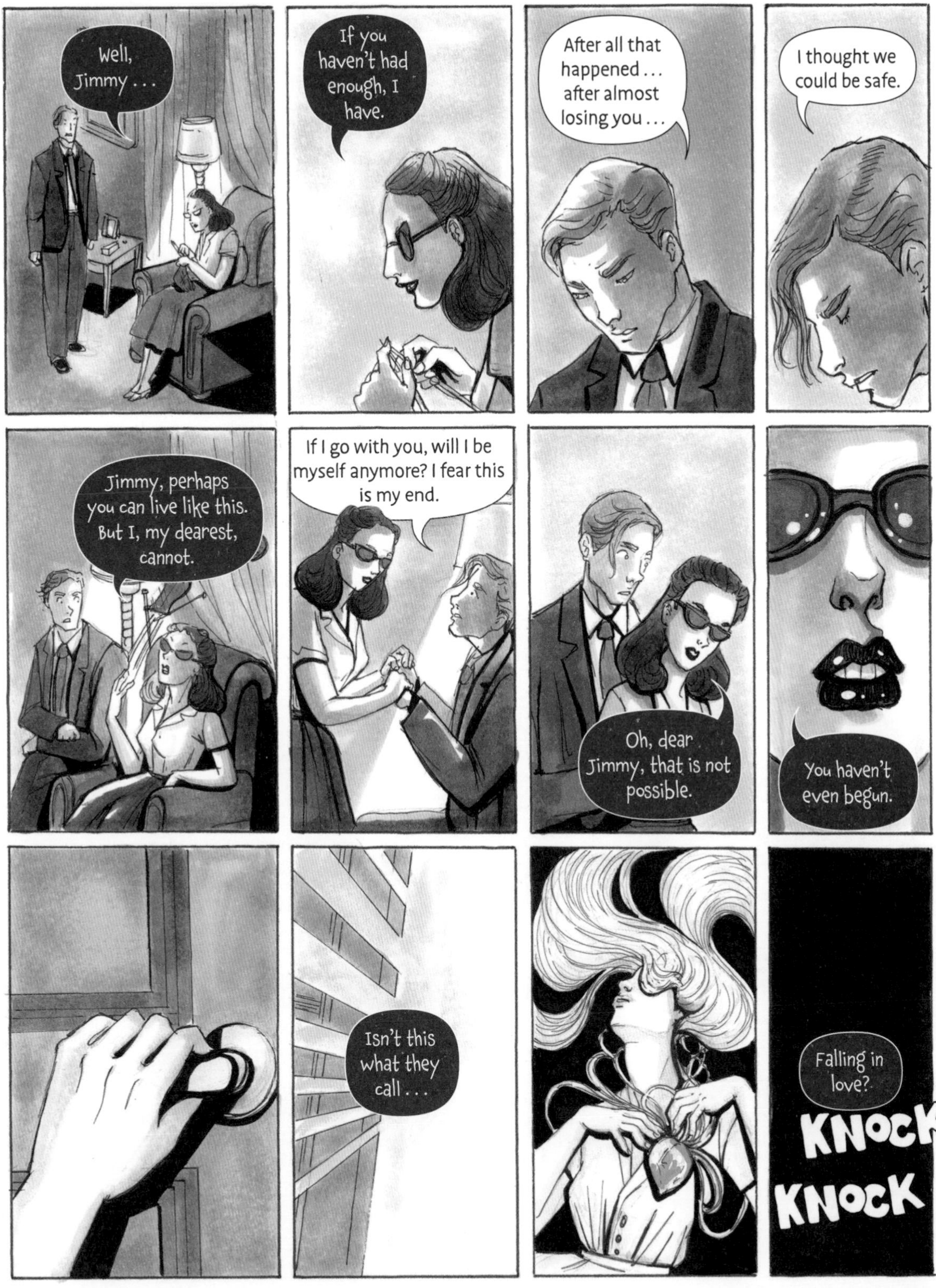
Well, Jimmy . . .
If you haven't had enough, I have.
After all that happened . . . after almost losing you . . .
I thought we could be safe.
Jimmy, perhaps you can live like this. But I, my dearest, cannot.
If I go with you, will I be myself anymore? I fear this is my end.
Oh, dear Jimmy, that is not possible.
You haven't even begun.
Isn't this what they call . . .
Falling in love?
KNOCK
KNOCK

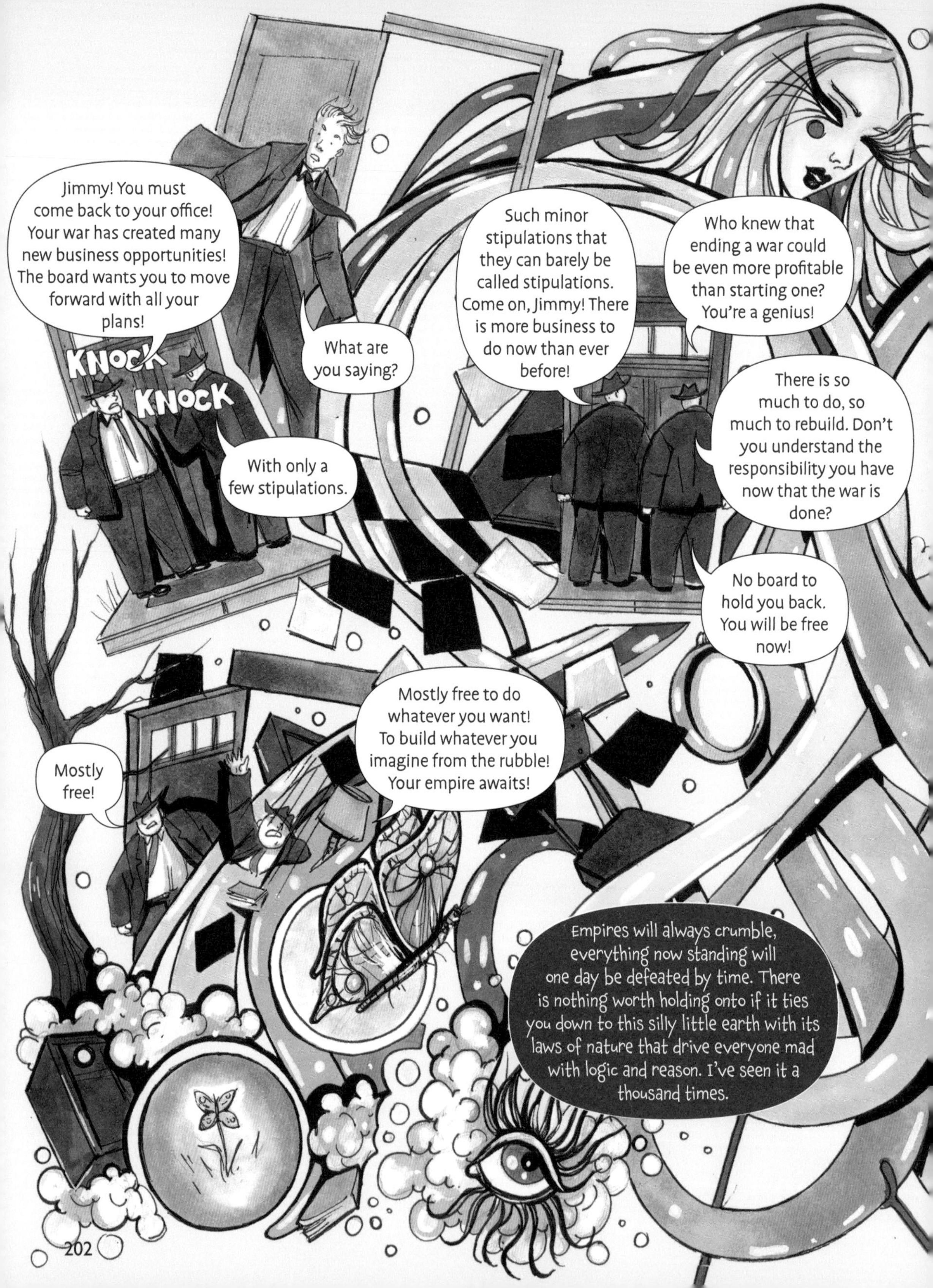
Jimmy! You must come back to your office! Your war has created many new business opportunities! The board wants you to move forward with all your plans!
KNOCK
KNOCK
What are you saying?
With only a few stipulations.
Such minor stipulations that they can barely be called stipulations. Come on, Jimmy! There is more business to do now than ever before!
Who knew that ending a war could be even more profitable than starting one? You're a genius!
There is so much to do, so much to rebuild. Don't you understand the responsibility you have now that the war is done?
No board to hold you back. You will be free now!
Mostly free!
Mostly free to do whatever you want! To build whatever you imagine from the rubble! Your empire awaits!
Empires will always crumble, everything now standing will one day be defeated by time. There is nothing worth holding onto if it ties you down to this silly little earth with its laws of nature that drive everyone mad with logic and reason. I've seen it a thousand times.

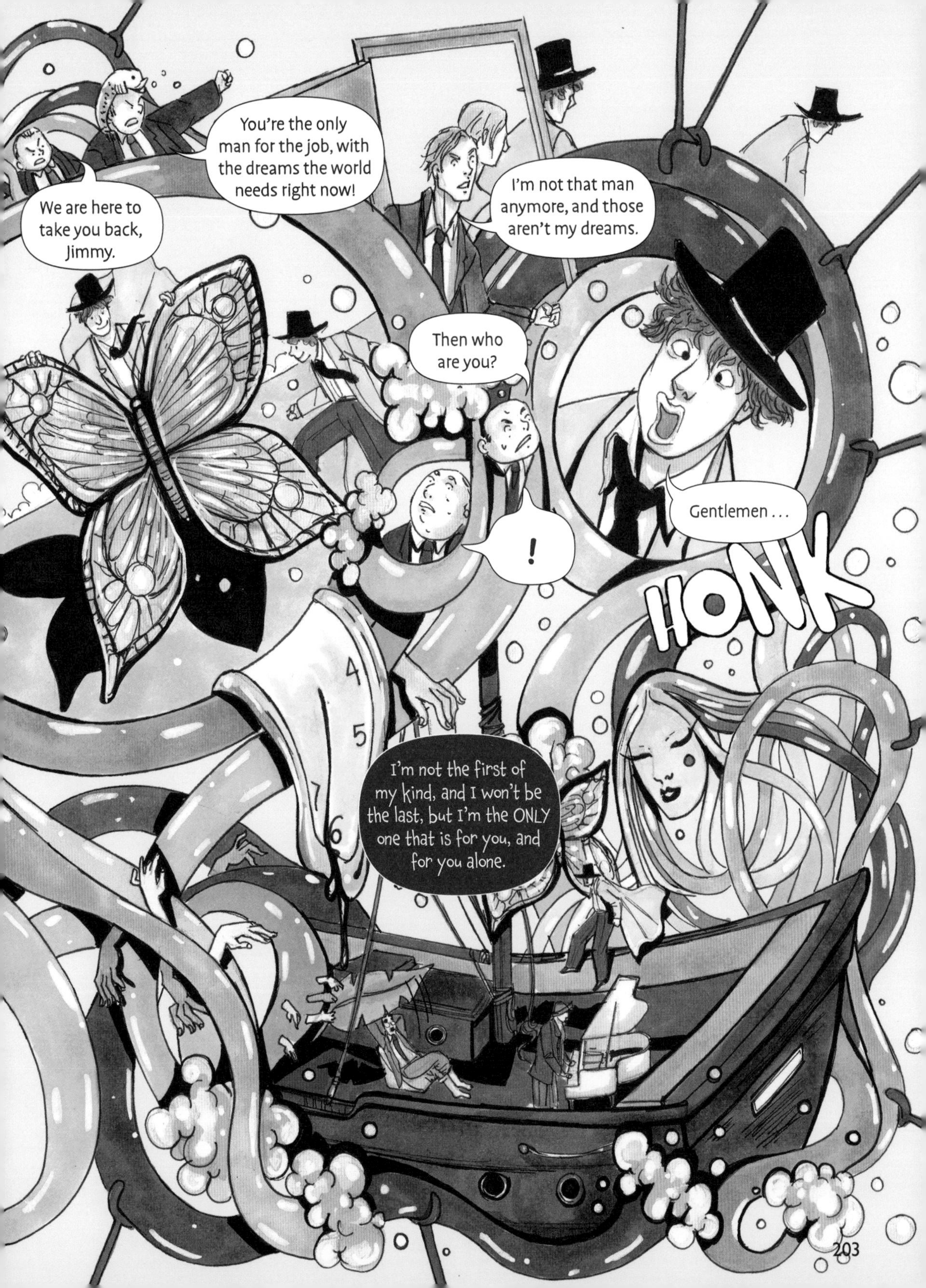
We are here to take you back, Jimmy.
You're the only man for the job, with the dreams the world needs right now!
I'm not that man anymore, and those aren't my dreams.
Then who are you?
!
Gentlemen . . .
HONK
I'm not the first of my kind, and I won't be the last, but I'm the ONLY one that is for you, and for you alone.

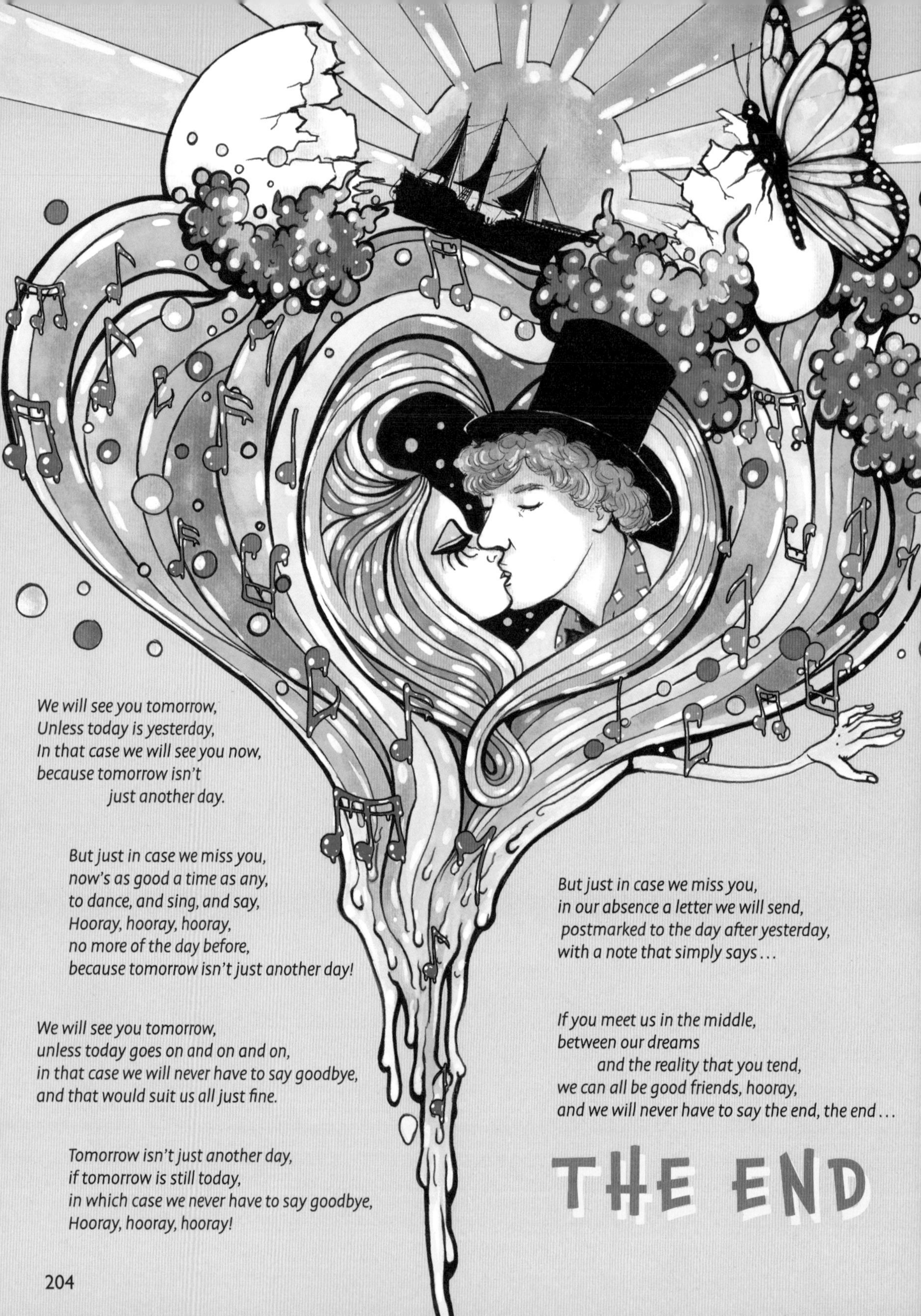

We will see you tomorrow,
Unless today is yesterday,
In that case we will see you now,
because tomorrow isn't
just another day.

But just in case we miss you,
now's as good a time as any,
to dance, and sing, and say,
Hooray, hooray, hooray,
no more of the day before,
because tomorrow isn't just another day!

We will see you tomorrow,
unless today goes on and on and on,
in that case we will never have to say goodbye,
and that would suit us all just fine.

Tomorrow isn't just another day,
if tomorrow is still today,
in which case we never have to say goodbye,
Hooray, hooray, hooray!

But just in case we miss you,
in our absence a letter we will send,
postmarked to the day after yesterday,
with a note that simply says . . .

If you meet us in the middle,
between our dreams
and the reality that you tend,
we can all be good friends, hooray,
and we will never have to say the end, the end . . .

THE END

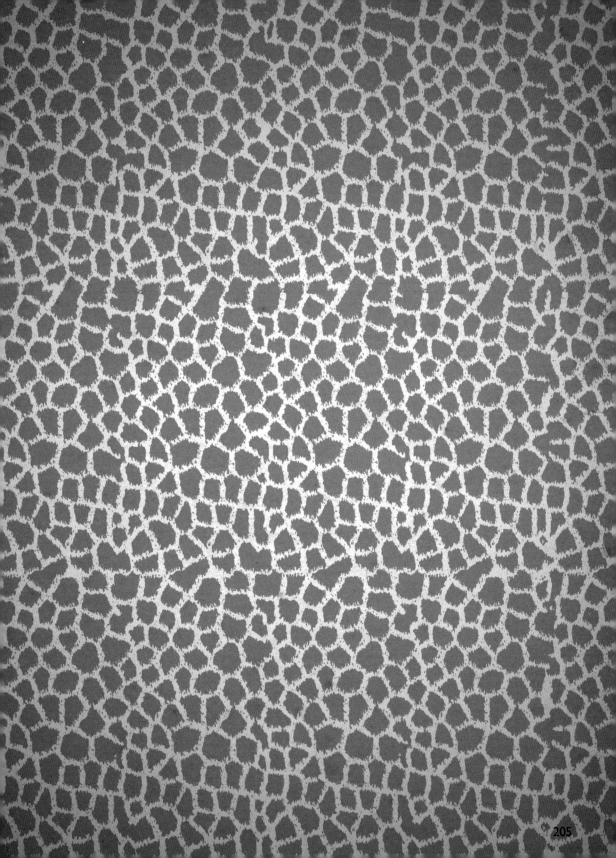

ALTERNATIVE ENDINGS

When Salvador Dalí returned to Spain in 1939, he and Gala found that their house in Port Lligat had been wrecked. War had left its scar on everythinge. Dalí kept in touch occasionally with Harpo, but he had moved on to the next phase of his artistic career. He painted, wrote, exhibited his art, and published his autobiography, The Secret Life of Salvador Dalí.

The final pages of his "Giraffes" notebook reveal the struggle of Dalí's artistic frustrations. He paints, with words, a world that is at odds with his vision. But he also searches for meaning in his failure, a plus to the world's minus, a balance.

Promiscuity always to his right, a labyrinth always to the left—Jimmy and Linda, and Jimmy and The Woman Surreal, Right left—destruction—annihilation—negative expenditure—biologically constructive wife—rigid structure—ugly structure—fertility—hammer and sickle—the broken wheel ideology—multiplication sign on which is inscribed the five year plan, with the head on the right and the tail on the left. The dead—the female and also the crescent moon—crushing diagonally and the death struggle of the workers and the fish and brutal antecedents and sensational in heraldry—mythographic perspective. Eternal fire, materialization of the solar myth symbol of the virgin. The street of fire—it is well known if we watch the sun a moment and close the eyes we see a sign both good and evil.

Yin and Yang: It goes together from the right and from the left and also they will bite their tails—because it is the sign of resentment—of totalitarian and territorial narcissism—The wheel of fire is consuming herself circumscribed to her geography. The 69 that everybody knows is an intrauterine cosmic symbol, it is the embryonic form of softs, right and left.

Back in his homeland at last, Dalí would sit for hours on the Port Lligat beachfront, staring out across the ocean. He had plenty to think about, including the film he never made. Years later, in a 1973 interview, Dalí would be asked by Joe Adamson (author of the 1983 book *Groucho, Harpo, Chico, and Sometimes Zeppo*) whatever became of his Marx Brothers script. Dalí purportedly became enraged and

began beating pigeons with his cane. "No one would DARE to do Dalí's script!" he screamed. When asked if there wasn't someone who found affection for his script, Dalí calmed and smiled and said, "Harpo, Harpo liked it."

That's one end of the story. But considering the surreal and sublime mind of Salvador Dalí, the failure of his Hollywood dream would not stop him from recutting that reality into a more fitting conclusion, one fit for a man living in surreality. If we reflect on the journey that he and Jimmy shared, it is not hard to imagine the alternate ending Dalí might have dreamed up in his weary head as he stared out at the vast and troubled sea.

EXTERIOR/DALÍ AND GALA'S HOME BY THE SEA/DAY

Gala stands on the pier overlooking the sea and then focuses her gaze on Dalí , who is staring into the space between the sea and the sky. Gala has had enough. She marches onto the beach and stands over Dalí ...

Speaking to both Gala and the sea, he whispers:

DALÍ: My film, it could have been eternal.

(The wind howls.)

DALÍ: I must render the experience of my life "classic." This is to endow it with a form, a cosmogony, a synthesis and architecture of eternity. Is it too late? For I may be dying.

(Dalí looks down at his naked feet and wiggles his toes.)

GALA: This is the spell of the tramontana* who speaks.

[*Northern wind]

DALÍ: Am I already more than half dead? Don't you see, there is something wrong, absolutely nothing that can frighten me, but I am afraid of being afraid. And the fear that I may be afraid, it frightens me.

GALA: This is where we sail off into the sunset. You have already written the end.

DALÍ: The end?

GALA: Are you ready?

DALÍ: Is this my end?

GALA: No. You have accomplished nothing yet. It is not time for you to die.

A long silence permeates. Gala takes a deep breath and then a long sigh. She turns to Dalí , eye to eye.

GALA: My love, perhaps you can live like this, but I, I cannot.

CUT TO:

Gala sets a long board on a rock facing the ocean, stands on it, and jumps. Dalí stands and follows her.

They land on a giant sailing ship. The Marx Brothers sit on the deck, playing music. They all play instruments, a bombastic tune. They sing and dance and laugh and . . .

Sail away.

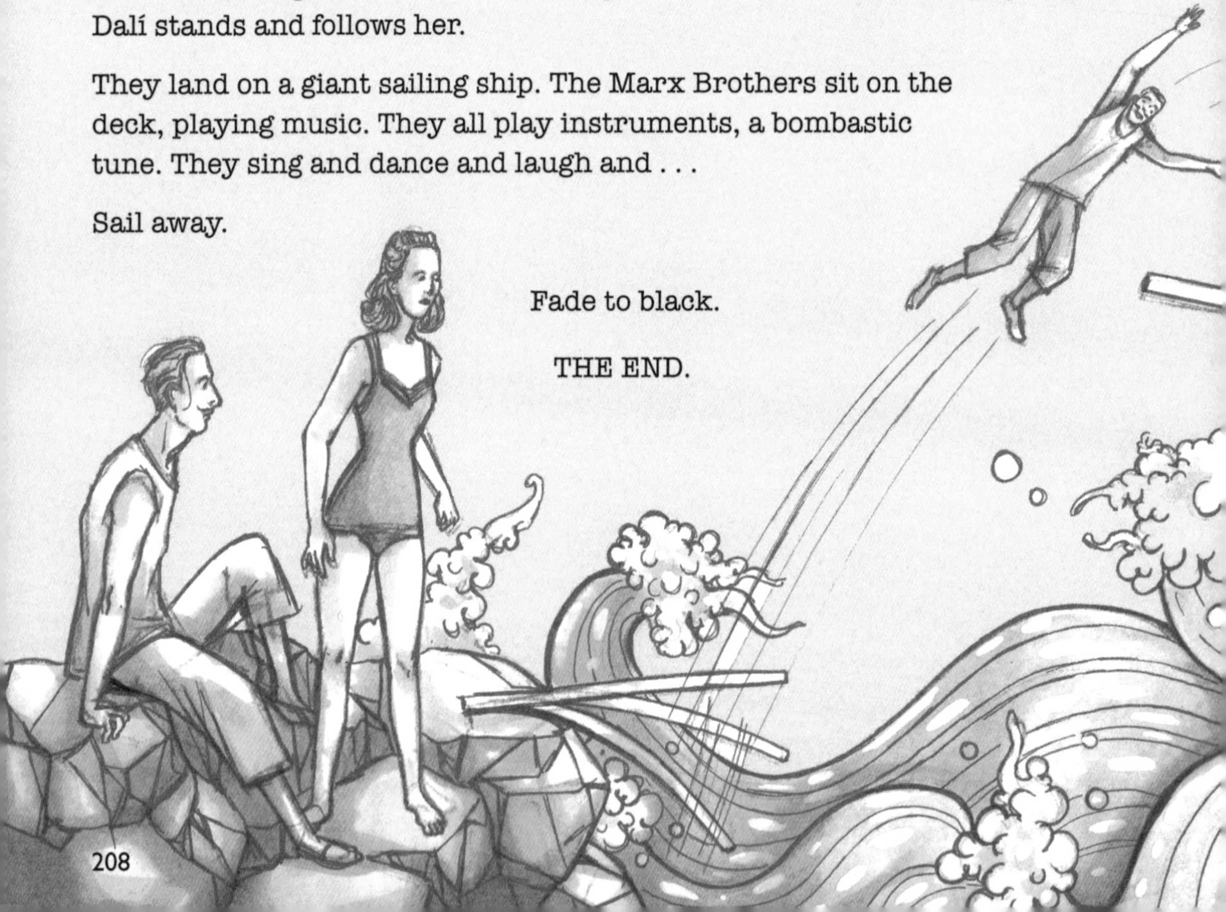

Fade to black.

THE END.

NOTES

The author relied on several primary sources and scholarly works in the telling of this story. The most important and revealing source was Salvador Dalí's "Giraffes" notebook, which is housed in the Centre Pompidou in Paris. It is written in French and was translated for the author by Louis Collin. The estate of Harpo Marx/Robert Bader personal archives also provided invaluable research help and documentation. Additional facts and details were drawn from the following:

Salvador Dalí, "Surrealism in Hollywood," *Harper's Bazaar*, June 1937.

Salvador Dalí, The Secret Life of Salvador Dalí (Dial Press, 1942).

Meredith Etherington-Smith, *The Persistence of Memory: A Biography of Dalí*
(Da Capo Press, 1995).

Elliott King, *Dalí, Surrealism and Cinema* (Oldcastle Books, 2007).

Harpo Marx, with Rowland Barber, *Harpo Speaks!*
(B. Geis Associates, 1961).

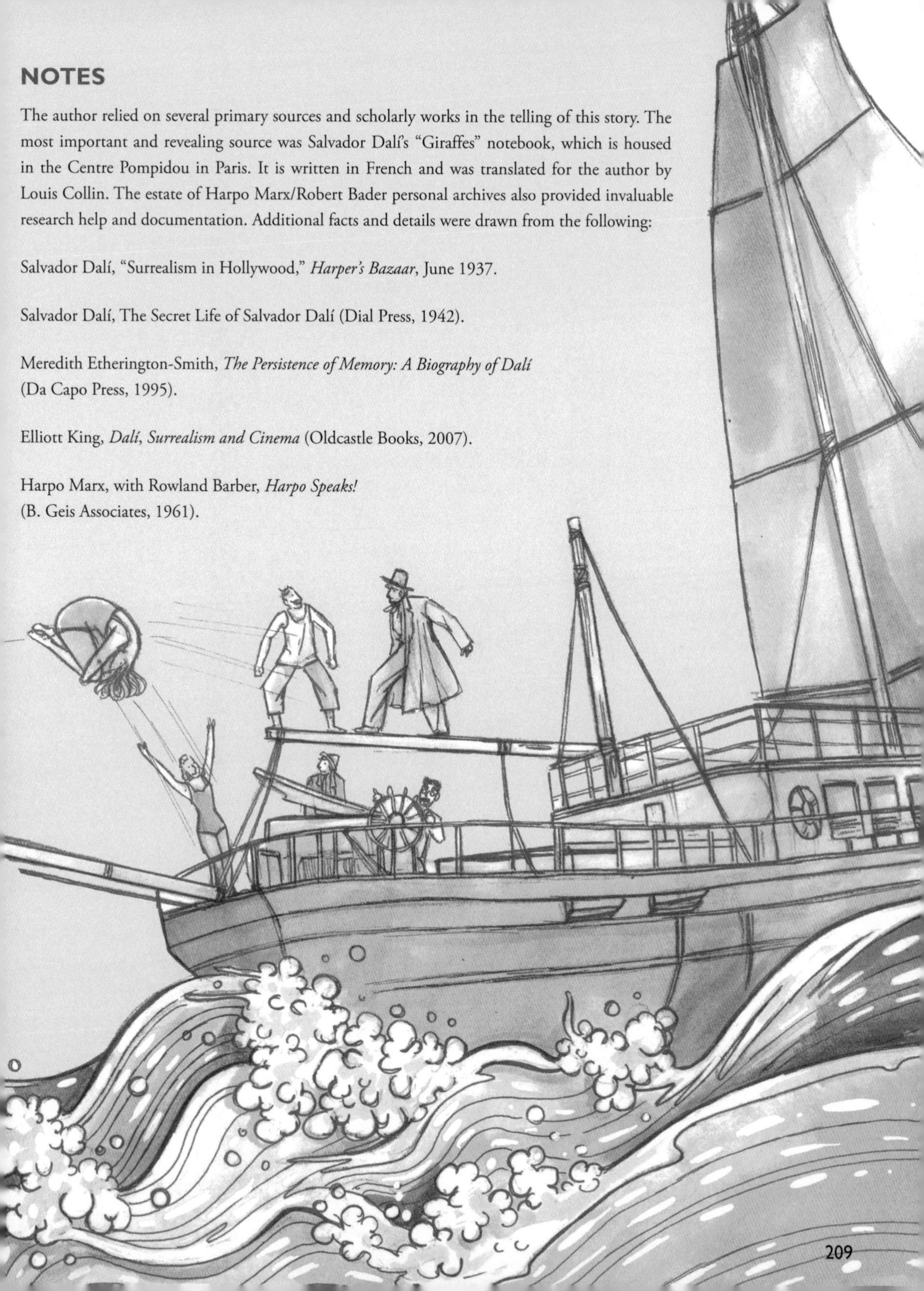

Living Legacy

PALM SPRINGS, CALIFORNIA, APRIL 2018—The Marx Brothers have been gone from this mortal earth for many decades now, though the world is in need of their counter-insanity now more than ever. When I imagine seeing them in person, what I most wish I could have experienced are Harpo's wild eyes, full of childlike sweetness and wonder, staring into me like he does all of us from the screen.

Which is why I was so excited to meet Harpo's son, Bill Marx. As I drove up to his home, I saw someone standing in the middle of the street, waving. It was not a mirage in the desert, it was Bill. He had come out to greet me. We entered his home and I quickly saw that it wasn't filled with Marx Brothers memorabilia, as I'd imagined it must be. Instead, the walls were covered with something truly surprising. And for the writer who was there to deliver a book about the untold story of Salvador Dalí and Bill's father, it was both a revelation and a fitting end for this amazing adventure.

What the walls were covered with was paintings, original paintings, all by Harpo. We walked through the house, and Bill showed me the evolution of Harpo's later-life talent. He explained that his father started painting shortly before he met Salvador Dalí. It is easy to see how a famous painter who worshiped Harpo Marx would be particularly exciting to Harpo, who had just started to dip brush into paint and spread it across a canvas. I believe that his time with Dalí gave Harpo inspiration and a continued commitment to learning the craft. When I first saw a picture of Harpo painting Dalí while Dalí painted Harpo, I assumed it was Harpo's funny idea for a press shot. But it wasn't. Harpo was painting *with* Dalí, because Harpo was becoming a painter.

Too soon, the day of my visit with Bill Marx was coming to an end, but Bill's day was far from over. Once a week, Bill played piano at a nearby retirement community's cabaret bar, and he invited me to come. I could not pass up the opportunity.

So that night I sat at table number 14 with my friend Melvin Rodriguez, who'd joined me for the drive to Palm Springs. (Mel, always ready for an adventure, was on hiatus from his day job acting on the TV show *Last Man on Earth*, where he and Will Forte channeled what I believe to be this generation's version of Laurel and Hardy.) About five minutes into Bill's set, I looked over at Mel and he was smiling ear to ear,

his eyes tearing up. I asked him if he was okay. He turned to me and said, "I see his father on that stage." Mel was absolutely right. It was exactly what I had been thinking.

At the end of Bill's last number, he looked over to Mel and me. He leaned into the microphone and widened his eyes until it seemed they might pop out of his head. Then he smiled a very familiar mischievous smile and said, "Thank you, boys. Thanks for coming to see me." He pointed to us before using the same finger to hit the final key.

I wish you all could have been there that night. I wish every fan of the Marx Brothers could see Bill play. I feel so lucky to have seen it twice! He thanked us again for coming, claiming that he was convinced we only ended up there because we took a wrong turn. That is Bill Marx—as far as I am concerned, the last living Marx Brother.

In the years after meeting Harpo, Salvador Dalí would go on to design scenes for Hollywood films, including a famous dream sequence for Alfred Hitchcock's *Spellbound*, and a short film with Walt Disney. Harpo would go on to become an accomplished painter. The two men crossed paths for a short time, but each clearly left an imprint on the other, a lasting legacy on canvas and celluloid. A legacy carried on in the flesh to this day by a piano man in the desert, who will play a song for any Marxists who take a wrong turn on the highway.

Hail Freedonia! Whim Wham. Quote, unquote, and quote. And two more hard boiled eggs.

PAGES FROM HISTORY

Please enjoy the first few pages of the only known copy of the Giraffes on Horseback Salad script and film treatment.
This is believed to be the document presented by Dalí and Harpo to MGM studios, typed and edited from Dalí's own notes.

Courtesy of the Marx Brothers Estate

1737

FILM BY MARX BROTHERS.

SCENARIO AND SETTINGS BY SALVADOR DALI.

Jimmy, a young Spanish aristocrat living in America because of political circumstances in hiw own country, occupies an important business position. Energetic to the point of violence, he hides under an appearance of calm assurance, an expansive sentimental temperament and even unsuspected inclinations towards fantasy and the most extravagant luxury. These inclinations may be explained by the heritages of his birth.

Linda, his fiancee personifies the highest possible degree of personal snobbery and vulgarity. All her actions mechanically obey the primary calculations of her social ambitions and her almost hysterical need of shining perpetually in the first rank.

After a day of exhausting work, Jimmy leaves the desk of a busy director's room. Until the end of the session, he has kept up an appearance of steel, dazzling the meeting by his daring projects. The minute he gets into his car, his face relaxes from the strain. Back home, he crosses several rooms in his apartment, filled with souvenirs of his past, and throws himself on his bed while the valet runs his bath. Just as he stretches out, the telephone rings, rousing him. It is his fiancee, chattering gaily, "How are you, darling? I am sure you are going to be late".

"I'll be over immediately".

"Take your time but don't bother to call for me. Come straight to the Restaurant. I know you've had a bad day".

Saying this, she glances at a young man stretched on her bed smoking. (The young man is the usual charming but unattractive type of gigolo).

Jimmy replies, "Terribla. But the idea of passing the evening alone with you makes up for it all. Where shall we have dinner"?

"Let's go to Chey Phoenix".

"Why that place? We shall see all our awful friends."

She; (very impatiently): "No, I have reserved a table and we only have .... (here she names six friends)".

He, (bitterly): "You are right. That makes only one less than there is in the office".

She: "You are nasty".

He: "Darling, remember I was hoping for a nice evening alone with you as you promixed. But I'll come in a good mood. So long".

2

Linda, (hurriedly): "Michael is with us, too. But you like him, don't
you"?

Jimmy: "Of course I do".

Jimmy goes across to his table where his friends are already waiting,
except for Linda and Michael who are late. They are all talking excitedly
of a certain very rich woman they call the "Surrealist woman". At the moment
everyone is curious about her because of her continuous fantastic actions.
All are ready to condemn them as cynicism, lack of taste, absurd exhibition-
ism and all are unanimously against her in spite of her obvious fascination.
Everyone admits that in spite of her madness, she is of unbelievable beauty.
Only Linda who has just arrived in a hurry with Michael says that she can
see nothing exceptional about her but that, on the contrary, she finds her
looks very ordinary.

Jimmy naively shows his curiosity and expresses a wish to get to know the
"Surrealist woman" but they all assure him it is impossible to see her and
that, once over the surprise of her appearance, no one bothers any more about
her.

The night club is now very full. Tables are put in the most inconvenient places.
The entrance is crowded and looks as if some demonstration is going on for
those who are arriving, wish to get in at any price in spite of the waiter's
protests.

Jimmy notices the unusual crush and asks the head waiter for an explanation.
The head waiter, with a condescending and ironic smile, bends down and says,
"Sir, they all want to see the "Surrealist woman'", and he points to the only
empty table where waiters are arranging quantities of very rare flowers which
are banked all around the table, closing it into a kind of a box.

Linda (in a petulant voice): "If I had known the 'Surrealist woman' was
going to appear, I would have ordered supper somewhere else".

They all look rather embarassed, knowing quite well that they are only there
because of the 'Surrealist woman'. So they change the subject and become
forcedly gay.

Outside, a powerful limousine drives up and out gets the 'Surrealist woman',
accompanied by Harpo and Groucho. (In the film the face of the 'Surrealist
woman' is never seen as she is always photographed from behind or in circumstances where the face is hidden, in order to increase the enigmatic atmosphere of her personality):

The crowd in the lobby open a way for them and they pass through the entrance
of the club amid curious glances. Two servants preceed them, carrying a large
luxurious-looking object which being opened, turns out to be a white satin
telescope tunnel of human height. This is spread from the door to the table
reserved for the "Surrealist woman", so as to permit the party to proceed to
their table without being seen by the public in the room. Like a caterpillar,

this tunnel twists round the tables to the general amazement of their
occupants. Some are outraged, some amused and others pay no attention.

A servant carrying a lighted candelabra preceeds the "Surrealist woman",
Harpo and Groucho. Their silhouettes can be seen reflected on the walls
of the satin tunnel.

Suddenly the "Surrealist woman" stops, pulls a zip-fastener which opens
a hole in the wall, and greets two young men seated at a table. They get
up and warmly kiss her hand. A few steps further, the three stop just
in front of the table occupied by Jimmy and his friends. Linda, imagining
hse is going to be greeted by the "Surrealist woman", moistens her lips and
prepares her face for her most welcoming smile. But this is immediately
frozen as the zip-fastener opening again, Groucho's face appears instead,
voluptuously puffing some smoke and showing only the whites of his eyes.

All three finally sit down behind the wall of flowers around the table,
through which one sees from time to time, the faces of Harpo and Groucho,
but only the brilliant jewelry and low-cut dress of the "Surrealist woman".
At Linda's table embarassment reaches its height.

Jimmy, who is the only one to be really annoyed, proposes leaving at once
and gets up but Linda takes his arm and quickly forces him to sit down
again.

"Why should that bother us? We mustn't give such importance to a mad
woman".

At the flowered table, the "Surrealist woman" and her friends greedily devour
the grilled lobsters which have just been served. These they eat with their
fingers, cracking the shells with their teeth, burning themselves and covering the table with shell and with sauce.

The waiters try to arrange the situation by changing the cloths but they have
no success because of the incredible increasing violence of those eating.

Groucho, on the other hand, with great laziness and indifference gives some
orders to the head waiter, who is obviously disconcerted and amazed until
Groucho pulls out and gives him a handful of dollar bills, when he immediately
becomes subservient. Groucho also pulls out of his pockets several leather
belts, which he gives him with his last orders.

The head waiter goes up to the orchestra and talks to the leader in a low
voice. He appears amused by and resigned to the requests he has just received.
At this point several waiters arrive carrying roast chickens. These are
quickly fixed by the straps on the head of each musician, except on to that
of the leader, who receives a magnificent pheasant decorated with feathers.
Chicken legs are also put on their choulders as epaulettes. This done, the
music plays a very sentimental tune and people begin to dance. The sight of
the musicians playing with chickens on their heads becomes uncomfortable,

embarassing and disgusting, for the juices from the roasted birds run
down their faces as the balancing of the chickens gets more and more
precarious, especially during the most syncopated moments. The fury,
ill concealed by a very artificial smile on the musicians' faces, gives
place to involuntary grimaces of real disgust each time they are obliged
to push back into place the chicken which is slipping sideways, at the
same time trying not to interrupt the music. This finishes and they are
relieved of their chickens. The musicians wipe their faces and shirt
fronts, which have been covered by the juice.

An announcer announces a cabaret in honor of the "Surrealist woman".
This is greeted by one or two claps.

(In colour) The curtain goes up on three panels of mirror, in the middle
of each of which there is a long oval ellipse made of quilted red satin.
Each ellipse is surrounded by holes cut in the glass.

Along the bottom of the middle panel there is a sofa in the form of a
mouth, also in quilted red satin. On this sofa, as if asleep, lies a
half naked dancer. (At this point the principal musical theme begins very
softly). As if aroused by this music, girls' arms begin to come out
like snakes from the holes in the mirrors and, following the rhythm of the
music, caress the body of the dancer. She, in her turn, awakes to the
rhythm which more and more takes control of her body. (The choreography
of this scene must be very carefully worked out).

The dancer has moments of great ecstasy, followed by calmer moments
during which she leans against the buttoned cushions while the hands caress
her body and her hair, as if to encourage her to continue the dance. When
this is brought to its close, the arms of the lower part of the mirror
lift her gently up into the buttoned satin ellipse into which she fits as
into a box. All the arms close round her body, covering her completely.

Harpo and Groucho, very excited by the dancer's good luck, throw themselves
on to the cushions each side, clutching onto the hands and forcing them to
hold and caress them. The arms resist, strike them and tear their clothes
but Harpo and Groucho retaliate by biting them, bending them and catching
them with their hands and knees, all of which calls forth cries of pain
from the owners of the arms in question, behind the mirrors.

Just as the confusion is at its heighth, Chico arrives bringing a harp
which he gives into Harpo's hands. Harpo begins to play and like a modern
Orpheus, charms successively all the arms which again begin to follow the
rhythm of his music and which end by being move submissive and caressing
than ever before.

As this lyricism is also communicated to the arms around Groucho, he profits
by giving his cigar to one of the hands to hold, kissing several at a time
and by making another scratch his leg. The scene finishes in a general
delirium of enthusiasm from the crowd filling the room.

NOTES FROM THE MASTER

Below are some excerpts from the "Giraffes" notebook, which Salvador Dalí kept during the planning phase of *Giraffes on Horseback Salad. Courtesy the Gala-Salvador Dalí Foundation and Centre Pompidou.*

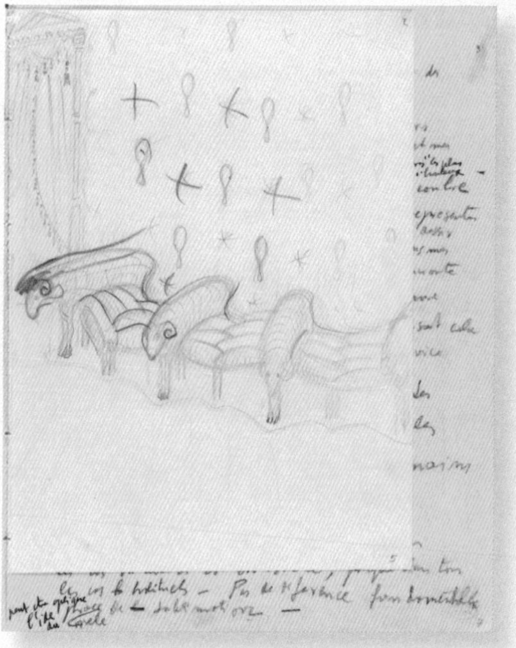

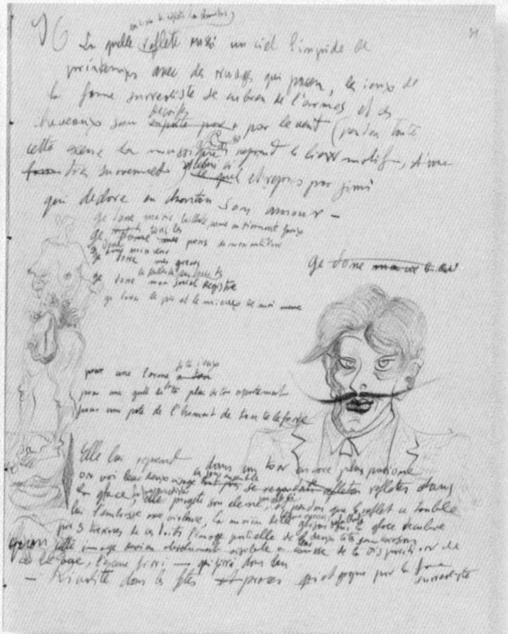

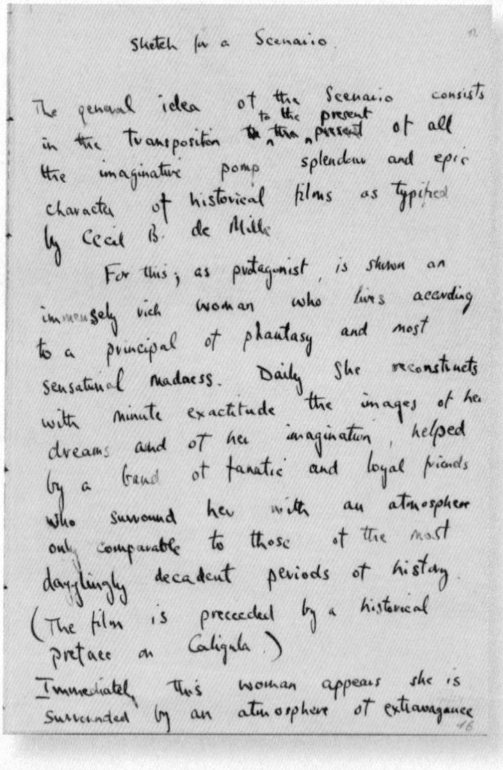

Sketch for a Scenario

The general idea of the Scenario consists in the transposition to the present of all the imaginative pomp splendour and epic character of historical films as typified by Cecil B. de Mille

For this, as protagonist, is shown an immensely rich woman who lives according to a principal of phantasy and most sensational madness. Daily she reconstructs with minute exactitude the images of her dreams and of her imagination, helped by a band of fanatic and loyal friends who surround her with an atmosphere only comparable to those of the most dazzlingly decadent periods of history. (The film is preceded by a historical preface on Caligula.)

Immediately this woman appears she is surrounded by an atmosphere of extravagance

46

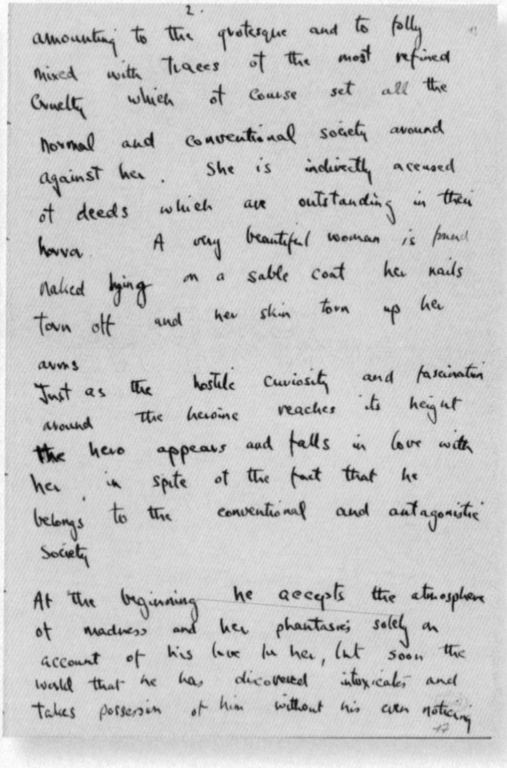

2.

amounting to the grotesque and to folly mixed with traces of the most refined cruelty which of course set all the normal and conventional society around against her. She is indirectly accused of deeds which are outstanding in their horror. A very beautiful woman is found naked lying on a sable coat her nails torn off and her skin torn up her arms

Just as the hostile curiosity and fascination around the heroine reaches its height the hero appears and falls in love with her in spite of the fact that he belongs to the conventional and antagonistic society

At the beginning he accepts the atmosphere of madness and her phantasies solely on account of his love for her, but soon the world that he has discovered intoxicates and takes possession of him without his even noticing

47

3.

All the sentimental and dramatic development of the plot is based on the continuous antagonism struggle between the imaginative life as depicted in the old myths and the practical and rational life of contemporary society. These struggles are so violent that they comprise the dramatic substance for the 2 characters for he always hopes for a normal life with her outside of this continuous hallucination in which they live.

The heroine is terribly disappointed not to be understood in the very essence of her self and in a blind fury there succeed one another a rupture and diplomatic intrigues on account of the personal influence he exerts over other powerful people. This ends by a declaration of war on his own country in order to avenge himself on the society of his former fiancée.

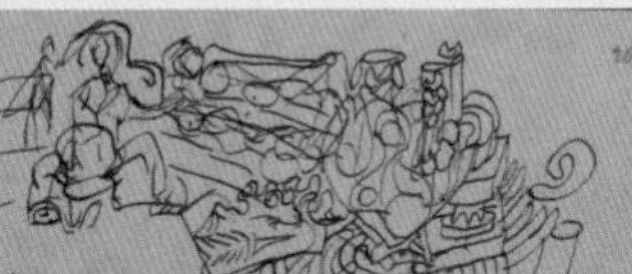

4.

After a short but disappointing attempt to readapt himself to his former life suddenly realises that he can no longer support the conventional normality of his before which now appear to him monstrously absurd without any justification.

After a decisive scene with his fiancee he forsakes everything, his duty, and his post at the war, and rushes to rejoin the heroine. But he is too late. The invasion of the enemy mixed with a general revolution ransacks the large palace where she had built up the strange world of her imagination.

(5)

On voi derriere le mur ou les 10 fmes sont couchés ~~il plonge dans~~ un profond someill un de leurs bras pendan leurs de chaque tiroir respectifs, Groucho vient un bon verre de bonbons narcotiques, on ~~voit~~ le voit ~~l'ofrir~~ dans la bouche d'une qui ~~n'est pas encore entierement endormi~~ se reveille legerement, l'aquelle aussi tot ~~et passe par~~ tombe entierement endormi ... Groucho reaparait de l'autre coté on pendant les bras ... sur le buret sont une lupe et un libre de quiromanci et comence a etudier dans toutes ces mains, il trouve dans une de celes quelque ~~chosse~~ qui l'equiete mais quil ne peu pas rien voir a cause de la lumiere il eseye de raprocher la lampe quil i a sur le bureau, mais cet une lampe solidemant fixe au buro, alors il tire brutallemant du bras mais naturellement il n'obance pas grand chosse, alors desapare et come s'il s'agisse de la chosse la plus naturelle de ce monde il prend de grand sisceau quil i a sur la table et va pour couper la main, au moment meme ... ... trombe dans la

(7) ~~Et~~ sort ~~une pere de~~ un melons melons coupes sur une ... la quelle monte tres lentement sur le ... ~~par le~~ corridor ... et ... d'une tortue, ... le gens qui traversent le corridor ne ... aucune attention a cet accident —

(8)

Groucho ofre a fumer, et a la place de cigarettes il i a des moustaches ...

(9) Groucho arpo et Chico ... ~~...~~ ... une noi sous i ... Groucho fait signe d'aprocher ... a une locomotive qui rentre lentement dans la piece, ... elle ... la noi avec des pinces ... en meme temps Chico ... une guillotine, ... la lame, et ... juste a ce moment il aparait un train qui arrive dans l'autre sens, pour ... Groucho il ... a travers la guillotine, qui ... tout juste de lui couper le ... Chico ... le train ... comme s'il ete un ... —

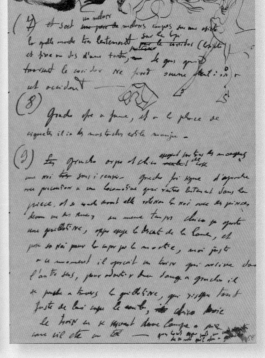

GIRAFFES **IN THE WILD**

Along with his long-undiscovered "Giraffes" notebook, Dalí explored ideas for his big Hollywood film debut in other works.
Here are some examples. *Images courtesy of the Fundació Gala-Salvador Dalí and the Salvador Dalí Museum*

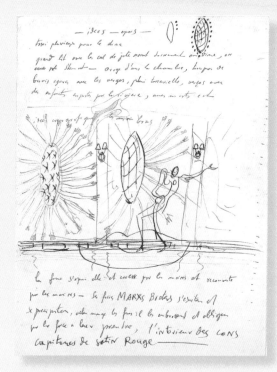

*Set Design for the Film with the
Marx Brothers, c. 1937*
Fundació Gala-Salvador Dalí, Figueres, Spain

This sketch (most likely originating from the "Giraffes" notebook found at the Centre Pompidou) is notable because it is a much more streamlined and focused design, compared to Dalí's more frantic and abstract sketches (see previous spread).

*Marx Brothers Orchestra (Drawing for a Film
Project with the Marx Brothers), 1937*
Salvador Dalí Museum, St. Petersburg, Florida

This sketch is one of a handful that define the imagery that would have been, and now is, *Giraffes on Horseback Salad*. In the triumphant finale, Jimmy, the Surrealist Woman, and the Marx Brothers sail off into the sunset after Jimmy and the Woman Surreal "win" their personal war against reality by choosing their own path into the horizon. Dalí created a number of these images for his film while writing the movie scenario and visiting with Harpo. They were his version of a movie shot list and the beginnings of a storyboard.

The Surrealist Piano, 1937
Fundació Gala-Salvador Dalí, Figueres, Spain

Depicted here is the film's protagonist, Jimmy, embracing the Surrealist Woman at a piano. Her is face hidden, in accordance with her enigmatic nature. This work was once owned by the Marx Brothers and was acquired by the Fundació Gala-Salvador Dalí in 2009.

Giraffes on Fire in the Desert (Drawing for a Film Project with the Marx Brothers), 1937
Salvador Dalí Museum, St. Petersburg, Florida

This drawing depicts the lavish dinner party at the Surrealist Woman's home, which Jimmy attends early in the story. Other notes describe the dinner guests feasting at a huge bed on which the Woman Surreal reclines. Dalí used the "giraffes on fire" image to represent the looming war, inspired by his own experience witnessing the turmoil of his country and the build-up to what would result in World War II.

FROM CONCEPT TO COMICS

Artist Maneula Pertega had the daunting task of translating surreal images and Marx Brothers comedy onto the comic book page. Here's a glimpse into her process.

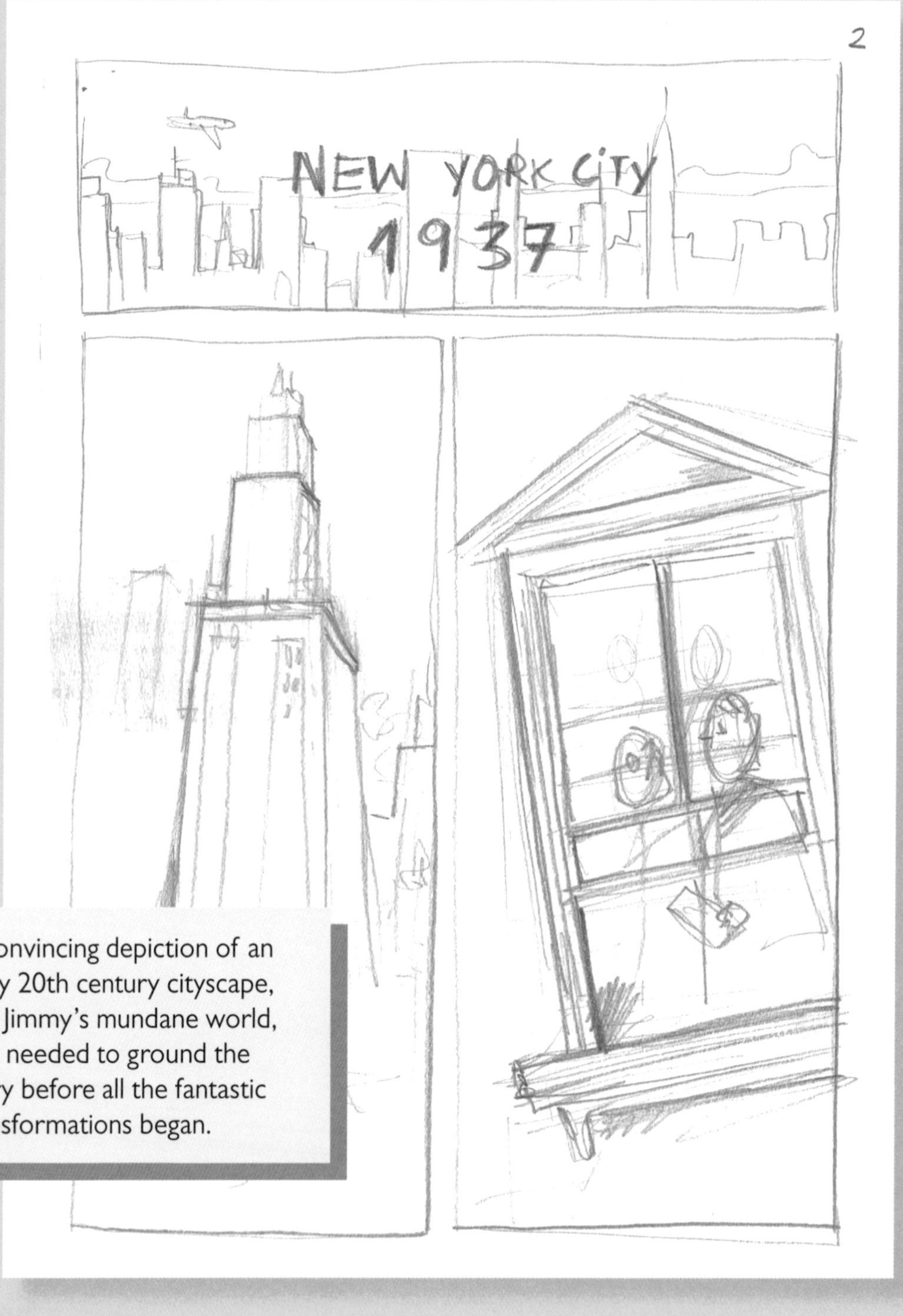
2
NEW YORK CITY
1937

A convincing depiction of an early 20th century cityscape, and Jimmy's mundane world, was needed to ground the story before all the fantastic transformations began.

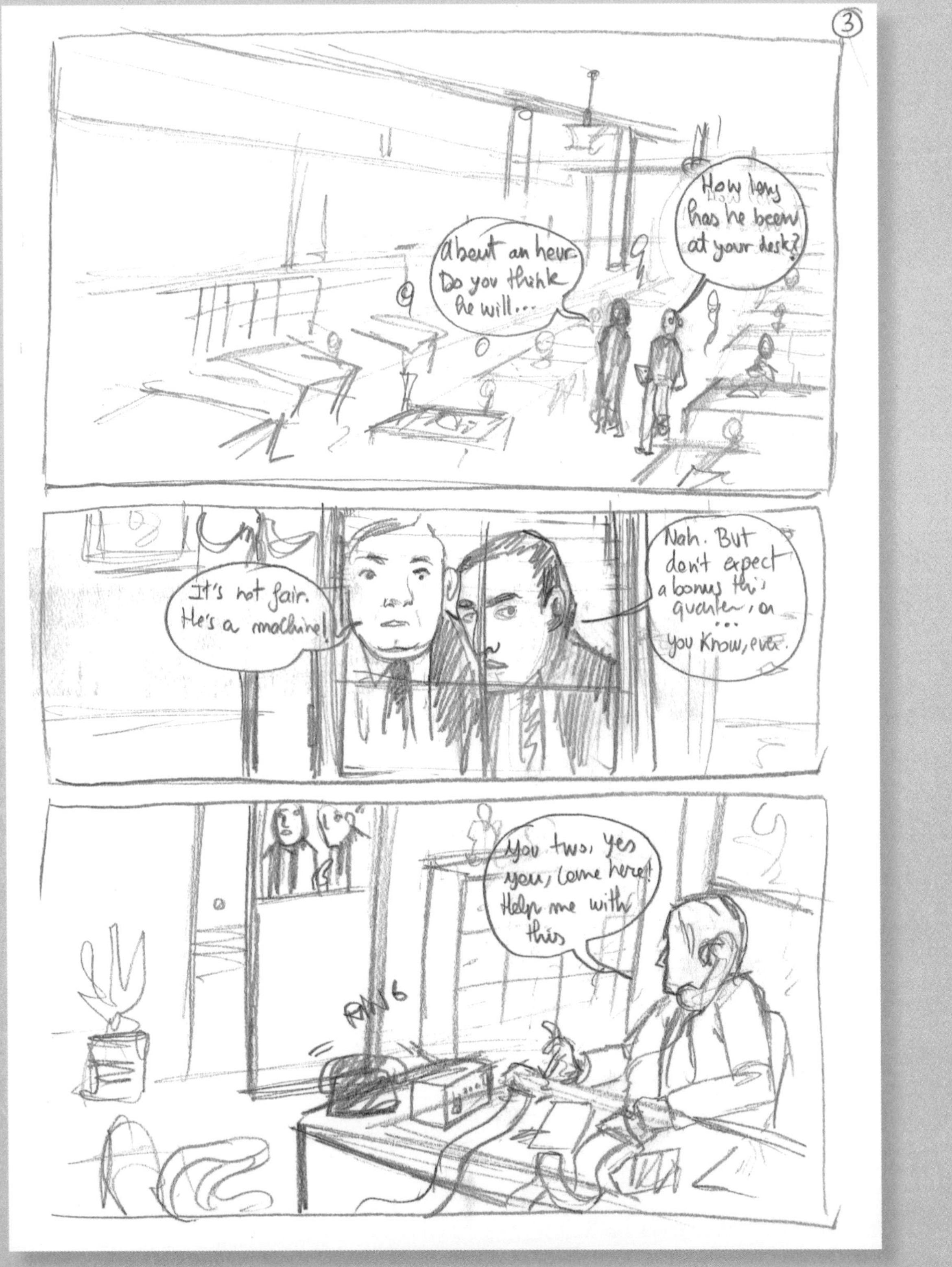
How long has he been at your desk?
About an hour. Do you think he will...
It's not fair. He's a machine!
Nah. But don't expect a bonus this quarter, or ... you know, ever.
You two, yes you, come here! Help me with this
RING

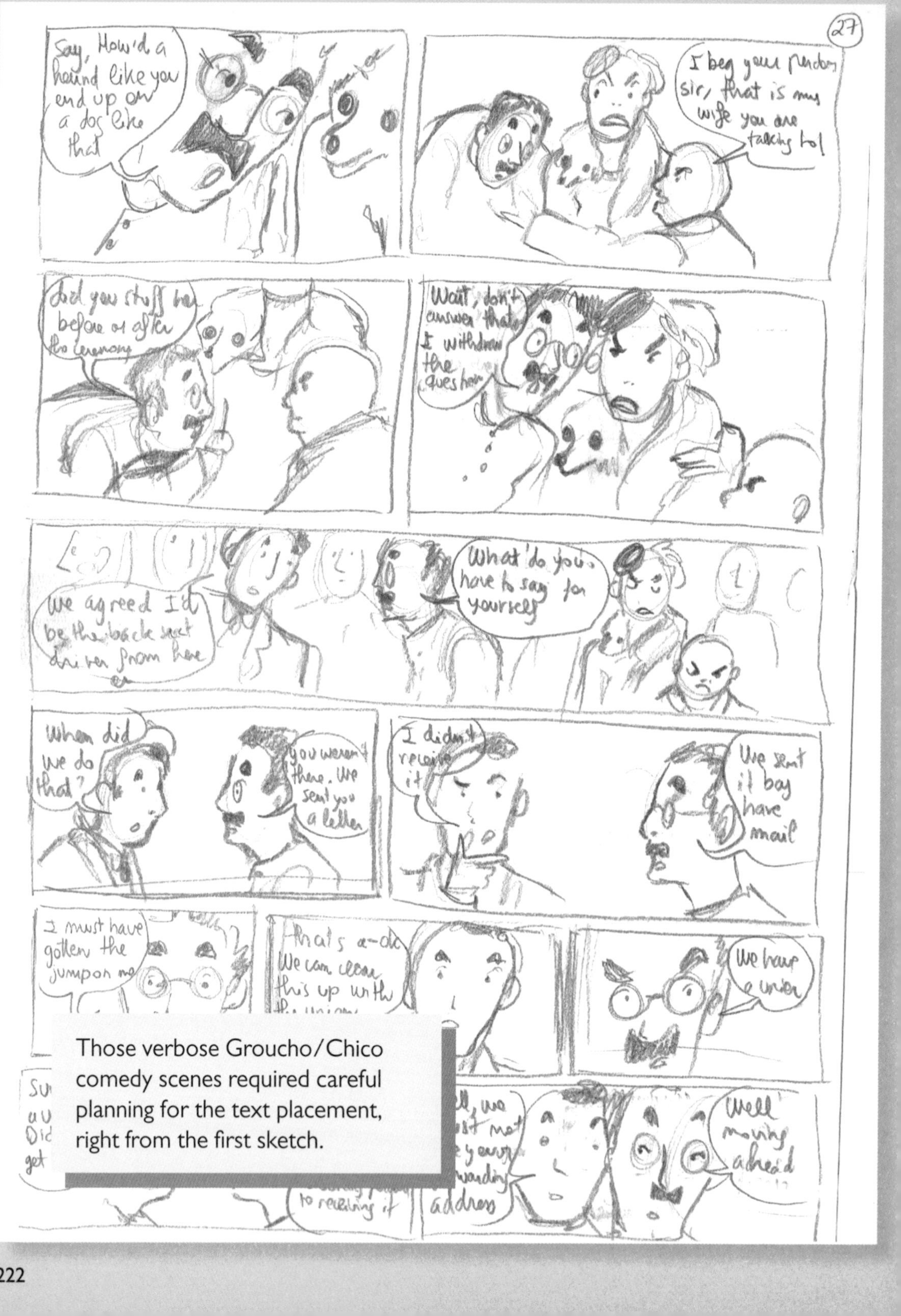

Say, How'd a hound like you end up on a dog like that
I beg your pardon sir, that is my wife you are talking to!
Wait, don't answer that I withdraw the question
We agreed I'd be the back seat driver from here
What do you have to say for yourself
When did we do that?
You weren't there. We sent you a letter
I didn't receive it
We have a union
Well moving ahead

Those verbose Groucho/Chico comedy scenes required careful planning for the text placement, right from the first sketch.

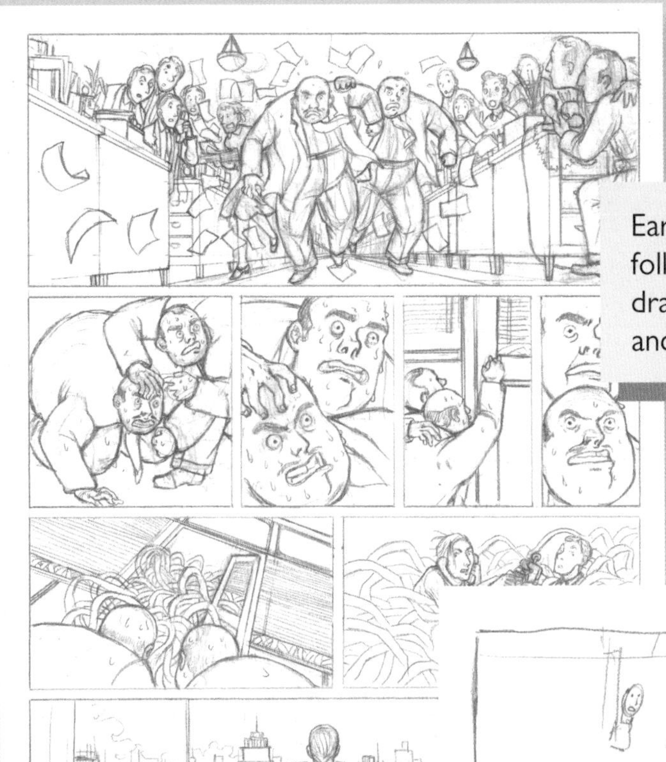

Early page treatments were followed by a tight page drawing before coloring and lettering were added.

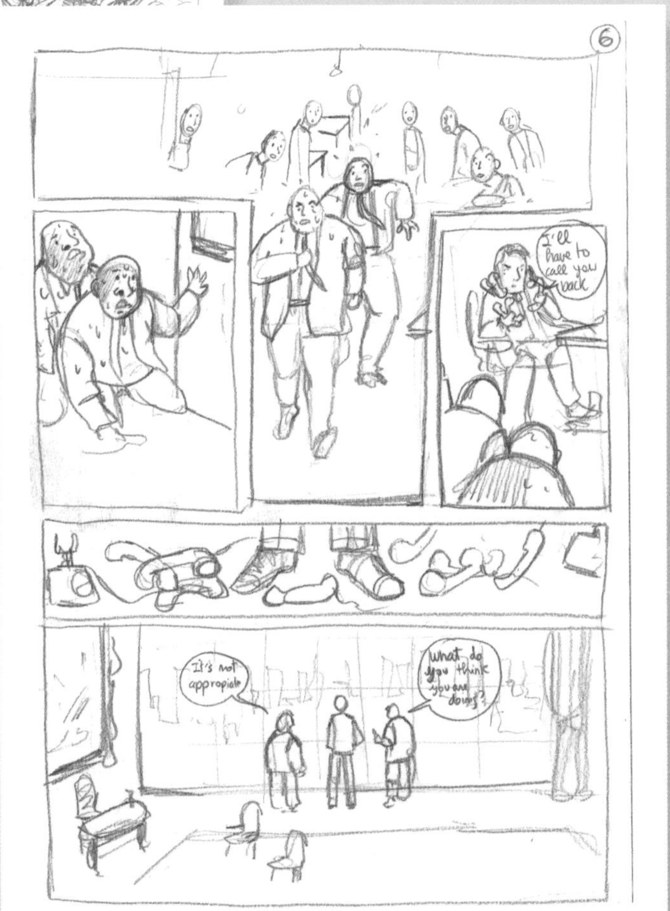
6
I'll have to call you back
It's not appropiate
What do you think you are doing?

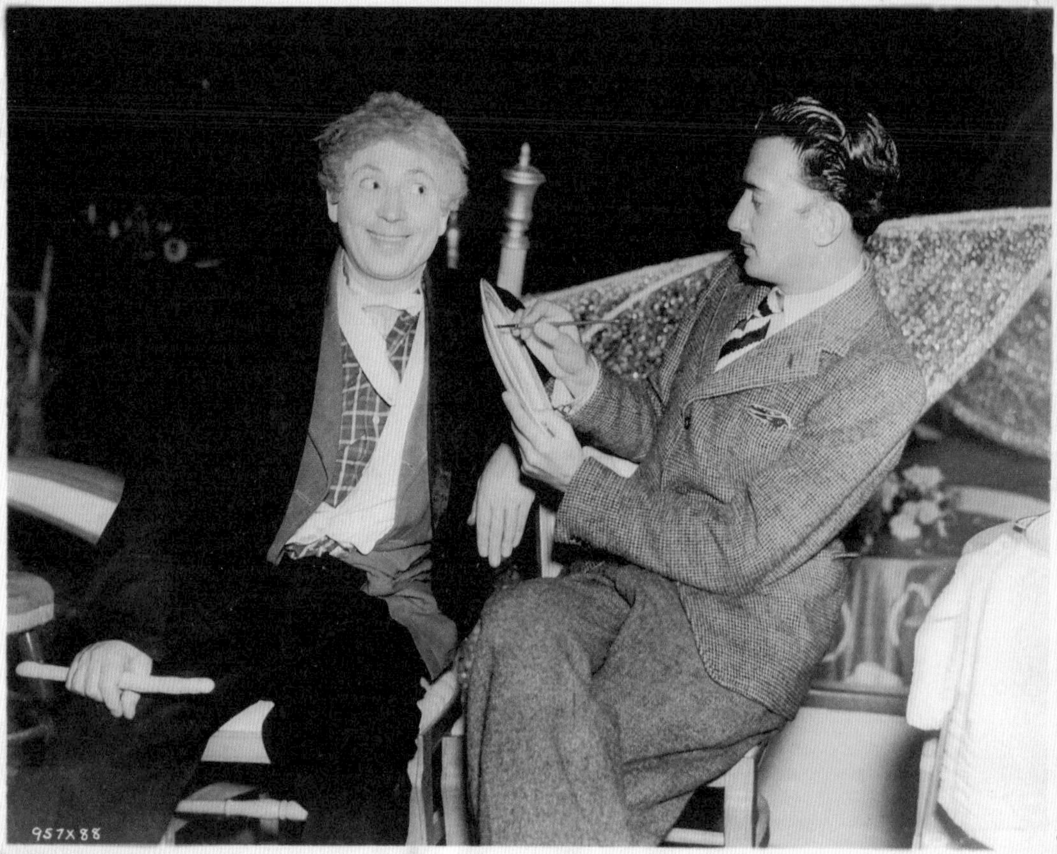
957X88
Photograph courtesy of the Marx family

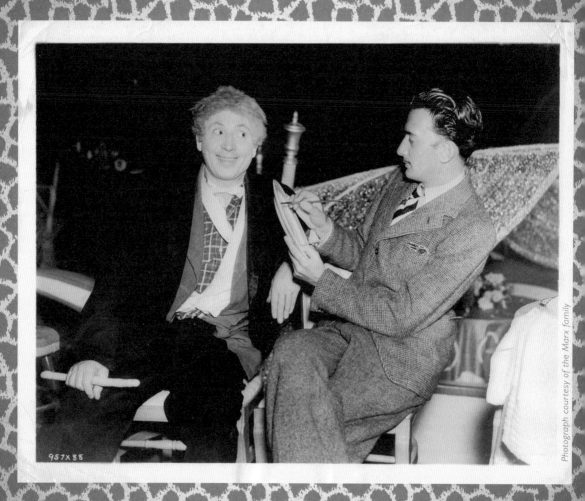